AN EXEGETICAL SUMMARY OF

PHILIPPIANS

J. Harold Greenlee

Summer Institute of Linguistics

© 1992 by the Summer Institute of Linguistics, Inc.
ISBN: 0-88312-828-4
Library of Congress Catalog Card Number: 92-80561
Printed in the United States of America

Summer Institute of Linguistics, Inc.
7500 West Camp Wisdom Road
Dallas, TX 75236

PREFACE

Exegesis is concerned with the interpretation of a text. To exegete the New Testament is to determine what the Greek text means. Translators must be especially careful and thorough in their exegesis of the New Testament so that they can accurately communicate its message in the vocabulary, grammar, and literary devices of another language. The questions that occur to translators as they study the Greek text are asked in this book. Then those questions are answered by summarizing how scholars have exegeted the text. This is information that should be considered by translators as they make their own exegetical decisions regarding the message they will communicate in their translations.

The Semi-Literal Translation

As a basis for discussion, a semi-literal translation of the Greek text is given so that the reasons for problems of interpretation can best be seen. When one Greek word is translated into English by several words, these words are joined by hyphens. When alternate translations of a Greek word are given, these are separated by slashes.

The Lexicon

The meaning of a key word in context is the first question to be answered. Words marked with a raised letter in the semi-literal translation are treated separately under the heading LEXICON. First, the lexicon form of the Greek word is given. Within the parentheses following the Greek word is the location number where, in the author's judgment, this word is defined in the *Greek-English Lexicon of the New Testament Based on Semantic Domains* (Louw and Nida 1988). Locations in bold type indicate that a translation of that particular verse is included there. If the specific reference is listed in *A Greek-English Lexicon of the New Testament and Other Early Christian Literature* (Bauer, Arndt, Gingrich, and Danker 1979), the outline location and page number is given. Then English equivalents of the Greek word are given to show how it is translated by commentators who offer their own translations of the whole text and, after a semicolon, by nine major translations. When reference is made to "all translations," this means all nine translations in the list of abbreviations. Sometimes further comments are made about the meaning of the word or the significance of a verb's tense, voice, or mood.

The Questions

Under the heading QUESTION, a question is asked that comes from examining the Greek text under consideration. Typical questions concern the identity of an implied actor or object of an event word, the antecedent of a pronominal reference, the connection indicated by a relational word, the meaning of a genitive construction, the meaning of figurative language, the function of a rhetorical question, the identification of an ambiguity, and the presence of implied information which is needed to understand the passage correctly. The question is answered with a summary of what commentators have said. If there are contrasting differences of opinion, the different interpretations are numbered and the commentaries which support each are listed. No attempt has been made to select which interpretation is best.

In listing support for various statements of interpretation, the author is often faced with the difficult task of matching the different terminologies used in commentaries with the terminology he has adopted. Sometimes he can only infer the position of a commentary from incidental remarks. This book, then, includes the author's interpretation of the views taken in the various commentaries. General statements are followed by specific statements which indicate the author's understanding of the pertinent relationships, actors, events, and objects implied by that interpretation.

The Use of This Book

This book does not replace the commentaries which it summarizes. Commentaries contain much more information about the meaning of words and passages. They often contain arguments for the interpretations which are taken, and they may have important discussions about the discourse features of the text. In addition, they have information about the historical, geographical, and cultural setting. Translators will want to refer to at least three commentaries as they exegete a passage. However, since no one commentary contains all the answers translators need, this book will be a valuable supplement. It makes available more sources of exegetical help than most translators have access to. Even if they had all the books available, few would have the time to search through all of them for the answers.

When many commentaries are studied, it soon becomes apparent that they frequently disagree in their interpretations. That is the reason why so many answers in this book are divided into two or more interpretations. The reader's initial reaction may be that all these different interpretations complicate exegesis rather than help it. However, before translating a problem passage, a translator needs to know exactly where there is a problem and what the exegetical options are.

Acknowledgments

This volume has been thoroughly reviewed by **Richard C. Blight**. He has studied the questions and answers and has made a significant contribution in determining their final forms. **Bob Sterner** helped with the preliminary research for the first chapter.

ABBREVIATIONS

COMMENTARIES AND LEXICONS

Alf   Alford, Henry. *The Greek Testament*. Vol. 3. London: Rivingtons, 1856.

BAGD Bauer, Walter. *A Greek-English Lexicon of the New Testament and Other Early Christian Literature*. Translated and adapted from the 5th ed., 1958 by William F. Arndt and F. Wilbur Gingrich, 2d English ed. revised and augmented by F. Wilbur Gingrich and Frederick W. Danker. Chicago: University of Chicago Press, 1979.

Bg   Bengel, John Albert. *Gnomon of the New Testament*. Vol. 4, 7th ed. Translated by James Bryce. Edinburgh: T. and T. Clark, 1877.

Ea   Eadie, John. *A Commentary on the the Greek Text of the Epistle of Paul to the Philippians*. Reprinted from 1884 edition. Grand Rapids: Baker, 1979.

EBC Kent, Homer A., Jr. *Philippians*. In *The Expositor's Bible Commentary*, edited by Frank E. Gaebelein, vol. 11. Grand Rapids: Zondervan, 1978.

EGT Kennedy, H. A. A. *The Epistle to the Philippians*. In *The Expositor's Greek Testament*, edited by W. Robertson Nicoll, vol. 3. New York: Doran, n.d.

El   Ellicott, C. J. *A Critical and Grammatical Commentary on St. Paul's Epistles to the Philippians, Colossians, and to Philemon*. 2d ed. London: Parker, Son, and Bourn, 1861.

GEL Louw, Johannes P. and Eugene A. Nida. *Greek-English Lexicon of the New Testament Based on Semantic Domains*. New York: United Bible Societies, 1988.

GNC Bruce, F. F. *Philippians*. A Good News Commentary, edited by W. Ward Gasque. San Francisco: Harper and Row, 1983.

HNTC Beare, F. W. *A Commentary on the Epistle to the Philippians*. Harper's New Testament Commentary, edited by Henry Chadwick. New York: Harper and Brothers, 1959.

ICC Vincent, Marvin R. *A Critical and Exegetical Commentary on the Epistles to the Philippians and to Philemon*. The International Critical Commentary, edited by Samuel R. Driver, Alfred Plummer, and Charles A. Briggs. Edinburgh: T. & T. Clark, 1897.

Lg   Braune, Karl. *The Epistle of Paul to the Philippians*. In
          Lange's Commentary on the Holy Scriptures, Vol. 11.
          Edited with additions by Hoiratio B. Hackett, the
          additions indicated by the abbreviation Lg(H). Reprinted
          from the 1870 edition. Grand Rapids: Zondervan, 1960.

Ln   Lenski, R. C. H. *The Interpretation of St. Paul's Epistles to the
          Ephesians and to the Philippians*. Minneapolis: Augsburg,
          1937.

Lt   Lightfoot, J. B. *Saint Paul's Epistle to the Philippians*. 7th ed.
          London: MacMillan, 1883.

MNTC   Michael, J. Hugh. *The Epistle of Paul to the Philippians*. The
          Moffatt New Testament Commentary, edited by James
          Moffatt. London: Hodder and Stroughton, 1928.

Mou   Moule, H. C. G. *Philippian Studies* Reprinted from 1927
          edition. Fort Washington, Penn.: Christian Literature
          Crusade, 1957.

My   Meyer, Heinrich August Wilhelm. *Critical and Exegetical
          Handbook to the Epistles to the Philippians and Colossians,
          and to Philemon*. Translated from the 4th. ed. n.d. by
          John C. Moore. Revised and edited by William P.
          Dickson, the additions indicated by the abbreviation
          My(D). Meyer's Commentary on the New Testament.
          New York: Funk and Wagnalls, 1885.

NIC   Muller, Jac. J. *The Epistles of Paul to the Philippians and to
          Philemon*. The New International Commentary on the
          New Testament, edited by F. F. Bruce. Grand Rapids:
          Eerdmans, 1955.

NOT   Greenlee, J. Harold. "Saint Paul–Perfect But Not Perfected;
          Philippians 3:12." In *Notes on Translation*, vol. 4, no. 4.
          Dallas: Summer Institute of Linguistics, 1990.

NTC   Hendriksen, Wiliam. *Exposition of Philippians*. New
          Testament Commentary. Grand Rapids: Baker, 1962.

Pl   Plummer, Alfred. *A Commentary on St. Paul's Epistle to the
          Philippians*. London: Robert Scott, 1919.

TH   Loh, I-Jin and Eugene A. Nida. *A Translator's Handbook on
          Paul's Letter to the Philippians*. New York: United Bible
          Societies, 1977.

TNTC   Martin, Ralph P. *The Epistle of Paul to the Philippians*.
          Tyndale New Testament Commentaries, edited by R. V.
          G. Tasker. Grand Rapids: Eerdmans, 1959.

WBC   Hawthorne, Gerald F. *Philippians*. Word Biblical
          Commentary, vol. 43, edited by Ralph P. Martin. Waco,
          Texas: Word, 1983.

WC   Jones, Maurice. *The Epistle to the Philippians*. Westminster Commentaries, edited by Walter Lock. London: Methuen and Co., 1918.

WEC   Silva, Moisés. *Philippians*. The Wycliffe Exegetical Commentary, edited by Kenneth Barker. Chicago: Moody, 1988.

GREEK TEXT AND TRANSLATIONS

GNT   Aland, Kurt, Matthew Black, Carlos Martini, Bruce Metzger, and Allen Wikgren. *The Greek New Testament*. 3d ed. (corrected). London, New York: United Bible Societies, 1983.

KJV   *The Holy Bible*. Authorized (or King James) Version. 1611.

NAB   *The New American Bible*. Camden, New Jersey: Thomas Nelson, 1971.

NASB   *The New American Standard Bible*. Nashville, Tennessee: Holman, 1977.

NIV   *The Holy Bible: New International Version*. Grand Rapids: Zondervan, 1978.

NJB   *The New Jerusalem Bible*. Garden City, New York: Doubleday, 1985.

NRSV   *The Holy Bible: New Revised Standard Version*. New York: Oxford University Press, 1989.

REB   *The Revised English Bible*. Oxford: Oxford University Press and Cambridge University Press, 1989.

TEV   *Holy Bible: Today's English Version*. New York: American Bible Society, 1976.

TNT   *The Translator's New Testament*. London: British and Foreign Bible Society, 1973.

GRAMMATICAL TERMS

act.	active	opt.	optative
fut.	future	pass.	passive
impera.	imperative	perf.	perfect
indic.	indicative	pres.	present
infin.	infinitive	subj.	subjunctive
mid.	middle		

EXEGETICAL SUMMARY OF PHILIPPIANS

DISCOURSE UNIT: 1:1–26 [Lt]. The topic is Paul's circumstances and the progress of the gospel in Rome.

DISCOURSE UNIT: 1:1–11 [EBC, HNTC, ICC, NTC, TH, WBC, WC, WEC; NASB, TEV]. The topic is the introduction [EBC, HNTC, TH, WBC, WC; TEV], prologue [ICC], opening [WEC], thanksgiving [NASB], Paul as a joyful servant [NTC], the intimate relationship of Christians to Christ [Mou].

DISCOURSE UNIT: 1:1–2 [Alf, EBC, EGT, HNTC, ICC, Lg, Ln, Lt, MNTC, NTC, Pl, TH, TNTC, WBC, WC, WEC; GNT, NAB, NIV, NJB]. All characterize this unit as Paul's address and greeting. It follows the convention of ancient usage: X to Y: greetings [HNTC, MNTC, NTC, Pl, TH, TNTC, WBC], expressed in Christian terms [TNTC, WEC]. The senders are first identified in the nominative case, then the recipients in the dative case, and words of greeting follow in the nominative case [Ln].

1:1
Paul and Timothy,

> QUESTION—What part does Timothy have in writing the letter?
> Although Timothy is spoken of as a joint writer [My] or joint sender [NIC, TH; TNT, WEC], all commentators agree that Paul is the sole author of the letter. Many support this by noting that Paul uses the first person singular throughout the rest of the letter and refers to Timothy in the third person [Alf, EBC, El, GNC, ICC, Lt, MNTC, Mou, My, NIC, NTC, Pl, TH, WBC, WC]. Reasons for including Timothy's name here are: Timothy was present with Paul [Alf, EBC, GNC, ICC, NTC, Pl, TNTC, WEC] and possibly wrote the letter at Paul's dictation [EBC, GNC, ICC, My, NIC, NTC, Pl, WC]; Timothy was well known to the Philippians, having been in their city at least twice [Alf, Ea, EBC, EGT, El, GNC, ICC, Lt, Mou, My, NIC, NTC, Pl, TH, TNTC]; he had helped found the church in Philippi, and had now discussed the situation with Paul and had some responsibility for the letter [WC, WEC]; he cared for them deeply [Ea, Lt, NTC]; he was about to be sent to Philippi [EGT, ICC, Lt, My, NIC, NTC, Pl, TH], and wanted to be included in the greeting [ICC]. By mentioning Timothy, Paul indicates that Timothy concurs with the contents of the letter [Ln, MNTC, My, NTC, WEC].

slaves[a] of-Christ Jesus,

LEXICON—a. δοῦλος (GEL 87.76) (BAGD 1.c. p. 184): 'slave' [BAGD, GEL, HNTC, Ln, Mou, WBC], 'bond-servant' [El, ICC, Pl; NASB], 'servant' [Ea, NTC, WEC; all translations except NASB].

QUESTION—How restricted is the designation of δοῦλοι 'slaves' and how are the nouns related in the genitive construction δοῦλοι Χριστοῦ Ἰησοῦ 'slaves of Christ Jesus'?

1. 'Slave' describes the relationship that all Christians have with Christ [Ea, EBC, El, GNC, HNTC, Ln, NTC, Pl, WBC]. The relationship focuses on ownership [Ea, El, Ln, Pl]: we belong to Christ; or on obeying and serving a master [EBC, GNC, HNTC, NTC, WBC]: we serve Christ.

2. 'Slave' is here used as a title for a restricted number of Christians who have been given a special task by Christ [EGT, ICC, Lg, MNTC, Mou, My, NIC, TH]: Paul and Timothy, slaves who work for their master Christ. This phrase is like 'servants of the Lord' in the Old Testament, a title of honor for the prophets [EGT, ICC, MNTC, TH]. The relationships under interpretation 1 are also included [Mou, NIC, TH].

QUESTION—Why does Paul not call himself an 'apostle' here, as in most of his letters to the churches?

It is because this is a more personal letter [Bg, Ea, EBC, EGT, El, ICC, Lg, Ln, Lt, MNTC, NIC, NTC, Pl, TH, WEC], and the Philippians did not need to be reminded of his position [Alf, Ea, GNC, ICC, Lg, My, NIC, NTC, Pl, WC].

to-all the saints[a] in[b] Christ Jesus the-
(ones) being[c] in Philippi,

LEXICON—a. ἅγιος (GEL 11.27): 'saints' [BAGD, Ea, El, HNTC, Ln, Lt, NTC; KJV, NASB, NIV, NRSV], 'God's people' [GEL, WBC; REB, TEV, TNT], 'holy ones' [Mou; NAB], 'God's holy people' [NJB], 'who are holy' [WEC], 'church' [EGT].

b. ἐν with dative object (GEL 89.119) (BAGD I.5.d. p. 259): 'in' [BAGD, GEL, Ea, HNTC, Ln, NTC; KJV, NAB, NASB, NIV, NJB, NRSV], 'incorporate in' [WBC; REB], 'in union with' [GEL; TEV], 'through their union with' [WEC], '(who) belong to' [TNT], 'in connection with' [Ln].

c. pres. act. participle of εἰμί (GEL 85.1): 'to be (at/in)' [Ea, GEL, HNTC, Ln, WBC; KJV, NASB, NRSV], 'to live (at)' [REB]. 'Being in' is translated 'at' [ICC; NAB, NIV, NJB], 'in' [WEC; TEV, TNT].

QUESTION—What relationship is indicated by ἐν 'in'?

1. It indicates an intimate personal relation or spiritual union with Christ [BAGD, Ea, EBC, EGT, El, HNTC, ICC, Ln, MNTC,

Mou, NTC, Pl, TH, WBC; REB, TEV]: saints who are in union with Christ.

2. It indicates ownership [TNT]: saints who belong to Christ.

with[a] (the) bishops[b] and/even deacons:[c]

LEXICON—a. σύν with dative object (GEL 89.107) (BAGD 4.b. p. 782): 'with' [Ea, HNTC, Mou, WBC; KJV, NAB, NRSV], 'including' [WEC; NASB, REB, TEV, TNT], 'together with' [BAGD, El, GEL, Ln, NTC; NIV, NJB], 'along with' [My].

b. ἐπίσκοπος (GEL 53.71) (BAGD 2. p. 299): 'bishop' [BAGD, Ea, El, HNTC, Mou; KJV, NAB, NRSV, REB, TNT], 'overseer' [ICC, Ln, Mou, My, NTC, WBC, WEC; NASB, NIV], 'presiding elder' [Ea; NJB], 'church leader' [GEL; TEV], 'superintendent' [BAGD, ICC, Mou], 'guardian' [BAGD].

c. διάκονος (GEL 53.67) (BAGD 1.c. p. 184): 'deacon' [BAGD, Ea, El, GEL, HNTC, Ln, Mou, My, NTC, WBC, WEC; all translations except TEV], 'minister' [ICC], '(church) helper' [TEV], '(one) who serves' [ICC, WBC], 'worker' [Mou].

QUESTION—What relationship is indicated by σύν 'with'?

The officers are mentioned in conjunction with the general members of the church [Alf, Ea, ICC, Ln, NTC, WBC]: to the church members and officers. This does not imply that the church officers are not saints or that they are not in Christ [TH]. Some think that special mention is made of the officers so as to include them in the greeting [GNC, My, Pl; NASB, REB, TEV, TNT]: to the saints, including the bishops and deacons; or it makes a special point to direct the greeting to them [El, NIC]: to the saints, especially to the bishops and deacons among them. Some suggestions for the reason for making special mention of the officers are that they would be the ones to whom the letter would be delivered and they would then have it read in church [EBC], Paul was endorsing their authority and they were responsible to see that Paul's instructions were carried out [EBC], Paul wanted to express his special appreciation to them because they were the ones that had been responsible for gathering money and sending it to Paul [EBC, EGT, El, Ln, Lt, MNTC, My, Pl, TH].

QUESTION—To whom do the terms ἐπισκόποις 'bishops' and διακόνοις 'deacons' refer?

They refer to two classes of office bearers [all commentaries except WBC]: to the bishops and the deacons. WBC favors the possibility that 'bishop' refers to the office and 'deacon' refers to the function of that office: to the overseers who serve. Some commentators think that ἐπίσκοπος 'bishop' (used here) and πρεσβύτερος 'elder' (used elsewhere) were differing terms for the same office and function at the early stage of church history [Ea, EBC, EGT, El,

GNC, HNTC, Ln, Lt, MNTC, Mou, My, NIC, NTC, Pl, TH, WBC].
One states that the bishops dealt with internal matters while the
deacons dealt with external matters [Bg].

1:2

Grace[a] to-you and peace[b]

> LEXICON—a. χάρις (GEL 88.66) (BAGD 2.c. p. 877): 'grace'
> [BAGD, Ea, GEL, HNTC, ICC, Ln, NTC, WBC, WEC; all
> translations], 'favor' [BAGD, Mou, Pl], 'kindness' [GEL].
> b. εἰρήνη (GEL 22.42): 'peace' [BAGD, Ea, GEL, HNTC, ICC,
> Ln, NTC, Pl, WBC, WEC; all translations], 'tranquility' [GEL].
>
> QUESTION—Why are 'grace' and 'peace' used in this greeting?
> Paul transforms the customary Greek and Hebrew letter salutations
> into a distinctly Christian greeting by the use of 'grace' and 'peace'
> [EBC, EGT, El, GNC, ICC, MNTC, NIC, Pl, TNTC, WBC, WC,
> WEC].
>
> QUESTION—What is the meaning of 'peace' here?
> 1. It encompasses all temporal and spiritual welfare and health
>   [GNC, MNTC, WC].
> 2. It is a wholeness and harmony brought about by reconciliation
>   with God [EGT, ICC, NTC, Pl, TH, TNTC, WBC].
> 3. It is an inner assurance and tranquility [EBC, Mou, NIC]. It is
>   caused by the fact of reconciliation with God [Mou, NIC].

from[a] God our Father and (the) Lord Jesus Christ.

> LEXICON—a. ἀπό with genitive object (GEL 90.15) (BAGD V.4.
> p. 88): 'from' [BAGD, Ea, GEL, HNTC, ICC, Ln, Mou, NTC,
> Pl, WBC, WEC; all translations except TEV], not explicit
> [TEV].
>
> QUESTION—What verb is implied here?
> Implicit is the idea that grace and peace are given by God the
> Father and the Lord Jesus. Paul's wish or prayer is that these
> blessings will be given to the Philippians [TEV]: may God our
> Father and the Lord Jesus Christ give you grace and peace.

DISCOURSE UNIT: 1:3–26 [Lg, Pl; NAB]. This unit is viewed as
historical and personal [Pl] and as Paul's example [NAB], Paul's situation
and work [Lg].

DISCOURSE UNIT: 1:3–11 [Alf, Lg, Lt, Mou, My, NIC, NTC, Pl, TH,
WBC, WC; GNT, NAB, NIV, NJB]. The topic is thanksgiving and prayer
for the Philippians [Lt, Mou, NIC, NTC, Pl, WBC, WC; NIV, NJB],
Paul's prayer for the Philippians [TH; GNT, TEV], gratitude and hope
[NAB], Paul's thankfulness and joy (and confidence [My]) over the church
[Lg, My].

DISCOURSE UNIT: 1:3–8 [EBC, EGT, HNTC, Ln, NIC, WEC]. The topic is thanksgiving [EBC, WEC], Paul's thankfulness and love for the Philippians and his confidence in them [EGT], Paul's prayer for the Philippians [HNTC, Ln].

DISCOURSE UNIT: 1:3–7 [MNTC, TNTC, WC]. The topic is thanksgiving [WC], Paul's thankfulness and confidence in the Philippians [MNTC, TNTC].

DISCOURSE UNIT: 1:3–5 [ICC, WEC]. The topic is thanksgiving [ICC].

1:3

I-thank[a] my God at/because-of[b] all[c] the remembrance/mention[d] of-you,

LEXICON—a. pres. act. indic. of εὐχαριστέω (GEL 33.349) (BAGD 2. p. 328): 'to thank' [Ea, GEL, ICC, Ln, NTC, Pl, WBC, WEC; all translations except NAB], 'to give thanks' [BAGD, HNTC; NAB].

b. ἐπί with dative object (GEL 67.33; 89.27) (BAGD II.2. p. 288): 'at' [Alf, BAGD], 'at the time of' [BAGD, GEL], 'on' [Ea, El, Pl], 'upon' [Ln; KJV], 'when' [GEL], 'in' [Alf, ICC, Mou, My, NTC; NASB], 'during' [BAGD], 'because of' [GEL], 'for' [WEC]. The phrase ἐπὶ πάσῃ τῇ μνείᾳ ὑμῶν 'at all the remembrance of you' is translated 'every time I make mention of you' [HNTC], 'every time I mention you' [WBC], 'every time I remember you' [WEC; NIV, NRSV], 'every time I think of you' [NAB, REB, TEV], 'whenever I think of you' [NJB, TNT].

c. πᾶς (GEL 59.23) (BAGD 1.c.β. p. 632): 'all' [GEL, ICC, Ln, Mou, NTC, Pl, WEC; NASB], 'whole' [Alf, Ea, EBC, El, My], 'every' [BAGD, WEC; KJV],

d. μνεία (GEL 29.18) (BAGD 2. p. 524): 'remembrance' [Alf, Ea, El, ICC, Ln, Mou, My, NTC, Pl, WEC; KJV, NASB], 'mention' [BAGD, HNTC, WBC].

QUESTION—What relationship is indicated by ἐπί 'at/because of'?

1. It indicates the time at which he thanks God [Bg, Blm, Ln, HNTC, MNTC, NIC, TH, TNTC, WBC, WEC; NAB, NIV, NJB, REB, TEV, TNT]: I thank my God when I remember/mention you. This implies that what he remembers about them is a reason for thanking God.

2. It indicates the reason he thanks God [Ea, EBC, EGT, El, Lg, Mou]: I thank my God because of what I remember about you.

3. It indicates what accompanies his thanksgiving [Alf, My]: I thank my God while remembering you.

QUESTION—What is the meaning of μνείᾳ 'remembrance/mention'?

1. It means 'remembrance' [Alf, Bg, Blm, Ea, EBC, EGT, El, GNC, ICC, Lg, Ln, Lt, Mou, My, NIC, NTC, Pl, TH, TNTC, WEC; all translations]: I thank my God when/because I remember you.
2. It means 'mention' [BAGD, HNTC, MNTC, WBC]: I thank my God when I mention you to him.

QUESTION—To what does πάσῃ 'all' refer?

1. It refers to the time of remembrance/mention [Blm, GNC, HNTC; all translations except KJV, NASB]: I thank my God every time I remember/mention you.
2. It refers to the content of what is remembered [Alf, Bg, Ea, EBC, EGT, El, ICC, Lg, Ln, Lt, Mou, My, NTC, Pl; KJV, NASB]: I thank my God when/because of all that I remember about you. Some commentators take it to mean that he is thankful for all that he remembers, that is, for everything that he remembers about them [Bg, Lt, Ln, NIC, NTC]. Others take this to mean, not every single thing he remembers, but what he remembers as a whole [Alf, EBC, EGT, El, ICC, Lg, Mou, My, Pl].

QUESTION—How are the event word and the persons related in the genitive construction τῇ μνείᾳ ὑμῶν 'the remembrance/mention of you'?

Many commentators mention the possibility of taking 'you' to be the actor of the event ('you remembered me'), but in fact all commentators and translations take 'you' to be the recipient of the event: I remember/mention you.

1:4

always[a] in every prayer[b] of-mine

LEXICON—a. πάντοτε (GEL 67.88): 'always' [Alf, BAGD, Ea, GEL, HNTC, ICC, Ln, NTC, WBC, WEC; KJV, NASB, NIV, NJB, REB], 'at all times' [BAGD, GEL, My], 'on all/every occasion(s)' [GEL, ICC, Pl], 'constantly' [NAB, NRSV], not specific [TEV, TNT].

b. δέησις (GEL 33.171) (BAGD p. 172): 'prayer' [Alf, BAGD, GEL, WBC, WEC; KJV, NAB, NASB, NIV, NRSV], 'supplication' [Ea, HNTC, ICC, NTC, Pl, TH], 'petition' [Ln, Mou], 'request' [GEL, Mou, My]. The phrase ἐν πάσῃ δεήσει μου 'in every prayer of mine' is translated 'every time I pray' [NJB, TEV], 'whenever I pray' [REB, TNT]. Δέησις 'prayer' is more specific than προσευχή, the general term for prayer or worship; δέησις implies petition or entreaty for the meeting of some present or future need [BAGD, Bg, EGT, ICC, Ln, Mou,

NIC, NTC, Pl, WBC]. However, one commentator thinks that
δέησις here is synonymous with προσευχή [WEC].

QUESTION—What is this phrase connected with?

1. It is connected with the following phrase, 'with joy making
   prayer' [El, ICC, Lg, Ln, WBC, WC; all translations except
   NAB]: in every prayer of mine, I always pray with joy; or, every
   time I pray, I pray with joy.

2. It is connected with the preceding verse [Lt, MNTC, My; NAB].

2.1 It gives the time of the thanksgiving [Lt, MNTC, My]: I thank
    my God always in every prayer of mine for you all.

2.2 It is a comment on the phrase 'in all my remembrance of you'
    [NAB]: I thank my God when I think of you (and I always
    think of you whenever I pray).

for[a] all of-you

LEXICON—a. ὑπέρ with genitive object (GEL 90.36): 'for' [Alf,
BAGD, Ea, GEL, HNTC, Ln, WBC; all translations except
NAB], 'on/in behalf of' [BAGD, GEL, NTC, WEC; NAB], 'for
the sake of' [BAGD].

QUESTION—What is this phrase connected with?

1. It is connected with the verb 'I thank' of the preceding verse
   [Lt, Pl]: I thank God for you all.

2. It is connected with the preceding reference to prayer 'in every
   prayer of mine' [Bg, El, Ln, MNTC, My, NTC, WEC; KJV,
   NASB, NIV, NJB, NRSV, REB, TEV]: in every prayer of mine
   for all of you.

3. It is connected with the following reference to prayer 'in joy
   making the prayer' [Alf, ICC, Lg, WBC; NAB, TNT]: I pray for
   all of you with joy.

with joy[a] the prayer[b] making,[c]

LEXICON—a. χαρά (GEL 25.123) (BAGD 1. p. 875): 'joy' [Alf,
BAGD, Ea, El, GEL, HNTC, ICC, Ln, NTC, WBC, WEC; all
translations except NAB, REB]. This noun is translated as the
participle 'rejoicing' [NAB] and as the adjective 'joyful' [REB].
This word occurs first for emphasis [Mou, Pl, WBC].

b. δέησις (GEL 33.171) (BAGD p. 172): 'prayer' [Alf, GEL,
WEC; NASB, REB], 'request' [GEL, Mou; KJV], 'supplication'
[Ea, HNTC, ICC, NTC], 'petition' [ICC, Ln, Mou], 'entreaty'
[NIC]. The phrase τὴν δέησιν ποιούμενος 'the prayer making' is
translated 'I pray' [WBC; NIV, NJB, TEV, TNT], 'praying'
[NRSV], 'as I plead' [NAB].

c. pres. mid. participle of ποιέω (GEL 90.45) (BAGD II.1. p. 683):
'to make' [Alf, Ea, GEL, HNTC, ICC, Ln, NTC, WEC; KJV],
'to offer' [NASB].

QUESTION—What is the significance of the article in the phrase τὴν δέησιν 'the prayer'?

1. It refers the reader back to the first mention of δέησις 'prayer' [Alf, Bg, Ea, El, Ln, Lt, Mou, My, WEC; NIV, NJB, NRSV, REB, TEV, TNT]: in my prayers I make these prayers with joy.

2. It indicates that Paul makes a particular petition [Blm, Lg(H)]; the first mention of δέησις 'prayer' without the article is more general [ICC; KJV, NAB]: in my prayers I make request for you.

QUESTION—What relationship is indicated by the use of the participial phrase τὴν δέησιν ποιούμενος 'making the prayer'?

1. This indicates the accompanying circumstance of Paul's thanksgiving [Ln, NTC; NAB, NASB, NIV, NJB, REB, TEV, TNT]: I thank God, and I pray for you with joy.

2. This amplifies the preceding phrase 'in every prayer of mine' [Lt]: whenever I pray for you, (and these prayers I offer with joy), etc.

1:5

for[a] your partnership[b] in[c] the gospel[d]

LEXICON—a. ἐπί with dative object (GEL 89.27): 'for' [ICC, NTC, Pl; KJV, NJB], 'because (of)' [GEL, WBC, WEC; NIV, NRSV, REB, TNT], 'on account of' [Ea, Mou], 'on the basis of' [GEL, Ln], 'in view of' [NASB], 'at' [NAB].

b. κοινωνία (GEL 34.5) (BAGD 1. p. 439): 'partnership' [NIV, NJB], 'fellowship' [Alf, Ea, GEL, HNTC, Ln, NTC, Pl; KJV], 'cooperation' [ICC], 'participation' [WEC; NASB], 'close relationship' [BAGD], 'close association' [GEL]. The phrase τῇ κοινωνίᾳ ὑμῶν 'your partnership' is translated 'the way you have all continually helped' [NAB], 'the way in which you have helped' [TEV], 'the way you have shared' [TNT], 'your sharing' [NRSV], 'the part you have taken' [REB], 'you have been partners' [WBC].

c. εἰς with accusative object (GEL 90.41) (BAGD 4.c.β. p. 229): 'in' [NTC, WBC; KJV, NASB, NIV, NJB, NRSV], 'in/to the furtherance of' [HNTC, Mou], 'in contributing to the spread of' [Pl], 'in promoting' [ICC], 'in proclaiming' [TNT], 'in the work' [WEC; REB, TEV], 'in favor of' [Ea], 'to promote' [NAB].

d. εὐαγγέλιον (GEL 33.217) (BAGD 1.a. p. 318): 'gospel' [BAGD, Ea, GEL, HNTC, ICC, Ln, NTC, WBC, WEC; all translations except TNT], 'good news' [BAGD, GEL; TNT].

QUESTION—What relationship is indicated by ἐπί 'for'?

1. It gives the reason for Paul's joy (1:4) [EBC, EGT, GNC, Ln, MNTC, TH, WBC; NAB, NIV, NJB, REB, TEV, TNT]: I pray

with joy because of your partnership in the gospel. This leaves
'I thank God' (1:3) without an explicit object, but it is implied
that Paul thanks God for the Philippians themselves [WBC].

2. It gives the reason for Paul's thanksgiving (1:3) [Alf, Bg, Ea, El,
   ICC, Lg, Lt, My, NIC, NTC, Pl, TNTC, WC, WEC]: I thank
   God because of your partnership in the gospel. One
   commentator takes 1:4 to be a parenthetical insertion between
   the thanksgiving of 1:3 and the reason for thanksgiving here
   [WC], but it natural to take 1:3–4 as the main clause with
   1:4b–5 as a subordinate clause so that 1:5 is a reiteration of the
   initial thought of thanksgiving [WEC].

QUESTION—There are two interrelated questions: Who are the ones
who are involved in the 'partnership/fellowship' and What is the area
of meaning of 'partnership/fellowship in the gospel'?

1. Paul is speaking of the Philippians' partnership with himself in
   all aspects of the work of propagating the gospel [Ea, EBC,
   EGT, El, GNC, Lt, MNTC, Mou, NIC, NTC, Pl, TH, TNTC,
   WBC, WEC; TEV, TNT]: your partnership with me in
   spreading the gospel. The reference is to financial support [all
   commentators], sympathy for his work [Ea, Lt, MNTC, NIC,
   NTC, TH], prayer for the progress of the gospel [Mou, NIC,
   NTC, WBC], and spreading the gospel themselves [El, GNC,
   NIC, TH, WBC].

2. Paul is speaking of the Philippians' fellowship with each other
   as they unitedly work for the spread of the gospel [Alf, ICC,
   My]: your fellowship with each other in the work of the gospel
   at Philippi.

3. Paul is speaking of the Philippians' partnership with all who
   had been involved in the work at Philippi from the beginning,
   including Paul, and of all the ways the partnership was
   manifested [Ln, WC]: your partnership with each other and me
   in the work of spreading the gospel.

4. Paul is speaking of the Philippians' fellowship with Christ
   through faith and their fellowship with one another in sharing
   the blessings of the gospel [Blm]: your fellowship with Christ
   and with other Christians.

from[a] the first day[b] until[c] now,[d]

LEXICON—a. ἀπό with genitive object (GEL 67.131) (BAGD II.2.b.
p. 87): 'from' [BAGD, Ea, GEL, HNTC, ICC, Ln, Lt, Mou,
NTC, Pl, WBC, WEC; all translations], 'since' [GEL].

b. ἡμέρα (GEL 67.178) (BAGD 2. p. 346): 'day' [BAGD, Ea,
GEL, HNTC, Ln, NTC, WBC; all translations]. The phrase τῆς
πρώτης ἡμέρας 'the first day' is translated 'the time it was first

preached among you' [ICC], 'the earliest days of your conversion' [Pl], 'the beginning of your faith' [WEC].
   c. ἄχρι with genitive object (GEL 67.119) (BAGD 1.a. p. 128): 'until' [BAGD, Ea, GEL, HNTC, ICC, Ln, NTC, WBC, WEC; all translations except NAB, NJB], 'down to' [Pl], 'up to' [NJB]. The phrase ἄχρι τοῦ νῦν 'until now' is translated 'continually' [NAB].
   d. νῦν (GEL 67.38) (BAGD 3.b. p. 546): 'now' [BAGD, Ea, GEL, HNTC, WBC; all translations except NAB, NJB], 'the present' [ICC, Ln, NTC; NJB], 'this very moment' [WEC], 'the present moment' [Pl].
QUESTION—What is this phrase connected with?
   1. It is connected with the preceding phrase 'your partnership in the gospel' and indicates uninterrupted partnership/fellowship [Alf, Ea, El, GNC, HNTC, ICC, Lg, Ln, Lt, MNTC, Mou, My, NTC, Pl, WEC; all translations]: your partnership in the work of the gospel continually, from the first day until the present.
   2. It is connected with the preceding phrase 'with joy making the prayer' [Blm]: I have been making this prayer since the first day of your fellowship in the gospel.
QUESTION—What is meant by 'the first day'?
   It means that the partnership continued from the very beginning of the Philippians' acquaintance with Paul, when they first believed the gospel he preached [EBC, El, GNC, ICC, Ln, Lt, MNTC, My, NIC, Pl, TH, WEC]: your partnership in the work of the gospel from the time it was first preached among you until the present.

DISCOURSE UNIT: 1:6–11 [ICC]. The topic is commendation and prayer.

DISCOURSE UNIT: 1:6–8 [WEC]. The topic is an expansion on the preceding thoughts.

1:6

being-confident-(of)[a] this very-thing,

   LEXICON—a. perf. act. participle of πείθω (GEL 33.301) (BAGD 2.b. p. 639): 'to be confident (of) [Ea, Ln, NTC, WEC; KJV, NASB, NIV, NJB, NRSV, REB], 'to be sure (of)' [BAGD, WBC; NAB, TEV], 'to be certain (of)' [BAGD], 'to be convinced' [GEL], 'to firmly believe' [TNT]. This entire phrase is translated 'in full confidence' [HNTC], 'with confidence' [ICC], 'I have this very confidence' [Pl].

QUESTION—What relationship is indicated by the use of the participle πεποιθώς 'being confident'?

1. It indicates the reason for thanking God (1:3) [Bg, ICC, Lg, Lt, NTC]: I thank God because I am confident that he will complete his good work in you.
2. It indicates the reason for praying with joy (1:4) [Blm, EGT]: I pray for you with joy because I am confident that he will complete his good work in you.
3. It indicates the reason for thanking God (1:3) and for praying with joy (1:4) [Ea, Ln, NIC, Pl, WC, WEC].
4. It indicates an accompaniment of thanksgiving [WBC]: I thank God for you and I am confident that he will complete his good work in you.
5. It indicates a conclusion to the previous clause [GNC, TH, TNTC; TEV]. The beginning of God's work in them is implied by their fellowship in the gospel from the first day and that leads to this expression of Paul's confidence that God will complete this good work [TNTC].

QUESTION—What does the phrase αὐτὸ τοῦτο 'this very thing' refer to?

1. It refers to the content of Paul's confidence that is stated in the following ὅτι 'that' clause [Ea, El, ICC, Ln, MNTC, NIC, NTC, Pl, TH, WEC; all translations except NJB, TEV]: the thing I am confident of is this, that, etc. The phrase is used for emphasis [Alf, Ea, El, ICC] or firmness [EGT, Mou].
2. It has no specific referent [HNTC, Lt, WBC; NJB, TEV]: I am confident that, etc. The phrase does not focus on an antecedent and means no more than 'I am confident with this confidence', meaning that he was sure of the following fact [WBC].
3. It refers to the reason for Paul's confidence which is stated in the preceding clause [My]: because of your partnership, I am confident that, etc.

that the-(one) having-begun[a] in[b] you a-good work

LEXICON—a. aorist mid. (deponent = act.) participle of ἐνάρχομαι (GEL 68.3) (BAGD p. 262): 'to begin' [BAGD, Ea, GEL, HNTC, ICC, Ln, NTC, WBC, WEC; all translations except REB], 'to start' [REB], 'to initiate' [Pl].

b. ἐν with dative object (GEL 83.13): 'in' [Ea, HNTC, ICC, Ln, NTC, Pl, WEC; all translations], 'through' [WBC].

QUESTION—What relationship is indicated by ὅτι 'that'?

It indicates the content of what Paul is confident about [Alf, Blm, EBC, El, GNC, HNTC, ICC, Lg, Lt, MNTC, Mou, My, NIC, NTC, Pl, TH, TNTC, WBC, WEC]: I am confident that he who has begun a good work will complete it.

QUESTION—Who is the implied actor of 'the one having begun'?
> God is the implied actor [Alf, Bg, Blm, Ea, EBC, El, HNTC, ICC, Lg, Ln, Lt, MNTC, My, NIC, NTC, TH, TNTC, WBC; TEV].

QUESTION—Why is this description of God given here?
> It provides the grounds for being confident that God will continue his work in them [EBC, HNTC, Ln, MNTC, My, NIC, NTC, Pl, WBC, WEC]. Since God started this work, he can be trusted to complete it [HNTC].

QUESTION—What is meant by ἐν 'in' you?
> 1. It refers to the location where the work was done and means in their hearts [Ea, EBC, El, ICC, Lg, Ln, MNTC, NTC, TH]: God began a good work in you.
> 2. It refers to the instruments God used [WBC]: God began a good work though you. This does not refer to the improvement of their characters, rather it refers to the sharing of their resources to help Paul promote the gospel [WBC].

QUESTION—What do the words ἔργον ἀγαθόν 'a good work' refer to?
> 1. They refer to the 'fellowship/partnership' mentioned in 1:4 [Alf, Ea, El, Lt, My, Pl, WBC]: he who began in you this good work of participation in the gospel. It may have a wider meaning as well [Pl, WBC].
> 2. They refer to the salvation/regeneration that came when the Philippians received the gospel and the development of their Christians lives [Bg, Blm, EBC, EGT, GNC, ICC, Lg, Ln, MNTC, Mou, NIC, NTC, TH, TNTC, WC]: he who began in you the good work of salvation. The absence of the article with 'work' implies a wider sense than just the gift they sent to Paul [EBC]. Their salvation resulted in their activity and close partnership for the promotion of the gospel [EBC, GNC, ICC, Ln, MNTC, NIC, NTC, TH, WC]. It includes God's work in their inner dispositions and their outward activity [NIC]. It is a work that gradually develops step by step until it is finally complete at the day of Christ [Lg].

will-complete[a] (it) until/at[b] (the)-day of-Christ Jesus.

TEXT—Instead of Χριστοῦ Ἰησοῦ 'Christ Jesus', some manuscripts read Ἰησοῦ Χριστοῦ 'Jesus Christ'. GNT does not deal with this variant. 'Jesus Christ' is read by KJV, NJB, and NRSV.

LEXICON—a. fut. act. indic. of ἐπιτελέω (GEL 68.22) (BAGD 1. p. 302): 'to complete', 'to perform' [Ea; KJV], 'to finish' [BAGD, Ln], 'to perfect' [NASB], 'to continue and complete' [TNT], 'to carry to completion' [HNTC], 'to carry through to completion' [NJB], 'to carry on toward completion' [NTC], 'to carry on to completion' [NIV], 'to bring to completion' [WBC,

WEC; REB, NRSV], 'to go on completing' [NJB], 'to bring to perfection' [Pl], 'to perfect and to show completed' [ICC], 'to carry on until it is finished' [GEL; TEV], 'to bring to an end' [BAGD]. The meaning is to bring to completion [EBC], to bring to a complete and perfect end [El], to present complete, fully done [NTC], to complete and consummate [ICC, TH].

   b. ἄχρι with genitive object (GEL 67.119) (BAGD 1.a. p. 128): 'until' [BAGD, Ea, GEL, HNTC, NTC, Pl; KJV, NASB, NIV, NJB], 'at' [WBC, WEC], 'up to' [Ln], 'right up to' [NAB], 'by' [NRSV, REB, TNT], 'on' [TEV], 'in' [ICC].

QUESTION—What is meant by ἡμέρας Χριστοῦ 'Ιησοῦ 'day of Christ Jesus'?

   1. It is the second coming of Christ [Alf, EBC, EGT, GNC, HNTC, ICC, Lg, Ln, Lt, MNTC, Mou, My, NIC, NTC, Pl, TH, TNTC, WBC]: until the day Christ Jesus returns. Aspects of that day specifically mentioned are Christ's glorious appearing [ICC, NTC], testing or judgment [EBC, EGT, GNC, HNTC, Lt, NIC, NTC, Pl, TH, WBC], consummation of salvation [EBC, GNC, HNTC, TH], the resurrection of believers [Ln], and vindication [EBC, NTC]. Some commentators think that this assumes that Christ would return soon [Ea, ICC, MNTC, My, TH] and that this does not refer to succeeding generations of Philippians or to their continued preparation after death [MNTC]. Others point out that God's work is not done in believers until the time of Christ's return when they receive resurrection bodies, are rewarded, and share in Christ's glory [EBC, Lg, Ln, WC].

   2. It is the decisive day for each individual, whether the person's death or the second coming of Christ [Blm, Ea, El]: until the day people meet Christ. Christ returns for believers at their death (John 14:1–2) [Ea].

1:7

Because[a] it-is right[b] for-me to-feel[c] this about[d] all of-you,

   LEXICON—a. καθώς (GEL 89.34; 64.14) (BAGD 3. p. 391): 'because' [GEL], 'for' [NASB], 'since' [BAGD], 'in so far as' [BAGD], 'just as' [GEL, NTC], 'even as' [Ea, Ln; KJV], 'indeed' [WBC], 'and indeed' [WEC], not explicit [HNTC, Pl; NAB, NIV, NJB, NRSV, REB, TEV, TNT].

   b. δίκαιος (GEL 66.5) (BAGD 5. p. 391): 'right' [BAGD, Ea, HNTC, Ln, NTC, WBC, WEC; all translations except KJV], 'proper' [GEL], 'natural' [REB], 'meet' [KJV].

   c. pres. act. infin. of φρονέω (GEL 26.16) (BAGD 1. p. 866): 'to feel' [BAGD, WBC, WEC; NASB, NIV, NJB, REB, TEV,

TNT], 'to have a feeling' [HNTC], 'to think' [BAGD, Ea; KJV, NRSV], 'to think in a particular manner' [GEL], 'to be minded' [ICC, NTC, Pl]. Φρονέω indicates a general disposition of mind rather than a specific thought [ICC, Mou, My]; it is a combination of feeling and thought [WBC].

    d. ὑπέρ with genitive object (GEL 90.24) (BAGD 1.a.δ. p. 838): 'about' [GEL, WBC, WEC; NASB, NIV, NRSV, REB, TEV, TNT], 'in/on behalf of' [BAGD, Ea, Ln, NTC, Pl], 'in (your) regard' [NAB], 'for' [HNTC], 'of' [KJV], towards [NJB].

QUESTION—What relationship is indicated by καθώς 'because'?

    1. It indicates the grounds for having confidence (1:6) [Alf, Ea, EGT, El, ICC, Lg, Lt, MNTC, My, NTC, Pl, TNTC; NAB]: I have this confidence in regard to you because it is right for me to feel this about you.

    2. It indicates the grounds for feeling thankful and joyful about them (1:3–4) [Blm, Mou]: I am thankful and joyful because it is right for me to feel this way about you.

    3. It indicates the grounds for his thankfulness, joy, and confidence about them (1:3–6) [Bg, Ln, WBC].

because-of[a] the to-have[b] I/me in the heart[c] you,

LEXICON—a. διά with accusative object (GEL 89.26): 'because of' [Ea, GEL, HNTC, Ln, NTC, Pl, WBC, WEC; KJV, NASB, NJB, NRSV, REB], 'for' [TNT, WEC], 'since' [NIV], not explicit [TEV].

    b. pres. act. infin. of ἔχω (GEL 18.6) (BAGD I.2.j. p. 333): 'to have' [BAGD, Ea, HNTC, Ln; KJV, NASB, NIV, NJB], 'to hold' [GEL, NTC, WBC, WEC; NAB, NRSV, REB]. This entire phrase is translated 'by my personal affection for you' [ICC], 'because you held me in such affection' [WBC], 'since I hold all of you dear' [NAB], 'because you hold me in such affection' [REB], 'for you are so very dear to me' [TNT], 'you are always in my heart' [TEV].

    c. καρδία (GEL 26.3) (BAGD 1.b.ζ. p. 404): 'heart' [Ea, GEL, HNTC, Ln, Lt, Mou, NTC, Pl; KJV, NAB, NIV, NJB, NRSV, TEV].

QUESTION—What relationship is indicated by διά 'because of'?

It indicates the grounds for saying that it was right to feel the way he did about them [Alf, Blm, ICC, Ln, Lt, WBC; all translations except TEV].

QUESTION—Who is in whose heart?

    1. Paul has the Philippians in his heart [Alf, Bg, Blm, Ea, EBC, El, GNC, HNTC, ICC, Lg, Ln, Lt, MNTC, Mou, My, NTC, Pl, TH, TNTC, WC, WEC; all translations except NRSV]: I have you in my heart.

2. The Philippians have Paul in their heart [WBC: NRSV]: you have me in your heart.

QUESTION—What is the meaning of having someone in one's heart?

1. It means to have a sincere affection for someone [Blm, Ea, EGT, ICC, Lg, My, Mou, WBC, WEC; NAB, REB, TNT].

2. It means to reflect and think deeply about them [Lt, MNTC, WC].

3. Both affection and thought are included [El, Ln, NIC, NTC, Pl].

both in[a] my bonds[b] and in[c] the defense[d] and confirmation[e] of-the gospel

LEXICON—a. ἐν with dative object (GEL 89.5; 89.119): 'in' [Ea, HNTC, ICC, Ln, Lt, Mou, NTC, Pl; KJV, NASB, NIV, NRSV, TEV], not explicit [NJB]. This entire phrase is translated 'both when I have been in chains and when I have defended and confirmed the gospel' [WEC], 'when I lie in prison or am summoned to defend the solid grounds on which the gospel rests' [NAB], 'both while I am kept in prison and when I am called on to defend the truth of the gospel' [REB], 'whether I am in chains or defending and confirming the gospel' [NIV], 'both now that I am in prison and also while I was free to defend the gospel and establish it firmly' [TEV], 'both of being in prison and of defending and vindicating the gospel' [WBC], 'both my chains and my work defending and establishing the gospel' [NJB].

b. δεσμός (GEL 37.115; 6.14) (BAGD 1. p. 176): 'bonds' [BAGD, Ea, GEL, HNTC, NTC; KJV], 'chains' [GEL; NIV, NJB], 'imprisonment' [BAGD, GEL, ICC, Ln, Pl; NASB, NRSV], 'prison' [BAGD, GEL, WBC; NAB, REB, TEV]. It may here refer to literal fetters or to imprisonment in general [EBC]. It refers to his entire imprisonment [Ln].

c. ἐν with dative object (GEL 89.5; 89.119): 'in' [Ea, HNTC, ICC, Ln, Lt, Mou, NTC, Pl, WEC; KJV, NASB, NRSV].

d. ἀπολογία (GEL 33.436) (BAGD 2.b. p. 96): 'defense' [BAGD, Ea, GEL, HNTC, ICC, Ln, NTC, Pl; KJV, NASB, NRSV]. This noun is also translated as a verb: 'to defend' [NIV, REB, TEV, TNT], or as a gerund: 'defending' [BAGD, WBC; NJB].

e. βεβαίωσις (GEL **28.44**) (BAGD p. 138): 'confirmation' [BAGD, Ea, GEL, Ln, NTC; KJV, NASB, NRSV], 'establishment' [BAGD, ICC, Pl], 'vindication' [HNTC], (to defend) the solid grounds on which the gospel rests' [NAB], '(to defend) the truth' [REB]. This noun is also translated as a verb: 'to confirm' [NIV], 'to establish' [TEV, TNT], and as a gerund: 'establishing' [NJB], 'vindicating' [WBC].

QUESTION—What is this clause connected with?
1. It is connected with the following phrase 'you all being partakers of grace' [Ea, EBC, EGT, El, HNTC, ICC, Lg, Lt, Mou, NIC, NTC, Pl, WBC, WC; all translations]: you are partakers of grace both in my imprisonment and in my defense of the gospel.
2. It is connected with the preceding phrase 'I have you in my heart' [Alf, Bg, Blm, Lg(H), MNTC, My]: I have you in my heart whether I am in prison or defending the gospel.

QUESTION—How are 'defense' and 'confirmation' to be understood?
1. 'Defense' and 'confirmation' are two distinct but related actions [Bg, Ea, EBC, El, HNTC, ICC, Ln, Lt, MNTC, My, NTC, Pl, WBC; all translations except NAB, REB]. 'Defense' has the meaning of answering objections or accusations [Ea, EBC, ICC, Pl] and 'confirmation' has the meaning of giving proofs or reasons [Ea, EBC, Ln, My, Pl]. Both are technical legal terms [EBC, EGT, HNTC, MNTC, Ln, WBC]. The defense of the gospel resulted in its confirmation [ICC]. Some take it to refer to a time that he was not in prison [NAB, NIV, REB, TEV]: when I am in prison or when I am defending and confirming the gospel.
2. 'Defense' and 'confirmation' are synonymous.
2.1 They refer to aspects of his trial [EGT; NAB, REB]: my defense and confirmation of the gospel in my trial.
2.2 They refer to his ministry in general [WEC]: my defense and confirmation of the gospel in my ministry in general.

QUESTION—When was the defense and confirmation made?
1. Paul defended and confirmed the gospel as an apostle [Ea, El, ICC, Lt, Pl; NJB, TEV]: my work of defending and confirming the gospel. His judicial defense may be included [ICC].
2. Paul made a special defense and confirmation of the gospel at his judicial hearing [EBC, EGT, GNC, HNTC, Ln, MNTC, NTC, WBC]: when I am summoned to defend and confirm the gospel. The defense and confirmation refer to Paul's time in Rome, whether in public at the trial or in private [Alf, Mou, My].

you all being partakers[a] of/with-me of-the grace.[b]
LEXICON—a. συγκοινωνός (GEL 34.6) (BAGD p. 774): 'partakers' [NTC, Pl; KJV, NASB], 'fellow-partakers' [Ea], 'joint-fellowshippers' [Ln], 'partners' [GEL], 'participants' [BAGD], 'sharers' [BAGD, ICC, WBC; NAB]. The phrase συγκοινωνούς . . . ὄντας 'being partakers' is translated 'to share' [HNTC; NIV, NJB, NRSV, REB, TEV, TNT], 'to participate' [WEC].

b. χάρις (GEL 88.66; 25.89) (BAGD 4. p. 878): 'grace' [Ea, GEL, HNTC, ICC, Ln, NTC, Pl, WEC; KJV, NASB, NIV, NJB, NRSV], 'privilege' [WBC; REB, TEV, TNT], 'gracious lot' [NAB], 'favor' [GEL].

QUESTION—What relationship is indicated by the use of the participle ὄντας 'being'?

1. It indicates the reason why Paul has the Philippians in his heart [Blm, EBC, El, WEC; KJV, NAB, NASB, NIV, NJB]: I have you in my heart because you are partakers.

2. It indicates a (second) reason why it is right for Paul to think as he does [TH, WBC; TEV]: it is right for me to think of you as I do because I have you in my heart and because you are partakers.

3. It explains what he remembered about them [MNTC, Pl]: it is right for me to remember you, that you are partakers.

QUESTION—Three interrelated questions are: What is the genitive μου 'of/with-me' connected with? What is meant by 'grace'? In what way are the Philippians 'partakers' with Paul?

1. The genitive μου 'of/with-me' is connected with 'partakers' [Blm, Ea, EGT, El, ICC, Lg, Ln, Lt, MNTC, NIC, NTC, Pl, TNTC; NASB, NIV]: you are partakers with me of God's grace. God's grace was given to them as well as to Paul [Blm, EBC, EGT, Lg]. Suggestions offered for the meaning of 'grace' here are God's grace in general [EGT, MNTC, WC], saving grace [EBC, Lg], grace for service [Ea, El, NIC], for suffering [Ea, El, ICC, Lt, NIC, Pl], for the defense and vindication of the gospel [Lt]. The Philippians shared this grace because they shared the same salvation as Paul [EBC, Lg, NIC], identified with Paul in the cause of the gospel's vindication [Ln, NIC], showed him love and kindness [EGT], prayed, sympathized, and gave financially to Paul [NTC], suffered and defended the gospel as Paul did [ICC], and had the same evangelical labor [Ea].

2. The genitive μου 'of/with-me' is connected with 'grace' [Alf, HNTC, Mou, My, WBC, WEC; KJV, NAB, NJB, REB, TEV, TNT]: you are partakers of my grace. 'Grace' here is the special enabling God gave Paul to be an apostle [BAGD, GNC, HNTC, Mou, TH, WBC, WEC]: partakers of the privileged work God has given me. Or, it is the grace God gave Paul to suffer and endure for the sake of the defense of the gospel [My, WBC, WEC]: partakers of the grace given to me in my suffering. The Philippians participated in the grace given Paul by identifying with Paul in praying for and sympathizing with him [HNTC, Mou], by sending financial gifts [Mou, WBC], or by being enabled to suffer for Christ as Paul was enabled [My].

DISCOURSE UNIT: 1:8–11 [MNTC, TNTC, WC]. The topic is Paul's longing for the Philippians and his prayer for their increase in love [MNTC], Paul's prayer for the Philippians [TNTC, WC].

1:8

For[a] my witness[b] (is) God,

> LEXICON—γάρ (GEL 89.23): 'for' [Ea, GEL, Ln, NTC, Pl, WBC; KJV, NASB, NJB, NRSV], not explicit [HNTC, ICC, WEC; NAB, NIV, REB, TEV, TNT].
>
> > b. μάρτυς (GEL 33.270) (BAGD 2.a. p. 494): 'witness' [BAGD, Ea, GEL, HNTC, ICC, Ln, NTC, WBC, WEC; NASB, NRSV, TEV], 'record' [KJV]. This phrase is translated 'God himself can testify' [NAB], 'God can testify' [NIV], 'for I call God to witness' [Pl], 'for God will testify' [NJB], 'God knows' [REB, TNT].
>
> QUESTION—What relationship is indicated by γάρ 'for'?
>
> > 1. It indicates the grounds for Paul's statement that he has the Philippians in his heart (1:7) [Alf, Blm, El, Lg, Lt, My, NIC, NTC, Pl]: I do have you in my heart for, God knows, I long to see you.
> > 2. It indicates the grounds for Paul's feeling of gratitude, joy, and confidence (1:3-6) as well as his longing (1:8) [Ln, WBC]: I do have these feeling toward you for, God knows, I long to see you.
>
> QUESTION—What is meant by the phrase 'God is my witness'?
>
> > This is an expression Paul uses on other occasions as well [BAGD, EGT, Lt, Mou, WEC]. God is witness that Paul is telling the truth [BAGD, Lt; TEV] and Paul appeals to him for the truth of his statement [Ea, EBC, NTC]. Only God can vouch for Paul's feelings [WC] as they are hidden from men [EBC, Ln, NIC, Pl, TH]. Paul uses the oath at times of intense emotion [GNC, ICC, Mou, NIC, Pl, TH]. Here he uses it to convince the Philippians of his love for them [Ln, MNTC, Mou, NTC, WBC], for 'all' of them [HNTC]. Perhaps the Philippians imagined that Paul did not really appreciate their gift to him [EGT], or some were not sure of his continued love [HNTC].

how/that[a] I-long-for[b] you all with[c] (the) affections[d] of-Christ Jesus.

> LEXICON—a. ὡς (GEL 89.86; 78.13) (BAGD IV.4. p. 889): 'how' [Ea, GEL, HNTC, ICC, Ln, NTC, Pl, WEC; NASB, NIV, NRSV, REB], 'in what manner' [GEL], 'how much' [GEL; NAB, NJB], 'how greatly' [KJV], 'that' [BAGD, WBC; TNT]. This phrase is translated 'when I say that my deep feeling for you comes from the heart of Christ Jesus himself' [TEV].
>
> > b. pres. act. indic. of ἐπιποθέω (GEL 25.18; 25.47) (BAGD p. 247): 'to long for/after [BAGD, Ea, GEL, HNTC, ICC, Ln;

all translations except TEV], 'to yearn for/after' [NTC, Pl,
WBC], 'to have a great affection for' [GEL].

c. ἐν with dative object (GEL 89.84): 'with' [GEL, ICC, NTC, Pl,
WBC, WEC; NAB, NASB, NIV, NRSV, REB, TNT], 'in' [Ea,
HNTC, Ln, Lt, Mou; KJV].

d. σπλάγχνον (GEL 25.49) (BAGD 1.c. p. 763): 'affection' [BAGD,
ICC; NAB, NASB, NIV], 'intense love' [WEC], 'love' [BAGD;
TNT], 'tenderness' [Pl], 'compassion' [GEL; NRSV], 'bowels'
[KJV], 'heart' [HNTC], 'deeply-felt affection' [NTC], 'deep
affection' [WBC], 'deep yearning' [REB], 'warm longing' [NJB].
Σπλάγχνον is literally a general term for body organs, especially
the heart, liver, and lungs [EBC, ICC, Ln, Mou, NTC, Pl,
WBC]. In a figurative sense it can be the seat of the emotions,
as we refer to the heart [EBC, GNC, ICC, Ln, Mou, My, NIC,
NTC, Pl, WBC], or it can be the emotion itself [EBC, NIC,
NTC].

QUESTION—What is meant by ὡς 'how/that'?

1. It indicates the intensity of Paul's longing [Ea, El, ICC, Lg, My,
NIC, TNTC; KJV, NAB, NJB]: God is my witness how much I
long for you all. He wants them to know the earnestness of his
longing, not just the fact of it [Ea].

2. It indicates the fact that Paul longs [MNTC, WBC; TEV,
TNT]: God is my witness that I long for you all. The depth of
the yearning is expressed by the addition of 'with the affection
of Christ Jesus' so here God's witness is to the fact of his
longing [MNTC, WBC].

QUESTION—What did Paul long for?

The compound verb ἐπιποθέω 'to long for' indicates the direction
of the longing, i.e., longing for someone [Ea, El, ICC, Lt, My, Pl,
WEC]. Paul longed to see the Philippians again [Ea, Lg, Lg(H),
Ln, MNTC, Mou, NTC, TNTC, WBC, WC] and to help them in
their faith [MNTC, WBC], or he longed for their eternal salvation
and welfare [El, Pl].

QUESTION—How are the nouns related in the genitive construction
σπλάγχνους Χριστοῦ Ἰησοῦ 'the affections of Christ Jesus'?

1. Paul longed for them with the same kind of affection that Christ
has for them [Blm, EBC, HNTC, ICC, Ln, Lt, NTC, Pl, TH,
TNTC, WC]: I long for all of you with the same affection that
Christ Jesus has for you.

2. Paul longed for them with an affection that Christ produced in
him [WBC; TNT]: I long for all of you with an affection that
Christ Jesus has given me for you.

3. Paul longed for them with a longing produced by Christ's affection for them [Bg, GNC, My; TEV]: I long for all of you because of Christ Jesus' affection for you.

DISCOURSE UNIT: 1:9–11 [Alf, EBC, EGT, HNTC, Ln, NIC, NTC, WEC; NIV, TEV]. The topic is intercessory prayer for the Philippians [Alf, EBC, EGT, HNTC, Ln, NIC, NTC, WEC].

1:9
And this I-pray,[a]

> LEXICON—a. pres. mid. (deponent = act.) of προσεύχομαι (GEL 33.178) (BAGD p. 714): 'to pray' [Ea, GEL, HNTC, ICC, Ln, WBC, WEC; KJV, NASB, TEV]. This phrase is translated 'my prayer is' [NAB], 'it is my prayer' [NJB], '(and) this is my prayer' [Mou, NTC; NIV, NRSV, REB, TNT], 'this then is the purport of my prayer' [Lt], 'and this is the substance of my prayers for you' [Pl], 'now this is what I am praying for' [WEC].
>
> QUESTION—What is καί 'and' connected with?
>
> It resumes the thought of prayer in 1:4 [Alf, Bg, Blm, Ea, El, GNC, ICC, Lg, Lt, MNTC, Mou, NTC, Pl, TH, WBC, WEC]: I pray for you, and this is what I pray. This follows naturally after expressing his longing for them in 1:8 [Alf, Ea].
>
> QUESTION—What does τοῦτο 'this' refer to?
>
> It refers to the content of Paul's prayer which follows [Alf, Bg, Ea, El, ICC, Lg, Ln, Lt, My, NIC, WBC, WC, WEC]: I am praying for this which follows. Τοῦτο 'this' is emphatic by forefronting [Ea, ICC, NIC].

that[a] **your love**[b] **still**[c] **more and more may-abound**[d] **with/in**[e] **knowledge**[f] **and all**[g] **discernment,**[h]

> LEXICON—a. ἵνα (GEL 90.22; 89.59) (BAGD II.1.e. p. 378): 'that' [Ea, HNTC, ICC, Ln, Lt, Mou, NTC, Pl, WBC, WEC; all translations except TNT]; not explicit [TNT].
>
>> b. ἀγάπη (GEL 25.43) (BAGD I.1.a. p. 5): 'love' [Ea, GEL, HNTC, ICC, Ln, Lt, Mou, NTC, Pl, WBC, WEC; all translations].
>>
>> c. ἔτι (GEL 67.128) (BAGD 2.b. p. 316): 'still' [HNTC, WBC; NASB], 'yet' [Ea, Ln; KJV], 'ever' [Lt, Pl; REB], not explicit [NTC, WEC; NAB, NIV, NJB, NRSV, TEV, TNT].
>>
>> d. pres. act. subj. of περισσεύω (GEL 78.31) (BAGD 1.a.δ. p. 651): 'to abound' [Ea, HNTC, ICC, Ln, NTC, WEC; KJV, NAB, NASB, NIV], 'to grow' [BAGD, Lt; NJB, TEV], 'to keep on growing' [GEL], 'to keep on increasing' [WBC], 'to be rich' [MNTC], 'to grow ever richer' [REB], 'to overflow' [NRSV], 'to

grow and overflow' [TNT], 'to abound and expand' [Pl], 'to do
so all the more' [GEL].

e. ἐν with dative object (GEL 89.5; 89.80): 'with' [NTC; NJB,
NRSV, TEV], 'in' [Ea, HNTC, ICC, Ln, Pl, WBC; KJV, NAB,
NASB, NIV, REB, TNT].

f. ἐπίγνωσις (GEL 28.2; 28.18) (BAGD p. 291): 'knowledge'
[GEL, HNTC, WEC; KJV, NIV, NJB, NRSV, REB, TNT],
'understanding' [NAB], 'full knowledge' [Blm, Ea, Ln, NTC],
'perfect knowledge' [Pl], 'deeper knowledge' [WBC], 'real
knowledge' [NASB], 'true knowledge' [TEV].

g. πᾶς (GEL 59.23; 58.28) (BAGD 1.a.β. p. 631): 'all' [Ea, HNTC,
Ln; KJV, NASB], 'total' [WEC], 'full' [NRSV], 'every kind of'
[BAGD; REB], not explicit [TNT]. The phrase πάσῃ αἰσθήσει
'all discernment' means 'keen discernment' [NTC], 'unfailing
discernment' [Pl], 'perfect judgment' [TEV], 'wealth of
experience' [NAB], 'broader perception' [WBC], 'depth of
insight' [NIV], 'complete understanding' [NJB].

h. αἴσθησις (GEL 32.28) (BAGD p. 25): 'discernment' [WEC;
NASB], 'judgment' [Ea; KJV], '(moral) experience' [BAGD],
'perception' [HNTC, Ln], 'capacity for understanding' [GEL],
'insight' [NRSV, REB], 'sensitiveness' [TNT].

QUESTION—What relationship is indicated by ἵνα 'that'?

1. It indicates the content of Paul's prayer [Bg, ICC, Ln, Lt, Mou,
My, NIC, Pl, WBC, WC, WEC]: I pray that your love may
increase.

2. It indicates both the content and the purpose of Paul's prayer
[Alf, Ea, EGT, El, Lg]: I pray that your love may increase in
order to bring this about.

QUESTION—Who is the implied object of love?

1. It is love in general, with no limiting object [Bg, Blm, Ea, EBC,
El, HNTC, Lg, Lt, MNTC, NIC, NTC, Pl, TH, WBC]: your love
for others, whether God or people.

2. It refers to love for fellow believers in Philippi [EGT, ICC, My;
NJB]: your love for one another.

QUESTION—What relationship is indicated by ἐν 'with/in'?

1. It indicates additional virtues that are to increase along with
love [Alf, Blm, EBC, GNC, ICC, NTC, Pl, TH, WBC; TEV]: I
pray for an increase of your love and also of your knowledge
and discernment. These two qualities guard love from being ill-
judged or misplaced [Alf]. Love should not be mere sentiment,
but it should be based on a knowledge of the principles of
God's word as illuminated by God's Spirit [EBC]. Love fosters
the growth of these qualities [GNC, WC].

2. It indicates the attributes or elements of love that are to increase [Ea, EGT, El, HNTC, Lg, Ln, MNTC, Mou, My, NIC, TNTC; KJV, NAB, NASB, NIV, REB]: I pray that your love may increase in knowledge and discernment. Love already existed among them, but it was deficient in these two qualities [Ea, El, My, MNTC, NIC]. Love is to increase in the sphere of these two important particulars [El, Lg].

QUESTION—What is meant by ἐπίγνωσις 'knowledge'?

Ἐπίγνωσις is knowledge that is accurate [Alf, Ea, El, Ln, Mou, NTC], firm [EGT], full [Ln, Mou, NTC, Pl], perfect [Lg, Lt], advanced [ICC, Lt, NIC, NTC, Pl, WBC]. It is concerned with truth that is general [Lg, Lt, MNTC], theoretical [El, My], practical [Alf, EGT, El, ICC, My, TH, WBC], moral [Alf, GNC, WBC], ethical [ICC, Lg, MNTC], religious [GNC, WBC], divine [ICC, My], spiritual [EGT, Ln, MNTC, Mou, NTC, TH], or scriptural [EBC].

QUESTION—What is meant by αἴσθησις 'discernment'?

Αἴσθησις is literally perception by the senses [Ea, EBC, EGT, ICC, Lg, Ln, MNTC, My]. Figuratively it can be discernment or sensibility that is moral [Ea, EBC, EGT, El, GNC, MNTC, My, NIC, Pl, TH, TNTC, WBC], spiritual [Blm, ICC, MNTC, NIC, Pl], practical [EBC, ICC, Lt, MNTC, Mou, NTC, Pl]. It is the practical outworking of knowledge [WEC]. 'All discernment' is extensive in meaning: 'every form of discernment' [El, ICC]. They need all kinds of discernment for all the kinds of situations that may occur [MNTC].

1:10

so-that[a] you may choose/approve/test[b] the-(things) being-excellent/differing,[c]

LEXICON—a. εἰς with an articular infinitive as its accusative object (GEL 89.57): 'so that' [Ea, HNTC, Ln, NTC, Pl, WEC; NAB, NASB, NIV, TEV], 'in order that' [WBC], 'that' [ICC; KJV], 'then' [TNT], 'to help' [NRSV], 'that will help' [NJB], 'enabling' [REB].

b. pres. act. infin. of δοκιμάζω (GEL 27.45; 30.114) (BAGD 2.b. p. 202): 'to choose' [TEV], 'to approve' [BAGD, GEL, ICC, NTC, Pl, WBC, WEC; KJV, NASB, TNT], 'to test' [GEL, Ln], 'to accept as proved' [BAGD], 'to determine' [NRSV], 'to distinguish' [Ea], 'to learn by experience' [REB], 'to discern' [NIV], 'to prove in practice' [HNTC], 'to value' [NAB]. Δοκιμάζω means not only to test those things, but to approve, value, and choose them [Bg, Hn, My, NIC, NTC, Pl, TNTC, WBC, WC, WEC; NAB, NASB, REB, TEV, TNT].

c. pres. act. participle of διαφέρω (GEL 58.41; **65.6**) (BAGD 2.b.
p. 190): 'to be excellent' [HNTC, NTC, Pl, WBC; KJV, NASB],
'to be more valuable' [**GEL**], 'to be best' [NIV, NRSV, TEV], 'to
be right' [TNT], 'to be supremely good' [ICC], 'to really matter'
[BAGD, WEC; NAB, REB], 'to differ' [Ea, GEL, Ln].

QUESTION—What relationship is indicated by εἰς 'so that'?

It indicates the purpose (anticipated result [Ln, Pl, TNTC]) that
Paul prays for (1:9) [Alf, Ea, El, HNTC, Lg, MNTC, Mou, My,
NTC, TH, WBC, WEC, WEC]: I pray that your love may abound
with/in knowledge and discernment in order that you may approve,
etc.

QUESTION—What does this phrase mean?

1. It means to approve or value the things that are excellent or
proper [Bg, My, NIC, NTC, Pl, TH, TNTC, WBC, WEC; KJV,
NAB, NASB, TNT].

2. It means to bring to the test the things that are excellent [El,
HNTC, WC], implying approval after testing [HNTC, WC].

3. It means to distinguish between things that differ and thus
discern what are the best things [Alf, Ea, EBC, EGT, ICC, Lg,
Ln, Mou; NIV, NJB, NRSV, REB, TEV]. This discernment is
for the purpose of choosing or approving the best things [Alf,
Ea, GNC, ICC].

so-that[a] you-may-be pure[b] and blameless/offenseless[c]

LEXICON—a. ἵνα (GEL 89.59): 'so that' [Ea, GEL, Ln; NASB, NJB,
NRSV], 'that' [HNTC, ICC; KJV], 'and thus' [Pl], 'then' [REB,
TEV], 'and' [NTC; NIV, TNT], not explicit [NAB].

b. εἰλικρινής (GEL **88.41**) (BAGD p. 222): 'pure' [BAGD, Ea,
HNTC, NTC, WBC, WEC; NIV, NRSV, TNT], 'flawless' [REB],
'innocent' [NJB], 'unalloyed' [Ln], 'sincere' [BAGD, GEL, ICC;
KJV, NASB], 'free from all impurity' [TEV], 'free from stain'
[Pl], 'with a clear conscience' [NAB].

c. ἀπρόσκοπος (GEL 88.318; 25.184) (BAGD 1. p. 102):
'blameless' [BAGD, GEL, ICC, NTC, WEC; NASB, NIV,
NRSV], 'offenseless' [Ea], 'without offense' [KJV], 'without
causing offense' [GEL], 'with blameless conduct' [NAB],
'without blame' [GEL; REB], 'free from all blame' [TEV], 'free
of any trace of guilt' [NJB], 'flawless' [TNT], 'unfaltering'
[HNTC], 'free from stumbling' [Pl], 'harmless' [WBC].

QUESTION—What relationship is indicated by ἵνα 'so that'?

1. It indicates the purpose of the preceding clause [Ln, Mou] or its
intended result [MNTC, Pl, TH; NJB, TEV]: you will approve
what is excellent so that you may be pure and
blameless/offenseless.

2. It indicates the purpose of what Paul prayed for (1:9) [Ea, El, Lg, My, WBC, WEC]: I pray that your love may abound with/in knowledge and discernment in order that you may be pure and blameless/offenseless. This is called a final purpose following the preceding immediate purpose [Ea, El, My, WEC].

3. It indicates the anticipated result of acquiring the virtues of knowledge and discernment [TNTC].

QUESTION—What is meant by εἰλικρινής 'pure'?

From the literal meaning of 'unmixed' [BAGD, EGT, GNC, Lt, NTC], it came to mean in the New Testament 'pure in a moral/ethical sense' [Alf, BAGD, EGT, GNC, Ln, NTC, WBC, WEC], pure regarding faith and doctrine [Blm], honest and open in relationships with God and people [WC].

QUESTION—What is meant by ἀπρόσκοπος 'blameless/offenseless'?

1. It means to be blameless [Alf, EBC, El, GNC, Ln, Lt, Mou, NTC, Pl, TH, WEC; all translations except KJV]. This is the corresponding negative virtue to 'pure' [Lt].

2. It has the active or transitive meaning of giving no offense to others [Ea, EGT, HNTC, ICC, Lg, MNTC, My, NIC, WBC, WC; KJV]. 'Pure' refers to their relationship to God, while 'offenseless' refers to their relationship to people [EGT, Lg, NIC].

for/until[a] (the)-day of-Christ,

LEXICON—a. εἰς with accusative object (GEL 67.117; 67.119; 67.160; 90.23) (BAGD 2.a.α. p. 228): 'for' [Ea, Pl, WEC], 'until' [BAGD; NASB, NIV], 'till' [KJV], 'up to' [NAB], 'in view of' [ICC], 'with a view to' [NTC], 'in regard to' [Ln], 'against' [HNTC], 'in preparation for' [WBC], 'when' [NJB, TNT], 'on' [REB, TEV], 'in' [NRSV].

QUESTION—What relationship is indicated by εἰς 'for/until'?

1. It means 'with reference to, for' [Alf, EBC, Ea, EBC, El, GNC, HNTC, ICC, Lg, Ln, Lt, MNTC, Mou, My, NIC, NTC, Pl, WBC, WC, WEC]: that you may be pure and blameless in view of the coming day of Christ. Because the day of Christ is coming, people should prepare for it [Ea, ICC, MNTC, WBC]. One's character will be made manifest on that day [Lg].

2. It has a temporal sense of 'until, on' [TH; KJV, NAB, NASB, NIV, NJB, REB, TEV, TNT]: so that you may be pure and blameless until/on the day of Christ.

3. It has both senses [EGT; some of the translations in 2. above, such as NJB, REB, TEV, and TNT may imply both senses]: so that, having prepared because you have the day of Christ in view, you may be pure and blameless on the day of Christ.

QUESTION—What aspects of the 'day of Christ' are in focus here?
Aspects mentioned are believers standing before the Lord to give
account of deeds [EBC], review and reward [GNC], revealing of
character [Mou, NTC], judgment [Lt, My, NIC, NTC, Pl, WBC].
(See 1:6 for the first mention of the 'day of Christ Jesus').

1:11

filled-(with)[a] fruit[b] of-righteousness[c] which (is) through[d] Jesus Christ,
TEXT—Instead of καρπόν (accusative singular) 'fruit', some
manuscripts read καρπῶν (genitive plural) 'fruits'. GEL does not
mention this variant. 'Fruits' is the translation given by Blm, NTC,
KJV, and NJB, although it is not certain that all of these have done so
because of the textual variant.
  LEXICON—a. perf. pass./mid. participle of πληρόω (GEL 59.37)
      (BAGD 1.b. p. 671): 'to be filled' [BAGD, Ea, GEL, ICC, Ln,
      NTC, Pl, WBC, WEC; KJV, NASB, NIV, NJB, TEV]. The
      phrase πεπληρωμένοι καρπόν 'filled with fruit' is translated 'to
      be found rich in the harvest' [NAB], and is considered by some
      to be a middle voice rather than passive [GNC, HNTC]:
      'bringing forth a full harvest' [HNTC], 'yielding the full harvest'
      [REB], 'to bear a harvest' [TNT], 'to produce a harvest' [NRSV].
      The perfect tense indicates the continuing results of having been
      filled [Lg, Ln, Pl]. It anticipates the day of Christ when, having
      been filled, the Philippians will be full [Mou; NJB, REB].
    b. καρπός (GEL 42.13) (BAGD 2.a. p. 404): 'fruit' [BAGD, Ea,
      ICC, Ln, Pl, WBC, WEC; NASB, NIV], 'fruits' (possibly
      following a different text) [NTC; KJV, NJB], 'deed' [GEL]. The
      phrase καρπὸν δικαιοσύνης 'fruit of righteousness' is translated
      'truly good qualities' [TEV].
    c. δικαιοσύνη (GEL 88.13) (BAGD 2.b. p. 196): 'righteousness'
      [BAGD, Ea, GEL, HNTC, ICC, Ln, Lt, Mou, NTC, Pl, WBC;
      KJV, NASB, NIV, NRSV, REB], 'uprightness' [BAGD; NJB,
      'right conduct' [WEC], 'goodness' [TNT], 'justice' [NAB].
    d. διά with genitive object (GEL 90.4): 'through' [HNTC, Ln,
      Mou, NTC, Pl, WEC; NASB, NIV, NJB, NRSV, REB], 'by' [Ea;
      KJV], not explicit [ICC]. The phrase τὸν διὰ Ἰησοῦ Χριστοῦ
      'which is through Jesus Christ' is translated 'that Jesus Christ
      produces' [WBC].
  QUESTION—What relationship is indicated by the use of the
  participle πεπληρωμένοι 'having been filled'?
    1. It restates the preceding clause more fully [Blm, El, GNC, ICC,
      Lg, My]: you will be pure and blameless/offenseless; that is,
      you will be filled with the fruit of righteousness. This gives the
      positive side to the preceding attributes [My].

2. It indicates an addition to the purpose of the prayer [TNTC, WBC; NAB]: I pray . . . so that you may be pure and blameless/offenseless and be filled with the fruit of right-eousness.

QUESTION—How are the nouns related in the genitive construction καρπὸν δικαιοσύνης 'fruit of righteousness'?

1. 'Righteousness' means righteous deeds or qualities, and these are the fruit [Alf, El, EBC, WBC, WEC; TEV]: fruit which consists of righteous deeds.
2. 'Fruit' is the result of righteousness.
2.1 'Righteousness' is justification by faith in Christ [GNC, HNTC, Lt, MNTC, Mou, NTC, TH]: the fruit (good deed/qualities) which justification by faith produces. The fruit is the product of the new life based on the righteousness given them, through faith in Christ [GNC].
2.2 'Righteousness' is moral uprightness [Ea, EGT, El, ICC, Lg, My, My(D), Pl]: the fruit (good deeds or qualities) which moral uprightness produces.
3. Righteousness is an attribute of fruit [Ln]: a fruit having a righteous quality. The fruit is described in Gal. 5:22 and is regarded by God as being righteous [Ln].

QUESTION—What relationship is indicated by διά 'through'?

It indicates the means by which the fruit is produced [Alf, Ea, EBC, EGT, El, GNC, HNTC, ICC, Lg, Ln, Lt, MNTC, Mou, My, NIC, NTC, Pl, WBC, WEC]: the fruit which results from righteousness which Jesus Christ enables us to manifest. The διά phrase is connected with 'fruit' [Alf, Ea, EBC, El, Ln, MNTC, My, WBC; KJV, NAB], since the article τόν agrees with καρπόν 'fruit' and not with δικαιοσύνη 'righteousness' [Ln, WBC]: fruit which is through Jesus Christ. Because of their union with Christ, they display these qualities [GNC, Pl]. These qualities are brought about through Christ's mediation [Blm, Lg, Ln]. Christ sends the Spirit who accomplishes this in the believer [Alf, Blm, Ea, EBC, El, My]. Christ's sacrifice brought believers to a new standing and state [NTC].

for[a] glory[b] and praise[c] of-God.

LEXICON—a. εἰς with accusative object (GEL 89.48; 89.57) : 'for' [Ln, WBC], 'to' [Ea, Mou, NTC, WEC], 'and redounds to' [HNTC], 'which shall redound to' [ICC], 'to promote' [Pl].
b. δόξα (GEL 33.357) (BAGD 3. p. 204): 'glory' [BAGD, all commentaries and translations], 'praise' [GEL].
c. ἔπαινος (GEL 33.354) (BAGD 1.b. p. 281): 'praise' [BAGD, GEL, all commentaries and translations].

QUESTION—What is this phrase connected with?

1. It is connected with 'filled with fruit of righteousness' [Alf, Ea, EBC, El, HNTC, Lg, MNTC, My, NIC, Pl]: I pray you may be filled with the fruit of righteousness for the glory and praise of God.
2. It is connected with everything back to the beginning of Paul's prayer (1:9) [ICC, Ln, NTC]: I pray all of this may happen in you for the glory and praise of God.
3. In addition to its more immediate function, it is connected with all of Paul's thanksgiving and prayer (1:3-11) as a doxology [GNC]: I end my thanksgiving and prayer with a desire for glory and praise to God.

QUESTION—What area of meaning is intended by δόξαν 'glory'?

It is a synonym of 'praise' [GEL, NTC, TH]. It is the manifestation of God's character [Ea, MNTC], majesty [El, My], power and grace [Lt, WBC], redeeming nature [ICC, My]. It is God's grace demonstrated in holy lives [Pl].

QUESTION—What area of meaning is intended by ἔπαινον 'praise'?

Praise results from recognizing God's glorious character [MNTC]. It is grateful homage [Ea, ICC, Pl]. Praise comes from the recipients of God's blessings [HNTC, Lg] and the whole creation [HNTC].

DISCOURSE UNIT: 1:12-2:30 [WBC]. The topic is news and instructions for the Philippians.

DISCOURSE UNIT: 1:12-30 [NTC, TH; GNT, NIV, TEV]. The topic is Paul's imprisonment [NTC, TH; NIV], the progress of the gospel resulting from Paul's imprisonment [NIV], Paul's situation and the future prospects [TH], living means Christ [GNT, TEV].

DISCOURSE UNIT: 1:12-26 [Alf, Ea, EBC, HNTC, ICC, Lg, Lt, NIC, Pl, TH, TNTC, WBC, WC, WEC]. The topic is Paul's situation in Rome [Alf, Ea, EBC, HNTC, ICC, Lt, NIC, Pl; NJB], living means Christ [TH], Paul's feelings and hopes [Alf, HNTC, ICC, Lt, Pl, TNTC], the progress of the gospel in Rome [ICC, Lg, Lt, Pl; NAB], Paul's situation and the advance of the gospel in Rome [WC], Paul's missionary report [WEC].

DISCOURSE UNIT: 1:12-20 [Mou; NASB]. The topic is Paul's situation [Mou], the proclamation of the gospel [NASB].

DISCOURSE UNIT: 1:12-18 [EBC, Ln]. The topic is the advance of the gospel through Paul's circumstances [EBC], Paul's joyful account of the first stage of his trial [Ln].

DISCOURSE UNIT: 1:12-18a [NTC]. The topic is the advance of the gospel because of Paul's imprisonment.

DISCOURSE UNIT: 1:12-17 [HNTC, WEC]. The topic is Paul's imprisonment which has encouraged the local church [HNTC], Paul's circumstances [WEC].

DISCOURSE UNIT: 1:12-14 [EGT, ICC, MNTC, My(D), NIC, Pl, TNTC, WEC]. The topic is Paul's situation [EGT], the influence which Paul's imprisonment has had [MNTC, Pl, TNTC], the advancement of the gospel through Paul's imprisonment [ICC, NIC], the unhindered advancement of the gospel [WEC].

DISCOURSE UNIT: 1:12-13 [WC]. The topic is the effect of Paul's circumstances on the advance of the gospel in Rome.

1:12
Now^a I-want^b you to-know,^c brothers,^d
> LEXICON—a. δέ (GEL 89.94; 89.124): 'now' [Ln, NTC, Pl, WBC, WEC; NASB, NIV, NJB], 'but' [Ea; KJV], not explicit [HNTC, ICC; NAB, NRSV, REB, TEV, TNT].
>> b. pres. mid. (deponent = act.) indic. of βούλομαι (**GEL 25.3**) (BAGD 2.a.δ. p. 146): 'to want' [BAGD, GEL, HNTC, Ln, NTC, WBC, WEC; all translations except KJV], 'to wish' [Ea, ICC], 'to will' (i.e., 'would have') [Pl; KJV].
>> c. pres. act. infin. of γινώσκω (GEL 28.1) (BAGD 6.c. p. 161): 'to know' [BAGD, Ea, GEL, HNTC, NTC, WBC, WEC; NAB, NASB, NIV, NRSV, TEV, TNT], 'to understand' [Pl; KJV, REB], 'to realize' [NJB], 'to inform (you)' [Ln], 'to assure (you)' [ICC]. This word is emphatic by forefronting [Lg].
>> d. ἀδελφός (GEL 11.23): 'brethren' [Ea, HNTC, Ln, Pl; KJV, NASB], 'brothers' [NTC, WEC; NIV, NJB, TNT], 'my brothers' [WBC; NAB, TEV], 'friends' [REB], 'beloved' [NRSV], not explicit [ICC].
> QUESTION—What relationship is indicated by δέ 'now'?
> It makes a transition to new subject matter [Ea, EGT, El, Lg, Ln, My, WEC]: at this point I want to tell you. The transition is from the affairs at Philippi to Paul's affairs in Rome [Lg].
> QUESTION—Why does Paul use the clause 'I want you to know'?
> This is a phrase common to letters of that time [EGT, GNC, Ln, MNTC, Pl, WBC, WC] and similar to phrases used by Paul in other epistles [EBC, GNC, ICC, NTC, WEC]. Paul uses the phrase to introduce important (or interesting [Blm]) information [EBC, ICC,

Ln, NTC, WBC, WEC]. This phrase and the addition of 'brothers' shows that Paul is speaking from his heart [Lg].

that[a] the-(things) pertaining-to[b] me rather[c] for[d] (the) advance[e] of-the gospel have-turned-out[f]

LEXICON—a. ὅτι (GEL 90.21): 'that' [Ea, HNTC, ICC, Ln, Mou, NTC, Pl, WBC, WEC; all translations].

  b. κατά with accusative object (GEL 89.4) (BAGD II.6. p. 407): 'pertaining to' [Ln], 'with regard to' [GEL], 'with' [Ea]. The phrase τὰ κατ᾽ ἐμέ 'the things pertaining to me' is translated 'the things that have happened to me' [NTC; TEV], 'what has happened to me' [NIV, NRSV, TNT], 'the things which happened unto me' [KJV], 'the things that happened to me' [WBC], 'my circumstances' [NASB], 'the circumstances of my present life' [NJB], 'my position and circumstances' [Mou], 'my situation' [NAB], 'this affair of mine' [HNTC], 'my adversities' [WEC], 'my condition of captivity' [Pl]. This phrase and the rest of this verse is translated 'the work of the Gospel has been helped on, rather than hindered, by this business of mine' [REB], 'the cause of the gospel has been promoted by reason of my imprisonment' [ICC].

  c. μᾶλλον (GEL 89.126) (BAGD 1. p. 489): 'rather' [Ea, HNTC, ICC, Ln, Mou, WBC, WEC; KJV, NJB, TNT], 'really' [Pl; NIV, TEV], 'in reality' [NTC], 'actually' [NRSV, REB], not explicit [NAB, NASB].

  d. εἰς with accusative object (GEL 89.43): 'for' [Ln, Mou, WEC; NASB], 'to' [Ea, HNTC, NTC; NAB], 'unto' [KJV]. The phrase εἰς προκοπήν 'for the advance' is translated as an infinitive 'to advance' [NIV]. The phrase εἰς προκοπὴν ἐλήλυθεν 'for the advance have turned out' is translated 'have helped the progress' [TEV], 'have advanced the progress' [WBC], 'have come to be a help to (its) advance' [Pl], 'has helped to spread' [NRSV].

  e. προκοπή (GEL 13.57) (BAGD p. 707): 'advance' [HNTC, GEL, Pl, WEC; NJB], 'advancement' [BAGD, Ln], 'advantage' [NTC], 'furtherance' [Ea; KJV, NAB], 'progress' [Mou, WBC; TEV], 'greater progress' [NASB].

  f. perf. mid. (deponent = act.) of ἔρχομαι (GEL 89.43) (BAGD I.2.c. p. 311): 'to turn out' [NTC, WEC; NASB], 'to come out' [Mou], 'to fall out' [KJV], 'to work out' [NAB], 'to serve' [Lt; NIV], 'to result in' [BAGD, Ea, GEL], 'to tend' [HNTC]. The perfect tense indicates that the results still continue [Lg].

QUESTION—What does the phrase τὰ κατ' ἐμέ 'things about me' refer to?

1. It refers to Paul's imprisonment generally [Blm, ICC, Lt, MNTC, Mou, My, Pl, TH, WEC]: my imprisonment.
2. It refers to new developments with regard to Paul's imprisonment and trial [EBC, EGT, Ln]: what has recently happened to me.

QUESTION—What is meant by μᾶλλον 'rather'?

1. It has the idea that what happened was contrary to what one would expect [Alf, Bg, EBC, EGT, El, ICC, Lg(H), Lt, MNTC, Mou, My, NIC, Pl, TNTC, WC, WEC; NJB, REB, TNT]: rather than being a hindrance, my circumstances have worked for the advance of the gospel.
2. It has the idea that what happened was both contrary to and more than one would expect under the circumstances [Ea, GNC, HNTC, Ln, NTC, WBC; NAB, NASB]: rather than being a hindrance to the spread of the gospel, my circumstances have worked for an even greater spread of the gospel.

1:13

so-that[a] my bonds[b] to-become known[c] in[d] Christ in all the praetorian-guard/praetorium[e] and all the rest;[f]

LEXICON—a. ὥστε (GEL 89.52) (BAGD 2.a.β. p. 900): 'so that' [BAGD, Ea, Ln, NTC, Pl; KJV, NASB, NRSV], 'as a result' [WBC; NIV, TEV], 'thus' [HNTC], not explicit [ICC, MNTC, WEC; NAB, NJB, REB].

b. δεσμός: 'bonds'. See this word at 1:7.

c. φανερός (GEL 28.28) (BAGD 1. p. 852): 'known' [BAGD, Ea, ICC; NRSV], 'well known' [GEL; NAB, NASB, NJB], 'widely known' [GEL], 'common knowledge' [REB], 'clear' [BAGD, NTC; NIV], 'manifest' [KJV], 'manifest influence' [Pl], 'published' [Ln].

d. ἐν with dative object: 'in' [Ea; KJV, NJB], 'in connection with' [Ln], 'in the power of' [Pl], 'in the cause of' [NAB, NASB, REB], 'for' [NTC; NIV, NRSV], 'for the sake of' [ICC].

e. πραιτώριον (GEL 55.12; 7.7) (BAGD p. 697): 'praetorian guard' [HNTC, NTC; NASB], 'band of the praetorian troops' [ICC], 'palace guard' [GEL; NIV, TEV], 'imperial guard' [NRSV], 'soldiers of the imperial guard' [Pl], 'my guards' [TNT], 'all at headquarters here' [REB], 'praetorium' [Ea, Ln, WBC; NAB, NJB], 'palace' [GEL; KJV].

f. λοιπός (GEL 63.21): 'rest' [Ea, GEL, ICC, Ln, NTC, Pl]. The phrase τοῖς λοιπός πᾶσιν 'all the rest' is translated 'all the others' [BAGD, HNTC; TEV], 'everyone/everybody else' [WBC;

NASB, NIV, NJB, NRSV, TNT], 'others as well' [NAB], 'the public at large' [REB], 'in all other places' [KJV].

QUESTION—What relationship is indicated by ὥστε 'so that'?

1. It introduces an explanation of the preceding reference to the advance of the gospel [Ea, EBC, El, Lg, Ln, MNTC, My, NIC, WBC, WEC]: what has happened to me has resulted in the advancement of the gospel; specifically, it has become known that my bonds are in Christ. The results of Paul's imprisonment show how the gospel has advanced [Ea, El, Ln, MNTC, My, WBC, WEC].

2. It indicates the result of the advancement of the gospel [Alf, ICC, TH]: the advancement of the gospel has caused it to be come known that my bonds are in Christ.

QUESTION—With what is ἐν Χριστῷ 'in Christ' connected?

1. It is connected with 'known' [Ea, EBC, EGT, El, GNC, HNTC, ICC, Lg, Ln, Lt, Mou, My, NTC, TH, TNTC, WBC, WEC]: it has become known that my imprisonment is in Christ. Φανερούς 'known' is emphatic by forefronting [Lg, Ea, El]. This indicates the cause of Paul's imprisonment [Ea, Ln, Mou, TH, WBC]. His bonds are endured for Christ's sake [Alf, EGT, NIC], in Christ's service [El], because he was a Christian [WBC], because of his connection with Christ [Ea, Ln, NTC].

2. It is connected with 'bonds' [WC]: my imprisonment, which is in Christ's cause, has become known.

QUESTION—Where was Paul imprisoned?

Most commentators think he was imprisoned in Rome [Alf, Bg, Ea, EBC, El, GNC, HNTC, ICC, Lg, Ln, Lt, Mou, My, NIC, NTC, Pl, TH, WC, WEC]. One thinks he was imprisoned in Ephesus [MNTC], and another thinks it was in Caesarea [WBC].

QUESTION—What is the meaning of πραιτώριον 'praetorium/praetorian guard'?

1. It means the military guard [EBC, GNC, HNTC, ICC, Ln, Lt, Mou, NIC, NTC, Pl, TH, WC, WEC].

2. It means a building [Alf, Ea, El, Lg, My, WBC; KJV, NAB, NJB, REB]. It refers to the barracks of the military guard [Alf, Ea, El, Lg, My], or the imperial palace if in Rome [Bg], or the residence of the provincial governor if outside of Rome [WBC].

QUESTION—What is the meaning of τοῖς λοιποῖς πᾶσιν 'all the rest'?

1. It means other persons. It refers to the general population of the city [Blm, ICC, Ln, MNTC, Mou, NTC, Pl, TH, WBC], or influential persons in the city [WC], or other persons connected with the military guard [GNC, HNTC].

2. It means 'all other places' [KJV].

DISCOURSE UNIT: 1:14–17 [WC]. The topic is how his imprisonment has affected the church in Rome.

1:14

and the majority[a] of-the brothers in (the) Lord having-become-confident[b] because-of-the bonds of-me,

> LEXICON—a. πλείων comparative of πολύς (GEL 59.1): 'majority' [BAGD, ICC, Pl, WEC], 'greater part' [Ea]. The phrase τοὺς πλείονας 'the majority' is translated 'most' [BAGD, HNTC, NTC, WBC; NAB, NASB, NIV, NJB, NRSV, REB, TEV, TNT], 'more' [Ln], 'many' [KJV].
>
> b. perf. act. participle of πείθω (GEL 31.82) (BAGD 2.a. p. 639): 'to be confident' [Ln], 'to gain confidence' [HNTC, NJB, TNT], 'to wax confident' [KJV], 'to take courage' [NAB], 'to be encouraged' [NIV], 'to be given confidence' [REB], 'to be given more confidence' [TEV], 'to be made confident' [NRSV], 'to make confident' [WBC], 'to find a ground for confidence' [Pl], 'to gain confidence' [WEC], 'to be heartened' [NTC], 'to have/put confidence in' [BAGD, Ea, GEL, ICC], 'to trust in' [BAGD, GEL; NASB], 'to have one's faith in God strengthened' [ICC]. The perfect tense indicates that they were already confident [Lg].

> QUESTION—What relationship is indicated by καί 'and'?
>
> It connects γενέσθαι 'to become' with τολμᾶν 'to dare' and indicates a second result of the advance of the gospel (1:12) [Alf, Ea, EBC, El, Lg, MNTC, NIC, NTC, Pl, TNTC, WBC]: what happened to me worked for the advance of the gospel. As a result my imprisonment has become known . . . and also the brothers have dared to speak boldly. It cannot be connected with ἐλήλυθεν 'have come' (1:12), since this finite verb cannot be parallel to an infinitive (τολμᾶν).

> QUESTION—What is implied by the comparative πλείονας 'most' of the brethren?
>
> 1. 'Most' implies that there was a minority that didn't take advantage of the opportunity [HNTC, ICC, Lt, MNTC, Mou, My(H), NIC, NTC, Pl, WBC, WC, WEC]: most but not all of the brethren. This minority consisted of Christians who were unfriendly to Paul [Mou].
>
> 2. 'Most' implies that so many had new courage that their action characterized the church there as a whole [GNC]: the believers in general. It does not contrast them with a minority [GNC].

> QUESTION—Two related questions are: With what is the phrase ἐν κυρίῳ 'in the Lord' connected? How are 'in the Lord' and 'my bonds' related to the confidence of the brethren?

1. 'In the Lord' is connected with 'brethren' [Alf, EBC, EGT, GNC, HNTC, Ln, Mou; KJV, NAB, NIV, NJB, REB, TNT]: brethren in the Lord. Paul's bonds/imprisonment is the object [Mou] or means [HNTC, Ln] of the new confidence of the brethren: the brethren in the Lord take courage from/because of my bonds.

2. 'In the Lord' is connected with 'being confident' [Bg, Ea, El, ICC, Lg, Lt, MNTC, My, NIC, NTC, Pl, TH, WBC, WC, WEC; NASB, NRSV, TEV]: being made confident in the Lord.

2.1 'The Lord' is the object of the brothers' confidence, and Paul's 'bonds/imprisonment' are the means which build that confidence [Ea, ICC, Lg, My, NIC, WC, WEC]: the brothers trust the Lord more because of the example of my imprisonment. Since the Lord had protected Paul, they trusted the Lord to protect them also [WC].

2.2 'In the Lord' is the basis, sphere, or agent of their confidence, and Paul's 'bonds/imprisonment' is the grounds of the brothers' confidence [Ea, Lg, MNTC, TH, WC]: because of the Lord, or by the power of the Lord, the brothers have stronger confidence because of my imprisonment. The Lord has caused them to become more confident [TH]. The Lord imparted courage to them and kept it alive [NTC]. His confidence is expressed in the "sphere" of the Lord [MNTC].

QUESTION—In what way were Paul's bonds the means or grounds of strengthening the confidence of the brothers?

The brothers gained confidence from his example in prison [Blm, EBC], including his courage [HNTC, MNTC, NIC, NTC], his endurance [Ea, HNTC, My, NIC, NTC, Pl], his confidence [MNTC, WC], his integrity [Ea], his convictions [Ea], his powerful witness [Ln], the safe-keeping of Paul by the Lord [Bg, NIC, NTC], the fact that his vindication was near [Ln], the truth and power of the word of God [My].

much-more^a to-dare^b without-fear^c to-speak^d the word.^e

TEXT—Following τὸν λόγον 'the word', many manuscripts add τοῦ θεοῦ 'of God'. GNT omits 'of God' with a D rating, indicating a very high degree of doubt. The phrase 'of God' is omitted by Alf, Ea, El, HNTC, Lg, Mou, My, TH, TNTC, WBC; KJV, NJB, NRSV, and TEV. The phrase is included by GNC, ICC, Ln, Lt, MNTC, NTC, Pl, WC; NAB, NASB, NIV, REB, and TNT.

LEXICON—a. περισσοτέρως comparative of περισσῶς (GEL 78.31) (BAGD 1. p. 651): 'much more' [KJV], 'far more.' [NTC; NASB], 'more and more' [HNTC; NJB, TNT], 'more abundantly' [Ea], 'so much the more' [BAGD], 'the more' [Ln], 'all the more' [GEL, WBC], 'further' [NAB]. The phrase περισσοτέρως τολμᾶν 'much more to dare' is translated 'more courageously' [NIV], 'are becoming exceedingly bold' [WEC], 'have gained still more abundant courage' [Pl], 'have had their boldness increased' [ICC], 'grow bolder all the time' [TEV], 'with extraordinary courage' [REB], 'with greater boldness' [NRSV].

b. pres. act. infin. of τολμάω (GEL 25.161) (BAGD 1.a. p. 821): 'to dare' [BAGD, GEL, Ln, WBC; NJB, NRSV, REB, TNT], 'to dare boldly' [HNTC], 'to be bold' [Ea, ICC; KJV], 'to have courage' [BAGD; NASB], 'to show courage' [NTC], 'to gain courage' [Pl], 'to be emboldened' [NAB].

c. ἀφόβως (GEL 25.253) (BAGD 1. p. 127): 'without fear' [BAGD, Ea, HNTC, WBC, WEC; KJV, NASB, NRSV], 'without any fear' [NJB], 'fearlessly' [BAGD, GEL, Ln, Pl; NAB, NIV, REB, TEV, TNT], 'without being afraid' [NTC].

d. pres. act. infin. of λαλέω (GEL 33.70) (BAGD 2.b. p. 463): 'to speak' [BAGD, Ea, GEL, ICC, Pl, WEC; KJV, NAB, NASB, NIV, NRSV, REB, TNT], 'to utter' [Ln], 'to tell' [GEL, NTC], 'to announce' [NJB], 'to preach' [HNTC, WBC; TEV].

e. λόγος (GEL 33.260) (BAGD 1.b.β. p. 478): 'word' [Ea, HNTC, ICC, Ln, Pl, WEC; KJV, NAB, NASB, NIV, NRSV, REB], 'message' [NTC; NJB, TEV, TNT], 'gospel' [GEL, WBC].

QUESTION—What is περισσοτέρως 'much more' compared with?

1. It compares the present situation with the situation previously [Alf, Bg, Ea, El, GNC, Ln, Lt, MNTC, Mou, NIC, NTC, TH, WBC, WC]: the brothers have more courage than before. The comparison is with the time before Paul was imprisoned Ea, El, GNC, My], to the early part of his imprisonment [NIC, NTC, Pl]. It does not mean that they had previously failed to preach because of fear, but merely that their courage was increased to a much greater degree [WBC].

2. It means that they are bolder than they would have been if Paul were not in prison [Lg]: the brothers are more courageous than if I were not in prison.

DISCOURSE UNIT: 1:15-20 [Pl]. The topic is the two classes of preachers—friendly and unfriendly.

DISCOURSE UNIT: 1:15-18 [MNTC, NIC, TNTC]. The topic is Paul's generous spirit in regard to differing motives [MNTC], the proclamation of Christ, whether sincerely or in pretence [NIC], sincere and mixed motives [TNTC].

DISCOURSE UNIT: 1:15-17 [EGT, ICC, My(D), WEC]. The topic is the result of Paul's circumstances [EGT], blessing mixed with problems [WEC].

1:15
Some indeed[a] even/also[b] because-of[c] envy[d] and rivalry,[e] but[f] some even/also[b] because-of[c] good-will[g] the Christ preach.[h]
LEXICON—a. μέν (GEL 89.136) (BAGD 1.c. p. 503): 'indeed' [Ea; KJV, REB], 'to be sure' [NTC; NASB], 'it is true' [NAB, NIV, NJB, TNT], 'the truth is' [Pl], 'of course' [TEV], 'it must be said' [HNTC], not explicit [Ln, WBC, WEC; NRSV]. The words μέν . . . δέ 'on the one hand . . . but on the other hand' relate items in contrast to each other [GEL].
  b. καί (GEL 89.93): 'also' [Ea], 'even' [KJV, NASB], 'actually' [Pl], 'indeed' [Ln], 'and yet' [WBC], not explicit [HNTC, NTC, WEC; NAB, NIV, NJB, NRSV, REB, TEV, TNT].
  c. διά with accusative object (GEL 90.44) (BAGD B.II.1. p. 181): 'because of' [Ln; TEV], 'from' [NTC; NASB, NRSV], 'from motives of' [NAB], 'motivated by' [WEC], 'out of' [BAGD, Pl, WBC; KJV, NIV, NJB], 'for' [Ea], 'in' [REB, TNT]. Διά 'from' here refers to motive [Alf, Ea, El, ICC, TH].
  d. φθόνος (**GEL 88.160**) (BAGD p. 857): 'envy' [BAGD, Ea, GEL, ICC, Ln, NTC, Pl, WBC, WEC; KJV, NAB, NASB, NIV, NRSV], 'jealousy' [BAGD, HNTC], 'malice' [NJB], 'a jealous spirit' [REB, TNT], '(they are) jealous' [TEV].
  e. ἔρις (GEL 33.447; 39.22) (BAGD p. 309): 'rivalry' [NTC; NAB, NIV, NJB, NRSV], 'strife' [BAGD, GEL, Ln, Pl, WEC; KJV, NASB], 'contention' [BAGD, Ea, HNTC, ICC], 'discord' [BAGD, GEL], 'a quarrelsome spirit' [REB], 'a hostile spirit' [TNT], 'a desire to stir up trouble' [WBC].
  f. δέ (GEL 89.136; 89.124): 'but' [Ea, HNTC, NTC, WBC, WEC; NAB, NASB, NIV, NJB, NRSV, TEV, TNT], 'and' [KJV], 'while' [Pl], not explicit [Ln; REB].
  g. εὐδοκία (BAGD 1. p. 319): 'good will' [BAGD, Ea, HNTC, Ln, NTC, WEC; KJV, NAB, NASB, NIV, NRSV, REB, TEV], 'good intentions' [WBC; NJB], 'benevolent purpose' [Pl]. The phrase δι' εὐδοκίαν 'because of good will' is translated 'sincerely' [TNT]. This word means 'determination to do the good thing' [Ln].
  h. pres. act. indic. of κηρύσσω (GEL 33.256) (BAGD 2.b.β. p. 431): 'to preach' [BAGD, Ea, GEL, HNTC, Ln, Pl, WBC, WEC; all translations except REB], 'to proclaim' [BAGD, ICC; REB], 'to herald' [NTC]. This is the usual word in the New Testament for the proclamation of the gospel [ICC].

QUESTION—Two related questions are: What is implied by καί 'even/also'? To whom does τινές 'some' refer?

1. Καί means 'also' and implies that τινές 'some' are a group of people other than those mentioned in 1:14 [Alf, Blm, Ea, EGT, El, ICC, Lg, My, NIC, NTC]: in addition to most of the brothers who fearlessly speak the word, there are also some people who preach Christ out of envy and rivalry. On this interpretation, those who have good will are those who were mentioned in 1:14 [Alf, Ea, EGT, El, My]. The mention of those speaking the word brings to mind some who are exceptions to those referred to in 1:14 [El]. Ideas offered as to who these people might be are the minority implied by the comparative of πολύς 'most' (1:14) [My], Christians who are hostile to Paul [Alf, NIC, TH], Jewish believers who were antagonistic to Paul [Ea], Christians who are vexed with Paul [EGT, ICC], Christians who are orthodox doctrinally [Lg, NIC, NTC], Christians who want to require practices of the Mosaic law [El, My], church leaders who lost prestige because of Paul [ICC, NTC], preachers in that city in general [NIC].

2. Καί indicates something unexpected and implies that τινές 'some' are part of those people mentioned in 1:14 [EBC, GNC, HNTC, Ln, Lt, MNTC, TH, TNTC, WBC, WC, WEC; NJB, TEV, TNT]: of those who fearlessly speak the word, some indeed preach Christ out of envy and rivalry. On this interpretation, those who have good will are the other part of those mentioned in 1:14 [EBC, GNC, HNTC, Ln, Lt, MNTC, TH, WBC]. Even preachers who were jealous of Paul could have gained courage by what happened to him [EBC]. Ideas offered as to who these might be are believers who differed theologically from Paul [WEC], doctrinally orthodox believers [EBC, GNC, HNTC, Ln, WBC, WC] who were opposed to Paul [WBC, WC], or Christians who want to require practices of the Mosaic law [Lt].

QUESTION—What verbal phrase is implicit in the first clause?
The words κηρύσσω Χριστός 'to preach Christ', which come at the end of the verse, are implicit in the first clause as well [Lg; REB]: some preach Christ from motives of envy and strife.

QUESTION—Whom did they envy?
They were jealous of Paul [Alf, Ea, EBC, EGT, GNC, ICC, Lg, Ln, My, NIC, NTC, TH, WBC] as well as of others who are rivals [MNTC].

QUESTION—What is implied in the concept of ἔρις 'rivalry'?
These people were envious of Paul's achievements and thought they could surpass his work now that he was in prison [GNC]. They

were devoted to their own party [MNTC], they intended to raise up discord in the Christian community [EBC], to dispute with Paul [Ln], or to hurt Paul by their preaching [Lg, WBC, WC].

QUESTION—Toward whom is the 'good will' of the second group directed?

It is directed toward Paul [Alf, Ea, EBC, El, ICC, MNTC, Mou, My, Pl, WBC]. It is also directed towards the work of the gospel [ICC, Pl, WC] or towards the Lord [Mou]. They wanted to share in Paul's ministry [GNC].

1:16

TEXT—Instead of the order of verses 16 and 17 in GNT, many manuscripts have the contents of these two verses reversed. GNT does not deal with this variant as a textual problem; the reverse order is read by Bg, Blm, and KJV. The reversal was probably made to preserve the order in which the two groups are mentioned in 1:15 instead of the chiastic structure of the text as found in GNT [EBC, WEC].

The-(ones) on-the-one-hand[a] (do it) out-of[b] love,[c]

LEXICON—a. μέν (GEL 89.136) (BAGD 1.c. p. 503): 'on the one hand' [GEL], 'indeed' [Ea, ICC], not explicit [HNTC, Ln, WBC; KJV, NAB, NJB, NRSV, REB, TEV, TNT].

b. ἐκ with genitive object (GEL 89.25): 'out of' [BAGD, Ea, ICC, NTC, Pl, WEC; KJV, NASB, NJB, NRSV], 'from' [Ln; NAB, TEV], 'because' [WBC; TNT], 'by' [HNTC; REB], 'in' [NIV].

c. ἀγάπη (GEL 25.43) (BAGD I.1.a. p. 5): 'love' [BAGD, Ea, GEL, HNTC, ICC, Ln, NTC, Pl, WEC; all translations except NAB, TNT], 'unaffected love' [NAB]. This noun is also translated as a verb: 'to love' [WBC; TNT].

QUESTION—To whom does the phrase οἱ μέν 'the ones' refer?

It refers to the second group of believers mentioned in 1:15 [Alf, Blm, El, GNC, Lg, Lt, NTC, TH, TNTC]: the latter, those who preach out of good will, do it because of their love.

QUESTION—What relationship is indicated by ἐκ 'out of'?

It indicates a cause for their action [Alf, Ea, GNC, Ln, Lt, MNTC, WBC; all translations]: the latter do so because of their love. Love is their motivation [El, HNTC, ICC; REB].

QUESTION—What is the implied verb in the clause 'the latter out of love'?

Translations add the following verbal ideas: 'to do (it/this/so) [MNTC, NTC, Pl; NASB, NIV, NJB, TEV], 'to proclaim Christ' [NRSV], 'to act' [NAB], 'to work' [Lt], 'to preach' [Ea, WBC, WC; TNT], 'to be moved (by)' HNTC, ICC; REB].

QUESTION—What is the implied object of ἀγάπη 'love'?

The implied object is Paul [EBC, GNC, Ln, MNTC, NIC, NTC, Pl, TH, WBC, WC; TNT] and Christ [Bg, NTC] and/or the gospel [EBC, NTC, WC]: out of love for me (and Christ and the gospel).

knowing[a] that for[b] defense[c] of-the gospel I-am-put-here/appointed/set;[d]

LEXICON—a. perf. act. participle of οἶδα (GEL 28.1): 'to know' [Ea, GEL, HNTC, ICC, Ln, NTC, Pl, WBC, WEC; all translations except NAB], 'to be aware' [NAB].

b. εἰς with accusative object (GEL 89.57): 'for' [Ea, HNTC, Ln, NTC; KJV, NASB, NIV, NRSV], 'in' [NJB]. The phrase εἰς ἀπολογίαν 'for defense' is translated 'to defend' [Pl, WBC, WEC; NAB, REB, TEV], 'of defending' [TEV].

c. ἀπολογία (GEL 33.436) (BAGD 2.b. p. 96): 'defense' [BAGD, Ea, GEL, HNTC, ICC, Ln, NTC; KJV, NASB, NIV, NJB, NRSV], 'vindication' [Mou]. This noun is also translated as a verb: 'to defend' [Pl, WBC, WEC; NAB, REB, TEV]. This word refers to Paul's legal trial [TNTC].

d. pres. mid. (deponent = act.) indic. of κεῖμαι (GEL 85.3) (BAGD 2.a. p. 426): 'to be put here' [WBC; NIV, NRSV], 'to be set here' [Pl], 'to be appointed' [BAGD, NTC; NASB], 'to be posted here' [HNTC], 'to be here' [TNT], 'to be where I am' [REB], 'to be set' [BAGD, Ea, ICC; KJV], 'to be divinely appointed' [WEC], 'to be destined for' [BAGD], 'to be given the work of' [TEV], 'to remain firm' [NJB]. This verb is also translated as 'my circumstances provide an opportunity' [NAB].

QUESTION—What relationship is indicated by the use of the participle εἰδότες 'knowing'?

It indicates the reason the believers preach Christ from love for Paul [Alf, Ea, El, ICC, Lg, MNTC, My, NIC, Pl; TEV, TNT]: the latter do this because they know that I am placed here/appointed in order to defend the gospel. They loved Paul because they appreciated his vocation and therefore sought to engage in the work to which he had devoted his life [Ea].

QUESTION—What is meant by κεῖμαι 'to be put/appointed/set'?

1. It means that Paul's present location and circumstances were appointed by God [Blm, EBC, GNC, HNTC, Lg, Ln, MNTC, Mou, Pl, WBC; NAB, NIV, NRSV, REB, TNT]: I am put here for the defense of the gospel.

2. It means that Paul has been appointed by God for defending the gospel as a ministry, or at this time [Alf, Ea, El, ICC, Lt, My, NIC, NTC, TH, WEC; KJV, NASB, TEV]: I am appointed for the defense of the gospel.

3. It means that Paul remains strong [TNTC, WC; NJB]: I remain firm in my defense of the gospel. 'To be set' is a military term

meaning to endure hardness as a soldier on duty does [TNTC, WC].

1:17

the-(ones) on-the-other-hand[a] out-of[b] partisanship[c] the Christ proclaim,[d]

LEXICON—a. δέ (GEL 89.136): 'on the other hand' [GEL], 'but' [Ea; TNT], not explicit [HNTC, ICC, Ln, WBC, WEC; KJV, NAB, NJB, NRSV, REB, TEV].

    b. ἐκ with genitive object (GEL 89.25): 'out of' [HNTC, NTC, Pl; NASB, NIV, NJB, NRSV], 'moved by' [WBC; REB], 'from' [Ln; TEV], 'in a spirit of' [ICC], 'from motives of' [Mou], 'of' [Ea; KJV], 'as' [NAB]. The phrase ἐξ ἐριθείας 'out of partisanship' is translated 'are nurturing selfish ambitions' [TNT].

    c. ἐριθεία (GEL **88.167; 39.7**) (BAGD p. 309): 'partisanship' [HNTC, Lt, Mou, Pl, WEC], 'envy, contention, and partisanship' [ICC], 'faction' [Ea, Mou], 'selfish ambition' [BAGD, GEL, NTC, WBC; NASB, NIV, NRSV, REB, TNT], 'a spirit of selfish ambition' [TEV], 'selfishness' [BAGD, EGT], 'self-seeking' [Ln], 'jealousy' [NJB], 'a feeling of rivalry' [GEL], 'a sense of hostility' [GEL], 'intrigue, party-spirit' [Lg], 'contention' [KJV]. This noun includes both the ideas of φθόνος 'envy' and ἔρις 'rivalry', which words Paul uses in 1:15 [Ea]. The noun comes from ἔριθος, which originally meant 'day-laborer' but came to mean 'mercenary' and the self-seeking ambition associated with such a person [Ea, EBC, EGT, GNC, ICC, Lg, Mou, NTC, Pl, WBC, WC].

    d. pres. act. indic. of καταγγέλλω (GEL 33.204) (BAGD 2. p. 409): 'to proclaim' [BAGD, GEL, HNTC, ICC, Ln, NTC, Pl; NASB, NJB, NRSV, TEV], 'to preach' [Ea, WBC; KJV, NIV, TNT], 'to announce' [GEL, Mou], 'to present' [REB], 'to promote' [NAB]. In this context there is no specific difference between this verb and κηρύσσω 'to preach' used in 1:15 [Ea, EGT, El, Ln, My].

QUESTION—To whom does the phrase οἱ δέ 'but the ones' refer?

It refers to the group of believers first mentioned in 1:15 [EBC, TH, TNTC, WEC]: the former, those who preach out of envy and rivalry. They preached the gospel, but with a wrong spirit [Lg, TNTC]. Some doctrinal differences were involved [WEC].

QUESTION—What relationship is indicated by ἐκ 'out of'?

This preposition is generally translated in the same way as the same preposition in 1:16. Here, as there, it indicates a cause for the group's action [Bg; all translations except REB]: the former proclaim Christ because of selfish ambition. It gives their motivation [El, ICC, My; REB].

QUESTION—Why is 'to proclaim/preach Christ' repeated in this verse?

By its proximity to 'partisanship' and the following phrase, 'not sincerely', it points out the contrast between the message and the motives of this group [ICC, Lt, MNTC, My, Pl].

not sincerely,[a] thinking[b] affliction[c] to-raise-up[d] to-my bonds.

TEXT—Instead of ἐγείρειν 'to raise up', some manuscripts read ἐπιφέρειν 'to bring upon'. GNT does not deal with this variant. 'To bring upon' is read by Bg, Blm, EGT, KJV, and possibly NJB.

LEXICON—a. ἀγνῶς (GEL 88.45) (BAGD p. 12): 'sincerely' [GEL, NTC; KJV, NIV, NRSV, TEV], 'in sincerity' [NJB], 'as a result of sincere motives' [GEL], 'from pure motives' [GEL; NAB, NASB], 'with pure motive' [Ln], 'purely' [Ea, Mou]. The phrase οὐχ ἀγνῶς 'not sincerely' is translated 'insincerely' [ICC], 'without sincerity' [WBC], 'with impure motives' [WEC], 'from mixed motives' [REB], 'with sadly mixed motives' [Pl], 'have mixed motives' [TNT], 'with unhallowed motives' [HNTC]. Their motives were mixed [ICC, Ln], having a degree of self-seeking with them [Ln].

b. pres. mid. (deponent = act.) participle of οἴομαι (GEL 31.29) (BAGD p. 562): 'to think' [BAGD, Ea, GEL, Ln, NTC, Pl, WBC; NAB, NASB, TEV, TNT], 'to suppose' [BAGD, WEC; KJV, NIV], 'to imagine' [GEL, HNTC], 'to expect' [BAGD], 'to think and mean' [Mou], 'to mean' [REB, NJB], 'to intend' [NRSV], 'to seek' [ICC].

c. θλῖψις (GEL 22.2) (BAGD 2. p. 362): 'affliction' [BAGD, Ea, ICC, Ln, NTC; KJV], 'distress' [NASB, REB, TNT], 'trouble' [BAGD, WBC; NIV], 'more trouble' [TEV], 'suffering' [GEL; NRSV], 'tribulation' [Mou], 'persecution' [GEL], 'pressure' [Pl, WEC], 'weight' [NJB]. The phrase θλῖψιν ἐγείρειν 'to raise affliction' is translated 'to increase the pressure' [Pl], 'that it will make even harsher' [NAB], 'to make galling to me' [HNTC].

d. pres. act. infin. of ἐγείρω (GEL 13.83) (BAGD 1.a.ε. p. 214): 'to raise up' [GEL, ICC, Ln, Mou, NTC], 'to stir up' [Ea, WBC; NIV], 'to make' [TEV], 'to cause' [BAGD; NASB, REB, TNT], 'to increase' [Pl; NRSV]; following a different text, 'to add to' [KJV, NJB].

QUESTION—What relationship is indicated by the use of the participle οἰόμενοι 'thinking'?

It indicates the reason for the preceding phrase, 'not sincerely' [Alf, Ea, El, ICC]: they proclaim Christ insincerely because they think that will stir up affliction. It also introduces their purpose [MNTC, TH, WC].

QUESTION—Two related questions are: Does οἴομαι 'thinking' imply that these believers deliberately intended to cause trouble for Paul? and What was the nature of the trouble they hoped to cause?

1. They deliberately tried to cause trouble for Paul [Alf, Bg, Blm, Ea, EGT, El, Lg, Lt, MNTC, My, NIC, TH, TNTC, WC, WEC; NJB, REB]: they proclaim Christ insincerely, because they think that this will cause trouble for me. They intended to cause Paul to have a troubled or jealous spirit by their actions [WEC], their deprecation of him, or their success [Alf, Ea, EGT, GNC, MNTC], or to cause further ill treatment of him by his opponents [Blm, El, My]. Also implied in the verb, however, is the idea that they did not succeed in their intentions [Alf, Bg, Ea, El, My, TH].

2. They did not deliberately try to cause trouble for Paul but thought that they were upsetting him [ICC, Ln, Mou]: they proclaim Christ insincerely, thinking that their actions may cause trouble for me. They thought that their actions or successes would cause Paul to be annoyed [ICC, Ln], but the verb implies that this thinking was erroneous [Mou, Pl]. Although they did not set out to increase Paul's suffering, they were glad for any annoyance their actions might cause him [ICC]. They wrongly thought that Paul's motives and feelings were like their own [Ln].

DISCOURSE UNIT: 1:18–26 [HNTC, ICC, WEC]. The topic is Paul's attitude concerning the situation [HNTC, WEC].

DISCOURSE UNIT: 1:18–20 [EGT, WC, WEC]. The topic is Paul's joy that Christ is preached and his conviction that his own cause will be successful [EGT], Paul's hopes and his fears [WC], joy in salvation [WEC].

1:18
Then[a] what?[b]

LEXICON—a. γάρ (GEL 91.1): 'then' [Ea, ICC, Ln, NTC, WBC, WEC; KJV, NASB]. The phrase τί γάρ 'Then what?' is translated 'What of it?' [NAB], 'What does it all amount to?' [TNT], 'What does it matter?' [NRSV, REB], 'But what does it matter?' [NIV, NJB], 'What matters it?' [Mou], 'What difference does that make?' [HNTC], 'Then what is the result?' [Pl], 'It does not matter!' [TEV].

b. τίς (GEL 92.14): 'what?' [Ea, ICC, Ln, NTC, WBC, WEC; KJV, NASB].

QUESTION—With what is this question connected?

It is connected with what Paul has just said [Alf, Ea, EGT, ICC, NIC, WC]: Considering what I have just said, what then? Specifically, it is connected with all of 1:17 [Ea, ICC, NIC] or the last clause, 'thinking affliction to raise to the bonds of me' [EGT]. It means that Paul chooses not to discuss the two groups further [Blm].

QUESTION—How do τί γάρ 'what then' and πλήν 'only' function in the sentence?

1. Τί γάρ is a rhetorical question, and πλήν introduces the answer [ICC, Ln, Lt, Mou, NIC, NTC, Pl, WBC; KJV, NASB, TNT]: What is the result of what they are thinking or trying to do to me? Only this, that Christ is preached. πλήν implies 'in either case' [Blm].

2. Τί γάρ is a rhetorical question with a negative answer implied, and πλήν introduces a positive result of the situation [Alf, Ea, El, HNTC, Lg, MNTC; NAB, NIV, NJB, NRSV, REB, TEV]: What does it matter what they are thinking or trying to do to me? It doesn't. The only important thing is that Christ is preached.

Only[a] that in-every way,[b] whether in-pretense[c] or in-truth,[d] Christ is-proclaimed,[e]

LEXICON—a. πλήν (GEL 89.130) (BAGD 1.d. p. 669): 'only' [BAGD, ICC, Ln, NTC, Pl; NASB, NJB], 'just (so/this)' [NRSV, TEV, TNT], 'except' [BAGD, GEL, WBC], 'in any case' [BAGD], 'notwithstanding' [KJV], 'but yet' [Ea], 'quite simply' [WEC], 'all that matters is' [HNTC; NAB], 'the important thing is' [NIV], not explicit [REB].

b. τρόπος (GEL 89.83) (BAGD 1. p. 827): 'way' [BAGD, GEL; all translations], 'manner' [BAGD]. The phrase παντὶ τρόπῳ 'in every way' is translated 'however this may happen' [WEC].

c. πρόφασις (GEL 88.230) (BAGD 2. p. 722): 'pretense' [Ea, GEL, HNTC, Ln, NTC, WEC; KJV, NASB], 'pretext' [ICC; TNT], not explicit [REB]. This noun is also translated 'with false motives' [BAGD, WBC; NJB], 'from false motives' [NIV], 'out of false motives' [NRSV], 'from wrong motives' [TEV], 'from specious motives' [NAB], 'by a mere show' [Pl]. The idea is that a professed motive is not the real motive [Alf, Ea, EBC, EGT, GNC, HNTC, ICC, Ln, Mou, My, NTC]. This noun is synonymous with οὐ ἁγνῶς 'not sincerely' in 1:17 [Ea].

d. ἀλήθεια (GEL 72.1) (BAGD 3. p. 36): 'truth' [GEL, HNTC, ICC, Ln, NTC, WEC; KJV, NASB], 'reality' [BAGD; TNT], 'sincerity' [Ea; REB]. This noun is also translated 'from true motives' [NIV], 'out of true motives' [NRSV], 'with true motives'

[WBC; NJB], 'from genuine motives' [NAB], 'from right
motives' [TEV]. This embodies the ideas of εὐδοκία 'good will'
(1:15) and ἀγάπη 'love' (1:16) [Ea].
   e. pres. pass. indic. of καταγγέλλω: 'to be proclaimed'. See this
   word at 1:17.
QUESTION—What is implied in the phrase 'in every way'?
   Implied is the idea 'of preaching' [Alf, Ea, El, ICC, Lg, NIC, WC]:
   in every way of preaching. This includes the motives of these
   preachers [Alf, Ea, El] as well as the ways in which they preached
   [Alf, NIC, TNTC]; it refers to the manner of presentation, not to
   the contents [Lg].
QUESTION—What relationship is indicated by the phrase 'in
pretense or in truth'?
   This phrase is an amplification of the phrase preceding it [El, ICC,
   My, NIC, NTC, TH]: in every way—that is, whether they pretend
   to be sincere or they truly are sincere.
QUESTION—What is indicated by the case of the nouns προφάσει
and ἀληθείᾳ 'pretense' and 'truth'?
   The nouns 'pretense' and 'truth' are in the dative case, which
   indicates the manner or motives of the preaching [Alf, Ea, El,
   WC]: in every way, whether with false motives or with true ones,
   Christ is proclaimed. These nouns relate to the character of the
   preacher [Lg].
QUESTION—What is meant by 'proclaiming Christ in pretense'?
   It means that they preached without sincerity (1:17) [Ea], with the
   motive described at the end of 1:18 [Alf]. They had a pretended
   zeal [Blm] which covered their personal and selfish ends [EGT,
   ICC, Lt, MNTC, NTC, TH]. Their hidden purpose was to attack
   Paul [EBC], diminish his standing [GNC], annoy him [HNTC,
   MNTC], and gain proselytes to the law [Lt].
QUESTION—What is meant by 'proclaiming Christ in truth'?
   It means that they preached with real sincerity [Alf, Blm]. They
   preached with good will for Paul and out of love (1:15) [Ea]. Their
   desire to spread the gospel was pure [GNC] and their only aim was
   to glorify Christ [NTC]. Their real motives were the same as their
   professed motives [MNTC].
and in[a] this I-rejoice.[b]
   LEXICON—a. ἐν with dative object (GEL 89.5; 89.26; 90.23): 'in'
   [Ea, HNTC, ICC, Ln, Mou, NTC; NASB, NRSV], 'for' [WEC;
   NJB, REB, TNT], 'because of' [NIV]. The phrase ἐν τούτῳ 'in
   this' is translated 'therein' [Pl; KJV], 'about it' [TEV]. This
   entire phrase is translated 'That is what brings me joy' [NAB],
   'This surely makes me glad' [WBC].

b. pres. act. indic. of χαίρω (GEL 25.125) (BAGD 1. p. 873): 'to rejoice' [BAGD, Ea, GEL, HNTC, ICC, Ln, NTC, Pl, WBC; KJV, NASB, NIV, NRSV, REB, TNT], 'to be glad' [BAGD, GEL], 'to be happy' [NJB, TEV]. This verb is also translated by the noun 'joy' [NAB].

QUESTION—What does ἐν τούτῳ 'in this' refer to?

It refers to Christ's being proclaimed [Ea, EGT, El, ICC, Lg, Ln, Lt, MNTC, My, TH, WBC]: in this, (that Christ is proclaimed), I rejoice. It is not the way in which Christ was proclaimed but the fact that he was proclaimed that caused Paul to rejoice [Lg, WBC].

DISCOURSE UNIT: 1:18b–26 [NTC]. The topic is the magnification of Christ by Paul's life or death.

1:18b
But[a] indeed/also I-shall-rejoice.[b]

LEXICON—a. ἀλλά (GEL 91.2; 89.96; 89.125): 'but'. The phrase ἀλλὰ καί 'but indeed/also' is translated 'yes, and' [HNTC, ICC, NTC, Pl, WBC; NASB, NIV, NRSV, REB], 'yea, and' [Alf, Ea; KJV], 'yea also' [Ln], 'aye and' [Mou], 'and too' [NJB], 'indeed' [WEC; NAB], 'and' [TEV], 'too' [TNT].

b. fut. mid. (deponent = act.) of χαίρω: See this verb in the preceding phrase.

QUESTION—With what is this clause connected?

1. It is connected with what precedes [Ea, HNTC, Ln, MNTC, My; KJV, NASB]. In this case a period is used at the end of this clause: in that I rejoice, yes, and I will rejoice. For I know that this will turn out for my deliverance.

2. It is connected with what precedes but more so with what follows [EGT, El, ICC, NIC, NTC, WBC; all translations except KJV, NASB] In this case a period, semicolon, or colon is used before the clause and a comma or period after it: in that I rejoice. Yes, and I shall rejoice, for I know that this will turn out for my deliverance. A transition, which ties what precedes to what follows, is being made at this point in the discourse [EBC]. Some translations begin a new discourse unit [NTC, WBC; NIV, NRSV, REB] with this clause.

QUESTION—What relationship is indicated by ἀλλά 'but'?

It indicates an addition to the preceding [EBC, HNTC, Ln, Lt, NTC, TH, WBC]: but, in addition, I will be glad for another reason. It is progressive and means 'what is more' [WBC]. It imparts an emphasis to the declaration [El]. This word implies an understood preceding clause, 'not merely do I now rejoice, but I will also rejoice in the future'. [Lg]. One commentator calls it "slightly adversative" since it stands between a present and a future tense of the verb [Ea].

DISCOURSE UNIT: 1:19–26 [EBC, Ln, MNTC, NIC, TNTC, WC]. The topics are Paul's circumstances resulting in salvation [EBC], Paul's desire that Christ would be glorified during the following part of his trial [Ln], Paul's confidence that he will be vindicated, and his calmness in facing the two alternatives, life or death [MNTC], Paul's dilemma and confidence in life or death [TNTC], Paul's hopes and fears [WC], Christ's glorification by Paul's life or death [NIC].

DISCOURSE UNIT: 1:19–20 [NIC]. The topic is Christ's glorification, whether by Paul's life or by his death.

1:19
For[a] I-know[b] that this for-me will-turn-out[c] for[d] deliverance/salvation[e]
   LEXICON—a. γάρ (GEL 89.23): 'for' [Ea, HNTC, ICC, Ln, NTC, Pl, WBC; KJV, NASB, NIV, NRSV, TNT], 'because' [WEC; NJB, TEV], not specific [REB]. The phrase οἶδα γάρ 'for I know' is translated 'in the conviction' [NAB].
      b. perf. act. indic. of οἶδα (GEL 28.1): 'to know' [Ea, HNTC, ICC, Ln, NTC, Pl, WBC; all translations except NAB, REB], 'to know well' [REB], 'to be confident' [WEC]. Some distinguish between γινώσκω 'to know' (1:12) and οἶδα (here) by saying that the latter is intuitive knowledge or assured conviction [ICC, NIC]. Others, however, say that Paul uses them synonymously [WBC].
      c. fut. mid. (deponent = act.) indic. of ἀποβαίνω (GEL 89.41) (BAGD 2. p. 88): 'to turn out' [BAGD, HNTC, ICC, Ln, NTC; NAB, NASB, NIV, NRSV], 'to turn' [KJV], 'to lead to' [BAGD, GEL], 'to fall out' [Ea], 'to result in' [GEL, Mou, WBC], 'to conduce' [Pl], 'the issue will be' [REB]. The phrase τοῦτό μοι ἀποβήσεται εἰς σωτηρίαν 'this for me will turn out for deliverance' is translated 'this is what will save me' [NJB], 'I shall be set free' [TEV, TNT].
      d. εἰς with accusative object (GEL 89.41): 'for' [HNTC, ICC, Ln, NTC], 'to' [GEL; BAGD, Pl; KJV], 'unto' [Ea], 'in' [WBC, WEC].
      e. σωτηρία (GEL 21.18) (BAGD 2. p. 801): 'deliverance' [GEL; NASB, NIV, NRSV, REB], 'salvation' [BAGD, Ea, HNTC, ICC, Ln, Mou, NTC, Pl, WEC; KJV, NAB], 'release' [WBC].
   QUESTION—What relationship is indicated by this word?
      It indicates the grounds for Paul's rejoicing [Bg, Ea, EGT, El, Ln, Mou, My, NTC, WBC]: I shall rejoice since I know that, etc. It is

connected either with the immediately preceding clause, 'yes, and I shall rejoice' [Bg, Ea, EGT, El, Mou, NTC, WBC; all translations except KJV, NASB] or with the two preceding clauses, 'in that I rejoice, yes, and I shall rejoice' [Ln, My; KJV, NASB].

QUESTION—To what does τοῦτο 'this' refer?

1. It refers generally to Paul's present circumstances [Blm, EGT, ICC, Lg, Lt, NIC, NTC, Pl, WBC, WC, WEC; NIV]: I know that my present circumstances will turn out for my deliverance. Paul was referring to the bad aspects of his situation [ICC], the harm intended for him [Blm], the opposition of his enemies [Lg], or to both the good and bad aspects [Pl, WBC]. In this case it refers back to τὰ κατ' ἐμέ 'the things about me' (1:12) [ICC].

2. It refers to Christ's being preached, even from false motives [Alf, El, My, TNTC]: I know that the preaching of Christ will turn out for my deliverance. In this case it refers back to ἐν τούτῳ 'in this' (1:18) [El, My].

3. It refers to the fact that Paul has joy when Christ is preached, in truth or even in pretense [Ea]: I know that my joy at the preaching of Christ will turn out for my deliverance.

4. It refers to Paul's trial [Ln]: I know that my trial will turn out for my deliverance.

QUESTION—What is meant by σωτηρία 'deliverance/salvation'?

1. It means Paul's release from prison [EGT, TH, WBC]: this will turn out for my release from prison. Included is the idea of Paul's vindication [TH, WBC]. The TEV and TNT are ambiguous for 'to be set free' could mean free from prison or free from his body.

2. It means vindication of Paul or his cause [EBC, HNTC, Ln, MNTC, TNTC]: this will turn out for my vindication. The Greek here has the exact wording of Job 13:16 in LXX, and some interpret the meaning of this word in the Philippians passage by the meaning in Job [EBC, GNC, HNTC, Ln, MNTC]. Here Paul has in view a present vindication of Christ and the gospel [Ln], his ultimate vindication before God [GNC, HNTC], or both his present and future vindication [EBC].

3. It means the salvation of Paul [Alf, Ea, El, GNC, ICC, Lt, Mou, NTC, Pl, WC]: this will turn out for my salvation. Some take this in the widest sense of the word 'salvation', including past, present, and future aspects [El, ICC, Lt, Pl, WC]. Others take it to mean the present aspects of salvation, particularly fruitfulness and magnification of Christ [Alf, NTC]. Others take it to mean the future aspect of salvation [GNC, Mou].

4. It means general, favorable results for Paul [Lg, My, NIC]: this will turn out for my general good.

5. It includes both release from prison and eternal salvation [Blm].

through[a] the of-you prayer[b] and (the) help/supply[c] of-the Spirit of-Jesus Christ,

LEXICON—a. διά with genitive object (GEL 89.76; 90.8): 'through' [Ea, HNTC, Ln, NTC, Pl, WEC; KJV, NASB, NIV, NRSV], 'by means of' [TEV], 'because (of)' [WBC; REB, TNT], 'thanks to' [NAB], 'in answer to' [ICC], 'with' [NJB]. The phrase διά τῆς ὑμῶν δεήσεως 'through your prayer' is translated 'because you are praying for me' [REB, TNT].

b. δέησις (GEL 33.171) (BAGD p. 171): 'prayer' [BAGD, GEL, HNTC, ICC, WBC, WEC; all translations except REB, TNT], 'supplication' [Ea, NTC], 'petition' [Ln], 'entreaty' [Pl], 'plea' [GEL]. This noun is also translated as a verb: 'to pray' [REB, TNT]. See 1:4 for discussion of this noun.

c. ἐπιχορηγία (GEL 35.31) (BAGD p. 305): 'help' [NTC, WBC; NIV, NRSV, TEV], 'supply' [Ea, ICC, Ln, Pl; KJV], 'support' [BAGD; NAB NJB, REB], 'provision' [HNTC, WEC; NASB]. This entire phrase is translated 'and because the Spirit of Jesus Christ is given me for support' [REB], 'and because Jesus Christ gives me his Spirit' [TNT], 'and what the Spirit of Jesus Christ will provide for' [GEL].

QUESTION—What relationship is indicated by διά 'through'?

It indicates the two means by which Paul's deliverance/salvation will come [EBC, El, ICC, Lg, Ln, NTC, TH, TNTC]: this will turn out for my deliverance/salvation by means of your prayers and by means of the help/supply of the Spirit of Jesus Christ.

QUESTION—What are the article τῆς 'the' and the genitive ὑμῶν 'of-you' (in the phrase 'through *the of-you* prayers and help/supply of-the Spirit of-Jesus Christ') connected with?

1. The article 'the' and the genitive 'of-you' are connected with both 'prayers' and 'help/supply' [Alf, Lg, Ln, Lt, MNTC, Pl]: through your prayers and the resulting help of the Spirit of Jesus Christ. The connection of the article and genitive with both nouns makes clear that the help of the Spirit is in answer to their prayers [Alf, Lt, MNTC, Pl].

2. The article 'the' and the genitive 'of you' are connected only with 'prayers' [Ea, EGT, El, ICC, My, TNTC, WEC; all translations]: through your prayers and the help of the Spirit of Jesus Christ. Paul is mentioning here two distinct sources of help, the prayers of the Philippians and the help of the Spirit [ICC, My]. This does not exclude, however, the idea that the

help of the Spirit comes as a result of the prayers of the Philippians [Ea, ICC, My].

QUESTION—Who is the implied beneficiary of the prayers?

Paul is the beneficiary of the Philippians' prayers [all commentaries; REB, TNT]: through your prayers for me. Just as Paul prays for the Philippians (1:4), so they pray for him [Ln, NTC]. Paul needs the help of the prayers of the Philippians [Alf, TNTC].

QUESTION—How are the two nouns related in the genitive construction ἐπιχορηγίας τοῦ πνεύματος 'help/supply of the Spirit'?

1. It means the help which the Spirit supplies [Ea, EBC, EGT, El, HNTC, ICC, Lg, Ln, My, NIC, NTC, TH, TNTC, WBC; NAB, NIV, TEV]: and through the help given by the Spirit of Jesus Christ. This is the help Jesus promised his disciples would receive when standing before accusers [WBC]. The Holy Spirit would help Paul face difficult circumstances [EBC].

2. It means that the Spirit is supplied to Paul [Alf, GNC, MNTC, Mou; TNT]: and through the Spirit who is given to me. This is a new outpouring of power by the Spirit on Paul [Mou]. The Philippians will supply Paul with the Spirit by their prayers and God's answering [Alf]. God supplies the Spirit, who will be Paul's advocate at the final judgment [GNC].

3. It means both the Spirit and the help which he gives [Lt; REB]: and through the Spirit who is given to help me.

QUESTION—How are the nouns related in the genitive construction τοῦ πνεύματος 'Ιησοῦ Χριστοῦ 'the Spirit of Jesus Christ'?

It means the Holy Spirit, who was with, or was possessed by, Jesus Christ [Ea, EGT, ICC, NTC, WBC], who was sent by Jesus Christ to be with believers [Ea, EBC, EGT, El, MNTC, Mou], who represents Christ [Ea], and reveals him [Mou]. This phrase is used as another name for the Holy Spirit [TH, WBC]. In either case all commentaries say this refers to the Holy Spirit.

1:20

according-to[a] the eager-expectation[b] and hope[c] of-me

LEXICON—a. κατά with accusative object (GEL 89.8): 'according to' [Ea, Ln; KJV, NASB], 'in accordance with' [GEL, HNTC, NTC, Pl, NJB], 'in harmony with' [WBC], 'such is' [WEC], 'and thus will be fulfilled' [ICC], not explicit [NRSV, REB, TEV]. This entire phrase is translated 'I eagerly expect and hope' [NIV], 'I hope and long' [TNT], 'I firmly trust and anticipate' [NAB].

b. ἀποκαραδοκία (GEL 25.64) (BAGD p. 92): 'eager expectation' [BAGD, GEL, NTC; NRSV], 'earnest expectation' [HNTC, ICC, Ln; KJV, NASB], 'firm expectation' [Ea], 'intense anticipation'

[Pl], 'deep desire' [TEV], 'eager desire' [GEL], 'confident hope' [NJB]. The phrase ἀποκαραδοκίαν καὶ ἐλπίδα 'eager expectation and hope' is translated 'eager hopeful expectation' [WBC], 'confident hope' [REB]. Depending on how the prefix ἀπο- is interpreted, the noun can imply looking with concentration, earnestness, ignoring other interests [EBC, EGT, ICC, TNTC, WBC, WC], or looking toward the future [TNTC], or having patience and persistence until something happens [Alf, Ea, El, Ln].

   c. ἐλπίς (GEL 25.59) (BAGD 2.b. p. 253): 'hope' [BAGD, GEL, all commentaries except WBC; KJV, NASB, NJB, NRSV], 'trust' [NJB]. In this context this word has been viewed as simple human expectation [WBC], or something surer than expectation [Ea].

QUESTION—What relationship is indicated by κατά 'according to'?

It indicates a comparison with the confidence Paul expresses in 1:19 [Alf, Ea, ICC, Lg, Ln, MNTC, Mou, My, NTC, WBC]: I know that this shall turn out for my salvation just as I am expecting and hoping that I will not be put to shame in anything.

QUESTION—How are the nouns in the phrase 'eager expectation and hope' related?

   1. They are two related but independent concepts [all commentaries except EBC, WBC; all translations except REB]: my eager expectation and hope. 'Eager expectation' describes Paul's more intense subjective longing; 'hope' describes the more objective grounds [Lg].

   2. They are aspects of a single concept, joined in the figure of speech known as hendiadys [EBC, My, WBC, WEC; REB]: eager hopeful expectation.

that in[a] nothing[b] I-shall-be-put-to-shame,[c]

LEXICON—a. ἐν with dative object (GEL 89.5): 'in' [BAGD, Ea, Ln, HNTC, ICC, NTC, WBC, WEC; KJV, NASB, NIV, NRSV]. The phrase ἐν οὐδενί 'in nothing' is translated 'never' [NAB, NJB, TEV, TNT]. This entire phrase is translated 'that nothing will daunt me' [REB].

   b. οὐδείς (GEL 92.23) (BAGD 2.b.γ. p. 592): 'nothing' [Ea, GEL, ICC; KJV, REB], 'no way' [BAGD; NIV], 'not any way' [HNTC, NRSV], 'not anything' [WBC; NASB], 'no respect' [BAGD], 'not a single respect' [NTC], 'thing' [Ln].

   c. fut. pass. indic. of αἰσχύνω (GEL 25.190) (BAGD 2. p. 25): 'to be put to shame' [BAGD, HNTC, ICC, NTC, WBC; NAB, NASB, NRSV], 'to suffer disgrace' [WEC], 'to feel disgraced' [GEL], 'to be disgraced' [BAGD], 'to be made ashamed' [Ln], 'to have to admit defeat' [NJB], 'to fail in one's duty' [TEV], 'to be ashamed' [Ea, GEL; KJV, NIV, TNT].

QUESTION—What relationship is indicated by ὅτι 'that'?

1. It introduces the object or content of Paul's hope [Alf, Ea, EBC, El, ICC, Lg, My]: my hope that I shall not be at all ashamed. This is the content of Paul's eager expectation as well [My].

2. It is connected with οἶδα 'I know' (1:19) and introduces the second thing of which Paul is convinced [WBC]: I know that this will turn out for my deliverance . . . and I know that in nothing I will be put to shame

QUESTION—In what way would Paul be put to shame?

Paul would be disgraced or made to feel ashamed if he did anything in his work unworthy of the Lord [Alf, EGT, MNTC, NIC], if he denied the Lord [EGT, HNTC, NTC, TH], if he failed to defend the gospel in his trial [EBC, Pl, WBC], if his efforts or hopes failed [Ea, El, ICC, Lg, Mou, My, NIC; NJB, TEV], if he failed to win the Lord's ultimate approval [EBC, GNC], or if God or the Spirit failed to help him [Alf, EGT, Ln].

but[a] with[b] all courage[c] as always also[d] now Christ will-be-magnified[e] in[f] my body,[g]

LEXICON—a. ἀλλά (GEL 89.125): 'but' [all commentaries except Pl, WBC, WEC; all translations except NAB, REB, TNT], 'but rather' [WBC], 'on the contrary' [Pl], not explicit [NAB, REB, TNT]. The phrase ἀλλ᾽ ἐν πάσῃ παρρησίᾳ 'but with all courage' is translated 'or prevent me from speaking boldly' [REB].

b. ἐν with dative object (GEL 89.84): 'with' [Ea, ICC, Pl, WBC, WEC; KJV, NASB, NJB, NRSV], 'by' [NTC], 'in' [HNTC, Ln], not explicit [REB, TEV, TNT]. The phrase ἐν πάσῃ παρρησίᾳ 'with all boldness' is translated 'freely' [BAGD], 'openly' [BAGD], 'I have full confidence' [NAB].

c. παρρησία (GEL 25.158) (BAGD 2. p. 630): 'courage' [GEL, NTC, WBC; TEV, TNT], 'fearlessness' [NJB], 'boldness' [Ea, GEL, ICC, Ln, Pl, WEC; KJV, NASB, NRSV], 'freedom' [HNTC]. The literal meaning of παρρησία is 'boldness of speech' [EGT, HNTC, ICC, Mou, WC]. It can be understood more generally as 'boldness' [El, ICC], 'courageous speech' [EBC, Ln], or 'free, public, open speech' [BAGD, GNC, NIC, WBC; TNT].

d. καί (GEL 89.93; 89.92) (BAGD II.3. p. 393): 'also' [Ln, Pl; KJV], 'even' [BAGD; NASB], 'especially' [TEV], 'and' [Ea, REB], not explicit [HNTC, NTC, WBC, WEC; NAB, NIV, NJB, NRSV, TNT].

e. fut. pass. indic. of μεγαλύνω (GEL 87.15) (BAGD 2. p. 497): 'to be magnified' [Ea, HNTC, ICC, Ln, NTC, Pl; KJV], 'to be

exalted' [BAGD; NAB, NASB, NRSV], 'to be glorified'
[BAGD; NJB], 'to be praised' [BAGD, WBC], 'to be held in
high honor' [GEL]. This passive is also translated actively:
'(Christ) will display his greatness' [REB].

f. ἐν with dative object (GEL 83.13; 89.26): 'in' [all commentaries
except WBC; KJV, NASB, NJB]. The phrase ἐν τῷ σώματί μου
'in my body' is translated 'because of me' [WBC], 'through me'
[NAB].

g. σῶμα (GEL 8.1; 9.8) (BAGD 1.b. p. 799): 'body' [Ea, GEL,
HNTC, ICC, Ln; KJV, NAB, NJB, NRSV], 'person' [NTC, Pl],
'me' [REB].

QUESTION—What relationship is indicated by ἀλλά 'but'?

It is contrastive [Alf, El, My]. It contrasts the phrase 'with full
courage' and the preceding phrase [Alf, El, ICC, Lg, My, Pl]: in no
way will I be ashamed, but with full courage Christ will be
honored. It introduces the positive side of his desire and hope
[MNTC].

QUESTION—Why does Paul use the passive of μεγαλύνω 'to be
magnified'?

Paul wishes to imply that he is not the agent lest he be glorifying
himself [Ln, Lt, MNTC, Pl]. The Spirit (mentioned in 1:19) or
Christ is the implied agent who brings honor to Christ through
Paul [EBC, EGT, Ln, Mou, My, NTC, WBC; REB].

QUESTION—How does Paul expect that Christ will be magnified?

He will bring honor to Christ by either living to serve him or by his
joyful death [Lg]. Through Paul's actions Christ's kingdom will
spread [Alf, El] and Christ's greatness and majesty will be shown to
men [Ea, GNC, MNTC, Mou, WBC]. People will praise Christ as a
result [Mou, WBC].

QUESTION—How does Paul use the term σῶμα 'body'?

1. He uses it in its literal sense because the body is directly
associated with physical life and death, which Paul goes on to
mention [Ea, GNC, ICC, Ln, MNTC, My, NIC, TNTC]: Christ
will be honored in my body. He says 'my body' rather than 'me'
because he is thinking of the possibility that he may die
violently [Lg(H)]. It was through Paul's body that others could
see the greatness of Christ [El, GNC, Mou, MNTC]. If he lived,
he would bring honor to Christ by the physical toil and
suffering he would endure for Christ's sake; if he was put to
death for Christ, he would bring honor to Christ by the joyful
spirit in which he would accept death [MNTC].

2. He uses it in the sense of the total person [EGT, NTC, Pl, TH,
WBC; NAB, REB, TEV, TNT]: Christ will be honored in my
person.

whether[a] through[b] life[c] or[a] through[b] death.[d]

LEXICON—a. εἴτε ... εἴτε (GEL 89.69): 'whether ... or' [Ea, GEL, HNTC, ICC, Mou, Pl, NTC, WBC; all translations], 'whether ... whether' [Ln], not explicit [WEC].

b. διά with genitive object (GEL 89.76): 'by' [Ea, NTC, WBC; KJV, NASB, NIV, NJB, NRSV], 'by means of' [Ln, Mou] 'through' [HNTC, WEC], not explicit [REB]. This entire phrase is translated 'whether I live or die' [ICC; NAB, TEV, TNT], 'whether I continue to live or am sentenced to death' [Pl].

c. ζωή (GEL 23.88) (BAGD 1.a. p. 340): 'life' [BAGD, Ea, GEL, HNTC, Ln, NTC, WBC; KJV, NASB, NIV, NJB, REB, NRSV]. This noun is also translated as a verb: 'to live' [ICC, Pl; NAB, TEV, TNT].

d. θάνατος (GEL 23.99) (BAGD 1.a. p. 350): 'death' [BAGD, Ea, GEL, HNTC, Ln, NTC, Pl, WBC; KJV, NASB, NIV, NJB, REB, NSV]. This noun is also translated as a verb: 'to die' [ICC; NAB, TEV, TNT].

QUESTION—What relationship is indicated by διά 'by'?

It indicates the means by which Christ will be honored [Alf, Ea, Ln, Mou]: Christ will be honored in my body by means of my life or my death.

QUESTION—What is implied in the terms 'life' and 'death'?

1. 'Life' implies further active service for Paul [Alf, Ea, EGT, El, Lg, Lt, MNTC, My, NIC, NTC, TNTC]. 'Death' implies courageous martyrdom [Ea, EGT, El, Lg, Lt, MNTC, My, NIC, NTC, TNTC] and/or being with Christ [Alf, Ea, My, NTC]. He did not know what the outcome of his trial would be [Bg, ICC].

2. The two terms together imply totalness [WBC]: that Christ will be honored by my entire existence. He already had stated that he would be released from prison (1:9) and that he had confidence that he would go on living (1:25) [WBC].

DISCOURSE UNIT: 1:21–30 [Mou; NASB]. The topic is the Christian's peace and his consistent behavior [Mou], living is Christ [NASB].

DISCOURSE UNIT: 1:21–26 [Pl, WC]. The topic is Paul's perplexed feelings and his hope [Pl], the choice of life or death [WC].

DISCOURSE UNIT: 1:21–24 [NIC, WEC]. The topic is whether Paul would choose to live or die [NIC], death not being a threat to Paul [WEC].

DISCOURSE UNIT: 1:21–23 [EGT]. The topic is death or life meaning Christ.

1:21
For

LEXICON—γάρ (GEL 89.23): 'for' [Ea, HNTC, ICC, Ln, NTC, Pl, WBC; all translations except NJB, TNT], 'because' [WEC], 'of course' [NJB], not explicit [TNT].

QUESTION—What relationship is indicated by this word?

1. It introduces the grounds for Paul's expectation and hope that is expressed in 1:20 [Alf, Blm, Ea, El, Lg, My, NTC, WBC, WC, WEC]: my hope is that Christ will be honored in my body, whether by life or by death, since, for me, to live is Christ and to die is gain. It states why Paul can speak with such boldness [WEC]. This is also an amplification of what is involved in life and death [El, My, WBC]. Christ was glorified by Paul's labor for him in life and by Paul's suffering death with the joyful courage produced by his certainty of the gain [My]. Christ would be honored by the death of one who had lived to honor him [Ea, WBC]. Christ would be honored in death because of Paul's praising and serving Christ as an immortal being in heaven [Ea].

2. It introduces an explanation of the previous phrase (1:20) [Ln, Mou, TH]: whether by life or death; that is, for me, to live is Christ and to die is gain. Christ would not be honored if living did not mean living for Christ, nor would he be honored by Paul's death if his dying was not gain [Ln].

3. It indicates the grounds for an implied comment [Blm, Lg] ; it does not matter to me whether I live or die because, for me, to live is Christ and to die is gain.

4. There is not a close logical connection between 1:20 and 1:21 [MNTC]. That death means gain does not give a reason why Paul could honor Christ by dying [MNTC].

to-me the to-live[a] (is) Christ,

LEXICON—a. pres. act. infin. of ζάω (GEL 23.88) (BAGD 2.b.α. p. 336): 'to live' [Ea, GEL, HNTC, ICC, Ln, NTC; KJV, NASB, NIV]. This verb is also translated by a noun: 'life' [BAGD, Pl, WEC; NAB, NJB, REB, TEV, TNT], and by a gerund: 'living' [WBC; NRSV]. The present tense indicates that Paul is referring to the continuation of his present, natural life [Alf, Ea, EBC, EGT, El, ICC, Lg, Ln, My, NTC, Pl, TH, WBC], or the action of living [Blm].

QUESTION—What is the significance of the pronoun ἐμοί 'to me'?

The form ἐμοι is emphatic in itself [El, TH], and it is further emphasized by being forefronted [Alf, Bg, Ea, EBC, EGT, El, Lg, Ln, MNTC, Mou, NTC, Pl, TH, TNTC, WBC, WC].

1. This pronoun focuses on Paul's personal situation [Bg, Ea, EBC, El, Mou, My, Pl, TH]: so far as it concerns me personally.
2. This pronoun indicates that Paul is thinking of a distinction between himself and others [EGT, Lg, Ln, Lt, MNTC, NTC, WBC, WC]: for me, in contrast with what others may think. The contrast may be with others who felt differently about life and death [EGT], with those who preached Christ from selfish motives [NTC], with Job, who is possibly quoted in 1:20 [MNTC], or with the Holy Spirit or God, who is the implied agent of magnifying Christ in 1:20 [Ln].

QUESTION—What does Paul mean by 'to me to live is Christ'?

Paul was completely identified with, or united with, Christ [EBC, EGT, El, GNC, Lg, Ln, Lt, NIC, WC]; Paul was so occupied with Christ that life for him was synonymous with Christ [Ea, MNTC, Pl, TH, WBC; NAB, TNT]; all of Paul's life, energy, and time was and would be spent for Christ [Alf, Blm, EBC, El, ICC, Lt, Mou, NIC, NTC, TNTC, WBC]; living would mean that Christ would be seen in him [CBC]. His life is wholly devoted to Christ [WEC].

and the to-die[a] (is) gain.[b]

LEXICON—a. aorist act. infin. of ἀποθνῄσκω (GEL 23.99) (BAGD 1.a.α. p. 91): 'to die' [BAGD, Ea, GEL, HNTC, ICC, Ln, NTC; KJV, NASB, NIV]. This verb is also translated by a noun: 'death' [Pl, WEC; NJB, REB, TEV, TNT], and a gerund: 'dying' [WBC; NAB, NRSV].

b. κέρδος (GEL 57.192) (BAGD p. 429): 'gain' [BAGD, GEL, all commentaries; KJV, NASB, NIV, NRSV, REB, TNT], 'so much gain' [NAB], 'positive gain' [NJB], 'more' [TEV], 'would result to my advantage' [WEC].

QUESTION—What relationship is indicated by καί 'and'?

1. It conjoins the two clauses of the verse [Blm, El, Ln, MNTC; all translations except NAB, NJB, TEV]: to me to live is Christ and to die is gain.
2. It introduces a conclusion [BAGD (see ζάω), Pl, TNTC, WC, WEC; NAB, NJB, TEV]: to me to live is Christ, therefore to die is gain. Since Paul's aim in life was to glorify Christ, if he were martyred, it would be a gain for Paul by closing his whole life in such a way of glorifying him [TNTC].

QUESTION—What does the aorist tense of the verb ἀποθανεῖν 'to die' indicate?

1. It indicates that the act of dying is meant [EBC, Lg, Ln, Mou, My, NTC, TH, TNTC, WBC, WEC]: to be put to death is gain. Paul's hope concerning the state after death is contained in the noun 'gain', not in the tense of the verb 'to die' [EBC]. The

event of dying will usher Paul into an existence of even more blessing [Mou].
2. It indicates that the state of death is meant [Alf, Ea, Lt, MNTC, Pl]: to be in the state of death is gain. For Paul the state of death meant blessing. [This can only be in the sense that the act of dying—aorist tense—leads to the state of death.]

QUESTION—In what way would dying be 'gain' for Paul?

He would be in the presence of Christ [Ea, EBC, Ln, My, NIC, NTC, TH, TNTC]; he would be in more complete union with Christ [EGT, El, GNC, ICC, Lg, Lt, TH, WBC, WC]; he would be removed from suffering and trials [Blm, Ea, WBC] or from the limitations of earthly life [MNTC]; he would have rest after a life of service for Christ [WC]; his death by martyrdom would promote the gospel [TH, TNTC]. The gain is explained further in 1:23 [Mou, Pl].

1:22
But

LEXICON—δέ (GEL 89.124): 'but' [Ea, ICC, Pl, WBC; KJV, NASB, TEV, TNT], 'on the other hand' [NAB, NJB], 'nevertheless' [WEC], 'now' [Ln, NTC], not explicit [HNTC; NIV, NRSV, REB].

QUESTION—What relationship is indicated by this word?

It introduces a contrast with what has just been mentioned [Blm, Ea, Mou, My]: to die is gain, but if I am to live, etc. He now deals with the first of the alternatives just mentioned [Bg]. In 1:21 Paul gives a personal point of view of life and death; here he speaks of life in view of his apostolic ministry [El, My].

if[a] the to-live[b] in[c] (the) flesh,[d]

LEXICON—a. εἰ (GEL 89.65): 'if' [all commentaries except Lt; all translations].
b. pres. act. infin. of ζάω: 'to live'. See this word at 1:21.
c. ἐν with dative object (GEL 83.13): 'in' [Ea, HNTC, Ln, Mou, NTC, Pl, WBC, WEC; all translations except TEV], not explicit [ICC; TEV]. The prepositional phrase ἐν σαρκί 'in flesh' is translated 'here on earth' [BAGD], 'here below' [MNTC].
d. σάρξ (GEL 8.63; 8.4) (BAGD 5. p. 744): 'flesh' [BAGD, Ea, HNTC, ICC, Ln, NTC, Pl, WEC; KJV, NAB, NASB, NRSV], 'body' [GEL, WBC; NIV, NJB, REB, TNT], not explicit [TEV].

QUESTION—What does εἰ 'if' govern?
1. It governs only 'to live in the flesh'; the consequence of this condition is 'this to me means fruit of labor' [EBC, EGT, GNC, HNTC, Ln, MNTC, Mou, NIC; NAB, NASB, REB, TNT]: if I am to continue to live, this will bring fruit.

1.1 The phrase 'and what I shall choose I do not know' is a further independent thought [HNTC, Ln, MNTC, Mou, NTC; KJV, NAB, NASB, NIV, NRSV, REB, TNT]: moreover/yet I don't know whether to choose life or death.

1.2 This latter phrase is a further consequence of the preceding part of the verse [GNC; TEV]: and therefore I don't know whether to choose life or death.

1.3 This latter phrase is a question [NIV, REB]: Which then shall I choose?

2. It governs 'to live in the flesh this is fruit of labor'; and 'what I shall choose I do not know' is the consequence [Blm, El, ICC, Lg, My, Pl, WBC, WC, WEC; NJB, TEV]: if by continuing to live I will produce fruit for Christ, in that case I don't know whether to choose life or death.

3. 'If' is interrogative, 'this to me is fruit of labor' is part of the interrogation, and the final part of the verse states the conclusion [Lt]: what if by continuing to live I will produce fruit for Christ? In fact, I don't know what to choose.

QUESTION—What is meant by τὸ ζῆν ἐν σαρκί 'to live in the flesh'?

Paul is speaking of the prolongation of his natural life on earth, which he mentioned at the beginning of 1:21 [Alf, Bg, Ea, El, Lg, Ln, Lt, Mou, My, NIC, NTC, Pl, TH, TNTC, WBC]. He adds 'in the flesh' since there is life even after physical death [Bg, Lg]. Implied in the word σάρξ 'flesh' may be the idea of physical limitations and weakness [EBC, EGT, Mou, NIC], but Paul doesn't imply the ethical sense 'sinful', which he does when he uses σάρξ in some other passages [NIC, TNTC].

this for-me (is) fruit[a] of-labor,[b]

LEXICON—a. καρπός (GEL 42.13) (BAGD 2.b. p. 405): 'fruit' [BAGD, Ea, HNTC, Ln, Mou, NTC; KJV], 'result of what has been done' [GEL], 'some good purpose' [WBC]. This noun is also translated as an adjective modifying 'labor': 'fruitful' [ICC, WEC; NAB, NASB, NIV, NJB, NRSV, REB], 'productive' [NAB], 'worthwhile' [TEV, TNT].

b. ἔργον (GEL 42.42) (BAGD 2. p. 308): 'labor' [BAGD, Ea, ICC, WEC; KJV, NASB, NIV, NRSV], 'work' [BAGD, GEL, Ln, Mou, NTC; REB, TEV], 'toil' [HNTC; NAB].

QUESTION—To what does τοῦτο 'this' refer?

It refers to the phrase 'to live in the flesh' [Ea, Ln, WBC]. It is emphatic here, directing attention to that phrase [Alf, BAGD, El, ICC, My]: that very living (in contrast with dying) means fruitful labor.

QUESTION—How are the nouns related in the genitive construction καρπὸς ἔργου 'fruit of labor'?

1. The fruit is the result of the labor [Blm, Ea, EGT, El, HNTC, ICC, Lg(H), Ln, Mou, NIC, Pl, NTC, WBC, WEC; NAB, NASB, NIV, NJB, NRSV, REB, TEV, TNT].

1.1 It refers to the result of Paul's work in the future [Blm, Ea, EGT, ICC, Ln, NIC, Pl, NTC, WBC, WEC]: that for me will mean results from the work I will be able to do. His life will be useful for the ministry of the gospel [Blm].

1.2 It refers to the result of Paul's labor in the past if he continues to live [HNTC]: that for me means reaping the results of work I have done in the past.

1.3 His continuing to live is the fruit of Paul's labor in the past [Lg, WC]: my continuing to live will be the fruit from my labor. His work in the past makes it desirable to continue to live for the sake of the church [WC].

2. The labor is the fruit [Bg]: the fruit of my continuing to live will be more labor for Christ.

then/and/yet[a] what I-shall-choose[b] I-know/make-known[c] not.

LEXICON—a. καί (GEL 89.92; 91.12): 'then' [ICC, Pl, WBC, WEC; REB, TEV], 'and' [Ea, Ln; NAB, NASB, NRSV], 'yet' [NTC; KJV, NIV], not explicit [HNTC; NJB, TNT].

b. fut. mid. indic. of αἱρέω (GEL 30.86) (BAGD 2. p. 24): 'to choose' [BAGD, Ea, HNTC, Ln, Mou, NTC, Pl, WBC; all translations except NAB, NRSV], 'to prefer' [BAGD, GEL; NAB, NRSV], 'to do' [WEC]. Paul is referring to his personal preference even though he does not have the power to make the choice [Bg, EBC]. The future indicative here has the force of the subjunctive, 'should choose' [EGT, Lg]. The middle voice refers to choosing for himself [Lg].

c. pres. act. indic. of γνωρίζω (GEL **28.1**; 28.26) (BAGD 2. p. 163): 'to know' [BAGD, Ea, GEL, HNTC, Ln, Mou; NAB, NASB, NIV, NJB, NRSV, TNT], 'to decide' [Pl], 'to be sure' [TEV], 'to wot' [KJV], 'to make known' [GEL]. This verb is also translated as a phrase: 'I cannot tell' [NTC, WBC; REB], 'I cannot decide' [WEC].

QUESTION—What relationship is indicated by καί 'yet/then/and'?

1. It introduces the consequence of what he has just said [ICC, Lg(H), Pl, WBC, WEC; REB, TEV]: if what I have just said is true, then I don't know what to choose.

2. It has its primary sense of 'and/also' [Alf, Ea, El, Mou, My]: and which I shall choose I cannot tell. It shows that what follows has a close connection with what precedes [Ea, El, Mou, My], or Paul is adding an additional idea to the one that 'to live is Christ' (1:21) [Alf].

3. It adds emphasis to what follows [Blm]: indeed, I do not know what I shall choose.

QUESTION—What is implied by τί 'what'?

Implied are the two eventualities possible for Paul [Alf, Lg, NIC]: which I shall choose, death which means gain or life which will mean fruitful work, I cannot tell. Τί 'what' is used in the sense of πότερον 'which (of the two)' [Lg, Pl].

QUESTION—What is meant by γνωρίζω 'to know/make known'?

1. Here it has its classical meaning 'to know, understand, or perceive' [Blm, Ea, El, GEL, Ln, Lt, Mou, TH, WBC, WEC; KJV, NAB, NASB, NIV, NJB, TEV, TNT]: which I should choose I do not know. It is a real dilemma to decide which alternative he prefers [TH]. He doesn't 'know' because God hasn't 'made it known' to him [Ln].

2. In the New Testament it most often means 'to make known or declare' and it means that here [EBC, EGT, GNC, ICC, MNTC, My, NIC, NTC, WC; REB]: which I should choose I cannot tell you. He cannot declare which he chooses because he is in a dilemma and doesn't know [MNTC, My, NIC]. It is not his perogative to make a choice [WBC], or he knows that he would prefer to die but doesn't want to express too strongly his own desire [ICC].

1:23

Now/But

TEXT—Instead of δέ 'but', some manuscripts have γάρ 'for'. GNT does not discuss this variant. Only KJV reads 'for'.

LEXICON—δέ (GEL 89.124; 89.94): 'now' [ICC], 'but' [Ea, Pl; NASB], 'so' [NTC], 'indeed' [WBC], 'moreover' [Ln], 'you see' [WEC], not explicit [HNTC; all translations except KJV and NASB].

QUESTION—What relationship is indicated by this word?

1. It indicates a contrast [Alf, Ea, EGT, El, Mou, Pl; NASB]: which to choose I do not know, but I am caught in a dilemma. It is a gentle contrast perhaps close to option 2 [El] or 3 [Mou] below.

2. It indicates the grounds for what Paul has just said [Bg, ICC, My]: which I shall choose I cannot say. Now the reason is that I am caught in a dilemma.

3. It conjoins additional information [Ln]: which I shall choose I do not know and I am caught in a dilemma.

I-am-hard-pressed[a] by[b] the two,

LEXICON—a. pres. act. indic. of συνέχω (GEL 19.45) (BAGD 5. p. 789): 'to be hard pressed' [BAGD, NTC; NASB, NRSV], 'to

be pressed' [Ea, GEL], 'to be held' [Ln], 'to be held in a strait'
[Pl], 'to be in a strait' [KJV], 'to be in straits' [WEC]. 'to be
drawn strongly' [HNTC], 'to be strongly attracted' [NAB], 'to be
pulled' [REB, TEV], 'to be torn' [WBC; NIV]. This entire
phrase is translated 'I am caught in this dilemma' [NJB], 'I am
in a dilemma' [TNT]. The basic idea of συνέχω is to be held
under pressure from two sides so that movement in either
direction is hindered [Blm, EBC, EGT, GNC, ICC, Lt, Mou,
TNTC]. Here Paul means that the attraction of either side is so
strong that it does not permit him to approach the other
[MNTC]. Present in this context may be the idea that the choice
brings stress to Paul [EBC, WBC].

b. ἐκ with genitive object (GEL 89.25; 89.77; 90.16): 'by' [NAB],
'from' [Ln; NASB], 'between' [NTC, Pl, WBC, WEC; NIV,
NRSV], 'betwixt' [KJV], 'on account of' [Ea]. The phrase ἐκ τῶν
δύο 'from the two' is translated 'in two directions' [TEV], 'both
ways' [HNTC], 'two ways' [REB].

QUESTION—To what does 'the two' refer?

1. It refers to the two possibilities mentioned previously [Alf, Ea,
El, ICC, Ln, Lt, My, Pl]: I am hard pressed to choose between
the two, that is, whether to live in the body, which means
Christ, or to die, which means gain.

2. It refers to the two possibilities that Paul is about to mention
[NTC, WBC]: I am hard pressed to choose between my desire
to depart and be with Christ and your need to have me stay.

having[a] the desire[b] for[c] the to-depart[d] and to-be with[e] Christ,

LEXICON—a. pres. act. participle of ἔχω (GEL 57.1) (BAGD I.2.e.β.
p. 332): 'to have' [BAGD, Ea, GEL, HNTC, ICC, Ln, NTC, Pl;
KJV, NASB]. The phrase τὴν ἐπιθυμίαν ἔχων 'the desire having'
is translated 'I want' [NJB], 'I want very much' [TEV], 'my
personal desire being' [Mou], 'my desire is' [NRSV, REB], 'I
desire' [WBC; NIV], 'I long' [NAB], 'For myself I am eager'
[TNT], 'because on the one hand I do wish' [WEC], 'If I should
consult only my own desire, I should wish' [ICC].

b. ἐπιθυμία (GEL 25.12) (BAGD 2. p. 293): 'desire' [GEL, Ea,
ICC, Ln, Mou, NTC, Pl; KJV, NASB, NRSV, REB], 'longing'
[BAGD, HNTC]. This noun can have either a good or a bad
sense; here it is used in a good sense [BAGD, GNC, Ln].

c. εἰς with accusative object (GEL 90.23): 'for' [Ea, Ln], 'in the
direction of' [Mou], 'towards' [Pl]. The phrase εἰς τὸ ἀναλῦσαι
'for departing' is translated 'to depart' [NTC, WEC; KJV,
NASB, NIV, NRSV, REB, TNT], 'to move on' [HNTC], 'to go'
[ICC], 'to be gone' [NJB], 'to leave this life' [GEL; TEV], 'to be
freed from this life' [NAB], 'to break camp' [WBC].

d. aorist act. infin. of ἀναλύω (GEL **23.101**) (BAGD 2. p. 57): 'to
depart' [BAGD, Ea, Mou, NTC, WEC; KJV, NASB, NIV,
NRSV, REB, TNT], 'to get to depart' [Ln], 'to leave' [GEL], 'to
strike camp' [Pl]. The literal meaning of this verb is 'to break
up', 'to unloose' [ICC], 'to break up one's camp' [TNTC, WC]. It
is a departure from life [Ea, ICC, TH, WBC; TEV] and from
this world [Alf]. It is used figuratively here as a euphemism for
'to die' [BAGD, all commentaries]. Another figurative meaning
possibly in Paul's mind was loosing an anchor for departure
[Alf, HNTC, TNTC, WC] or breaking up a camp [ICC, Ln, Lt,
My, Pl]. Paul may have had in mind either of those meanings
[Ea, El, GNC, MNTC, Mou, NTC, WBC].

e. σύν with dative object (GEL 89.107): 'with' [Ea, HNTC, ICC,
Ln, Mou, NTC, Pl, WBC, WEC; all translations].

QUESTION—What relationship is indicated by the use of the
participle ἔχων 'having'?

It indicates the reason for his dilemma which he has just
mentioned [My]: I am perplexed because I have the desire to die.

QUESTION—What is implied in the phrase σὺν Χριστῷ εἶναι 'to be
with Christ'?

Paul is saying that were he to die he would immediately be in the
presence of Christ having fellowship with him [EBC, ICC, Lg, Lt,
MNTC, NIC, NTC, TNTC, WBC]. Death cannot interrupt life in
Christ [EGT, GNC]. Grammatically, the phrases 'to depart' and 'to
be with Christ' are closely connected [Pl, TH, WBC].

for[a] (that is) by-much[b] more[c] better.[d]

TEXT—Some manuscripts omit γάρ 'for'. GNT places it in brackets,
indicating considerable doubt concerning its inclusion. Γάρ is not
explicitly translated by WBC; KJV, NIV, NJB, REB, TEV, TNT, but
this may be merely stylistic and may or may not mean that they do not
accept this word in their Greek text.

LEXICON—a. γάρ (GEL 89.23): 'for' [Ea, HNTC, ICC, Ln, Mou,
NTC, Pl; NAB, NASB, NRSV], 'since' [WEC], not explicit
[WBC; KJV, NIV, NJB, REB, TEV, TNT].

b. πολύς (GEL 59.11) (BAGD I.2.c.α. p. 689): 'much' [GEL]. The
phrase πολλῷ μᾶλλον 'more by much' is translated 'far' [KJV,
NAB, NRSV, TEV, TNT], 'far, far' [Mou, Pl], 'very far' [Ln,
NTC], 'by far' [ICC; NIV, NJB, REB], 'far and away' [HNTC],
'much by far' [Ea], 'much' [WEC], 'much indeed' [BAGD], 'very
much' [WBC; NASB].

c. μᾶλλον (GEL 78.28) (BAGD 1. p. 489): 'more' [GEL].

d. κρείσσων (GEL 65.21) (BAGD 2. p. 450): 'better' [BAGD, Ea,
GEL, ICC, Ln, Mou, NTC, Pl, WEC; KJV, NASB, NIV, NRSV,

REB, TNT], 'the better' [HNTC], 'the better thing' [ICC; NAB], 'a better thing' [WBC; TEV], 'the stronger desire' [NJB].

QUESTION—What relationship is indicated by γάρ 'for'?

It indicates the reason or grounds for Paul's strong desire [El]: I desire to depart and be with Christ, because that is far better.

QUESTION—What is implied in the phrase 'by much that is more better'?

Implied is the exuberant desire Paul feels [Ea, El, MNTC, Mou, My]. To the comparative κρείσσων 'better' is added the comparative adjective μᾶλλον 'more, rather' and both words are intensified by πολύς 'much' to form a triple comparative [Ea, EBC, HNTC].

QUESTION—What comparison is implied by κρεῖσσον 'better'?

Paul implies that it is better to die and be with Christ than to remain alive in the body [GNC, NIC, NTC], even if that life is one of serving Christ [MNTC, Mou].

DISCOURSE UNIT: 1:24–26 [EGT]. The topic is Paul's thought that he may visit them again.

1:24
But

LEXICON—δέ (GEL 89.124): 'but' [Ea, HNTC, ICC, NTC, Pl; NIV, NRSV, REB, TEV, TNT], 'yet' [Ln; NAB, NASB], 'and yet' [NJB], 'and' [WBC], 'nevertheless' [KJV], 'on the other hand' [WEC].

QUESTION—What relationship is indicated by this word?

1. It indicates a contrast with what precedes [Ea, El, HNTC, ICC, Lg, NTC, Pl, TH, TNTC; NIV, NRSV, REB, TEV, TNT]: for my sake to depart and be with Christ is far better, but for your sake for me to remain is more necessary. The departing from life to be with Christ would be better for Paul, while Paul's remaining in life would be more necessary for the Philippians [Ea, El, Ln, Lt, My, NIC, NTC]. Paul's use of 'for the sake of you' later in the verse indicates that the sentiment in this verse is in contrast with his desire for himself (1:23) [Ea, My].
2. It indicates contraexpectation with what precedes [KJV, NAB, NASB, NJB]: although to depart and be with Christ is far better, yet to live on is more necessary.
3. It conjoins the two aspects of the desire Paul mentions in 1:23 [WBC]: I desire both to depart . . . which is far better, and to remain . . . which is more necessary.

the to-remain[a] in[b] the flesh[c] (is) more-necessary[d] for-the-sake-of[e] you.

TEXT—Some manuscripts omit ἐν 'in'. GNT places this word in brackets, indicating considerable doubt that it is part of the text. ICC, Lt, Mou, and Pl omit ἐν. EGT says there is basically no difference of meaning whether or not it is included (but see the question on 'in the flesh').

LEXICON—a. pres. act. infin. of ἐπιμένω (GEL 68.11; 85.55) (BAGD 1. p. 296): 'to remain' [BAGD, GEL, HNTC, Ln, NTC, WEC; NIV, NRSV, REB], 'to remain alive' [WBC], 'to remain on' [NASB], 'to stay alive' [NJB], 'to abide' [Ea, ICC, Pl; KJV]. The phrase ἐν τῇ σαρκί 'the remaining in the flesh' is translated 'to go on living' [TNT], 'to remain alive' [NAB, TEV]. The prefix ἐπι- on the verb implies continuance, 'staying on' [Alf, El, Mou, My].

b. ἐν with dative object (GEL 13.8; 83.13): 'in' [Ea, HNTC, Ln, NTC, WBC, WEC; KJV, NASB, NIV, NJB, NRSV, REB], 'by' [ICC Pl].

c. σάρξ: 'flesh'. See this word at 1:22.

d. ἀναγκαιότερος (GEL 71.39) (BAGD 1. p. 52): 'more necessary' [BAGD, Ea, ICC, Ln, NTC, Pl; NASB, NIV, NRSV, TNT], 'necessary' [GEL, MNTC], 'more needful' [HNTC; KJV], 'more urgent' [NAB], 'much more important' [TEV], 'greater need' [REB], 'a more urgent need' [WBC; NJB].

e. διά with accusative object (GEL 89.26; 90.38): 'for the sake of' [HNTC, ICC, NTC; NAB, NASB, NJB, REB, TEV, TNT], 'on account of' [Ea, Ln, Mou, Pl], 'for' [WBC; KJV, NIV, NRSV], 'because of' [WEC].

QUESTION—What is meant by ἐν τῇ σαρκί 'in the flesh'?

The similar phrase 'in flesh', without the article (1:22), refers in general to a Christian's living; here, with the article, it specifically refers to Paul's continuing to live [Alf, El, ICC]: that I should continue to live in the body. Those who prefer the textual reading which omits ἐν 'in' see yet a further distinction: to continue to live by the flesh is to cling to life with all its consequences [Lt, Pl].

QUESTION—With what is ἀναγκαιότερον 'more necessary' related?

At the end of 1:23 Paul uses the emphatic comparative by 'much more better'; here he maintains the emotion with 'more necessary' [ICC, Ln, Lt]. Both comparatives are equal in intensity [WBC], or the second comparative (1:24) is even more forceful that the former [Ea, El], i.e., Paul is more obligated to stay than to depart [Bg, Lg, MNTC, TNTC, WC].

QUESTION—What is implied in 'more necessary for the sake of you'?

It was more necessary for Paul to stay alive so he could continue his pastoral ministry of guidance, advice and help for this young church [Alf, Bg, EBC, Lg, NIC, NTC, TNTC, WC] and other churches and converts related to Paul [GNC, HNTC, MNTC, My].

DISCOURSE UNIT: 1:25-26 [My(D), WEC]. The topic is reassurance [WEC].

1:25
And[a] convinced[b] of-this,

LEXICON—a. καί (GEL 89.92): 'and' [Ea, HNTC, ICC, Ln, NTC, Pl; KJV, NASB], 'so' [WEC], not explicit [WBC; NAB, NIV, NJB, NRSV, REB, TEV, TNT].

b. perf. act. participle of πείθω (GEL 33.301) (BAGD 2.b. p. 639): 'to be convinced' [BAGD, GEL, NTC, WBC; NASB, NIV, NRSV], 'to be confident' [ICC, Ln, Pl], 'to be persuaded' [Ea, HNTC], 'to be well aware of' [WEC], 'to be sure' [TEV, TNT]. This entire phrase is translated 'confidence' [KJV]; this phrase plus the following verb οἶδα 'I know' is translated 'this fills me with confidence' [NAB], 'this convinces me' [REB], 'this much I know for certain' [NJB]. The perfect tense indicates a settled state of confidence [Lg].

QUESTION—What relationship is indicated by the participle πεποιθώς 'convinced'?

1. It indicates the grounds for what Paul is going to say [Lg, WBC, TEV]: since I am convinced of this, therefore I know that . . .

2. It gives the manner of his knowing [Bg, Blm]: I confidently know this.

QUESTION—To what does τοῦτο 'this' refer?

1. It refers to the preceding thought [Alf, Ea, EGT, El, ICC, Lg, Ln, MNTC, My, WBC; all translations except NJB, REB]: I am convinced that my continuing to live is more needful for you, therefore I know that I shall remain.

2. It refers to the following statement [Bg, Blm, HNTC, Lt; NJB, REB]: I am convinced of this, namely that I know that I shall remain.

QUESTION—What is meant by οἶδα 'I know'?

Paul is not saying that he knows absolutely that he will continue to live [Ln], but he is expressing his full expectation on the basis of what seems necessary or probable [Blm, EBC, El, ICC, Lt, MNTC, NTC, Pl, TNTC, WEC]: it is my definite opinion or conviction. Paul is certain because he knows that God's plan for him involves meeting the needs of his converts [EGT, GNC, HNTC, Lg, WBC]. He knows by prophetic inspiration [Bg].

I-know[a] that I-shall-remain[b] and I-shall-continue-with[c] you all,

TEXT—Instead of παραμένω 'to remain (at one's side)', some manuscripts have συμπαραμένω 'to remain (with someone) to help'. GNT does not deal with this variant. The sense of the two words is sufficiently similar that only if the Greek word is mentioned can it be clear which word the commentary has used. The variant συμπαραμένω is specifically read by Bg, Blm, Lg, My.

LEXICON—a. perf. act. indic. of οἶδα (GEL 28.1): 'to know' [all commentaries except WEC; all translations except NAB, REB], 'to be confident' [WEC], 'to be sure' [REB].

    b. fut. act. indic. of μένω (GEL 85.55) (BAGD 1.c.α. p. 504): 'to remain' [Ea, GEL, HNTC, Ln, NTC; NASB, NIV, NRSV, REB], 'to remain alive' [BAGD], 'to stay' [GEL, WBC, WEC; NJB, TEV, TNT], 'to stay with' [NAB], 'to abide' [KJV], 'to bide' [Pl].

    c. fut. act. indic. of παραμένω (GEL 85.56): 'to continue with' [BAGD; KJV, NASB, NIV, NRSV], 'to continue in company with' [HNTC], 'to remain with' [Ea, GEL, NTC, WEC], 'to remain by the side of' [Ln], 'to remain on' [WBC], 'to stay on with' [TEV], 'to be with' [TNT], 'to stand by' [NJB, REB], 'to persevere with' [NAB], 'to abide with' [Pl].

QUESTION—What is the difference between μένω 'to remain' and παραμένω 'to continue with'?

Μένω is used in the general sense of 'to remain alive' and παραμένω (or συμπαραμένω) is used in the relative sense of 'to remain with someone, in their company' [Bg, Blm, Ea, EBC, GNC, ICC, Lg, Ln, Lt]. The second verb amplifies the first [ICC, Ln].

for[a] the progress[b] of-you and joy[c] of-the faith,[d]

LEXICON—a. εἰς with accusative object (GEL 89.57): 'for' [Ea, ICC, Ln, NTC; KJV, NAB, NASB, NIV, NRSV], 'to further' [HNTC], 'to encourage' [NJB], 'to add to' [TEV], 'so that' [WEC], 'to promote' [Pl], 'in order that' [WBC], 'to (help)' [TNT], 'to ensure' [REB].

    b. προκοπή (GEL 13.57) (BAGD p. 707): 'progress' [BAGD, HNTC, ICC, Mou, NTC, WBC, WEC; NAB, NASB, NIV, NRSV, REB, TEV], 'furtherance' [BAGD; KJV], 'advancement' [BAGD, Ea, GEL, Ln], 'advance' [NJB]. This noun is also translated as a verb: 'to help' [TNT].

    c. χαρά (GEL 25.123) (BAGD 1. p. 875): 'joy' [BAGD, Ea, GEL, HNTC, ICC, Ln, Mou, NTC; all translations].

    d. πίστις (GEL 31.102) (BAGD 2.d.α. p. 663): 'faith' [BAGD, Ea, HNTC, ICC, Ln, Mou, NTC; all translations].

QUESTION—What relationship is indicated by εἰς 'for'?

It indicates the purpose of his remaining [Lg, Ln, WBC, WEC]: I shall continue with you all in order that, etc.

QUESTION—With what is ὑμῶν 'of you' connected?

1. It is connected with both of the nouns 'progress' and 'joy' [Blm, ICC, Lg, My, TNTC, WC, WEC; NAB, NJB, REB, TNT]: for your progress and your joy.

2. It is connected only with 'progress' [Ln]: for your progress and the joy about the faith.

QUESTION—With what is the phrase τῆς πίστεως 'of the faith' connected?

1. It is connected with both of the nouns 'progress' and 'joy' [Alf, Blm, Ea, El, GNC, ICC, Lg, Lt, Mou, My, Pl, TH, TNTC, WBC, WC, WEC]: I shall remain for your progress in the faith and your joy in the faith. The faith of the Philippians will be advanced through Paul's continued presence and ministry [Alf, Ea, EBC]. They will increasingly appreciate, understand, and practise the things he teaches [WBC]. Specifically they will progress in love, knowledge, fruitfulness, and obedience [NTC].

1.1 'Faith' relates in the same way to 'progress' and 'joy' [Alf, Ea, ICC, My]: I shall remain with you all in order that your faith may advance and that your faith may have joy.

1.2 'Faith' relates in a different way to 'progress' and 'joy'; faith is first subject, then origin [El]: I shall remain with you all in order that your faith may advance and that joy may come from your faith.

2. It is connected only with 'joy' [EGT, Ln; REB]: for your progress and to add joy to your faith. Faith is the object of joy [Ln]: joy about the faith or over what you believe. MNTC says that the sense in this option 2 is the same as that in 1 above, because even here it would be the progress 'in their faith' that Paul would be concerned about.

1:26

so-that[a] the cause-for-glorying/glorying[b] of-you may-increase[c]

LEXICON—a. ἵνα (GEL 89.59) (BAGD I.1.d. p. 377): 'so that' [HNTC, ICC; NASB, NIV, NJB, NRSV, REB, TEV], 'in order that' [BAGD, Ln, NTC, Pl, WBC], 'so' [TNT], 'that' [Ea; KJV], not explicit [NAB].

b. καύχημα (GEL **25.203**; 33.368) (BAGD 1. p. 426): 'cause for glorying' [HNTC], 'glorying' [ICC, WEC], 'reason for boasting' [Ln, Pl], 'matter of boasting' [Ea], 'what (you) can be proud of' [BAGD], 'pride' [BAGD; NJB, REB], 'boasting' [WBC; NRSV], 'proud confidence' [NASB], 'joy' [NIV], 'rejoicing' [KJV], 'exultation' [NTC], 'cause for pride' [REB], 'reason to be proud' [GEL; TEV], 'to be made proud' [NAB], 'to take pride in' [TNT].

c. pres. act. subj. of περισσεύω (GEL 59.52) (BAGD 1.a.β. p. 650): 'to increase' [Ln, WBC], 'to abound' [Ea, GEL, ICC, NTC, WEC; NASB], 'to overflow' [NIV], 'to increase to overflowing' [NJB], 'to be present in abundance' [BAGD], 'to be more abundant' [Pl; KJV], 'to share abundantly' [NRSV], not explicit [REB].

QUESTION—What relationship is indicated by ἵνα 'so that'?

1. It indicates purpose [Ea, EGT, El, ICC, Lg, Ln, My, NTC, TH, WBC]: I shall continue with you all in order that your cause for boasting may increase. 1:26 may be seen as a specific definition of the generic purpose 'for your progress and joy in the faith' (1:25) [El, ICC, My, NTC] or it may be an additional purpose [Ea, WBC]. In any case it is Paul's ultimate purpose for continuing with the Philippians [Ea, ICC, My, TH]. It is the purpose of your progress and joy (1:25) [Lg].

2. It indicates result [MNTC; TNT]: I shall continue with you all with the result that your cause for boasting will increase.

QUESTION—What is meant by καύχημα 'cause for glorying/glorying'?

1. It speaks of the *basis for* or *object of* one's pride or joy [Alf, Ea, EBC, El, EGT, HNTC, ICC, Ln, Lt, MNTC, My, NIC, Pl, TNTC, WBC; NASB, NIV, NJB, REB, TEV]: so that your reason to be proud may increase. The idea of pride is present in καύχημα [WBC; NAB, TNT].

2. It speaks of the *act* of glorying or rejoicing [Blm, Lg, NTC, WC; KJV]: so that your rejoicing may increase.

QUESTION—What is the basis for the Philippians' pride or joy?

The basis for, or object of, their pride and joy is Christ Jesus [Blm, ICC, NIC, NTC, WBC, WC; NIV, NJB] and the gospel [Blm], Paul (especially through his return to them) [Alf, GEL, ICC, MNTC, NIC, NTC, TNTC, WC; NAB, NASB, REB, TEV, TNT], the Philippians' knowledge and possession of the gospel [Alf, EGT, El], their 'progress and joy in the faith' (1:25) [Ea, EBC, Lg, Ln], their joy as Christians [My].

in[a] **Christ Jesus in/on-account-of**[b] **me,**

LEXICON—a. ἐν with dative object (GEL 13.8; 89.26): 'in' [Ea, HNTC, ICC, Ln, Mou, NTC, WBC, WEC; KJV, NASB, NIV, NJB, NRSV, REB], 'in union with' [TEV], 'because of your relation to' [Pl].

b. ἐν with dative object (GEL 13.8; 89.26): 'in' [Ea, HNTC, ICC, Pl; NASB], 'on account of' [NIV], 'because of' [WBC], 'in connection with' [Ln, NTC], 'for' [KJV], not explicit [NRSV].

The phrase ἐν ἐμοί is translated 'through my ministry' [WEC], 'on my account' [NJB, REB].

QUESTION—With what is the phrase ἐν Χριστῷ 'Ιησοῦ 'in Christ Jesus' connected?

1. It is connected with the preceding verb περισσεύῃ 'may increase' [Ea, El, ICC, Lg, Ln, My, Pl; KJV, NASB, REB]: your pride may increase in Christ Jesus.
2. It is connected with the noun καύχημα 'cause for glorying/glorying' [Blm, NTC, WBC; NIV, NJB]: your joy in Christ Jesus or your pride in Christ Jesus.
3. It is connected with both the noun and verb [HNTC, MNTC; NAB, TEV, TNT]: you will have more cause to be proud of me in Christ Jesus, or, in me you will have more cause to be proud in Christ.

QUESTION—What is meant by 'in Christ Jesus'?

It is the sphere in which the blessing of the gospel is found and increases [EGT, El, Lg, Ln, Lt, My]. It indicates that this is a matter of Christian rejoicing or boasting, not of human happiness or pride [Alf, ICC, MNTC, Mou, My].

QUESTION—With what is the phrase ἐν ἐμοί 'in me' connected?

1. It is connected with the whole preceding phrase 'your reason for pride may increase in Christ Jesus' [Ea, EBC, El, HNTC, Ln, Lg, MNTC, NTC, Pl, WBC; KJV, NIV, NJB, REB]: your reason for pride may increase in Christ Jesus because of me.
2. It is connected with καύχημα 'cause for glorying/glorying' [NAB, NASB, TEV, TNT]: your pride in me.

QUESTION—What is meant by 'in me'?

In Paul was the immediate occasion of their increasing pride or rejoicing [EBC, ICC, Lt, Mou, My]: because of me. He was the representative of Christ's cause [ICC]. Grammatically, this and the following phrase are emphatic [Ln].

through[a] the my coming[b] again[c] to[d] you.

LEXICON—a. διά with genitive object (GEL 89.76): 'through' [HNTC, ICC, Ln, Pl, WBC; NASB, NIV, REB], 'because of' [NTC], 'on account of' [Ea], 'by' [KJV]. This entire phrase is translated 'when I come back to you' [WEC; NRSV].

b. παρουσία (GEL 15.86; 85.25) (BAGD 2.a. p. 630): 'coming' [BAGD, Ea, GEL; KJV, NASB, NRSV], 'arrival' [HNTC], 'presence' [Ln, Pl, WBC], 'being (present)' [ICC, NTC; NIV], not explicit [REB, NRSV]. The literal meaning of παρουσία is 'presence' but it came to mean 'coming' [Mou].

c. πάλιν (GEL 67.55) (BAGD 1.a. p. 606): 'again' [Ea, GEL, HNTC, ICC, NTC, Pl; KJV, NASB, NIV, NRSV], 'back' [BAGD, Ln], 'once again' [WBC], not explicit [REB].

      d. πρός with accusative object (GEL 84.18; 89.112) (BAGD III.7. p. 711): 'to' [Ea; KJV, NASB, NRSV, REB], 'with' [BAGD, ICC, Ln, NTC, Pl, WBC; NIV], 'among' [HNTC; NJB].

QUESTION—What relationship is indicated by διά 'through'?

      1. It indicates means [Alf, Ea, El; KJV, NASB, NIV]: by my being with you again, your pride/rejoicing will increase.

      2. It indicates reason [EGT; NAB, NJB, TEV, TNT]: your pride/rejoicing will increase because I will again be with you.

QUESTION—What is implied by the adverb πάλιν 'again'?

      It is implied that Paul had been in Philippi before [NIC, NTC, TNTC].

DISCOURSE UNIT: 1:27–2:30 [WEC]. The topic is an exhortation to sanctification.

DISCOURSE UNIT: 1:27–2:18 [Alf, EBC, HNTC, Lg, NIC, Pl, TNTC, WBC, WC; NAB]. The topic is exhortations to be firm, to be in agreement, to be humble, and to be earnest in the faith [Alf], an exhortation to be in agreement [HNTC], an exhortation to Christian heroism [NAB], exhortation and example [TNTC], exhortations [EBC, NIC, WC], hortatory and doctrinal comments [Pl], instructions for the church [WBC], Christ's example for the church to follow [Lg].

DISCOURSE UNIT: 1:27–2:4 [Lt, NIC, Pl, WC, WEC]. The topic is a plea for unity and self-denial [Lt, Pl, WC], an exhortation to be united, steadfast, and humble [NIC], Christian citizenship [WEC].

DISCOURSE UNIT: 1:27–30 [CBC, EBC, EGT, HNTC, ICC, Lg, Ln, MNTC, NIC, NTC, TH, TNTC, WBC; NAB, NJB]. The topic is an exhortation to unity and obedience by behavior worthy of Christ [CBC], an exhortation to be in agreement and to be courageous (and steadfast [Ln, NTC]) in the face of enemies of the gospel [EBC, HNTC, Ln, NTC, TNTC], an exhortation to live in a manner worthy of the gospel [MNTC] in view of conflicts [EGT], a plea to be steadfast in all situations of life [NIC], an urging to stand firm for the faith [TH; NAB], a plea to contend for the faith [NJB], a plea for stability in the faith [WBC], the Philippians' Christian behavior as the condition of Paul's joy [Lg].

DISCOURSE UNIT: 1:27–28 [WEC]. The topic is steadfastness.

1:27
Only[a] worthily[b] of-the gospel of-the Christ conduct-yourselves,[c]

      LEXICON—a. μόνον: 'only' [Ea, HNTC, ICC, Ln, Mou, NTC, Pl, WBC; KJV, NASB, NRSV, REB], 'then' [NAB], 'now' [TEV], 'but' [NJB], 'whatever may happen' [TNT], 'whatever happens [NIV], not explicit [WEC].

b. ἀξίως (GEL 65.17; 66.6) (BAGD p. 78): 'worthily' [GEL, Pl], 'in a manner worthily of' [HNTC, NTC, WEC; NASB, NIV, NRSV], 'in a way worthy of' [Ln, Mou; NAB], 'in a way that is worthy' [NJB], 'as it becometh' [KJV]. The phrase ἀξίως πολιτεύεσθε 'worthily conduct yourselves' is translated 'let your conduct be worthy' [REB], 'let your conversation be worthy' [Ea], 'let your daily life with your fellowmen be worthy' [TNT], 'show yourselves to be good citizens, worthy' [WBC]. The phrase ἀξίως τοῦ εὐαγγελίου τοῦ Χριστοῦ 'worthily of the gospel of Christ' is translated 'as becomes members of a Christian community' [ICC]. The phrase ἀξίως τοῦ εὐαγγελίου τοῦ Χριστοῦ πολιτεύεσθε 'worthily of the gospel of Christ conduct yourselves' is translated 'the important thing is that your way of life should be as the gospel of Christ requires' [TEV].

c. pres. mid. impera. of πολιτεύω (GEL 41.34) (BAGD 3. p. 686): 'to conduct oneself' [NAB, NASB, NIV], 'to behave' [WEC; NJB], 'to order one's life' [HNTC, Mou], 'to bear oneself' [ICC] 'to live' [GEL, Pl], 'to continue conduct' [Ln], 'to exercise one's citizenship' [NTC], 'to let one's conversation be' [KJV]. The original sense of living as a citizen of a state [EBC] came to mean generally to conduct oneself [Ea, EGT, Mou]; here it refers to the Philippians' public life [Ea], or their life in community [Ln], or their membership in the Christian community [EBC, ICC, Lg, Lt, My, NIC, TH, WEC]. It is used intentionally to emphasize the idea of the Philippians' fellow-citizenship in a heavenly community [El, HNTC, NTC, Pl], or to their life both as citizens of their community and as citizens of the Kingdom of Heaven [TNTC, WBC]. It is related to his comment in 3:20 that they were citizens of heaven [GNC].

QUESTION—What is meant by μόνον 'only'?

It is a transitional word bringing up an important matter that concerned Paul [WEC]. It means that what follows is the one thing Paul is emphasizing [Alf, Bg, Ea, El, ICC, Ln, MNTC, My, NIC, WBC]. Regardless of what may happen to him this is what they are to do [Pl]. This is the one thing which will bring Paul joy regarding them, as the emphatic position of this word points out [Lg, TNTC].

QUESTION—What is the significance of the word order in this clause?

The phrase 'worthily of the gospel of Christ' is emphatic [Alf] since it precedes the verb 'conduct yourselves'.

QUESTION—How are the two nouns related in the genitive construction τοῦ εὐαγγελίου τοῦ Χριστοῦ 'the gospel of Christ'?

1. It is an objective genitive [El, ICC, TH]: the gospel which tells about Christ.
2. It is a genitive of origin [Ea, Ln]: the gospel which has its origin in Christ.
3. It is both a subjective and objective genitive since both are true [NIC]: the gospel which comes from Christ and tells about him.

in-order-that[a] whether[b] having-come and having-seen you or-whether[b] being-absent I-may-hear the-(things) concerning[c] you,

TEXT—Instead of ἀκούω 'may be hearing' (present subj.), some manuscripts read ἀκούσω 'I may hear' (aorist subj.). GNT does not deal with this variant, and most versions would not distinguish between these two forms. A number of commentaries read ἀκούσω, but only Ln, who accepts ἀκούσω, comments on the difference between the two forms; NIC and WEC prefer ἀκούω but say the two forms have essentially the same meaning.

LEXICON—a. ἵνα (GEL 89.59): 'in order that' [Ea, Ln], 'so that' [HNTC, Mou, Pl, WEC; NASB, NJB, NRSV, REB, TEV], 'that' [NTC; KJV], 'then' [WBC; NIV], not explicit [ICC; NAB, TNT].

　　b. εἴτε . . . εἴτε (GEL 89.69): 'whether . . . or whether' [Ea; NJB, TNT], 'whether . . . or' [HNTC, ICC, Mou, NTC, Pl, WBC, WEC; NAB, NASB, NIV, NRSV, REB, TEV], 'whether . . . or else' [KJV], 'whether . . . whether' [Ln]. This expression implies 'whatever may happen regarding my arrival' [Bg].

　　c. περί with genitive object (GEL 90.24) (BAGD 1.i. p. 645): 'concerning' [Ln], 'about' [HNTC, Mou, Pl, WBC, WEC; NAB, NIV, NJB, NRSV, REB], 'of' [Ea, NTC; KJV, NASB], not explicit [ICC; TEV, TNT].

QUESTION—What relationship is indicated by ἵνα 'in order that'?

It introduces the purpose of Paul's exhortation to live worthily of the gospel [Ea, Lg]: live worthily in order that I may hear, etc.

QUESTION—What relationship is indicated by the εἴτε . . . εἴτε 'whether . . . or whether' phrase?

1. The grammar is irregular; the full sense would be 'whether I come and see you, or whether I am absent and hear', the verb 'to hear' being related only to 'whether I am absent' [Alf, EBC, GNC, MNTC, Mou, NTC; NAB, NIV, NJB]: if I am absent I may hear the things concerning you. The sense requires that it be related only to εἴτε ἀπών 'or being absent' [Alf, GNC, MNTC, Mou, NTC; NAB, NASB, NIV, NJB], even though the structure of the clause implies that it is related to 'whether

coming and seeing you' as well [Alf]. The obvious semantic parallel to ἀκούω 'I may hear' is ἰδών 'seeing' [Alf].

2. The full sense would be 'whether I come and see you or am absent, (in either case) I will hear', the verb 'to hear' being related both to 'coming and seeing' as well as to 'being absent' [Bg, Blm, Ea, Lg, Lt, My, TH; KJV, NASB, REB, TEV, TNT]: whether I come and see you or am absent, in either case I may hear that you are standing firm. The verb 'I may hear' is related to 'coming and seeing you' as well as to 'being absent' [Bg, Blm, Ea, ICC, Lg, Lt, My; KJV, NASB, TEV, TNT] and is therefore the verb related to ἵνα 'in order that' [TH; KJV]. By a common Greek figure of speech 'I may hear' may be related to both aspects even though it grammatically applies only to the latter one [Blm]. The verb that would have followed the first 'whether' phrase ("I may find out" or something similar) is omitted and only the verb 'I may hear' is used [Ea, Lt], which implies his absence [Ea], since his probable absence is prominent in Paul's mind [ICC, MNTC]. The two alternatives 'whether . . . or' do not refer respectively to the possibility of Paul's being freed or not being freed; he assumes that he will be freed but is not certain that he would then come to them or would need to go somewhere else [My, WEC].

that^a you-are-standing^b in^c one spirit,^{d}

LEXICON—a. ὅτι (GEL 90.21): 'that' [Ea, HNTC, Ln, Mou, NTC, Pl, WBC, WEC; all translations].

b. pres. act. indic. of στήκω (GEL 13.30) (BAGD 2. p. 768): 'to stand' [Ea, GEL], 'to stand firm' [HNTC, Ln, Mou, NTC, Pl, WBC; all translations except KJV], 'to stand fast' [KJV], 'to stand steadfast' [WEC]. The basic sense of this word is simply 'to stand,' but the context in which Paul uses it always implies the sense of standing firm [ICC, MNTC, TH]. The present tense is important, indicating that they are now standing firm [Ln].

c. ἐν with dative object (GEL 13.8): 'in' [Ea, HNTC, ICC, Ln, Mou, NTC, Pl, WEC; all translations except TEV], 'with' [WBC; TEV].

d. πνεῦμα (GEL 30.6) (BAGD 3.a. p. 675): 'spirit' [Ea, HNTC, Ln, NTC, Pl, WBC, WEC; all translations except TEV], 'disposition' [GEL], 'purpose' [TEV], 'Spirit' [Mou].

QUESTION—What relationship is indicated by ὅτι 'that'?

It tells what Paul meant by the preceding phrase τὰ περὶ ὑμων 'the things concerning you' [Alf, Ea, El, ICC, Lg, My, NTC, TH]: the things concerning you, namely that you are standing firm. The ὅτι 'that' clause limits the phrase τὰ περὶ ὑμῶν 'the things concerning you' to what is mentioned in this clause [Ea].

QUESTION—What is the meaning of πνεῦμα 'spirit' here?

1. The following phrase, μιᾷ ψυχῇ 'in one soul/mind' shows that πνεῦμα here refers to the human spirit, not to the Holy Spirit [Ea, EBC, EGT, El, ICC, Ln, Lt, MNTC, My, NIC, TH, WBC, WEC; all translations]. It refers to the higher aspect of our spiritual nature [Lt], in which the Holy Spirit works [Ea, EBC, EGT, El, ICC], or to the functions of thinking and reflecting [NIC, TH]. One commentary apparently makes the phrase 'in one spirit' parallel to the following phrase 'with one soul' and joins both to the following verb 'striving together' [HNTC]. To stand 'in one spirit' refers to unity of their human spirits [Alf, El]: united in purpose in your spirits. At the same time, it is the Holy Spirit which inspires this unity [Alf, El].

2. It refers to the Holy Spirit [Mou, TNTC].

with-one soul[a] striving-together[b] for-the faith[c] of-the gospel,

LEXICON—a. ψυχή (GEL 26.4) (BAGD 1.b.γ. p. 893): 'soul' [Ea, Ln, Mou, NTC, Pl, WEC], 'mind' [GEL, HNTC, WBC; KJV, NASB, NRSV, REB], 'accord' [NAB], 'desire' [TEV]. The phrase μιᾷ ψυχῇ 'with one soul' is translated 'as one man' [NIV, REB], 'with a single aim' [NJB]. The ψυχή 'soul' is the area of the emotions and moral energies [Alf, Ea, El, ICC, Lt, My, NIC, TH], or of the senses [EBC].

b. pres. act. participle of συναθλέω (GEL 42.50) (BAGD p. 783): 'to strive together' [KJV, NASB], 'to strive' [Ea], 'to strive side by side' [HNTC, NTC; NRSV], 'to toil with' [GEL], 'to exert oneself' [NAB], 'to wrestle side by side' [Mou], 'to fight side by side' [Pl], 'to fight together' [TEV], 'to contend' [NIV], 'to contend together' [Ln], 'to struggle together' [WBC], 'to struggle jointly' [WEC], 'to battle as a team' [NJB], 'in the struggle' [REB]. This word implies promoting the gospel and also that there will be adversaries to face [EBC, NTC]. The prefix συν- 'together with' implies their striving together in cooperation.

c. πίστις (GEL 31.104) (BAGD 2.c. p. 663): 'faith' [Ea, GEL, HNTC, Ln, Mou, NTC, Pl, WBC, WEC; all translations]. The dative case of 'faith' indicates striving for the faith as the object of their striving [Alf, Ea, EGT, El, Lg, Ln, MNTC, Mou, My, NIC, TH, TNTC, WBC, WC; all translations]. It means to strive together with the Faith (personified) [Pl]. It refers to the contents of the gospel [EBC, EGT, Lt, NIC, Pl]. Faith is the governing principle of their life [ICC].

QUESTION—What is the phrase μιᾷ ψυχῇ 'with one soul' related to?

1. It is related to συναθλοῦντες 'striving together' [Alf, Ea, El, ICC, Lg, MNTC, My, Pl; all translations except REB]: striving together with one soul. It is not related to the preceding verb

'you are standing firm' [Ea, ICC]. It is emphatic by word order
[El, Lg, My, Pl].

2. It is related to the preceding verb 'you are standing firm' and
   parallel with 'in one spirit' [REB]: you are standing firm in one
   spirit, with one mind, striving for the faith.

QUESTION—What relationship is indicated by the use of the present
participle συναθλοῦντες 'striving together'?

1. It states the means by which they are standing firm [WEC]: you
   are standing firm by striving together.
2. It states an action in addition to standing firm [NAB, TEV]:
   you are standing firm and striving together.

QUESTION—With whom are the Philippians exhorted to 'strive
together'?

1. They are to strive together in cooperation with one another [Alf,
   Ea, EBC, El, GNC, ICC, Ln, MNTC, Mou, My(D), NTC, TH,
   TNTC, WBC, WC, WEC; all translations]: strive together in
   cooperation with one another. The word ἀλλήλοις 'one another'
   is the implied object [WBC].
2. They are to strive together in cooperation with Paul [Bg, Lg,
   My]: strive together in cooperation with me.

QUESTION—How are the two nouns related in the genitive
construction τῇ πίστει τοῦ εὐαγγελίου 'the faith of the gospel'?

1. It means the faith which characterizes the gospel [ICC, WEC].
   It makes it specific that the faith is in reference to the gospel
   [Lg].
2. It means the faith which is based on the gospel [TH].
3. It means the faith which has resulted from preaching the gospel
   [MNTC].
4. It means the faith produced by the gospel [WBC].

1:28

and not being-frightened[a] in[b] nothing[c] by[d] the-(ones) opposing,[e]

LEXICON—a. pres. pass. participle of πτύρω (GEL 25.263) (BAGD
p. 727): 'to be frightened' [BAGD, NTC; NIV], 'to be scared'
[BAGD, HNTC, Ln, Mou, Pl], 'to be terrified' [Ea; KJV], 'to be
alarmed' [NASB], 'to be intimidated' [GEL, WBC, WEC; NAB,
NRSV]. The phrase μὴ πτυρόμενοι ἐν μηδενί 'not frightened in
anything' is translated 'undismayed' [NJB]. This entire phrase is
translated 'in no way letting your opponents intimidate you'
[WBC], 'don't be afraid of your enemies; always be courageous'
[TEV], 'meeting your opponents without so much as a tremor'
[REB], '(bear yourselves as becomes members of a Christian
community) in your courage in the face of your adversaries'
[ICC], '(I would like to hear) that you are facing your

opponents quite unafraid' [TNT]. The reference is to the fear of being persecuted by opponents of the gospel [Blm].

b. ἐν with dative object (GEL 89.5): 'in' [Ea, HNTC, Ln, Mou, NTC, WC; KJV, NAB, NASB, NIV, NRSV], not explicit [WEC; NJB, REB].

c. μηδείς (GEL 92.23): 'nothing' [GEL]. The Greek double negative μὴ . . . ἐν μηδενί 'not . . . in nothing' is translated 'not . . . in anything' [NTC], 'not . . . in any situation' [NAB], 'never . . . in any way' [HNTC], 'without . . . in any way' [NIV], 'refusing . . . in anything' [Mou], 'in nothing' [Ea, Ln; KJV], 'in no way' [WBC; NASB, NRSV], 'never' [Pl], not explicit [WEC; NJB, REB].

d. ὑπό with genitive object (GEL 90.1): 'by' [Ea, HNTC, Ln, Mou, NTC, Pl, WEC; KJV, NAB, NASB, NIV, NJB, NRSV].

e. pres. pass. (deponent = act.) participle of ἀντικεῖμαι (GEL 39.1) (BAGD p. 74): 'to oppose' [GEL, HNTC, Pl; BAGD, NIV]. This participle is also translated as a noun: 'opponent' [BAGD, Mou, WBC, WEC; NAB, NASB, NJB, NRSV, REB, TNT], 'adversary' [Ea, ICC, Lg, Ln, NTC; KJV], 'enemy' [TEV]. The reference is to those around them who oppose the Christian faith, whether Jews or pagans [Alf, Ea, EBC, EGT, El, ICC, Lg, Mou, My, NIC, NTC, Pl, TNTC, WC], unbelieving Jews [WBC], only pagans [GNC, Ln, MNTC, TH], including authorities [GNC, Ln].

QUESTION—What relationship is indicated by the use of the present participle μὴ πτυρόμενοι 'not being frightened'?

1. It is parallel to συναθλοῦντες 'striving together' (1:27) [Ea, Ln]. The grammar requires that both of these verbs be interpreted as indicatives, since they expand στήκετε 'you are standing'. It is an additional explanation of 'standing firm' [Lg]: you are standing firm; that is, you are striving together and not being frightened.

2. It stands for an imperative verb semantically [Blm; NAB, TEV]: don't be frightened.

which[a] is for-them evidence[b] of-destruction,[c] but of-you of-salvation,[d]

TEXT—Instead of the genitive plural ὑμῶν 'of you' some manuscripts read the dative plural ὑμῖν 'to you' and other manuscripts read the dative plural ἡμῖν 'to us'. GNT does not these alternatives and the difference between 'of you' and 'to you' is not necessarily reflected in the versions. 'To you' is read by Blm, El, ICC, Lg, Mou, WC; KJV, NAB, NASB, NJB, REB, although it is not certain that all of the versions are following the Greek dative text; 'of you' is read by Alf, Ea, EBC, EGT, HNTC, Ln, Lt, MNTC, My, NTC, Pl, WBC, WEC; NRSV; none accept 'to us'. If the genitive 'of you' is read, then most

commentaries and versions interpret it to mean that the 'evidence' to
the opponents includes both their destruction and the Christians'
salvation. If the dative 'to you' is read, then most interpret it to mean
that the 'evidence' to the opponents is for their destruction and the
'evidence' to the Christians is for their salvation.

LEXICON—a. ὅστις (GEL 92.18): 'which' [Ea, ICC, Ln, NTC; KJV,
   NASB], 'this' [HNTC; NIV, NJB, NRSV, REB, TEV, TNT],
   'such' [Mou], not explicit [Pl, WBC, WEC; NAB]. This pronoun
   introduces an explanation or opinion here [Ea, EGT, El, ICC,
   Lg, Ln, Lt, My, Pl, TH]. It is feminine gender by attraction to
   the gender of the following word ἔνδειξις 'evidence' [Alf, Ea,
   EGT, El, ICC, Lg, Ln, Lt, NIC, Pl, WEC].
   b. ἔνδειξις (GEL 28.52) (BAGD 1. p. 262): 'evidence' [Mou;
   NRSV], 'indication' [Ln], 'clear indication' [GEL], 'clear
   intimation' [Pl], 'sign' [WEC; BAGD, NASB, NIV], 'clear sign'
   [NTC; NJB], 'sure sign' [REB], 'token' [Ea], 'manifest token'
   [HNTC], 'evident token' [KJV], 'omen' [BAGD], 'proof' [WBC].
   The phrase ἐστὶν ἔνδειξις 'is evidence' is translated
   'foreshadows' [NAB], 'will prove' [TEV], 'will show' [TNT], 'will
   demonstrate' [ICC]. The Philippians' conduct actually is
   evidence for their opponents even if the opponents do not
   realize it [Alf, EBC, ICC, Lg, My, NTC]; this is implied by the
   emphatic word order of ἐστίν 'is' [Lg]. This word indicates
   proof based on factual evidence [MNTC, TH].
   c. ἀπώλεια (GEL 20.31) (BAGD 2. p. 103): 'destruction' [BAGD,
   GEL, NTC; NASB, NRSV, REB], 'perdition' [Ea, HNTC, Ln,
   Mou, Pl; KJV], 'downfall' [NAB], 'doom to destruction' [ICC].
   This word is also translated as a phrase: 'that they will be
   destroyed' [WEC; NIV, TNT], 'that they are to be lost' [NJB],
   'that they will lose' [TEV], 'that you will perish' [WBC]. The
   destruction is spiritual [Alf, Ea, ICC, Lg], referring to final
   doom [HNTC, ICC, Lg, Ln, MNTC, My, WC, WEC].
   d. σωτηρία (GEL 21.25; 21.26) (BAGD 2. p. 801): 'salvation'
   [BAGD, Ea, GEL, HNTC, ICC, Ln, Mou, NTC, Pl; KJV, NAB,
   NASB, NRSV, REB]. This word is also translated as a phrase:
   'that you are to be saved' [NJB]. The phrase ὑμῶν σωτηρίας 'of
   your salvation' is translated 'that you will be saved' [WBC; NIV,
   TNT], 'that you will receive salvation' [WEC], 'that you will win'
   [TEV]. The salvation is spiritual [Alf, ICC], referring to their
   final salvation [El, HNTC, ICC, Ln, MNTC, My, TNTC, WEC]
   and God's care in their difficulties [TNTC], or both to earthly
   victory and final salvation [WC].

QUESTION—What is the word ἥτις 'which' connected with?

1. It refers back to Paul's exhortation that they should not be frightened by their adversaries [Alf, Blm, Ea, EBC, El, ICC, Lg, MNTC, Mou, My, NIC, WC; KJV, NASB, TEV]: your not being frightened by your adversaries is evidence. Its reference also includes 'striving together' and 'standing firm' [Ln]. The Philippians' lack of fear will show their adversaries that they cannot prevail against the Christians, and in this way their spiritual ruin is made clear.

2. It refers back to συναθλοῦντες 'striving together' [Bg]: your striving together is evidence.

3. It refers to the opposition of their adversaries [NAB]: your adversaries' opposition is evidence.

4. It refers to πίστει 'faith' (1:27), with which it agrees in gender and number [WBC]: your adherence to the faith for which you strive is evidence.

QUESTION—What is αὐτοῖς 'to them' related to?

1. It is related to ἔνδειξις 'evidence' [Alf, Blm, Ea, EBC, El, NIC, WBC, WEC; all translations except NAB, NASB]: this is evidence to your opponents. 'To them' is in emphatic position [Ln]. However, Paul's comment is intended for the encouragement of the Philippian Christians [NTC]. For most of those who follow the reading ὑμῶν 'of you' in the following phrase, it is evidence to the opponents both of the opponents' fate and of the salvation of the Christians [EBC, EGT, HNTC, MNTC, My, NTC, WEC; NIV, NRSV, REB]: evidence to them that they will be lost and that you will be saved. For those who follow the reading ὑμῖν 'to you' in the following phrase [plus Alf, Ea, GNC], it is evidence to the adversaries only of their own destruction, and it is evidence to the Christians that they themselves will be saved [Alf, Blm, Ea, El, GNC, ICC, Lg, Mou, WC; KJV, NASB, NJB]: evidence to them that they will be lost, and evidence to you that you will be saved. Some do not state to whom the evidence appears [TNTC; NAB]. One commentator reconstructs the text to give the interpretation 'evidence to your adversaries that you will be destroyed and evidence to you that you will be saved' [WBC].

2. It is related to ἀπωλείας 'destruction' [NAB, NASB]: this is evidence of their destruction.

QUESTION—How are the two nouns related in the genitive construction ἔνδειξις ἀπωλείας 'evidence of destruction'?

1. It is evidence to the adversaries that they will be destroyed [EBC, EGT, HNTC, Ln, My, MNTC, NIC, NTC, WEC; NIV, NRSV].

2. It is evidence to the adversaries that the Christians will be destroyed [WBC]. Instead of a contrast between 'their destruction' and 'your salvation', there is a contrast between the perceptions of the two groups: the believers' striving for the faith of the gospel is perceived by the opponents as an indication that the believers will be destroyed, but the believers see it as an indication that they will be saved.

QUESTION—How are the pronoun and noun related in the genitive construction ὑμῶν σωτηρίας 'of you of salvation'?

It is 'you' who possess the salvation [Ln], or it signifies that they will be saved [NIC]: evidence that you are/will be saved. 'Of you' is emphatic by word order [Ln, Pl, TH].

and this-(thing) from[a] God;

LEXICON—a. ἀπό with genitive object (GEL 90.7; 90.15): 'from' [Ea, Ln, Mou, NTC, Pl, WEC; NASB, NJB, REB], 'by' [HNTC, WBC; NIV], 'of' [KJV], not explicit [ICC]. The phrase ἀπὸ θεοῦ 'from God' is translated 'as God intends' [NAB]. This entire phrase is translated 'God himself will show them' [TNT], 'because it is God who gives you the victory' [TEV], 'and this is God's doing' [NRSV]. This word shows that God is the source of their standing firm and not being afraid [Ln], the agent of their victory [TH], the agent of the entire situation [TNTC]. This condition, involving conflict and fearlessness, is God's purpose [Mou]. This evidence, of their lostness and of the Christians' salvation, is actually God's gift to the adversaries [MNTC].

QUESTION—What relationship is indicated by the word καί 'and'?

It introduces the phrase which adds emphasis to what follows [ICC, My]: your conduct is not only evidence, it is evidence from God.

QUESTION—What does τοῦτο 'this thing' refer to?

1. It refers to all the preceding part of the verse [Ea, El, ICC, Ln, Mou, NTC], namely that it is God who has given them their courage to stand firm [EBC, Pl, TH]: your lack of fear and the evidence that this shows is all from God.
2. It refers to ἔνδειξις 'evidence', the evidence to the adversaries [Alf, HNTC, Lt, MNTC; REB, TNT]: this evidence is from God.
3. It refers to the perdition of the opponents and the salvation of the believers [Lg, WC]: this perdition and salvation are both from God.
4. It refers only to 'your salvation' [My, TH, WBC]: your salvation is from God.

DISCOURSE UNIT: 1:29–30 [WEC]. The topic is suffering.

1:29

because[a] to-you has-been-granted[b] the on-behalf-of[c] Christ,

LEXICON—a. ὅτι (GEL 89.33): 'because' [Mou, Pl], 'for' [Ea, HNTC, ICC, NTC, WBC; all translations], 'since' [WEC], 'seeing that' [Ln].

    b. aorist pass. indic. of χαρίζομαι (GEL 57.102) BAGD 1. p. 876): 'to be granted' [Ea, GEL, HNTC, NTC; NASB, NIV, REB], 'to be graciously granted' [Ln, NRSV], 'to be granted the privilege' [NJB], 'to be granted as a boon' [Mou], 'to be given' [GEL; KJV], 'to be given the privilege' [TEV], 'to have a privilege conferred upon one' [ICC], 'to be conferred the privilege' [Pl]. In most passages this verb is deponent, 'to give freely or graciously as a favor' [BAGD]. The phrase ὑμῖν ἐχαρίσθη 'to you it has been granted' is translated 'it is your special privilege' [NAB], 'God has given you the privilege' [TNT], 'God has graciously given you the privilege' [WBC], '(it) is God's gracious gift to you' [WEC]. The subject of this verb is all the rest of the verse [Lg]. It is self-evident that God is the agent of the giving [My, TH, WBC]. The use of the passive voice here is due to the phrase ἀπὸ θεοῦ 'from God' in 1:28 [Lg]. The aorist tense refers to God's dealings as a whole, not as merely one act [Alf]; it refers to the time when the grace was first given [El, ICC, Ln, MNTC], or indefinitely to an early time in their Christian lives [Ea]. The verb receives secondary emphasis [Alf]; or it receives the principal emphasis [Bg]; or it is not emphasized [Lg]. The verb implies that their suffering is a privilege granted by God [Blm, EBC, EGT, El, GNC, HNTC, ICC, Lt, Mou, NIC, NTC, TH, TNTC, WBC, WC, WEC], and therefore they should thank God for the privilege [GNC]. Paul means that their gift of new life from God was something which would bring them into collision with the evil world [MNTC, WBC] but also gave them a spirit which would enable them to resist the opposition [MNTC].

    c. ὑπέρ with genitive object (GEL 90.36): 'on behalf of' [Ea, GEL, NTC, WEC; NIV], 'in behalf of' [Ln], 'in the behalf of' [KJV], 'for the sake of' [BAGD, GEL, Mou], 'for' [BAGD], not explicit [ICC, WBC; REB, TEV, TNT]. The phrase τὸ ὑπὲρ Χριστοῦ 'on behalf of Christ' is translated 'on Christ's behalf' [Pl], 'for Christ's sake' [HNTC; NASB, NJB], 'to take Christ's part' [NAB]. This word implies the reason or moving cause [EBC].

QUESTION—What relationship is indicated by ὅτι 'because'?

1. It introduces the proof that the evidence mentioned in 1:28 is from God [Alf, Ea, El, ICC, Lg, MNTC, My, NTC, Pl, TNTC, TH, WEC; NAB, NJB]: the evidence is from God, because he has granted you the privilege of believing in Christ and suffering for him. It refers to the evidence given to the opponents of the salvation of the Christians [MNTC, My, TH] and of their own lostness [MNTC, TH]. To suffer with Christ proves their union with him and this union insures their salvation [ICC]. The fearlessness that furnishes the evidence was God's gift since the suffering that gave rise to their courage was God's gift to them [MNTC].
2. It indicates the reason why they should not be frightened by their adversaries [EGT]: you should not be frightened, because your suffering is a gift of God's grace.
3. This explains the entire content of 1:28 [TH]: all this will happen because you have been given the privilege of suffering for Christ.

QUESTION—What is implied by the position of ὑμῖν 'to you'?

It is emphatic [Alf, Ea, El, ICC, Lg, MNTC, My, TH]: it is to you that this has been granted. Paul is contrasting the Christians' privilege with the situation of their adversaries [MNTC].

QUESTION—What is the phrase τὸ ὑπὲρ Χριστοῦ 'on behalf of Christ' connected with?

1. It is primarily connected with πάσχειν 'to suffer' [Alf, Ea, EGT, El, ICC, Lg, Lt, My, Pl, WEC]: it has been granted to you to suffer on behalf of Christ. Paul inserts the phrase 'not only to believe in him' to heighten the emphasis on suffering for Christ [MNTC, My], or to state the basis upon which the suffering must rest in order to lead to salvation [Lg].
2. It is connected with both 'to believe' and 'to suffer' [GNC, Ln, Mou, NIC; REB]: it has been granted to you to believe in Christ and to suffer for him.
3. It is connected with ἐχαρίσθη 'it has been granted [HNTC, NTC; KJV, NASB, NIV, NJB]: for Christ's sake this has been granted to you.

QUESTION—What is the use of the article τό 'the' to introduce the two ὑπέρ 'in behalf of' prepositional phrases?

The article makes a substantive of the prepositional phrase, giving the meaning 'this matter of *for the sake of Christ*' [EBC, Ln].

not only the to-believe[a] in[b] him

LEXICON—a. pres. act. infin. of πιστεύω (GEL 31.102) (BAGD 2.a.β. p. 661): 'to believe' [BAGD, Ea, GEL, HNTC, Ln, Mou, NTC, WBC; all translations], not explicit [ICC]. The believing includes the initial act of faith and also continuing to believe [EBC]. Believing in Christ implies union with him in surrender and trust [ICC, NIC, WBC] and therefore fellowship with his suffering [ICC]. The present tense implies continuation [Ln, TH].

b. εἰς with accusative object (GEL 84.22): 'in' [HNTC, Ln, NTC, WBC; all translations except KJV, NIV], 'on' [Ea, Mou; KJV, NIV], not explicit [ICC, WEC]. The phrase τὸ εἰς αὐτὸν πιστεύειν 'the to believe in him' is translated 'in faith surrender to Him' [Pl], 'your faith' [WEC]. It refers to the soul's union with Christ by faith [EGT, NTC, WBC]. The prepositional phrase εἰς αὐτόν 'in him' precedes the verb for emphasis.

QUESTION—Why is this phrase mentioned?

It serves to heighten the emphasis on the aspect of suffering for Christ [El, Pl]: not only to believe in him, but also to suffer for him. The value of suffering for Christ is emphasized by comparing it with believing in him, which the Philippians would recognize as being of supreme value [EGT]. The principal emphasis is upon the thought of suffering for Christ [NTC].

but also the to-suffer[a] on-behalf-of[b] him,

LEXICON—a. pres. act. infin. of πάσχω (GEL 24.78) (BAGD 3.a.β. p. 634): 'to suffer' [BAGD, Ea, GEL, HNTC, ICC, Ln, Mou, NTC, Pl, WBC; all translations]. The phrase τὸ πάσχειν 'the to suffer' is translated 'your suffering' [WEC]. Suffering in itself is not a privilege [NTC, WEC], but suffering for the sake of Christ is a privilege [HNTC, NTC]. The present tense implies continued or repeated suffering [Ln, TH].

b. ὑπέρ with genitive object (GEL 90.36) (BAGD 1.d. p. 839): 'on behalf of' [Ea, WEC], 'in behalf of' [Ln], 'for the sake of' [BAGD], 'for' [BAGD, HNTC, ICC; NAB, NIV, NJB, NRSV, REB, TEV, TNT]. The phrase τὸ ὑπὲρ αὐτοῦ 'in behalf of him' is translated 'in his behalf' [NTC], 'on his behalf' [Pl], 'for his sake' [Mou; KJV, NASB], 'in his stead' [WBC]. This word implies the reason or moving cause [EBC]. The prepositional phrase ὑπὲρ αὐτοῦ 'in behalf of him' precedes the verb for emphasis.

1:30

having[a] the same struggle[b]

LEXICON—a. pres. act. participle of ἔχω (GEL 90.65) (BAGD I.2.i. p. 333): 'to have' [Ea, GEL, Ln; KJV, NRSV], 'to experience' [GEL, Mou, WEC; NASB], 'to be engaged in' [NTC], 'to be partaker of' [ICC], 'to go through' [NIV], 'to carry on' [HNTC], to be in' [WBC; TNT], not explicit [Pl; NAB, REB].

b. ἀγών (GEL **39.29**) (BAGD 2. p. 15): 'struggle' [BAGD, GEL, WBC; NAB, NIV, NRSV, TNT], 'conflict' [Ea, ICC, Ln, Mou, NTC, Pl, WEC; KJV, NASB], 'contest' [HNTC; REB]. The phrase τὸν αὐτὸν ἀγῶνα ἔχοντες 'having the same struggle' is translated 'you are fighting the same battle' [NJB], 'Now you can take part with me in the battle' [TEV]. This word is commonly used of athletic contests [EGT, HNTC, ICC, Lt, MNTC, NIC, TH, WBC, WC, WEC] or gladiatorial contests [Lt, MNTC], as is συναθλοῦντες in 1:27 [HNTC, Lt]; Paul pictures Christians as engaged in a spiritual wrestling match [HNTC, MNTC] or a gladiatorial contest [MNTC]. This figurative use of 'struggle' is appropriate in connection with the words στήκετε 'you are standing fast' and συναθλοῦντες 'striving together' [EGT].

QUESTION—What relationship is indicated by the use of the participial form ἔχοντες 'having'?

It further explains the meaning of the preceding word πάσχειν 'to suffer' [Ea, El, ICC, Lg, MNTC, My, WBC]: to suffer for Christ by having the same struggle as I have.

QUESTION—What is the participle ἔχοντες 'having' related to?

1. It is related to the dative ὑμῖν 'you (plural)' in 1:29 [Alf, Ea, EGT, El, Lt, My, Pl, TH, WBC, WEC], but is in the nominative case because Paul was thinking of 'you' as a subject and thus in the nominative case [Alf, Ea, El, ICC]: it has been granted to you . . . You have the same struggle.
2. It is related to the subject ὑμεῖς 'you (plural)' implied by πάσχειν 'to suffer' [Lg]: you suffer; that is, you have the same struggle as I.
3. It is related to the subject of πολιτεύεσθε 'conduct yourselves' [EBC Ln] or στήκετε 'you are standing fast' [Bg, EBC, Mou] in 1:27: conduct yourselves properly/you are standing fast, having the same struggle.

QUESTION—What is implied by τὸν αὐτὸν ἀγῶνα 'the same struggle'?

It means that their struggle was of the same nature and for the same cause as that of Paul [Alf, Ea, EBC, GNC, HNTC, ICC, Lg, Ln, MNTC, My, NIC, NTC, TNTC, WBC, WEC]. The emphasis is on the word 'same' [TH, TNTC]. However, the Philippians were not being actively persecuted as Paul was [Ln, MNTC].

which[a] you-saw in[b] me and now hear in[b] me.

LEXICON—a. οἷος (GEL 64.1) (BAGD p. 562): 'which' [Ea, ICC, NTC, Pl; KJV, NAB, NASB, NJB], 'that' [NRSV], 'as that which' [HNTC], 'such as' [Ln], 'in kind as that which' [Mou], not explicit [WBC, WC; NIV, REB, TEV, TNT]. This qualitative relative pronoun, 'of such sort', is used instead of the ordinary relative pronoun ὅς 'who/which', implying that the Philippians' conflict was not identical to that of Paul [Pl]. It is 'the same sort' of conflict [MNTC].

   b. ἐν with dative object (GEL **90.6**): 'in' [Ea, Ln, Mou; KJV, NASB, REB]. The two phrases ἐν ἐμοί 'in me' are translated 'me having' [NTC], 'I had . . . that I have' [NIV, NRSV], 'me engaged in . . . that I am engaged in' [GEL], 'me engage in . . . I am engaged in' [WBC], 'I am engaged . . . about me' [HNTC], 'me engaged in . . . that I am caught up in' [NAB], 'me contending . . . of my contending' [Pl], 'me go through . . . that I am still experiencing' [WEC], 'me undergo . . . my waging' [ICC], 'me fighting . . . I am fighting' [NJB, TEV], 'me struggling . . . that I am doing so' [TNT]. The struggles took place in his person; he is struggling personally [ICC, Lg, TH].

QUESTION—Why is this clause mentioned?

   1. It is to remind them that Paul is not terrified by the struggle, implying that they do not need to be terrified [Bg, Blm, Ea]: you have the same struggle that I have; I am not terrified, so you do not need to be.

   2. It explains what Paul means by 'the same struggle' [Lg]: you have the same struggle which you saw and now hear concerning me.

QUESTION—What relationship is indicated by the two prepositional phrases ἐν ἐμοί?

They refer to Paul's struggle as an example [Alf, Ea]: you saw that I was engaged in this struggle and now you hear that I am engaged in it. They had seen his struggle when he was with them [Alf, Ea, Blm, EBC, El, GNC, ICC, Lg, Ln, Lt, MNTC, Mou, My, NIC, NTC, Pl, TH, WBC], and now they are hearing (from others [Alf, EBC, MNTC, TNTC]—specifically, from Epaphroditus [Hn, ICC, Lg, MNTC, My, NIC, WBC]—and/or by this epistle [Alf, Ea, El, GNC, Hn, ICC, Lg, MNTC, My, NIC, Pl, TNTC]) of his difficulties [Alf] in Rome [Blm, Ea, EBC, EGT, ICC, Ln, Mou, TH] or in Ephesus [MNTC] or in Caesarea [WBC]. The conflict is with personal adversaries or with unbelievers [Ea].

DISCOURSE UNIT: 2:1-18 [NTC, TH; NASB]. The topic is bearing the cross in humility [NTC], being like Christ [NASB], an exhortation to be united, humble, and to bear witness [TH].

DISCOURSE UNIT: 2:1-11 [EBC, Lg, Ln, Mou, TH; GNT, NAB, NIV, NJB, TEV]. The topic is an exhortation to be united in spirit and to be humble toward fellow Christians [EBC; NJB], Christ as the example of humility for Christians [GNT, NAB, NIV], Christ's example of exaltation through humility [Lg, TH; TEV], Christ's example of unity through relinquishing one's own rights [Mou], an exhortation to relinquish their rights in humility for the sake of fellow Christians [Ln].

DISCOURSE UNIT: 2:1-4 [EGT, HNTC, ICC, MNTC, NIC, NTC, TNTC, WBC, WEC]. The topic is an appeal by Paul as a humble bearer of the cross [NTC], an exhortation to be united in spirit [WEC] and humble [EGT, NIC, WBC] in view of a possible factious spirit within [TNTC], an appeal for harmony based on concern for fellow Christians and not insisting on one's rights [HNTC, MNTC], unity and love for one another [ICC].

2:1

If[a] therefore[b] (there is) any encouragement/exhortation[c] in[d] Christ,

LEXICON—a. εἰ (GEL 89.65): 'if' [Ea, GEL, HNTC, ICC, Ln, Mou, NTC, Pl, WBC, WEC; KJV, NASB, NIV, NJB, NRSV, REB], not explicit [NAB]. This clause is translated 'your life in Christ makes you strong' [TEV], 'if you belong to Christ are you not strong?' [TNT].

b. οὖν (GEL 89.50): 'therefore' [ICC, Mou, NTC, Pl, WBC, WEC; KJV, NASB], 'then' [HNTC; NRSV, REB], 'accordingly' [Ln], 'so' [NJB], not explicit [Ea; NAB, NIV, TNT].

c. παράκλησις (GEL 25.150) (BAGD 3. p. 618): 'encouragement' [BAGD, GEL, NTC, WBC; NAB, NASB, NIV, NRSV], 'consolation' [KJV], 'comfort' [Mou], 'exhortation' [BAGD, Ea, HNTC, WEC], 'power of exhortation' [ICC], 'admonition' [Ln], 'power to persuade you' [Pl] 'anything to stir the heart' [REB], 'anything that will move you' [NJB]. This word means persuasive and helpful speech [My]; it includes both consolation and exhortation [EBC, EGT].

d. ἐν with dative object (GEL 89.119): 'in' [Ea, HNTC, ICC, Mou, NTC, Pl, WBC; all translations except NIV, TNT], 'from union with' [WEC], 'from being united with' [NIV], 'in connection with' [Ln].

QUESTION—What relationship is indicated by οὖν 'therefore'?
1. It indicates a conclusion based on 1:27 [Bg, Ea, Blm, EBC, El, ICC, My(D), TNTC, WC]: since they must live worthily of the gospel, standing in one spirit and striving together, they must make Paul's joy complete by being of the same mind, etc.
2. It indicates a conclusion based on 1:30 [My]: since they are engaged in the same conflict as Paul, they should fulfil his joy.

QUESTION—What relationship is indicated by εἰ 'if' in the four clauses of this verse?
1. The clauses indicate the incentive for the exhortation that follows in 2:2 [Alf, Bg, Blm, Ea, EBC, GNC, HNTC, Lt, MNTC, Mou, My, NIC, NTC, WEC; all translations]: since, etc., therefore complete my joy. 'If' here does not assume doubt; rather, it assumes that the condition is true [Ea, Blm, EBC, GNC, HNTC, Lg, Ln, My, NTC, TH, TNTC, WBC].
2. Each 'if' clause contains its own apodosis; the verb 'let it be' is implied [Ln]: if (there is) any admonition, (let it be) in connection with Christ; if (there is) any solace, (let it be) of love; if (there is) any fellowship, (let it be) of spirit; if (there is) any (such fellowship, let it be) with tender mercies and compassion.

QUESTION—What verb is to be understood in these four 'if' clauses?
Most supply the verb 'to be' [Bg, Blm, Ea, EBC, Lg, Ln, Mou, My, NIC, NTC, WBC; KJV, NASB, NJB, NRSV]: if there is . . . Alternatives are: 'if you have . . .' [NIV], 'if . . . has the power to move you' [HNTC], 'if . . . exists among you' [Ea].

QUESTION—What is meant by encouragement/exhortation in Christ?
1. Encouragement comes from their being in Christ [Alf, Mou, NTC, WBC]. They are encouraged because they are in union with Christ [Mou, NTC]. They are Christians who have been encouraged by appeals from Paul, a fellow Christian, and should therefore respond to his present appeal [WBC].
2. Exhortation comes from their being in Christ [EBC, ICC, Lt, My, NIC, WEC]. The fact that they are in Christ has power to exhort them to concord [ICC]. Being Christians, they are obligated to respond to orders from Christ and his apostles [EBC]. Brother exhorts brother from a living fellowship with Christ [My].
3. Exhortation is characterized as being in Christ [Ea, El, HNTC, MNTC]. 'In Christ' is its sphere and element [El]. Paul makes his exhortation to them in the sphere of Christ [MNTC]. Paul speaks to them within the sphere of grace into which they have access through Christ [HNTC].
4. It means that Christ appeals to them [WC].

if (there is) any consolation/encouragement[a] of-love,[b]

LEXICON—a. παραμύθιον (GEL **25.154**) (BAGD p. 621): 'consolation' [BAGD, GEL, HNTC, ICC, Mou; NASB, NRSV, REB],
'comfort' [Ea; KJV, NIV], 'solace' [Ln; NAB], 'encouragement'
[BAGD, Pl, WEC], 'persuasive appeal' [NTC], 'incentive' [NJB],
'power to move you' [TNT]. This entire phrase is translated 'if
in any way my love has consoled you' [WBC], 'if his love
consoles/encourages you' [GEL], 'his love comforts you' [TEV].
This word refers to encouragement by speaking [Ea]. It includes
the quality of tenderness [EGT]. Their love for Christ and for
one another should lead them to work together and to avoid
divisiveness of any kind [EBC].

b. ἀγάπη (GEL **25.43**) (BAGD I.1.a. p. 5): 'love' [BAGD, Ea,
GEL, HNTC, ICC, Ln, Mou, NTC, Pl, WBC, WEC; all
translations].

QUESTION—How are the two event words related in the genitive
construction παραμύθιον ἀγάπης 'consolation of love'?

1. Consolation is given from love [Ea, EGT, El, HNTC, ICC, Lg,
Ln, Mou, My, NTC, WBC, WC, WEC; NAB, NIV, NJB, NRSV,
TEV, TNT]. They are consoled by Christ's love for them
[HNTC, ICC, TH; TEV]. They are consoled by Paul's love for
them [EGT, MNTC, WBC]. They are consoled by others loving
them [Ea, EBC, WC]. Love has a persuasive power to move
them to concord [ICC].

2. Encouragement is given from love [NIC, NTC]. It is a
persuasive appeal they receive from Christ's love for them
[NTC].

if (there is) any fellowship[a] of-Spirit/spirit,[b]

LEXICON—a. κοινωνία (GEL **34.5**; **57.98**) (BAGD 1., 2. p. 439):
'fellowship' [BAGD, Ea, GEL, HNTC, ICC, Ln, NTC, Pl, WBC,
WEC; KJV, NAB, NASB, NIV, NJB, TEV], 'sharing' [Mou;
NRSV, TNT], 'participation' [REB].

b. πνεῦμα (GEL **12.18**; **26.9**; **30.6**) (BAGD 5.d.β. p. 677): 'Spirit'
[BAGD, Ea, HNTC, ICC, Mou, NTC, Pl, WBC, WEC; all
translations except NAB], 'spirit' [Ln; NAB].

QUESTION—How are the two nouns related in the genitive
construction κοινωνία πνεύματος 'fellowship of Spirit'?

1. They fellowship with the Holy Spirit [ICC, Lt, Pl, TH, TNTC,
WC; NJB, TEV].

2. The Spirit causes them to fellowship with one another [Ea,
EBC, GNC, WBC, WEC]: if there is any fellowship produced
by the Holy Spirit. The Spirit produces like-mindedness [Ea].

3 It is both subjective and objective [HNTC, NTC]: if there is any
participation in the Spirit and fellowship produced by the Spirit.

4. They participate in the gifts and influence of the Spirit [El].
5. They fellowship with one another in regards to their spirits [Lg, Ln; NAB]: if there is any fellowship of your spirits.

if (there is) any compassion[a] and mercies,[b]

LEXICON—a. σπλάγχνα (GEL 25.49) (BAGD 1.b. p. 763): 'compassion' [GEL; NAB, NRSV, TNT], 'tender mercy' [ICC, Ln, NTC], 'tenderness' [HNTC, Pl, WBC; NIV], 'affection' [BAGD; NASB], 'kindness' [TEV], 'warmth' [NJB], 'warmth of affection' [REB], 'heart' [BAGD, Mou], 'bowels' [Ea; KJV]. The phrase σπλάγχνα καὶ οἰκτιρμοί 'compassion and mercies' is translated 'the compassion that flows from the heart' [WEC]. This word relates to the affections in general [Alf], or the seat of the emotions [TNTC]. This word together with the following word οἰκτιρμοί 'mercy' are qualities which would make unity of spirit the normal thing [EBC].

b. οἰκτιρμός (GEL 88.80) (BAGD p. 561): 'mercy' [BAGD, Ea; KJV], 'compassion' [BAGD, GEL, ICC, Ln, Mou, NTC, Pl, WBC; NASB, NIV, REB, TEV], 'sympathy' [NJB, NRSV], 'pity' [BAGD, HNTC; NAB, TNT]. This word relates specifically to the emotion of compassion [Alf]. It relates to the outward expression of the emotions [TNTC].

QUESTION—How is the singular pronoun τις 'any' related to the plural nouns σπλάγχνα καὶ οἰκτιρμοί 'compassion and mercies'?

The singular pronoun is used because the two plural nouns are generic and thus singular in sense, and the two nouns together express one common idea [Ea]: if there is any compassion, any mercy. Paul probably intended to follow this τις 'any' with another singular word but then switched over to these two plurals to express his meaning [Pl].

QUESTION—What relationship is indicated by the phrase σπλάγχνα καὶ οἰκτιρμοί 'compassion and mercies'?

1. They are distinct qualities [EBC, El, Mou, NTC; all translations] but closely related [HNTC, ICC]: tenderness and mercy. The first noun is the source of the feelings, the second noun is their manifestation [Lg, Lt, TH]. The second noun carries the idea of pity more strongly than does the first noun [MNTC].
2. The phrase is a hendiadys [TNTC, WBC]: merciful compassion/ affectionate sympathy.

QUESTION—Who are the participants in the event words here?

The reference is to compassion and mercy for one another [Ea, EBC, HNTC, ICC, Mou, TH, WC]: if you have compassion and mercy for one another. It may focus either on their compassion for Paul or for Paul's compassion for them [MNTC]. It means God's

compassion for them [WBC]: if you know God's compassion and
mercy, respond by doing what I request. It means that if they
believe in compassion and mercy, they should do what Paul
requests [WC].

2:2
complete[a] my joy[b]

LEXICON—a. aorist act. impera. of πληρόω (GEL 59.33) (BAGD 3.
p. 671): 'to complete' [ICC, Pl], 'to make complete' [GEL,
WBC, WEC; NAB, NASB, NIV, NJB, NRSV], 'to bring to
completion' [BAGD], 'to fulfill' [Ea, Ln; KJV], 'to make full'
[Mou, NTC], 'to bring to the full' [HNTC]. This entire phrase is
translated 'make me completely happy' [TEV, TNT], 'fill up my
cup of happiness' [REB]. This verb receives the emphasis [Alf].
Paul already had joy in the Philippians (at their conversion
[Blm]), but he wants that joy to become complete [Alf, Blm, Ea,
HNTC, Lg, Lt, MNTC, Mou, My, NIC, NTC, TH].

b. χαρά (GEL 25.123) (BAGD 1. p. 875): 'joy' [Ea, GEL, HNTC,
ICC, Ln, Mou, NTC, Pl, WBC, WEC; KJV, NAB, NASB, NIV,
NJB, NRSV], 'happiness' [GEL; REB].

QUESTION—What is this clause connected with?

It is an exhortation based on the preceding 'if' clauses in 2:1
[HNTC, MNTC, Mou, My, NTC, WEC]. It is defined by the
following phrases [Blm, Ea], showing that the joy Paul is seeking is
the joy of knowing that the Philippian Christians are living in
harmony and unity of spirit [Ea, MNTC, WBC]: fulfill my joy,
which will come when I hear that you are living in harmony and
unity. The first two phrases refer to Paul's appeal to them; the last
two refer to the qualities which they should have [Lg].

that[a] the same-(thing)[b] you-should-think,[c]

LEXICON—a. ἵνα (GEL 90.22): 'that' [Ea, Ln; KJV].

b. αὐτός (GEL 58.31): 'same' [Ea, GEL, HNTC, Ln, Mou, NTC,
Pl, WEC; NASB, NRSV, TEV]. The phrase ἵνα τὸ αὐτὸ
φρονῆτε 'that you should think the same thing' is translated
'that ye be like-minded' [KJV].

c. pres. act. subj. of φρονέω (GEL 26.16): 'to think' [BAGD, Ea],
'to think in a particular manner' [GEL], 'to mind' [Ln], 'to have
an attitude' [GEL]. This entire phrase is translated 'by being of
the same mind' [Mou, NTC, Pl; NASB, NRSV], 'by being of a
single mind' [NJB], 'by being of one mind' [TNT], 'by being like-
minded' [NIV], 'by showing the same disposition' [HNTC], 'by
thinking and feeling alike' [REB], 'by having the same thoughts'
[TEV], 'by your unanimity' [NAB], 'think alike' [WBC], 'adopt
the same frame of mind' [WEC]. This phrase and all the rest of

this verse is translated 'by your unanimity and your love to each
other' [ICC]. It means to have a settled opinion or a particular
mindset [GNC, HNTC, TH], to be united in sentiments [MNTC,
My, WBC].

QUESTION—What relationship is indicated by ἵνα 'that'?

1. It indicates a specification of what fulfilling Paul's joy would
consist of [EBC, EGT, El, ICC, NIC, WBC, WEC]: fulfill my
joy, which will consist of your minding the same thing, etc. It is
not the purpose but the means (or content [WEC]) which is
being expressed [NIC, TH, WEC]. To insist on making ἵνα
always mean purpose [as Alf] ignores the usage of later Greek
[El].

2. It indicates the purpose [My] or the contemplated result of their
unity [Alf, Ea, Mou]: fulfill my joy in order that/looking to the
result that you will mind the same thing. Ea, after insisting that
the clause states purpose and anticipated result, expresses the
thought in terms of content, "He besought them to fulfill his
joy." Mou and My also state the clause in a form which
corresponds to 1. above.

QUESTION—What are the phrases following ἵνα 'that' connected
with?

1. There are four separate phrases [Blm, EGT, Lt, Pl, TNTC,
WBC, WC; KJV, NASB, NJB, NRSV, TNT]: thinking the same
thing, having the same love, being harmonious, thinking the one
thing. They are each separate designations showing how Paul's
joy may be fulfilled [Blm, Pl, TNTC, WBC, WC; TNT]: fulfill
my joy by doing the following things.

2. There are three separate phrases, σύμψυχοι 'harmonious' being
joined with τὸ ἕν φρονοῦντες 'thinking the one thing' [Alf, Bg,
Blm, EBC, El, HNTC, ICC, Lg, Ln, My, NIC, NTC, TH; NAB,
NIV, REB, TEV]: in harmony think the one thing. Σύμψυχοι
'harmonious' illustrates (or is the basis for [HNTC]) the
following participial phrase [El, ICC, My]. This interpretation
preserves the literary parallels of the four participles in 2:2-4
[EBC, NTC].

QUESTION—How is this clause related to the following phrases?

This phrase is general [Blm, EGT, Lt, WC; TNT]. The next two
phrases (one, for those who combine σύμψυχοι 'harmonious' with
the final phrase) are specifics, and the final phrase is a stronger
expression and a climax [Blm, MNTC]. The phrases τὸ αὐτὸ
φρονῆτε 'think the same thing' and τὸ ἕν φρονοῦντες 'thinking the
one thing' are essentially synonymous, the latter phrase being
stronger and serving to reinforce Paul's exhortation [Ea, EBC, El,
MNTC] or being a more abstract form [El]. The participial phrase

'having the same love' is dependent on 'that you should think the same thing' [Bg]: think the same thing, shown by having the same love.

QUESTION—What is implied by 'thinking the same thing'?

It includes matters which relate to the church, not to everything possible [Ea]: be agreed in your thinking regarding matters related to the church. This clause is more specifically defined by the two following participial phrases 'having the same love' and 'thinking the one thing' [Blm, Ea, EGT, El, MNTC, WC].

having[a] the same love,[b]

LEXICON—a. pres. act. participle of ἔχω (GEL 90.65) (BAGD I.2.e.β. p. 332): 'to have' [BAGD, Ea, GEL, HNTC, Ln, NTC; KJV, NIV, NRSV], 'to feel' [Mou], 'to share' [WEC; TEV], 'to possess' [BAGD; NAB], 'to maintain' [NASB], not explicit [Pl; NJB, REB].

  b. ἀγάπη (GEL 25.43) (BAGD I.1.a. p. 5): 'love' [Ea, GEL, HNTC, Ln, Mou, NTC, Pl, WEC; all translations except TNT]. This entire phrase is translated 'love alike' [WBC], 'love one another' [TNT].

QUESTION—What is meant by this phrase?

It means having mutual love [Alf, Ea, El, HNTC, ICC, MNTC, My, NIC, TH, WBC, WC] and the love of God [ICC, NIC] based on the love of Christ [WC].

harmonious,[a] thinking[b] the one-(thing),

TEXT—Instead of ἕν 'one', some manuscripts read αὐτό 'same'. GNT accepts 'one' with a B rating, indicating some degree of doubt. No commentary or translation clearly reads 'same'.

LEXICON—a. σύμψυχος (GEL 26.6) (BAGD p. 781): 'harmonious' [BAGD], 'being one in spirit' [GEL], 'united in spirit' [BAGD; NASB, TNT], 'united in soul' [HNTC], 'with union of soul' [Ea], 'souls united' [NTC], 'of one soul' [WBC], 'joined in soul' [Ln], 'knit together in soul' [Pl], 'soul and soul together' [Mou], 'one in heart' [NJB], 'of one accord' [KJV], 'in full accord' [NRSV], not explicit [WEC]. This entire phrase is translated 'united in spirit and ideals' [NAB], 'being one in spirit and purpose' [NIV], 'with a common attitude of mind' [REB], 'being one in soul and mind' [TEV]. It means to have the same point of view in their mutual interests [EGT, My]. Occurring first in its phrase, this word has the emphasis [Ln, My].

  b. pres. act. participle of φρονέω (GEL 26.16): 'to think', 'to mind' [Ea, Ln], 'to set one's mind on' [NTC], 'to adopt a frame of mind' [WEC]. The phrase τὸ ἕν φρονοῦντες 'thinking the one thing' is translated 'of one mind' [KJV, NRSV], 'one in mind' [NJB], 'by being of one mind' [Pl], 'be of one mind' [WBC], 'in a mind which is unity itself' [Mou], 'intent on one purpose' [NASB], 'one in disposition' [HNTC], 'always agree with one another' [TNT].

QUESTION—How is σύμψυχοι 'harmonious' related to the other phrases?

1. It is a separate item [Blm, EGT, Lt, Pl, TNTC, WBC, WC]: harmonious, and minding the one thing.
2. It is joined with the following phrase [Alf, Bg, Ea, EBC, El, HNTC, ICC, Lg, Ln, MNTC, My, NIC, NTC, TH]: like-minded by minding the one thing.

QUESTION—What relationship is indicated by the phrase τὸ ἕν φρονοῦντες 'minding the one thing'?

1. It is practically synonymous with the earlier phrase τὸ αὐτὸ φρονῆτε 'mind the same thing' [Blm, Ea, EBC, Lt, My, NIC, Pl, TH, WBC], perhaps stated more abstractly than the former phrase [El, Lt, NIC], more concretely [NIC], more strongly [Blm, Ea, Lt, TH, WBC]: set your mind on the one thing, harmony of spirit, which I mentioned in 'mind the same thing'.
2. It further defines 'mind the same thing' [El]: like-mindedly mind the one thing.

2:3

(thinking/doing) nothing in-accord-with[a] selfish-ambition[b] nor in-accord-with[a] conceit[c]

TEXT—Instead of μηδὲ κατά 'nor in accord with', some manuscripts read ἤ 'or'. GNT does not deal with this variant, and the difference is not necessarily reflected in the translations. μηδὲ κατά 'nor in accord with' is clearly read by Ea, EGT, El, ICC, Lg, Ln, Lt, Pl, WBC, WEC; TEV, while ἤ 'or' is clearly read by Alf, Blm, My; KJV.

LEXICON—a. κατά with accusative object (GEL 89.4; 89.8) (BAGD II.5.b.β. p. 407): 'in accord with' [Ln], 'in the spirit of' [Ea], 'out of a spirit of' [WBC], 'in the way of' [Mou], 'under the influence of' [Pl], 'characterized by' [WEC], 'moved by' [HNTC], 'out of' [NAB, NIV, NJB], 'from' [ICC, NTC; NASB, NRSV, TEV], 'through' [KJV], not explicit [REB]. This entire phrase is translated 'you must never be ambitious or foolishly proud' [TNT]. This preposition tells in what way the action of the supplied participle is to take place [Ea, ICC], the circumstances or the occasion for it [El].

b. ἐριθεία (GEL 88.167) (BAGD p. 309): 'selfish ambition' [GEL, NTC; NIV, NRSV, REB, TEV], 'self-seeking' [Ln], 'selfishness' [WEC; NASB], 'rivalry' [GEL, WBC; NAB], 'strife' [KJV], 'faction' [Ea, ICC], partisanship' [HNTC, Pl], 'jealousy' [NJB], 'personal/party spirit' [Mou]. The meaning of this word is self-seeking to secure preeminence [Ea], inordinately seeking the advantage for one's own group [MNTC], to have no interest in pleasing others [Bg].

c. κενοδοξία (GEL **88.221**) (BAGD 1. p. 427): 'conceit' [BAGD; NAB, NRSV], 'empty conceit' [NTC, WBC; NASB], 'empty pride' [GEL], 'vain conceit' [WEC; NIV], 'vanity' [BAGD; NJB, REB], 'personal vanity' [Pl], 'vainglory' [Ea, ICC, Ln; KJV], 'vain ambition' [HNTC], 'cheap desire to boast' [TEV], not explicit [Mou]. The meaning is the (mistaken [WBC]) insistence that one's own ideas are always best [Ea, WBC], boastful pride [EGT], a conceited claim of deserving honor [ICC], groundless conceit [MNTC], to be too anxious to please others [Bg].

QUESTION—What verb is to be supplied for μηδέν 'nothing'?

1. The participle φρονοῦντες 'thinking' is to be supplied [Ea, EGT, WEC] from the preceding phrase in 2:2 [Alf, El, ICC, Lg, My, NIC, Pl]. 'Thinking' fits better in the train of thought [Ea, NIC], which pertains to moral attitudes rather than to actions [ICC]. To make a break and supply the imperative 'do' is unacceptable, since the following participle after ἀλλά 'but' shows that it must be balanced with a preceding participle [My], although semantically the participle implies a command or exhortation. There is not much difference in meaning between 'thinking' and 'doing' [Pl].

2. The sense of 'to do' is to be supplied [EBC, Lt, TH; all translations except REB, TNT]: doing/do nothing. There is a break from the preceding verse; the implied verb is the imperative 'do' [Lt]: do nothing. This is more natural and carries more force than to understand a repeated φρονοῦντες 'thinking' from the preceding phrase [Lt].

3. The verb 'to act' is to be supplied [WBC]: do not act out of rivalry.

but[a] in-the humility[b] considering[c] one-another being-more-superior[d] to-yourselves,

LEXICON—a. ἀλλά (GEL 89.125): 'but' [Ea, HNTC, ICC, Ln, NTC; KJV, NASB, NIV, NRSV, REB, TEV], 'rather' [Mou, WBC, WEC; NAB], 'instead' [NJB], 'on the contrary' [Pl], not explicit [TNT]. This word marks the strong contrast with what precedes [Lg].

b. ταπεινοφροσύνη (GEL 88.53) (BAGD p. 804): 'humility' [BAGD, Ea, GEL, HNTC, WBC, WEC; NIV, NRSV], 'humility of mind' [NASB, NJB], 'humble-mindedness' [Mou, NTC], 'lowly-mindedness' [Ln], 'lowliness of mind' [ICC, Pl; KJV], 'without arrogance' [GEL]. This noun is also translated as an adverb: 'humbly' [NAB, REB], as a phrase: 'be humble toward one another' [TEV], 'be humble enough' [TNT].

c. pres. mid. (deponent = act.) participle of ἡγέομαι (GEL 31.1) (BAGD 2. p. 343): 'to consider' [BAGD, GEL, Ln, WBC; NIV, TEV], 'to regard' [BAGD, Ea, GEL, Pl, WEC; NASB, NRSV, TNT], 'to account' [ICC], 'to count' [HNTC, NTC], 'to reckon' [Mou; REB], 'to esteem' [KJV], 'to think of' [NAB]. The phrase ἀλλήλους ἡγούμενοι ὑπερέχοντας ἑαυτῶν 'considering one another superior to yourselves' is translated 'everyone should give preference to others' [NJB]. This verb refers to a conscious judgment based on weighing the facts [ICC].

d. pres. act. participle of ὑπερέχω (GEL 65.4) (BAGD 2.b. p. 841): 'to be superior' [Pl], 'to surpass' [BAGD, GEL], 'to be better' [GEL], 'to be above' [Ln]. This participle is also translated as an adjective: 'better' [GEL, Ea, HNTC, ICC, NTC, WBC; KJV, NIV, NRSV, REB, TEV, TNT], 'more excellent' [WEC], 'superior' [Mou; NAB], 'more important' [NASB]. The meaning is to consider others superior in their abilities and in their rights [Bg] to the extent to which the facts will permit [Blm]. With the variety of gifts which God gives believers, there is always something in other people which can be appreciated [NIC]. It does not mean to consider others as better than ourselves even though we know many are not better; it means to defer to others and to give honor to others above ourselves [Ln], the recognition of our unworthiness and a willingness to rejoice in the good qualities in others [MNTC]. The word ἑαυτῶν 'yourselves' is plural, which shows that Paul is thinking of parties and party leaders in this exhortation rather than of individuals [WC].

QUESTION—What is τῇ ταπεινοφροσύνῃ 'in the humility' connected with?

It is connected with ἡγούμενοι 'considering' [Ea, My]: in humility considering others. The dative case gives the sense of 'under the influence of humility' [El], 'as regards your humility' [Mou]; it is instrumental, 'by means of humility' [My].

QUESTION—What is indicated by the article in the noun phrase τῇ ταπεινοφροσύνῃ 'the humility?

1. The article is used in a generic sense [EGT] with the abstract noun to focus on the virtue of humility [Ea, ICC, My]: in the specific virtue of humility in general.
2. It implies the humility which is appropriate for each person [El]: in the appropriate attitude of humility.
3. It implies the possessive pronoun ὑμῶν 'your' [Lt, Mou]: in your humility.

QUESTION—What relationship is indicated by the use of the participial form ἡγούμενοι 'considering'?

It is semantically an imperative [Mou]: consider one another as better than yourselves. The participle, together with the two participles in the preceding verse, are related to the indirect exhortation ἵνα φρονῆτε 'that you should mind' and are semantically of the same mood, although none of the commentaries mention this point.

QUESTION—What is meant by ταπεινοφροσύνη 'humility'?

The meaning is self-denial of one's own rights [Bg], unostentatious modesty [Blm]. This humility is a distinctive characteristic of the Christian faith [Ea, TH]; it is based on dependence upon God for everything [Ea], with an awareness of one's own lacks and of the gifts of others which may be superior to one's own [El, NIC, Pl]. This quality does not include undue depreciation of oneself or one's gifts which God has given him [Ea]. It means that we should place our consideration for others above concern for ourselves [EBC, Ln], rejoicing in honor given to others more than in honor given to ourselves [GNC]. It does not mean to regard everyone as superior in every respect to oneself [NTC].

2:4

not each-one looking-to[a] the-(things) of-yourselves[b] but[c] each-one (looking-to) the-(things) of-others also.[d]

TEXT—Instead of the participle σκοποῦντες 'looking to', some manuscripts have the second person plural imperative σκοπεῖτε '(you) look' or the third person singular imperative σκοπείτω 'let him look'. GNT does not mention these alterative readings; KJV evidently accepts the third person singular imperative; Blm accepts the second person plural imperative. Some translations have a finite verb here for stylistic reasons although they doubtless accept the participle in the Greek text.

LEXICON—a. pres. act. participle of σκοπέω (GEL 27.36) (BAGD p. 756): 'to look to' [Ea, Mou, NTC, WBC; NAB, NIV, NRSV, REB], 'to look on' [KJV], 'to look out for' [BAGD, WEC; NASB, TEV], 'to watch out for' [Ln], 'to be concerned about' [GEL], 'to consider' [HNTC; TNT], 'to pursue' [NJB], 'to study' [ICC], 'to adopt as one's aim' [Pl].

　　b. ἑαυτοῦ (GEL 92.25): 'of yourselves' [WBC], 'his own' [HNTC, NTC; KJV, NAB], 'your own' [Ea, ICC, Mou, Pl, WEC; NIV, NRSV, REB, TEV, TNT], 'your own personal' [NASB], 'their own' [Ln], 'selfish' [NJB].

c. ἀλλά (GEL 89.125): 'but' [Ea, HNTC, Ln, Mou, NTC, Pl,
WEC; KJV, NASB, NIV, NJB, NRSV, TNT], not explicit [ICC,
WBC; NAB, REB, TEV].

d. καί (GEL 89.93): 'also' [Ea, HNTC, Ln, Mou, NTC, WC; KJV,
NASB, NIV, TNT], 'beyond them' [Pl], not explicit [ICC, WBC;
NAB, NJB, NRSV, REB, TEV].

QUESTION—Why is this clause mentioned?

It is an exhortation to give their attention to more than their own
affairs [Alf, Bg, Blm, El, MNTC, Mou, NIC, Pl]; Paul is not
forbidding taking proper care of their own affairs [Ea, EBC, El,
MNTC, Pl]. The καί 'also' softens the contrast, showing that Paul
does not mean that one should not take care of his own affairs at
all [Alf, Ea, El, ICC, Lg, Ln, Lt, My, NIC, Pl, WEC]. It is an
exhortation to unselfishness [Ea, EBC, EGT, El, Lg, Ln, MNTC,
My]. It is an exhortation to modesty [Blm] or humility [ICC, Ln,
TNTC], to enable the readers to do more effectively what Paul has
exhorted them to do in 2:2–3 [Blm].

QUESTION—What relationship is indicated by the use of the
participial form σκοποῦντες 'looking'?

1. It is an additional explanation of thinking the same thing (2:2)
[Blm, EBC, EGT, El, Pl, TNTC, WBC, WC]. Each of the
participial clauses elaborates on the general statement [EBC].

2. It explains the preceding phrase by telling how we should
consider others above ourselves [Ea, ICC, Ln].

QUESTION—What are the 'things' referred to in this verse?

1. They are matters of well-being [NTC, TH], or personal virtues
[GNC, Lg, MNTC, My], or the right to high position in the
church [HNTC].

2. They are spiritual matters [Ea, TNTC].

3. They include both spiritual and material matters, because
spiritual interests extend into material interests for Christians
[Ln].

DISCOURSE UNIT: 2:5–11 [EGT, HNTC, MNTC, NIC, NTC, Pl, TNTC,
WBC, WC, WEC]. The topic is Christ's glorification [EGT, HNTC],
Christ's example [MNTC, NTC, TNTC], Christ's demonstration of
humility and unselfishness [Pl, WBC, WC], Christian humility [WEC].

DISCOURSE UNIT: 2:5–8 [ICC, NIC]. The topic is Christ's example in
his condescension [NIC].

DISCOURSE UNIT: 2:5 [WEC]. The topic is Paul's exhortation.

2:5
Think[a] this-(thing) in/among[b] you which (was/you-think) in Christ Jesus also,

TEXT—Some manuscripts introduce this clause with γάρ 'for'. GNT rejects γάρ with a C rating, indicating a considerable degree of doubt. Γάρ is included by Alf, Ea, Blm, El, Lg, My.

TEXT—Instead of φρονεῖτε 'you (pl.) think', the second person plural present active imperative of φρονέω, some manuscripts have φρονείσθω 'let (this) be thought', the third person singular present middle/passive imperative. GNT does not mention this variant. Some translations do not make it clear which text has been used; only Alf, Bg, Blm, My, WBC and KJV clearly read the middle/passive form.

LEXICON—a. pres. act. impera. of φρονέω (GEL **26.16**) (BAGD 3. p. 866): 'to think', 'to mind' [Ln], 'to have a (certain) attitude' [GEL; NAB, NASB, NIV, TEV], 'to have a (certain) mind' [Mou], 'to have a (certain) disposition' [HNTC], 'to cherish a (certain) disposition' [ICC], 'to have (certain) inmost thoughts' [TNT], 'to make one's mind (thus)' [NJB], 'to set one's mind on (a certain thing)' [NTC], 'to let a (certain) mind be (in one)' [Ea; KJV], 'to reflect in one's mind' [Pl], 'to adopt a (certain) way of thinking' [WBC], 'to adopt a (certain) frame of mind' [WEC], 'to take to heart' [REB]. See this word at 2:2.

b. ἐν with dative object (GEL 83.13; 83.9): 'in' [Ea, HNTC, Ln, Mou, NTC, Pl, WEC; KJV, NASB, NRSV], 'among' [REB], 'by' [WBC], not explicit [ICC; NAB, NIV, NJB, TEV, TNT].

QUESTION—What relationship is indicated by γάρ 'for' (for the commentaries which include it)?

It introduces the grounds for the exhortation which precedes [Alf, Ea, El, Lg(H), My]: do these things, because you should have this attitude.

QUESTION—To what does τοῦτο 'this thing' refer?

1. It refers to the generosity and humility exhorted in the preceding verses [Ea, EBC, GNC, HNTC, Lg, Ln, My, NTC, TNTC, WBC]: have this attitude of generosity and humility in your inner thoughts. It is emphatic by word order [Ea].

2. It refers to what follows [TH; probably NAB, NIV, NJB, NRSV, REB, TEV, TNT]: have the same attitude Christ had as shown by the following.

QUESTION—What is meant by ἐν ὑμῖν 'in/among you'?

1. It refers to the inner attitudes of each person [Alf, Ea, EBC, El, ICC, Lg, Ln, Lt, Mou, My, NTC, Pl; all translations except REB, NRSV]: let this attitude be in your minds.

2. It refers to their attitudes toward one another in daily affairs [EGT, GNC, HNTC, MNTC, TH, TNTC, WC, WEC]: let this attitude be among you in your relations with one another.
3. It expresses personal agent by the group [WBC]: let this way of thinking be adopted by you toward one another.

QUESTION—What is meant by ὃ καὶ ἐν Χριστῷ Ἰησοῦ 'which (was/you-think) in Christ Jesus also'?

1. It refers to the attitude of mind which Christ had (and continues to have [Mou]) [Alf, Bg, Ea, EBC, El, GNC, ICC, Lg, Ln, Lt, Mou, My, NTC, Pl, TH, TNTC, WBC; all translations]: let the attitude of mind in you be the same attitude which was in Christ Jesus. The meaning is 'in' individuals, not 'among' you [Alf, Ea], referring to their inner thoughts [Ea]. It means that the Philippians should have the same disposition which Christ had [El, TH].
2. It refers to the Philippian Christians' affairs in relation to Christ Jesus [EGT, MNTC, WC]: let the attitude you have among one another be the attitude of mind which you have in your relations with Christ Jesus. It is an exhortation to manifest the same attitude in their day-by-day community affairs which they manifest in their spiritual activities [EGT, WC]. This interpretation avoids the otherwise superfluous use of the phrase ἐν ὑμῖν 'in you', gives a vivid force to καί 'also', and implies the same verb to be understood in the second half of the verse as was used in the first half [EGT].
3. It means appropriateness to their life in Christ [HNTC, WEC]: let the attitude you have among one another be as is appropriate for those who are in union with Christ.

DISCOURSE UNIT: 2:6–8 [WEC]. The topic is the humiliation of Christ.

2:6

QUESTION—Why is the passage 2:6–8 mentioned?

It gives the grounds for referring to Christ as the example of unselfishness in 2:5 [Bg, GNC, Lg, MNTC, My(D)]: (follow Christ's example,) because he did these things. The point is that Christ was more concerned about rescuing sinful human beings than holding on to his heavenly glory [Ea].

who, existing[a] in[b] (the) form[c] of-God,

LEXICON—a. pres. act. participle of ὑπάρχω (GEL 13.77) (BAGD 2. p. 838): 'to exist' [Ea, Ln, NTC, WEC; NASB], 'to be' [Ea, HNTC, WBC; KJV, NAB, NIV, NJB, NSV, REB], 'to subsist' [Mou], 'to exist from eternity' [ICC], 'to share from the beginning' [TNT], 'to be by nature' [Pl]. The phrase ὃς ἐν μορφῇ θεοῦ ὑπάρχων 'who, existing in the form of God' is translated 'he always had the nature of God' [TEV]. This verb means to be originally [Alf, WC], to be by nature [EGT, TH], to be from eternity [El], implying Christ's pre-existence [Lg, Lt]; his eternal existence is also implied in the context [Lt]. The present tense indicates that this was a continuing condition [EBC, NTC, Pl, TH, WC] both in his preincarnate existence and his existence afterward [NIC].

b. ἐν with dative object (GEL 13.8): 'in' [Ea, HNTC, ICC, Ln, Mou, NTC, Pl, WBC, WEC; all translations except TEV, TNT], not explicit [TNT].

c. μορφή (GEL **58.2**) (BAGD p. 528): 'form' [BAGD, Ea, HNTC, Ln, NTC, Pl, WBC, WEC; KJV, NAB, NASB, NJB, NSV, REB], 'nature' [GEL; TEV], 'very nature' [GEL; NIV, TNT], 'a state of equality' [ICC]. The phrase μορφῇ θεοῦ 'form of God' is translated 'God's manifested Being' [Mou].

QUESTION—What relationship is indicated by the use of the participial form ὑπάρχων 'existing'?

1. It is concessive [Bg, Blm, El, ICC, Lg, Lt, MNTC, NTC; NAB, NASB, NRSV, REB]: although he continually existed in the form of God, yet he did not consider, etc.

2. It is causative [Mou, WBC]: because he existed in the form of God, he therefore considered equality with God not a matter of getting, but of giving up.

3. It is temporal [My]: when he existed in the form of God, he did not consider, etc. It merely narrates his heavenly position; the time is that of Christ's preincarnate state [My].

4. It is not concessive; it is merely a statement [Ea] or description [Ln]: he existed in the form of God.

QUESTION—What is meant by μορφῇ θεοῦ 'the form of God'?

It refers to the outward form which properly reflects the true nature [EBC, EGT, GNC, HNTC, ICC, Lg(H), Ln, Lt, MNTC, Mou, My, NIC, NTC, TH]; that is, that Christ had the position, condition, and glory of God, the character and nature of God [WBC], the form and glory of God [TNTC]. It means to have the attributes of divinity [Pl]. It refers to the characteristics by which God's appearing is recognized, the splendor of deity [Bg], not the nature of deity, although it clearly implies that Christ had the nature of God as well [Ea, Lt, MNTC]. It includes the divine nature [NIC, WC], but also the full sense of Heb. 1:3, the radiance of God's glory and the exact representation of his being [Alf, My], the nature and essence of God [Blm, EBC], one with God and equal to God the Father [Blm]. The word is used in a popular, not a philosophical, sense [EGT]. Paul does not state that Christ was the form of God, but rather that he existed in the form of God, suggesting that the form of God was the clothing in which Christ existed [WBC].

QUESTION—How are the two nouns related in the genitive construction μορφῇ θεοῦ 'form of God'?

1. It means that the form which Christ had in heaven was deity [El, HNTC, Lg, Mou], not specifically 'God the Father' [Bg, Lg, Mou], but rather the outward manifestation of God's glory [Bg], deity in the full sense [Mou]: Christ existed in the form which was deity.

2. It means that the form which Christ had in heaven was the form which God the Father had [Blm, EBC, EGT, GNC, MNTC]: Christ existed in the same form which God the Father had.

considered[a] (as) not something-to-be-grasped[b] the being equal[c] to-God,

LEXICON—a. aorist mid. (deponent = act.) indic. of ἡγέομαι (GEL 31.1) (BAGD 2. p. 343): 'to consider' [BAGD, GEL, Ln, WBC; NIV, TNT], 'to regard' [BAGD, GEL, ICC, Pl; NASB, NRSV], 'to think' [BAGD; KJV, TEV], 'to deem' [NAB], 'to count' [HNTC, NTC; NJB], 'to reckon' [Mou]. The phrase οὐχ ἁρπαγμὸν ἡγήσατο 'he considered not as something to be grasped' is translated 'he laid no claim' [REB], '(he) took no advantage' [WEC]. It expresses a resolution or decision [Lg].

b. ἁρπαγμός (GEL 57.235; 57.236) (BAGD 1., 2. p. 108): 'something to be grasped' [NIV, NJB], 'something to be grasped at' [NAB], 'a thing to be grasped' [NASB], 'a prize to be eagerly grasped' [ICC], 'grounds for grasping' [WBC], 'a prize to be strenuously secured' [Pl], 'a thing of snatching' [Ln], 'something to be held on to forcibly' [GEL], 'something to cling to' [NTC], 'something to be taken by force' [GEL], 'something to be exploited' [NRSV], 'to try by force' [TEV], 'plunder' [HNTC], 'plunderer's prize' [Mou], 'robbery' [KJV]. It is also translated as a phrase: 'that he must cling to' [TNT]. It is emphatic by word order [Alf, El, My].

c. ἴσος (GEL 58.33) (BAGD p. 381): 'equal' [GEL, Ln, NTC, WBC; KJV, TEV], 'on an equality' [Mou, Pl], not explicit [ICC]. The phrase τὸ εἶναι ἴσα 'the being equal' is translated 'equality' [HNTC, WEC; all translations except KJV, TEV]. The neuter singular form ἴσα of this adjective is used as an adverb [BAGD, Bg, Ea, EBC, EGT, El, ICC, Lg, Ln, Lt, My, NTC]; it states the manner in which Christ existed [EBC, NTC]. This being 'equal' with God implies the fullness and the exaltation of God [Bg], possessing the attributes and perfections of God the Father [Blm].

QUESTION—What is meant by the phrase τὸ εἶναι ἴσα θεῷ 'the being equal to God'?

1. It implies having the same attributes and the exalted state of God [Bg, Blm, HNTC]: Christ had the same attributes and exalted state as God the Father had and existed in this manner.
2. It means existence in the manner equal to God [ICC, NIC, NTC, TH], showing or making known the form of God which he possessed [Bg, Ea, TNTC, WC]: he existed in the manner in which God the Father existed.
3. It means having the acknowledgment of the honor of his exalted position [TNTC].
4. It refers to his existence in his divine-human condition [Ln].

QUESTION—What is meant by 'he considered the being equal with God as not something to be grasped'?

1. He already was equal with God [Alf, Ea, EBC, El, GNC, HNTC, ICC, Lt, Mou, My, NIC, NTC, TNTC, WBC, WC, WEC; TNT].
1.1 He was willing to relinquish that existence of equality with God in order to come to earth as a human being [Alf, Ea, EBC, El, GNC, ICC, Lt, Mou, NIC, NTC, WC, WEC]: he did not regard his equality with God as something which he should hold on to. As such, this clause focuses the emphasis upon Christ's utter unselfishness in laying aside his equality with God [Alf].
1.2 He was equal to God but subordinate to him [My]. He rejected any thought of taking advantage of his coming to earth to seize power and glory and no longer be subordinate to the Father [My, TNTC]; instead, he chose to secure this equality by his incarnation and humiliation [TNTC].
1.3 He did not accept the thought that being equal with God meant that he could take all power and glory to himself [WBC].
1.4 He did not consider that he was robbing God of his glory by being equal with God [Blm].
2. He was not equal with God [Bg, EGT, Ln, MNTC; REB, TEV].
2.1 On earth he was not fully equal with God, but he did not desire to seize that equality for himself [Bg, EGT, MNTC]: he did not regard full equality with God as something which he should seize for himself. He was not willing to use his miraculous powers to force men to recognize him as God, but rather submitted to death and resurrection as the means for securing this recognition [EGT]. It was the equality that he received at his exaltation that is in view here [MNTC].

2.2 He did not consider that his existence in his divine-human condition allowed him to display his equality with God as a prize to be exhibited [Ln].

QUESTION—How is the phrase ἐν μορφῇ θεοῦ ὑπάρχων 'being in the form of God' related to the phrase τὸ εἶναι ἴσα θεῷ 'the being equal to God'?

1. They are not completely equal [Bg, Ea, EBC, EGT, ICC, Lg, MNTC, My, NIC, TH, TNTC, WC]. The former phrase refers to Christ's nature [EGT, MNTC, NIC, TH, TNTC, WC] as to its form and pre-existence [El, ICC, My]; the latter phrase refers to a relationship [EGT], to God's position [TH], to the state and continuation of the relationship [El, MNTC], to his existence in the same manner as God [ICC; NIC], to Christ's internal nature [My], to the fullness and exaltation of God [Bg], to the acknowledgment of his position [TNTC], to making his glory known [WC]. The former phrase is further explained as 'being equal with God'; however, although the nature does not change, the way in which it is manifested may change [EBC]. The former phrase refers to Christ's existence apart from the world and prior to the world; the latter refers to his existence as king of his people at the Father's right hand [Lg]. However, the two phrases are not essentially different [My, TH].

2. The two phrases are essentially equal [Blm, El, HNTC, WBC, WEC]. The article τό preceding the infinitive εἶναι 'to be' refers back to something previously mentioned, in this case to ἐν μορφῇ θεοῦ 'in the form of God' [WBC]; it implies a definiteness which allows the rendering 'his equality' [WEC]. The article simply introduces the articular infinitive.

2:7

but[a] he-emptied[b] himself, taking[c] (the) form[d] of-a-slave,[e]

LEXICON—a. ἀλλά (GEL 89.125): 'but' [GEL, HNTC, ICC, Ln, NTC; KJV, NASB, NIV, NJB, NRSV, REB], 'on the contrary' [GEL, Pl, WBC], 'rather' [Mou; NAB], 'instead' [GEL, WEC], 'instead of this' [TEV], 'no' [TNT].

b. aorist act. indic. of κενόω (GEL 87.70) (BAGD 1. 428): 'to empty' [BAGD, GEL, Ln, NTC; NAB, NASB, NJB, NRSV, TNT], 'to pour out' [WBC], 'to make nothing' [WEC; NIV, REB], 'to make void' [Mou], 'to strip' [HNTC], 'to divest of position' [GEL], 'to lay aside' [ICC], 'to make of no reputation' [KJV]. The phrase ἑαυτὸν ἐκένωσεν 'he emptied himself' is translated 'of his own free will he gave up all he had' [TEV], 'of his own free will he divested himself of his glory' [Pl]. The active voice shows that the emptying was voluntary [HNTC,

WBC]. This verb emphasizes his complete renunciation [ICC, MNTC].

   c. aorist act. participle of λαμβάνω (GEL 49.10) (BAGD 1.a. p. 464): 'to take' [Ea, HNTC, ICC, Ln, Mou, NTC, WBC; all translations except REB, TNT], 'to assume' [Pl, WEC; REB, TNT], 'to put on' [GEL]. It forms a contrast with ὑπάρχων in 2:6 [Lt, Pl]. The aorist tense indicates an action simultaneous to the verb ἐκένωσεν 'he emptied' [Alf, Ea, El, Lg, Ln, MNTC, My, NIC, Pl, TH, TNTC, WBC, WEC]. This verb shows that the 'taking' was voluntary [Pl].

   d. μορφή: 'form'. See this word at 2:6.

   e. δοῦλος (GEL 87.76) (BAGD 1.e.β. p. 205): 'slave' [BAGD, GEL, HNTC, Ln, WBC; NAB, NJB, NRSV, REB], 'bond-servant' [GEL, Mou, Pl; NASB], 'servant' [Ea, NTC, WEC; KJV, NIV, TEV, TNT].

QUESTION—What relationship is indicated by ἀλλά 'but'?

   1. It indicates the opposite of the preceding clause [Alf, Bg, EGT, El, GNC, Lg, Ln, Lt, MNTC, My, NTC, Pl, TH, WBC, WC, WEC; NAB, TEV, TNT]: he did not consider equality with God as something to be seized/retained; on the contrary, he emptied himself. This word introduces the rest of 2:7 and 2:8 [Bg].

   2. It indicates a partial contrast with the preceding clause [Blm, Ea, EBC, Mou, NIC]: he considered that he was entitled to retain his equality with God; however, he emptied himself.

QUESTION—What is meant by ἑαυτὸν ἐκένωσεν 'he emptied himself'?

   1. He emptied himself of his mode of existence as God [Alf, Blm, Ea Lg, Mou, My, TH]: he emptied himself of the form of existence as God. He willingly became incarnate as a helpless child, not as a theophany [Ea]. On earth he did not show forth the glory of the Father [Alf, Lt, TNTC]. He retained the fullness which he had in heaven [EBC, TH] and took on the form of a slave in addition to his nature of deity [EBC], but conducted himself as if he were empty and did not use his rights [Bg, Lt]. It means that he emptied himself of his glory and majesty which he had in heaven in his equality with God [El, GNC, HNTC, Lt, NTC], or although he was not equal with God [MNTC]. The emptying was Christ's voluntary act after his incarnation, not a decision he made in heaven [MNTC]. 'Himself' is emphatic by word order [Alf, Bg, Ea, El, Lg, Ln, Lt, Mou, My], pointing to the fact that it was his own self which he emptied [El] instead of seizing something for himself [Bg, Lg, My], the fact that it

was not himself but us for whom he was concerned [Ln], the fact that his humiliation was voluntary [Lt, Mou, Pl, TH, WBC].

2. Paul does not mean that Christ emptied himself of something, referring to either form or likeness [NIC, WBC, WC, WEC]. At his incarnation, he retained the form of God and he 'emptied himself' by taking the form of a slave [NIC]. The sense is 'he poured himself out', denying himself of his rights for the sake of others [WBC, WC], thus indicating how complete his self-denial was [WEC]. It simply means 'he made himself nothing' [WEC].

QUESTION—What relationship is indicated by the use of the participial form λαβών 'taking'?

1. It indicates the means by which he emptied himself [Alf, Blm, Ea, EBC, El, HNTC, ICC, Lg, Lt, MNTC, Mou, My, NIC, NTC, TH, WEC]: he emptied himself by taking the form of a slave.

2. It defines the phrase ἐκένωσεν ἑαυτόν 'he emptied himself' [Bg, EGT, GNC, Ln, Pl]: he emptied himself; that is, he took the form of a slave.

QUESTION—How are the two nouns related in the genitive construction μορφὴν δούλου 'form of a slave'?

It means the form and nature which human beings have [Alf, EBC, Mou, NIC, TNTC], including both resemblance and attributes [Lt, MNTC, Pl, WBC], since human beings also are servants of God [Alf]: he took the form which human beings have. Paul does not deal with the question of whose slave Christ became; the word simply points out the humility of his incarnate state [EGT]. It means the form of a servant, not a slave [ICC, NTC], referring to his life of service [ICC]. It means the form of a slave [Mou, WBC] with no rights of his own [WBC]. This phrase is explicitly contrasted with μορφὴ θεοῦ 'form of God' [Ea, EBC, Pl]. However, it does not mean that his inner divine nature was changed [EGT, NIC]. He retained the nature of God but manifested it in (or added to it [NIC]) the nature of a servant [GNC, Ln, NIC, NTC]. The word 'slave' here is stronger than 'men' which is used in the next phrase [Lt, NIC]. This phrase is in contrast with equality with God [Alf, ICC, TH] and implies a servant of God [Alf, MNTC, Mou, My, Pl], not a slave of man [Alf]. It refers to the form and existence of a bondservant or slave [ICC, MNTC, WBC], pointing to Christ's complete submission to God's will [MNTC, TH].

becoming[a] in[b] (the) likeness[c] of-men.[d]

LEXICON—a. aorist mid. (deponent = act.) participle of γίνομαι (GEL 13.48) (BAGD II.4.a. p. 160): 'to become' [GEL, NTC, WEC; NJB, TEV, TNT], 'to come to be' [Mou], 'to get to be' [Ln], 'to be made' [Ea, HNTC, ICC; KJV, NASB, NIV], 'to be born' [Pl, WBC; NAB, NRSV], 'to bear' [REB]. This word is in contrast with ὑπάρχων 'being' in 2:6 [ICC, Lt, Pl, WBC, WC] and refers to the addition of his human nature to his divine nature [Lt], to the contrast between what he became and what he always was [WBC]. By being born, he received a human form [Alf, My], and this means the same as 'being born' [HNTC, Pl]. The use of this participle makes it clear that the preceding participle λαβών 'taking' is more than an outward appearance [Lg]. The action is simultaneous to 'taking the form of a slave' [NIC, WEC].

b. ἐν with dative object (GEL 13.8): 'in' [Ea, GEL, HNTC, ICC, Ln, Mou, Pl, WBC; KJV, NAB, NASB, NIV, NRSV], not explicit [NTC; REB]. The phrase ἐν ὁμοιώματι ἀνθρώπων 'in the likeness of men' is translated 'incarnate' [WEC], 'like a person' [GEL], 'like human beings' [NTC], 'like man' [TEV], 'as human beings are' [NJB], 'a man like one of us' [TNT]. It indicates Christ's location as a human being [El, Lg].

c. ὁμοίωμα (GEL 64.3) (BAGD 4. p. 567): 'likeness' [Ea, GEL, HNTC, ICC, Ln, WBC; KJV, NAB, NASB, NIV, REB, NRSV], 'similitude' [Mou], 'guise' [Pl]. 'Likeness' indicates similarity of appearance to other human beings [Bg, ICC, My, TH, WBC], including both similarity and reality [Blm]. It includes both inner and outer life [Lg]. It does not imply any lack of reality [TH, WBC], but it implies that there is more involved than the likeness [HNTC, Pl], namely his divine nature [ICC].

d. ἄνθρωπος (GEL 9.1) (BAGD 1.a.β. p. 68): 'man' [BAGD, Ea, HNTC, ICC, Ln, Mou; KJV, NAB, NASB, TEV, TNT], 'human being' [BAGD, GEL, NTC, WBC; NJB]. This genitive noun is also translated as an adjective: 'human' [Pl; NIV, NRSV, REB]. In this verse, this word defines δοῦλος 'slave' more specifically [Lg].

QUESTION—What relationship is indicated by the use of the participial form γενόμενος 'becoming'?

1. It is related to what precedes [Alf, Bg, Blm, Ea, El, EBC, EGT, HNTC, ICC, Ln, Lt, Mou, My, NIC, NTC, Pl, WBC, WC, WEC; KJV, NAB, NASB, NIV, NJB, NRSV].

1.1 It expresses the means by which Christ emptied himself, parallel to λαβών 'taking' above [Alf, Blm, EBC, WBC, WEC]: he emptied himself by taking the form of a slave; i.e., by becoming in the form of men. It defines the preceding phrase more specifically [Alf, ICC, WBC, WEC].

1.2 It indicates the means by which he took the form of a slave [Ea, El, My, Pl]: he took the form of a slave by becoming like human beings. In taking the form of a servant, he took the likeness of human beings [NTC]. This participle, like the preceding one, is simultaneous to ἐκένωσεν 'he emptied' [My].

1.3 The participle is temporal [Ln]: he took the form of a slave when he became like human beings.

1.4 It gives the reason why he was able to take the form of a slave [Bg]: he took the form of a slave because he had become like human beings.

2. It relates to what follows [MNTC, TH; REB, TEV].

2.1 It relates to what follows, including 2:8 [MNTC; REB]: coming to be like men and being found in form as a man, he humbled himself.

2.2 It relates only to the following phrase [TH; TEV]: he took the nature of a servant; he became like man and appeared in human likeness.

QUESTION—How are the two nouns related in the genitive construction ὁμοιώματι ἀνθρώπων 'likeness of men'?

It means that he was like a human being and was a true human being [Bg, Blm, GNC, Mou, My, WBC]: he was a human being and had the flesh and nature of human beings. This phrase further defines the preceding phrase 'form of a slave' [My], but the differences between the two phrases is largely stylistic [WEC]. The plural 'men' identifies him with the entire human race [Lt, Pl, TH, WC]. He was not merely a human being, but rather was the Son of God manifested in human flesh and nature and with the appearance of human beings [Alf, Ea, EBC, El, Lg, Ln, My]. He was therefore not completely identical with other human beings [Ea, EBC, EGT, My, NTC].

QUESTION—How are the three phrases μορφὴν δούλου 'form of a slave', ἐν ὁμοιώματι ἀνθρώπου 'in the likeness of men', and σχήματι ὡς ἄνθρωπος 'in form as a man' related?

The first phrase is more comprehensive [Ea]; it relates to Christ's humiliation [EGT, Ln, WBC, WC], pointing out that he came as a servant of men [ICC], focusing on the form which human beings have [Alf, EBC, MNTC, Mou, My], including human attributes [Lt, MNTC]; he retained the nature of God but manifested it in the nature of a servant [GNC, ICC, Ln, NTC], implying his true humanity [Lt]. The first two phrases contrast what Christ was with what he became [Lt]. The second phrase relates to his incarnation [Ln, WBC, WC], focusing on his similarity to other human beings [Bg, EBC, EGT, GNC, ICC, Lt, MNTC, Mou, My], relating to the manner of his emptying himself [Ea], stating what Christ actually was [EBC]; but it keeps his deity in mind which means that he was not absolutely identified with human beings [ICC]. This phrase thus stands midway between the first and the third [Lt]. The third phrase (2:8) repeats the contents of the first and second phrases [TNTC], is an emphatic repetition of the second phrase [Alf]; it shows the extent and nature of his humiliation [Blm, Ea]; it shows how he appeared to people in his outward form [EBC, ICC, Lt]. From the σχῆμα 'appearance' in the third phrase, the ὁμοίωμα 'likeness' in the second phrase may be inferred, and both of these words serve to explain the sense of μορφή 'form' in the first phrase [Ea].

and[a] in-appearance[b] being-found[c] as[d] a-man,

TEXT—This phrase is part of 2:7 in ICC, Lg, My, TH, WBC, WEC; GNT, NAB, NJB, NRSV, TEV, and TNT. It is part of 2:8 in Alf, Bg, Blm, Ea, EBC, EGT, El, HNTC, Ln, Lt, Mou, MNTC, NIC, NTC, Pl, TNTC, WC; KJV, NASB, NIV, and REB.

LEXICON—a. καί (GEL 89.87; 89.92): 'and' [Ea, GEL, HNTC, ICC, Ln, Mou, Pl, WBC, WEC; KJV, NASB, NIV, NJB, NRSV, TEV], 'and then' [GEL], 'so' [NTC], not explicit [NAB, REB, TNT].

b. σχῆμα (GEL **58.17**; 58.7) (BAGD 1. p. 797): 'appearance' [**GEL**; NASB, NIV], 'outward appearance' [BAGD], 'likeness' [TEV], 'form' [BAGD, GEL; TNT], 'fashion' [Ea, ICC, Ln, NTC; KJV], 'shape' [BAGD, HNTC], 'form' [NRSV], 'guise' [Mou], 'estate' [NAB], 'all that is external' [Pl], not explicit [WBC]. This entire phrase is translated 'sharing the human lot' [REB]. This word relates to external appearance [Bg, EBC, EGT, El, ICC, Lt, MNTC, My, TH, WBC, WC], clothing, and manner of speaking, etc. [Alf, Bg, Ea, Mou, My, WC]; it is emphatic [Alf]. In this context this word combines with μορφή 'form' and ὁμοίωμα 'likeness' to emphasize Christ's full identity with mankind [WBC]. This word can refer only to Christ's humanity, not to his deity [Pl]. The use of this word does not imply that the appearance differed from the reality [HNTC, TH]. The dative case indicates reference—in reference to his appearance [El, Ln], and is emphatic by word order [Ln].

c. aorist pass. participle of εὑρίσκω (GEL 13.7) (BAGD 2. p. 325): 'to be found' [BAGD, Ea, HNTC, ICC, Ln, Mou; KJV, NASB, NIV, NRSV], 'to be found to be' [GEL], 'to be known to be' [NAB], 'to be recognized' [NTC, Pl, WBC], 'to appear' [TEV, TNT]. The phrase σχήματι εὑρεθείς 'in appearance being found' is translated 'being in every way' [NJB], 'having appeared' [WEC]. It means that he appeared and behaved in such a manner [Bg, My] and was seen to be such by those who saw him [Ea, EBC, EGT, El, ICC, Ln, My, NTC, Pl, WC].

d. ὡς (GEL 64.12) (BAGD III.1.c. p. 898): 'as' [Ea, GEL, HNTC, ICC, Ln, Mou, NTC, Pl, WBC, WEC; KJV, NASB, NIV], 'like'

[GEL; NJB], not explicit [NAB, NRSV, TEV, TNT]. It indicates manner [Ea]. It indicates that Christ was truly a man [TNTC], that he behaved as if he were no more than (or different from [EBC]) an ordinary man [Bg, My]. He was a perfect man, but he was not merely a man [El]. It focuses on how he was seen to be rather than upon what he actually was [ICC, Lt].

QUESTION—What relationship is indicated by καί 'and'?

1. It introduces a further development subsequent to the preceding [Alf, Ln, My(D), NTC, WEC; KJV, NASB, NIV, NJB, NRSV], thus joining ἑαυτὸν ἐκένωσεν 'he emptied himself' and ἐταπείνωσεν ἑαυτόν 'he humbled himself' [Bg, ICC, Ln, WEC]: he emptied himself; furthermore, he humbled himself. This verse describes the humiliation of Christ, as the preceding verse describes his emptying himself [Blm, El]. Καί introduces the contrast between what Christ actually was and what he appeared to be [EGT].

2. It joins the two participial phrases [Lg, MNTC, My, WBC; TEV]: becoming in the likeness of men and being found in appearance as a man. It is the third of the participial phrases which define 'he emptied himself' [WBC].

QUESTION—What relationship is indicated by the use of the participial form εὑρεθείς 'being found'?

It is evidently temporal, but none of the commentaries or translations point this out: and when he was found in appearance as a man, he humbled himself.

QUESTION—What is the participial phrase σχήματι εὑρεθεὶς ὡς ἄνθρωπος 'being found in appearance as a man' connected with?

1. It is connected with the following verb phrase ἐταπείνωσεν ἑαυτον 'he humbled himself' [Alf, Bg, Ea, ICC, Ln, My(D), NTC, WEC; all translations except TEV]: being found in appearance as a man he humbled himself. This phrase summarizes the two preceding phrases and gives the setting for ἐταπείνωσεν ἑαυτόν 'he humbled himself' [WEC].

2. It is connected with the preceding participial phrase(s) [Lg, MNTC, My, WBC; TEV]: (taking the form of a servant,) becoming in the likeness of men, and being found in form as a man.

2:8

he-humbled[a] himself

LEXICON—a. aorist act. indic. of ταπεινόω (GEL 87.62; 88.56) (BAGD 2.a. p. 804): 'to humble' [BAGD, Ea, GEL, HNTC, ICC, Mou, NTC, Pl, WBC, WEC; all translations except NJB, TEV], 'to be humble' [NJB, TEV], 'to lower' [Ln]. This verb is first in its clause, indicating emphasis on the act [Ea, El, ICC, Lg, My, Pl, TH], the aorist tense indicating the act rather than the continuing attitude [TH]. It is a voluntary action [GNC, Ln, WC] which took place after the incarnation [MNTC, NIC, Pl, WBC].

QUESTION—How is ἐταπείνωσεν ἑαυτόν 'he humbled himself' related to the preceding ἑαυτὸν ἐκένωσεν 'he emptied himself'?

1. 'He humbled himself' implies a further level of humiliation after emptying himself [Alf, Bg, Ea, EBC, EGT, El, ICC, Ln, Mou, TNTC, WBC, WC; NJB]; it is not the same as ἐκένωσεν 'he emptied' [El, ICC]: after emptying himself to become man, he then humbled himself. It is something Christ did after coming to earth [Ea, El]. It refers to his entire earthly life, but in particular to the climax of his humiliation on the cross [TNTC, WBC]. This humbling is far more profound than even his emptying himself to become man [Ln]. It is not the climax, for the humiliation of his descent from heaven to become man is far greater than his descent in human state to the cross [Ea].

2. 'He humbled himself' describes what is meant by 'he emptied himself' [Lg]: he emptied himself, that is, he humbled himself to become man.

3. 'He humbled himself' is included in 'he emptied himself', the latter being more comprehensive [My]: he emptied himself, which includes humbling himself to death.

becoming[a] obedient[b] to-the-point-of[c] death, even/and[d] death of-a-cross.

LEXICON—a. aorist mid. (deponent = act.) of γίνομαι (GEL 13.48): 'to become' [Ea, GEL, HNTC, ICC, Mou, NTC, Pl, WBC, WEC; KJV, NASB, NIV, NRSV], 'to get to be' [Ln], 'to be' [REB]. The phrase γενόμενος ὑπήκοος 'becoming obedient' is translated 'he walked the path of obedience' [TEV], 'in obedience' [TNT]. The phrase γενόμενος ὑπήκοος μέχρι θανάτου 'becoming obedient to the point of death' is translated 'obediently accepting even death' [NAB], 'even to accepting death' [NJB]. The action of this participle is simultaneous to 'he humbled himself' [My, TH, WEC].

b. ὑπήκοος (GEL 36.16): 'obedient' [Ea, GEL, HNTC, ICC, Ln, Mou, NTC, Pl, WBC, WEC; KJV, NASB, NIV, NRSV, REB]. The obedience is to God [Ea, El, GNC, ICC, Lg, Mou, My, NIC, NTC, Pl, TH]; it is to God and in service to people [WBC]; it is to the power of the elemental spirits [HNTC].

c. μέχρι with genitive object (GEL 78.51) (BAGD 1.c. p. 515): 'to the point of' [GEL, WBC, WEC; NASB, NRSV, REB, TNT], 'all the way to' [TEV], 'to the extent of' [GEL, NTC], 'which extended to' [Pl], 'as far as' [Ln], 'even so far as' [ICC], 'to the

length of' [Mou], 'unto' [Ea, HNTC; KJV], 'to' [NIV]. This
preposition expresses the degree or extent of his obedience [Ea,
El, Lg, My, TH, WBC, WC] and indicates that death was the
climax of Christ's obedience [Alf, My].

    d. δέ (GEL 89.94): 'even' [KJV, NASB, NIV, NRSV], 'and' [GEL],
'and that' [HNTC], 'but' [Pl], 'yes' [NTC], 'yea' [ICC, Ln], 'aye'
[Mou], 'ay' [Ea], 'and that of all things' [WBC], 'and no less
than' [WEC], not explicit [NAB, NJB, REB, TEV, TNT]. It
introduces a more specific aspect of the humiliation [ICC, Lg,
Lt, Pl, TH, WBC]. In a context like this, used with the repeated
word θανάτου 'death', it makes its phrase emphatic [Ea, El, Ln]
and calls attention to the kind of death [Alf, EBC, EGT, NTC,
WEC]. The cross was the punishment for slaves [Bg, Lg, Ln, Lt,
Pl, WBC] and criminals [Ea, Lg, Lt, TH, WBC], a type of
punishment not permitted for Roman citizens [EBC, Pl], the
most degrading [WEC], painful and shameful manner of death
[Ea, Lt, Mou, NIC, Pl, TH, WBC]. This is the ultimate
degradation and humbling of himself [MNTC, WBC].

QUESTION—What relationship is indicated by the use of the
participial form γενόμενος 'becoming'?

    1. It indicates the means by which he humbled himself [Alf, Ea,
El, ICC, Pl, TH, WBC; NAB, NASB]: he humbled himself by
becoming obedient.

    2. It explains what is meant by ἐταπείνωσεν ἑαυτόν 'he humbled
himself' [HNTC, Ln, MNTC, Mou, My, NTC]: he humbled
himself, that is, he became obedient to the point of death.

    3. It indicates the extent of his humiliation [NJB]: he humbled
himself to the point of accepting death.

QUESTION—What is the phrase μέχρι θανάτου 'to the point of death'
connected with?

    1. It is connected with ὑπήκοος 'obedient' [Alf, Ea, EBC, El, Lg,
Ln, MNTC, My, NIC, NTC; KJV, NAB, NASB, NIV, TEV]:
obedient to the point of death.

    2. It is connected with ἐταπείνωσεν 'he humbled' [NJB]: he
humbled himself to the point of accepting death.

    3. It is connected with both ἐταπείνωσεν 'he humbled' and
ὑπήκοος 'obedient' [Bg]: he humbled himself, and became
obedient, both to the point of death.

QUESTION—How are the two nouns related in the genitive
construction θανάτου σταυροῦ 'death of a cross'?

    The cross is the means or the place of the death [EBC, HNTC,
ICC, Lg, NTC, Pl, TH, WBC, WEC; all translations except KJV]:
death on/by means of a cross. The absence of the article with

σταυροῦ 'of a cross' calls attention to the nature of such a death [MNTC].

DISCOURSE UNIT: 2:9–11 [ICC, NIC, WEC]. The topic is Christ's exaltation [NIC, WEC] and the recognition that he is Lord [NIC].

2:9

Therefore[a] God also[b] highly-exalted[c] him and gave[d] him the name[e] the-(one) above[f] every name,[e]

TEXT—Instead of τὸ ὄνομα 'the name', some manuscripts read simply ὄνομα 'a name'. GNT does not deal with this variant. Only Alf, Bg, El, and KJV read 'a name'.

LEXICON—a. διό (GEL 89.47): 'therefore' [GEL, HNTC, NTC, WBC; NASB, NIV, NRSV, REB], 'wherefore' [Ea, Ln, Mou; KJV], 'therefore in consequence of this' [Pl], 'as a consequence, therefore' [WBC], 'because of this' [NAB], 'on this account' [ICC], 'and for this' [NJB], 'for this reason' [GEL; TEV], 'for this very reason' [GEL, WEC], 'that is why' [TNT].

b. καί (GEL 89.93): 'also' [GEL, HNTC, Ln, Mou; KJV, NASB, NRSV], 'too' [Ea], 'in consequence of this' [Pl], not explicit [ICC, NTC, WBC, WEC; all translations except KJV, NASB, NRSV]. It emphasizes the contrast with what Christ did [Ea, El]; it indicates the result corresponding to the humiliation [EGT, ICC]. It implies that the conclusion is the logical outcome of Christ's humiliation [WBC, WC].

c. aorist act. indic. of ὑπερυψόω (GEL **87.16**) (BAGD 1. p. 842): 'to exalt highly' [Ea, Ln; KJV, NAB, NASB, NRSV], 'to exalt to the highest place' [WBC; NIV], 'to exalt to the highest station' [HNTC], 'to exalt supremely' [Mou, Pl], 'to exalt above all things' [WEC], 'to exalt above all creatures' [ICC], 'to raise to the highest place' [TEV, TNT], 'to raise to the heights' [REB], 'to raise to the loftiest heights' [BAGD, NTC], 'to raise high' [NJB], 'to give exceptional honor' [GEL]. The prefix ὑπέρ- gives emphasis to the verb [Alf, Bg, Ea, HNTC, NTC, WBC]; the exaltation is great in dignity (in superlative measure [ICC, Ln, My, NIC, TH, WBC]) just as Christ's humiliation was great [Ea, El, WBC]. It expresses the opposite of Christ's humbling himself [Lg]. This verb should not be translated 'has highly exalted' [Alf] but rather as a simple historical past 'highly exalted' [Alf, El]. The aorist tense implies that his exaltation occurred at the time of his resurrection and ascension [WBC].

d. aorist mid. (deponent = act.) indic. of χαρίζομαι (GEL **57.102**) (BAGD 1. p. 872): 'to give' [Ea; KJV, NIV, NJB, NRSV, TEV], 'to grant' [Ln], 'to grant as a gift' [WEC], 'to bestow' [GEL,

ICC, NTC; NAB, NASB, REB], 'to confer' [HNTC, Mou, Pl, WBC; TNT]. This verb implies giving freely and graciously [El, HNTC, MNTC, NIC, NTC, TH], bestowing as a gift [Ea, ICC, My, TNTC] what had been voluntarily renounced [ICC, My] but without denying that it was a reward [Ea].

   e. ὄνομα (GEL 33.126) (BAGD I.4.c.β. p. 572): 'name' [BAGD, GEL, Ea, HNTC, ICC, Ln, Mou, NTC, Pl, WBC, WEC; all translations]. The definite article with this noun indicates that it is a name which is known and honored [Ea].

   f. ὑπέρ with accusative object (GEL 87.30) (BAGD 2. p. 839): 'above' [BAGD, GEL, Ea, HNTC, ICC, Ln, Mou, NTC, Pl, WBC, WEC; all translations except TEV], 'greater than' [TEV] 'superior to' [GEL].

QUESTION—What relationship is indicated by διό 'therefore'?

It indicates the consequence (the reward [My(D)]) of Christ's actions mentioned in 2:8 [Alf, Bg, Blm, Ea, El, GNC, ICC, Lg, Ln, Lt, MNTC, My, NIC, NTC, Pl, TH, TNTC, WBC]: he humbled himself and became obedient to the point of death; therefore God highly exalted him.

QUESTION—What is the first καί 'also' connected with?

   1. It is connected with the following ὁ θεός 'God' [Alf, Lg, Lt, Pl; KJV]: Christ emptied himself; God, for his part, exalted him. The καί 'also' indicates that God, for his part, responded to Christ's actions [Pl]. It points out what God, on his part, has done because of Christ's obedience [Alf, Lg, Lt]. 'God' is emphatic by forefronting [Ea], and so is αὐτόν 'him' [Pl].

   2. It is connected with διό 'therefore' [Ea, ICC, WEC; NASB]: therefore also. It strengthens the meaning of διό 'wherefore' [WEC].

   3. It is connected with ὑπερύψωσεν 'he exalted highly' [El, HNTC]: God also exalted him highly. It points out the contrast between Christ's humbling himself and God's exalting him [El].

QUESTION—In what way did God exalt Christ?

The exaltation is to his kingly throne and office [Alf, ICC, TNTC, WC] at God's right hand [My, TNTC] with the highest possible honor [GNC, ICC, Lg, MNTC, NIC, NTC, TH, TNTC] and authority [WBC], to the position which was always rightfully his but which he could only possess after his earthly ministry and humiliation [TNTC], to the position of Son of Man with the full divine power which he had before [El], to the position of mediator between God and men [Ea], to equality with God the Father [Bg, TNTC], to his being raised from the dead, ascending to heaven, and being glorified there with all he had previous to his incarnation plus much more [EBC]. This must be an exaltation of Christ's human nature from his condition of humiliation [Blm, HNTC, Ln, My(D), TH, WC], since only his human nature could suffer the humiliation [Ln] and since as God he could not actually be further exalted [Blm]; his deity has not changed [WC].

QUESTION— What was the name God gave him?

1. It is 'Lord' [Blm, EBC, EGT, GNC, HNTC, Lt, MNTC, NIC, Pl, TH, TNTC, WBC]. Christ already had the name 'Jesus' during his incarnation [EBC]. It is equal to God, the highest possible title and authority [EBC, EGT, GNC, HNTC, MNTC, NIC, TNTC, WBC], the equivalent of Yahweh [GNC, Mou, Pl]. It involves not merely a title but also full authority [HNTC, WBC].

2. The name is 'Jesus', which God has made to be the most exalted and glorious of all names [Alf, El, My(D), WEC] with full divine power and lordship combined [El, My(D)].

3. It is 'Jesus Christ', combining the human and the Messianic names [ICC].

4. It is 'Jesus Christ the Lord' with the full implications of each of the components [WC].

5. It does not refer to a specific name but to rank and dignity [Lt].

QUESTION—What relationship is indicated by the second καί 'and'?

1. It joins the two things which God did for Jesus [ICC, WBC; KJV, NASB, NJB]: God exalted him, and he gave him the name. The second phrase is parallel to the first phrase and indicates the extent of the exaltation [WBC].

2. It introduces the explanation of the exaltation [Bg, Ea, GNC, Lg, WEC]: He exalted him, that is, he gave him the name; or, he exalted him by giving him the name.

2:10

in-order-that[a] at/in[b] the name of-Jesus every knee[c] of-(beings)-in-heaven[d] and (beings)-on-earth[e] and (beings)-under-the-earth[f] should-bow[g]

LEXICON—a. ἵνα (GEL 89.59) (BAGD I.2. p. 377): 'in order that' [WBC], 'so that' [GEL, Mou, Pl, WEC; NAB, NJB, NRSV, TNT], 'that' [Ea, HNTC, ICC, Ln, NTC; KJV, NASB, NIV, REB], 'and so' [TEV]. It has the sense of purpose [BAGD].

b. ἐν with dative object (GEL 67.33; 89.5): 'at' [all translations except TEV], 'in' [Ea, HNTC, ICC, Ln, Mou, NTC, Pl], 'in honor of' [TEV], 'before' WBC, WEC]. This prepositional phrase is emphatic by forefronting, as the basis of what follows [Alf, Lg, My].

c. γόνυ (GEL 8.47; 9.16) (BAGD p. 165): 'knee' [BAGD, Ea, GEL, HNTC, ICC, Ln, Mou, NTC, Pl, WBC; all translations except TNT], 'person' [GEL], 'everyone' [TNT], not explicit

[WEC]. 'Bow the knee' is put for worship as a whole [Bg]; it implies the act of adoration [Lg, My].

d. ἐπουράνιος (GEL 1.12) (BAGD 2.b. p. 306): 'beings in heaven' [ICC, Pl; TEV], 'beings in the heavens' [NJB], 'dwellers in heaven' [GEL, HNTC], 'such as are in heaven' [Ln], 'things in heaven [KJV], 'those in heaven' [NTC], 'those who are in heaven' [NASB], 'everyone in heaven' [TNT], 'in heaven' [GEL; NIV NRSV, REB,], 'in the heavens' [NAB], 'heavenly beings' [BAGD, WBC], 'beings heavenly [Ea], 'in the sky' [GEL], 'celestial' [GEL], 'things celestial' [Mou]. The phrase πᾶν γόνυ ἐπουρανίων καὶ ἐπιγείων καὶ καταχθονίων 'every knee of heavenly beings/things and beings/things upon earth and beings/things under the earth' is translated 'the whole universe' [WEC].

e. ἐπίγειος (GEL 1.41) (BAGD 2.b. p. 290): 'beings on earth' [GEL, Pl; NJB, TEV], 'dwellers on earth' [HNTC], 'such as are on earth' [Ln], 'beings in earth' [ICC], 'earthly beings' [WBC], 'beings earthly' [Ea], 'things in earth' [KJV], 'things terrestrial' [Mou], 'those on earth' [NTC], 'those who are on earth' [NASB], 'everyone on earth' [TNT], 'on earth' [NIV, NRSV, REB], 'on the earth' [NAB].

f. καταχθόνιος (GEL 1.17) (BAGD p. 420): 'beings under the earth' [BAGD, Ea, Pl, WBC], 'those under the earth' [GEL, NTC], 'those who are under the earth' [NASB], 'such as are under the earth' [Ln], 'things under the earth' [KJV], 'things subterranean' [Mou], 'everyone under the earth' [TNT], 'under the earth' [NAB, NIV, NRSV], 'in the depths' [REB], 'beings in the underworld' [NJB], 'dwellers in the underworld' [HNTC], 'beings in the world below' [TEV], 'beings in Hades' [ICC].

g. aorist act. subj. of κάμπτω (GEL 53.61) (BAGD 2. p. 402): 'to bow' [Ea, GEL, HNTC, ICC, Ln, Mou, Pl, WBC; KJV, NASB, NIV, REB], 'to bend' [NRSV], 'to worship' [GEL], 'to bow in adoration' [WEC], 'to bow in worship' [TNT], 'to bend' [BAGD, NTC; NAB, NJB], 'to fall on (one's knees)' [TEV]. Bowing the knee is a symbol of religious devotion [GEL], adoration [Blm, El, ICC, Lg, MNTC, My, NIC, Pl], worship [Bg, El, TNTC], homage [Ea, Lt, NTC, TNTC], reverence [Lt], submission [Ea]. It is an act that recognizes Christ's sovereignty [EBC].

QUESTION—What relationship is indicated by ἵνα 'in order that'?

It introduces the purpose of Christ's exaltation [Alf, EBC, El, ICC, Lg, Ln, MNTC, My, NTC, TH, WBC]: God exalted Christ in order that every knee should bow to Christ.

QUESTION—How are the two nouns related in the genitive construction τῷ ὀνόματι Ἰησοῦ 'the name of Jesus'?

    1. It means the name which has been given to Jesus by God in his exaltation [Blm, EBC, Ln, Lt, MNTC, Mou, My, Pl, NTC, TNTC, WBC]: the name which God gave to Jesus. (See 1:9 for the identification of this name.)

    2. It means the name 'Jesus' [Ea, WC, WEC].

    3. It means Jesus himself [NIC, TH]: in honor of Jesus.

QUESTION—What relationship is indicated by ἐν 'in' in the phrase 'in the name of Jesus'?

    1. It indicates the time when they bow [all translations except TEV]: at the mention of the name of Jesus every knee will bow, or, when the name of Jesus is proclaimed every knee will bow [GEL, p. 6, fn 6].

    2. It states the basis for the worship and confession concerning Jesus which follows [Alf, Blm, Ea, EGT, GNC, My, Pl, TH, WC, WEC]: on the basis of the name of Jesus every knee will bow and every tongue should confess. The worship is given to him as Lord [EGT]. The worship is given to honor the name of Jesus [GNC, TH; TEV]. They bow in virtue of his dignity [Blm].

    3. It means that Jesus is the recipient of the homage [Lt, WBC]: they pay homage to the name of Jesus. This is also explained as bowing before Jesus [WBC].

    4. It is the sphere or area in which prayer is to be made [El, ICC]: in the name of Jesus.

QUESTION—What is meant by the phrase ἐπουρανίων καὶ ἐπιγείων καὶ καταχθονίων 'of beings/things in heaven and beings/things on earth and beings/things under the earth'?

It is intended to emphasize the fact that all beings/things of every kind in the universe are subject to Jesus [Blm, Ea, EBC, GNC, ICC, Lg, Ln, Lt, Mou, NTC, Pl, TH, WC, WEC]: every created being/thing in the universe is subject to Jesus. Most commentators take these three adjectives to refer to beings, not things [Alf, Bg, Blm, Ea, EBC, GNC, HNTC, ICC, Lg, Ln, My, NIC, NTC, TH, TNTC, WBC; NASB, NJB, TEV, TNT]. Since the words can be neuter, another view is that they refer to the whole universe, including both animate and inanimate objects [Lt, WC, WEC], so that there is a personification of universal nature [Lt]. The following are views as to the identity of the beings *in heaven*: angels [Alf, El, ICC, Lg, My, TH, TNTC, WBC], both angels and glorified human beings [Ea, EBC, Ln, NTC], spirits [EGT, NIC, WEC], ruling spirits [HNTC]. The following are views as to the identity of those *on earth*: human beings living on earth [Alf, Ea, EBC, EGT, El, ICC, Lg, Ln, My, NIC, NTC, TH, TNTC, WBC,

WEC], terrestrial spirits who rule over earth [HNTC]. The
following are views as to the identity of those *under the earth*:
human beings in general who have died [Alf, Blm, EGT, El, GEL,
ICC, Lg, My, NIC, TH, WEC] and are thought to be living in a
dark region underground [GEL], lost souls [Ea, EBC, Ln, NTC],
lost souls and demons [TNTC, WBC], spirits who rule over the
underworld [HNTC]. Those who include impenitent human beings
and the demons among those who will bow say that all will submit
to God, whether in true worship or not [Ea, EBC, GNC, Ln, NIC,
NTC, TNTC]. The angels and redeemed humans will do so joyfully,
but the damned will do so ruefully [NIC]. One other view is that
this verse expresses only a purpose that will not be realized by all
beings [WBC].

QUESTION—How are the noun and the substantivized adjectives
related in the genitive phrase πᾶν γόνυ ἐπουρανίων καὶ ἐπιγείων καὶ
καταχθονίων 'every knee of beings/things in heaven and beings/things
on earth and beings/things under the earth'?

The adjectives are qualitative [Ln]: the knees of all these kinds of
beings/things.

QUESTION—Who is implied as the object of bowing the knee?
1. Jesus is the one to whom the knee is bowed in prayer and
   worship [Alf, Ea, EGT, El, ICC, Lt, MNTC, Mou, My, NIC,
   TH, WBC, WEC]: that every knee should bow in submission to
   Jesus.
2. God the Father is the one to whom the worship is given
   [HNTC]: that every knee should bow in submission to God the
   Father.

2:11
**and every tongue[a] should-confess[b] that Jesus Christ (is) Lord for[c] (the)
glory[d] of-God (the) Father.**

LEXICON—a. γλῶσσα (GEL **9.18**; 8.21) (BAGD 2. p. 162): 'tongue'
[GEL, HNTC, Ln, Mou, NTC, Pl, WBC, WEC; all translations
except TEV, TNT], 'person' [BAGD, **GEL**], 'being' [ICC; TEV].
The phrase πᾶσα γλῶσσα 'every tongue' is translated 'everyone'
[TNT]. 'Every tongue' is a poetic expression meaning 'everyone'
[TH, WBC].

b. aorist mid. subj. of ἐξομολογέομαι (GEL **33.275**) (BAGD 2.b.
p. 277): 'to confess' [GEL, Ln, Mou, NTC, WEC; KJV, NASB,
NIV, NRSV], 'to confess freely' [Pl], 'to acknowledge' [BAGD,
ICC; NJB], 'to acknowledge openly and thankfully' [WBC], 'to
proclaim' [NAB], 'to proclaim openly' [TEV], 'to acclaim'
[HNTC; REB], 'to declare openly' [TNT]. This verb indicates
an open profession of faith [TH, WBC], a public acknowledg-

ment in religious adoration [Blm]. The ἐξ- compound gives added force to the idea of the confession [Ea, El]. This confession will occur at the final judgment [Ln].

c. εἰς with accusative object (GEL 89.57): 'for' [Ln, WEC], 'for the purpose of' [GEL], 'to' [Ea, HNTC, Mou, NTC, WBC; all translations], 'to promote' [Pl], not explicit [ICC].

d. δόξα (GEL 33.357; 87.4) (BAGD 3. p. 204): 'glory' [Ea, HNTC, Ln, Mou, NTC, Pl, WBC, WEC; all translations], 'praise' [BAGD, GEL], 'honor' [BAGD, GEL]. The phrase εἰς δόξαν 'for the glory' is translated 'and glorify' [ICC].

QUESTION—What relationship is indicated by καί 'and'?

1. It introduces the second part of the purpose clause which was introduced by ἵνα 'in order that' (1:10) [EBC, Lg, TH, WBC, WEC]: in order that every knee should bow and every tongue confess. In addition to the silent worship of bowing the knee is added the vocal confession [Lg]. This verse expresses God's purpose, but it does not state whether or not this purpose will be fulfilled [WBC].

2. It introduces the result of every knee bowing (1:10) (reading the future indicative ἐξομολογήσεται 'will confess' instead of the aorist subjunctive ἐξομολογήσηται 'should confess' [Alf]: every knee should bow and as a result every tongue shall confess.

QUESTION—What relationship is implied by the word πᾶσα 'every'?

It implies confession by every moral being [Ln, TNTC, WBC], including Christ's enemies [EBC] and angels and demons [NIC, TNTC]: every person without exception will acknowledge Christ as Lord, willingly or unwillingly. It includes the same three categories as those mentioned in 1:10 and is not limited to rational beings [Lg].

QUESTION—What relationship is indicated by the word ὅτι 'that'?

It introduces the content of the confession [Ea, Lg, MNTC, NTC, TH, WBC]: should confess that Jesus Christ is Lord.

QUESTION—What is meant by κύριος 'Lord'?

The word signifies supremacy as Lord over every person and thing [Blm, Ea, El, Mou, NTC, TH]. This word is the predicate, not the subject [Lg, Ln, My], and is forefronted for emphasis [El, Lg, My, Pl, TH].

QUESTION—What relationship is indicated by εἰς 'for' in the phrase 'for the glory of God the Father'?

1. It indicates the purpose of the confession [Alf, EGT, El, Lg, MNTC, My, NIC, Pl, TH, WC]: everyone should confess that Jesus Christ is Lord for the purpose of bringing glory to God.

2. It indicates the result of the confession [Ea, EBC, NTC]: everyone should confess that Jesus Christ is Lord, with the result that God is glorified.
3. It gives the place where Jesus Christ is located [Bg]: should confess that Jesus Christ is Lord, since he is in the glory of God.

QUESTION—How are the two nouns related in the genitive construction δόξαν θεοῦ 'glory of God'?

God is the recipient of the glory [EBC, Ln, TH, WEC]. When the Son is glorified, the Father is also glorified [ICC, Mou, Pl, NTC]. Having such a Son brings glory to the Father [Blm, El, GNC, WC]. The Son's authority is derived from the Father's authority [TH, TNTC]. The fulfillment of God's purpose brings him glory [EBC].

DISCOURSE UNIT: 2:12–18 [EBC, HNTC, ICC, Lg, Ln, MNTC, Mou, NIC, NTC, Pl, TH, TNTC, WBC, WEC; GNT, NAB, NIV, NJB, TEV]. The topic is an exhortation to work out their salvation [EBC, MNTC; NJB], an exhortation to be and behave as bearers of light [Ln], an exhortation to shine as lights in the world [TH; GNT, TEV], the shining of their spiritual lights will bring joy to them and to Paul [NTC], Paul's farewell exhortation [HNTC], an exhortation to irreprovable behavior [NIC], an exhortation to unity and submission [Pl], God's help from seeking to imitate Christ [Lg], the Lord's power in the life of Christians [Mou], the preceding exhortation applied, and Paul's personal example [TNTC], instructions on obedience [WBC, WEC], the innocence of Christians [NAB], urging imitation of the humility of Christ [NIV].

DISCOURSE UNIT: 2:12–16 [EGT, Lt, WC]. The topic is the necessity of awe and watchfulness as in the presence of God's operation [EGT], following Christ's example [Lt], an exhortation to obedience, spiritual effort, and peace with one another [WC].

DISCOURSE UNIT: 2:12–13 [My(D), NTC, WEC]. The topic is an exhortation to work out their own salvation [NTC], the Christian's responsibility [WEC].

2:12
Therefore,[a] my beloved-(ones),[b] just-as[c] always you-have-obeyed,[d]

LEXICON—a. ὥστε (GEL 89.52) (BAGD 1.b. p. 899): 'therefore' [BAGD, GEL, WEC; NIV, NRSV], 'wherefore' [Ea, ICC; KJV], 'so' [BAGD, GEL, HNTC, Mou; NJB, REB], 'so then' [NTC, Pl; NAB, NASB, TEV], 'and so' [Ln], 'well then' [WBC], not explicit [TNT].

b. ἀγαπητός (GEL 25.45) (BAGD 2. p. 6): 'beloved one' [Mou, Pl], 'beloved' [BAGD, GEL, HNTC, Ln, NTC; KJV, NASB, NRSV], 'dearly beloved' [NAB], 'beloved brethren' [ICC], 'one who is loved' [GEL], 'loved one' [WEC], 'friend' [REB], 'dear friend' [WBC; NIV, NJB, TEV, TNT].

c. καθώς (GEL 64.14): 'just as' [GEL, HNTC, Mou, Pl, WBC; NASB, NRSV], 'even as' [ICC, Ln, NTC], 'as' [Ea; KJV, NAB, NIV, REB, TEV], 'in the same way that' [WEC], not explicit [NJB, TNT].

d. aorist act. indic. of ὑπακούω (GEL 36.15) (BAGD 1. p. 837): 'to obey' [BAGD, Ea, GEL, HNTC, Mou, NTC, WBC; KJV, NASB, NIV, NRSV, TEV, TNT], 'to be obedient' [NJB, REB], 'to show ready obedience' [Pl], 'to show an obedient attitude' [WEC], 'to manifest a spirit of obedience' [ICC]. This verb is also translated as an adjective: 'obedient' [NAB].

QUESTION—What relationship is indicated by ὥστε 'therefore'?

1. It indicates an exhortation based on Christ's example [Alf, Bg, Blm, Ea, EGT, El, GNC, ICC, Lg, Lt, MNTC, My, Pl, TH, TNTC, WBC, WC]: since you have Christ's example, obey me now by working out your own salvation. Since Christ obeyed, they should obey [GNC, TH, TNTC, WBC, WC] and there is an implied step of logic: 'as you have always obeyed, so continue to obey now' [WBC, WC]. Christ's obedience resulted in his exaltation, therefore they should obey for their salvation [EGT, ICC, My, NTC]. They are bound by their Christian profession to follow Christ's example [Ea].

2. It marks the paragraph as being last in the group of admonitions in 1:27–2:18 [Ln, NIC]. It advances the appeal to stand fast [Ln]. Paul returns to exhortation to the church after interrupting with citing the example of Christ [NIC].

QUESTION—Who is the implied object of ὑπηκούσατε 'you have obeyed'?

1. The obedience is to God [Alf, EGT, El, GNC, Lt, Pl]: as you have obeyed God.

2. The obedience is to Paul [Blm, HNTC, NIC, TH, TNTC, WBC; NAB, TEV, TNT]: as you have obeyed me.

3. The obedience is primarily to God and secondarily to Paul [Ea, EBC]: as you have obeyed God, but also me (and your church officials).

4. The obedience is to both Paul and God [Bg, MNTC]: as you have obeyed both me and God.

5. The obedience is to the gospel [Ln, My]: as you have always obeyed the gospel.

6. The reference is to a spirit of obedience, not to the person to be obeyed [ICC]: as you have always shown an obedient spirit in general.

not as[a] in[b] my presence[c] only but[d] now more by much in[b] my absence,[e]

TEXT—Some manuscripts omit ὡς 'as'. GNT includes this word with a B rating, indicating some degree of doubt. Alf, Blm, Ea, EGT, El, GNC, HNTC, ICC, Lg, Ln, Lt, Mou, My, NIC, NTC, WBC, WC, WEC; KJV, and NASB include 'as'. Pl; NAB, NIV, NJB, NRSV, REB, TEV, and TNT omit 'as'. EBC is unclear.

LEXICON—a. ὡς (GEL 64.12; 67.139): 'as' [GEL, HNTC, Ln, Mou, NTC; KJV, NASB], 'while' [GEL], 'in light of' [WBC], not explicit [Ea, Pl, WEC; NAB, NIV, NJB, NRSV, REB, TEV, TNT]. The phrase ὡς ἐν τῇ παρουσίᾳ μου is translated 'as though I were present' [ICC].

b. ἐν with dative object (GEL 67.136) (BAGD II.2. p. 260): 'in' [Ea, HNTC, Ln, Mou, NTC, WBC(2nd occurrence); KJV, NASB, NIV, NRSV], 'during' [GEL, Pl, WEC(2nd occurrence)], not explicit [WBC(1st occurrence)]. The phrase ἐν τῇ παρουσίᾳ μου 'in my presence' is translated 'when I am present' [WEC; NJB], 'when I was with you' [REB, TEV], 'when I have been with you' [TNT], 'when I happen to be with you' [NAB].

c. παρουσία (GEL 85.25) (BAGD 1. p. 629): 'presence' [BAGD, Ea, GEL, HNTC, Ln, Mou, NTC, Pl; KJV, NASB, NIV, NRSV], 'coming' [WBC].

d. ἀλλά (GEL 89.125): 'but' [Ea, GEL, HNTC, ICC, Ln, Mou, NTC, WBC, WEC; KJV, NAB, NASB, NIV, NRSV], 'on the contrary' [Pl], not explicit [NJB, REB, TEV, TNT]. It is the strong contrast, 'on the contrary' [My].

e. ἀπουσία (GEL 85.28) (BAGD p. 101): 'absence' [BAGD, Ea, GEL, HNTC, ICC, Ln, Mou, NTC, Pl, WBC, WEC; KJV, NASB, NIV, NRSV]. The phrase νῦν ἐν τῇ ἀπουσίᾳ μου 'now in my absence' is translated 'now that I am absent' [NAB, NJB, REB], 'now I am away from you' [TNT], 'now while I am away from you' [TEV].

QUESTION—What is this entire phrase connected with?

1. It is connected with the following verb κατεργάζεσθε 'work out' [Alf, Blm, Ea, EBC, El, GNC, HNTC, ICC, Lg, Lt, MNTC, Mou, My, NIC, NTC, Pl, WBC, WC, WEC; NAB]: work out your own salvation, not only as when I was with you but now while I am absent. The negative μή 'not' requires the connection with the imperative κατεργάζεσθε 'work out' and not with the indicative ὑπηκούσατε 'you have obeyed' [Alf, EBC, HNTC, ICC, Lg, Mou, My, NTC, WBC]. Moreover, it is doubtful that they had been more obedient in Paul's absence than when he

was with them [Blm, ICC]. This entire phrase is emphatic by forefronting, since it is the real basis for Paul's following exhortation [My(D)].

2. It is connected with the verb ὑπηκούσατε 'you have obeyed [Ln; NIV, NJB, REB, TEV, TNT]: just as you have obeyed, not only as when I was with you but now while I am absent.

QUESTION—What is meant by ὡς 'as' in the phrase 'as in my presence'?

1. The meaning implied is 'not as if it were something to be done only when I am with you' [Alf, El, ICC, Lg, Lt, My, NIC, NTC, WEC] or prompted only by Paul's presence [GNC]. It cautions against behavior based on Paul's presence rather than on heart motivation [Ea, El, ICC, Lg, NTC].

2. 'As' modifies both phrases, 'in my presence' and 'in my absence' and has no negative connotation [Ln]: you have obeyed as in my presence and as in my absence.

3. This word here means 'in view of' [WBC]: work out your salvation, not only in light of my anticipated coming to you again, but even more in my absence from you.

QUESTION—What is meant by παρουσία 'presence'?

1. It refers to Paul's previous presence with them [Alf, Blm, Ea, El, EBC, GNC, ICC, Lg, Ln, Lt, Mou, My, NIC, NTC, Pl, TNTC, WC, WEC]: when I was with you previously.

2. It refers to Paul's possible future return to be with them [WBC]: when I come to be with you in the future.

3. It refers to Paul's presence with them in general during his lifetime [HNTC, MNTC]: at any time when I am with you.

QUESTION—What is meant by πολλῷ μᾶλλον 'more by much, much more'?

It means that they should endeavor more earnestly while he was absent from them [Alf, Blm, Ea, EBC, El, My, NIC, NTC, TH, WBC, WEC], because his absence places the responsibility more directly upon them [Ea, Lg, Lt, MNTC, Mou, My, NTC], because their renewal was so important [WBC].

QUESTION—What is meant by ἀπουσία 'absence'?

1. The reference is to Paul's absence from them as he was writing [Alf, Blm, Ea, EBC, El, GNC, ICC, Lg, Ln, Lt, Mou, My, NIC, NTC, TH, TNTC, WBC, WC, WEC]: now that I am absent from you.

2. It refers to his death [HNTC, MNTC]: when I have died and thus am no longer with you.

with[a] fear[b] and trembling[c] work-out[d] the of-yourselves[e] salvation;[f]

LEXICON—a. μετά with genitive object (GEL 89.79) (BAGD A.III.1. p. 509): 'with' [BAGD, Ea, GEL, HNTC, ICC, Ln, Mou, NTC,

Pl, WEC; all translations except NJB, REB], 'in' [NJB, REB].
The phrase μετὰ φόβου καὶ τρόμου 'with fear and trembling' is
translated 'obediently' [WBC].
b. φόβος (GEL 25.251) (BAGD 2.b.α. p. 863): 'fear' [Ea, GEL,
HNTC, Ln, Mou, NTC; all translations except NAB], 'godly
fear' [Pl], 'reverence' [BAGD], 'respect' [BAGD], 'conscientious
caution' [ICC]. The phrase φόβου καὶ τρόμου 'fear and
trembling' is translated 'anxious concern' [NAB], 'all godly fear'
[WEC].
c. τρόμος (GEL 16.6) (BAGD p. 827): 'trembling' [BAGD, Ea,
GEL, HNTC, Ln, Mou, NTC; all translations except NAB],
'trembling anxiety' [Pl], 'self-distrust' [ICC].
d. pres. mid. (deponent = act.) impera. of κατεργάζομαι (GEL
13.9; 42.17) (BAGD 2. p. 421): 'to work out' [BAGD, HNTC,
Ln, Mou, NTC, Pl; KJV, NASB, NIV, NJB, NRSV, REB], 'to
work to achieve' [NAB], 'to work at achieving' [WBC], 'to work
to complete' [TEV, TNT], 'to carry out' [Ea, ICC], 'to effect'
[GEL], 'to accomplish' [GEL], 'to bring about' [WEC]. The
κατα- compound is intensive, implying carrying out to
fulfillment [Ea, EBC, EGT, El, MNTC, My, Pl, TH, WBC]. The
present tense indicates continued effort [NTC, WBC]. Their
attitude, humility and obedience, are primary here rather than
moral effort [EGT].
e. ἑαυτοῦ (GEL 92.25): 'of yourself' [GEL, Ln], 'your own' [Ea,
HNTC, ICC, Mou, NTC, WEC; KJV, NRSV, REB], 'your' [Pl;
NAB, NASB, NIV, NJB, TEV, TNT], not explicit [WBC]. This
word is emphatic because it is God's free gift to them [GNC],
or in contrast to what God is doing (1:13) [ICC], or because
Paul is directing attention to their need to obey to accomplish
their own salvation [Blm, EGT, El, GNC, Lg, MNTC, Mou], just
as Christ obeyed and achieved his exaltation [Alf]. It is
emphatic in contrast both with the preceding reference to Paul
and to the following reference to God [Lt]. It is not emphatic
[Ln].
f. σωτηρία (GEL 21.26) (BAGD 2. p. 801): 'salvation' [BAGD,
Ea, GEL, HNTC, ICC, Ln, Mou, NTC, Pl, WEC; all
translations], 'spiritual health' [WBC].
QUESTION—What is meant by the phrase μετὰ φόβου καὶ τρόμου
'with fear and trembling'?
1. It means with true concern for the possibility of failure [Alf, El,
ICC, Lt, My, Pl]: work out your own salvation with fear and
trembling concerning the possibility of failure. It is the
recognition in God's presence that no effort can be too great
[Lg]. The 'fear' is based on realization of the possibility of

failure; the 'trembling' is the concern associated with that possibility [El, ICC]. This phrase is emphatic by forefronting [Ln, My(D), NTC].

2. It indicates reverential devotion to God [GNC, TH, TNTC] and realization of their responsibility to God [EGT, GNC]: work out your own salvation with reverence and devotion to God. It is a common Old Testament expression meaning humble reverence, dependence, and devotion to God [TH].

3. It indicates both reverential fear of God and fear of the possibility of sin [Blm, EBC, Ea, HNTC, Ln, Mou, NIC, WC, WEC]; it is emphatic [HNTC]. This phrase is connected with the verb 'work out' [Blm].

4. It is an idiom for an attitude of obedience to God [WBC].

5. It refers to their behavior toward the other persons of the community [MNTC].

QUESTION—What is meant by ἑαυτῶν 'your own' and what is meant by working out their salvation?

1. The reference is to each individual's responsibility for the carrying out of the salvation which they have already received by faith [Alf, Bg, Blm, Ea, EBC, EGT, El, HNTC, ICC, Ln, My, NIC, NTC, Pl, WC, WEC]: work for the full realization of your salvation in your life. It refers to their spiritual growth and progress [EBC]. Justification is carried on to a life of experiential sanctification [EBC], one of holy obedience [Alf]. They must apply their salvation to daily life [NTC]. Salvation includes the manifestation of righteousness which is lived out by personal activity [WEC].

2. They are to work out their salvation as a community, not individually, and this refers to restoring spiritual health to the community [GNC, MNTC, TH, TNTC, WBC]: each of you work together to restore full spiritual health to your community. Each of them and all of them together must pay attention to the health and well-being of the congregation as a whole [GNC]. Their community is threatened with disruption [MNTC].

2:13

for[a] God is the-(one) working[b] in/among[c] you both the willing/to-will[d] and the working/to-work[e] concerning[f] the good-pleasure.[g]

TEXT—Some manuscripts add the article ὁ before θεός 'God' at the beginning of this verse. This variant is not dealt with by GNT; the article is included only by Bg, Blm. Without the article, θεός 'God' would normally be the predicate; with the article it could be either subject or predicate.

LEXICON—a. γάρ (GEL 89.23): 'for' [Ea, GEL, HNTC, Ln, Mou, NTC, Pl, WBC; KJV, NASB, NIV, NRSV, REB, TNT], 'because' [GEL, ICC, WEC; TEV], not explicit [NAB, NJB].

b. pres. act. participle of ἐνεργέω (GEL 13.9) (BAGD 2. p. 265): 'to work' [Ea, Ln, NTC, Pl; KJV, NIV, REB], 'to be at work' [NASB, NRSV, TEV, TNT], 'to work effectively' [WBC], 'to produce' [BAGD, WEC], 'to beget' [NAB], 'to effect' [Mou], 'to act effectively' [HNTC], 'to energize' [ICC], 'to give' NJB]. The phrase ὁ ἐνεργῶν ἐν ὑμῖν 'the one working in you' is translated 'is causing you' [GEL]. The phrase ὁ ἐνεργῶν ἐν ὑμῖν καὶ τὸ θέλειν καὶ τὸ ἐνεργεῖν 'the one working in you both the willing and the working' is translated 'energizes your will and stimulates you to work' [ICC]. This word refers to effective working [EBC, EGT, ICC, Lt, MNTC, TH, TNTC, WBC]. The present tense implies continuous working [TH].

c. ἐν with dative object (GEL 83.13) (BAGD I.5.a. p. 259): 'in' [BAGD, Ea, GEL, Ln, Mou, NTC, Pl, WEC; all translations except NJB], 'among' [HNTC, WBC], not explicit [ICC; NJB].

d. pres. act. infin. of θέλω (GEL 25.1; 30.58) (BAGD 2. p. 355): 'to will' [BAGD, Ea, HNTC, NTC; KJV, NASB, NIV, NRSV], 'to be willing' [GEL(13.9), TEV], 'to want' [GEL; TNT], 'to desire' [GEL], 'to purpose' [GEL]. The infinitive phrase τὸ θέλειν 'the willing' is translated 'the willing' [Ln], 'your willing' [Mou]. This infinitive is also translated as a noun: 'the will' [BAGD, Pl, WEC; REB], 'the intention' [NJB], 'the desire' [WBC]. The phrase καὶ τὸ θέλειν καὶ τὸ ἐνεργεῖν 'both the willing and the working' is translated 'any measure of desire or achievement' [NAB]. This verb implies determination [EGT, ICC, Lg] or specific purpose [ICC]. The use of the articular infinitive rather than the noun focuses on the aspect of active energy [ICC].

e. pres. act. infin. of ἐνεργέω (GEL 42.3) (BAGD 1.a. p. 265): 'to work' [Ea, GEL, NTC; NASB, NRSV, TNT], 'to do' [KJV], 'to act' [NIV], 'to act effectively' [HNTC], 'to make (one) able' [TEV]. The infinitive phrase τὸ ἐνεργεῖν 'the working' is translated 'the working' [Ln, WEC], 'your effecting' [Mou]. This infinitive is also translated as a noun: 'the action' [BAGD], 'the power' [Pl], 'the powers to act' [NJB], 'the drive' [WBC], 'the deed' [REB]. This word focuses on ability rather than on results [Ea, El], on the personal exertion [EGT, Lg], on effective working [Lt]. The use of the articular infinitive rather than the noun focuses on the aspect of active energy [ICC].

f. ὑπέρ with genitive object (GEL 90.24) (BAGD 1.e. p. 839): 'concerning' [GEL], 'in behalf of' [Ln], 'for' [NTC; NASB, NJB,

NRSV, REB], 'for the accomplishment of' [HNTC], 'for the sake of' [Mou, WEC], 'in fulfillment of' [Pl], 'according to' [NIV], 'in consequence of' [Ea], 'of' [KJV], 'in' [NAB], 'to promote' [WBC], not explicit [ICC; TEV, TNT].

g. εὐδοκία (GEL **25.88**) (BAGD 1. p. 319): 'good pleasure' [Ea, ICC, Ln, Mou, NTC; KJV, NASB, NRSV], 'good will' [BAGD, WBC; NAB], 'gracious will' [HNTC, WEC], 'good purpose' [NIV], 'generous purpose' [NJB], 'chosen purpose' [REB], 'benevolent purpose' [Pl], 'purpose' [TEV], 'what pleases' [GEL], 'things which please' [TNT].

QUESTION—What relationship is indicated by γάρ 'for'?

1. It gives encouragement that they can fulfill what is urged in 2:12 [Alf, Blm, Ea, EBC, El, GNC, HNTC, ICC, Ln, Lt, MNTC, My, NIC, NTC, Pl, WBC, WC, WEC]: you can do this, for God is helping you. It implies that they can do it since God will enable them [EBC, Ln, Lt, My, NTC, WBC, WC, WEC]. They are not left alone because God will work in them [Alf]. They have better help than Paul's help, since God is working in them [Pl].

2. It emphasizes the fact that in their salvation they are dealing with God, not with Paul, and it emphasizes the necessity of working 'with fear and trembling', since to fail means to reject God's purpose for them [EGT, Lg, MNTC]: do this, for it is God with whom you are dealing.

QUESTION—What is implied by the absence of the article with θεός 'God'?

It focuses on God as deity rather than upon him as a person [Ea]; 'God' is forefronted for emphasis [Ea, EGT, ICC, Pl, TH, WC, WEC]: deity, divine grace, is at work in you. 'God' is the subject as the agent [My, TH]. Greek grammar would normally make ὁ ἐνεργῶν 'the one working' (with the article) the subject and θεός 'God' (without the article) the predicate, but only WBC and WEC imply this: the one who is working in you is God.

QUESTION—What is the meaning of ἐν 'in/among'?

1. The meaning is in each individual [Alf, Ea, El, ICC, Lg, Mou, My, NIC].

2. It has the corporate meaning, 'among' [HNTC, TH, TNTC, WBC].

3. It means both individually and collectively [GNC].

QUESTION—What is the significance of the double καί 'both . . . and'?

It gives emphasis to the two verbs [Ea, El, ICC, Lt, My]: both the willing and also the working.

QUESTION—What relationship is indicated by ὑπὲρ 'in behalf of'?
1. It indicates the goal of their willing and working [Alf, GNC, HNTC, Ln, TH, TNTC, WBC; KJV, NASB, NRSV, TEV, TNT]: God is working in you to make you both to will and to work for his good pleasure.
2. It indicates God's purpose for working in them [Alf, ICC, Lg, Lt, Mou, My, NIC, NTC, WC]: God is working in you in order to carry out his good pleasure.
3. It indicates the reason God works in them [Blm, Ea, EGT, Pl, WEC; NAB, NJB, REB]: God is working in you because of his good pleasure to do so.

QUESTION—Whose good pleasure is implied?
The definite article implies the possessive 'his' and relates back to the subject of the clause, God [Alf, Bg, Ea, GNC, ICC, Ln, Mou, WEC]: God's good pleasure, the things which please God.

DISCOURSE UNIT: 2:14–18 [My(D), NTC]. The topic is producing mutual joy [NTC].

DISCOURSE UNIT: 2:14–16 [WEC]. The topic is being blameless.

2:14
Do everything without[a] complaining[b] and arguing,[c]
LEXICON—a. χωρίς with genitive object (GEL 89.120) (BAGD 2.b.β. p. 890): 'without' [BAGD, Ea, GEL, HNTC, ICC, Ln, Mou, NTC, WBC, WEC; all translations except NJB, TNT], 'free of' [NJB], not explicit [Pl]. The phrase πάντα ποιεῖτε χωρίς 'do everything without' is translated 'whatever you do, avoid' [TNT]. This preposition indicates separation; the Philippians must be distant from complaining and arguing [Lg].
b. γογγυσμός (GEL 33.382) (BAGD 1. p. 164): 'complaining' [BAGD; NIV, TEV], 'complaint' [GEL], 'grumbling' [Ln, WBC; NAB, NASB, REB, TNT, WEC], 'murmuring' [Ea, HNTC, ICC, Mou, Pl; KJV, NJB, NRSV], 'muttering' [NTC]. It implies moral rebellion against God [Lt]. It refers to an unwilling spirit [Lg]. It refers to a spirit of insubordination [Blm], dissatisfaction [Ea].
c. διαλογισμός (GEL 33.446) (BAGD 2. p. 186): 'arguing' [WBC; NAB, NIV, NRSV, TEV], 'argument' [GEL, HNTC; REB, TNT], 'argumentation' [NTC], 'dispute' [BAGD, Mou], 'disputing' [KJV, NASB], 'quarreling' [WEC], 'complaining' [NJB], 'criticizing' [ICC], 'reasoning' [Ln], 'questioning' [Pl], 'doubt' [Ea]. It implies intellectual rebellion against God [Lt]. It refers to attempts to avoid what one should do by introducing doubts and magnifying difficulties [Blm], unwarranted hesitation

concerning their duty [My], a doubtful spirit [Lg], questioning, not disputing [My(D)].

QUESTION—Why is this clause mentioned?

It continues his appeal for harmony and good will [WBC]. It introduces further details concerning what their conduct should be [Alf, TH], how they should carry out what he has urged them to do [My].

QUESTION—Who is the implied object of the phrase χωρὶς γογγυσμῶν καὶ διαλογισμῶν 'without complaining or arguing'?

1. It refers to complaints against other Christians [Alf, Bg, EGT, MNTC, Pl, TH, TNTC], including their leaders [Blm]: without complaining against fellow-Christians. It refers to secret talk and arguments against fellow-Christians [WBC], open disagreements [Pl].
2. It refers to complaints against God [El, ICC, Lt, My, NIC, WC]: without complaints against God.
3. It refers to a general attitude [Ea, EBC, Lg]: without an attitude of complaining or arguing. It refers to complaints against both members of the Christian community and God [Ea, EBC].

2:15

in-order-that[a] you-may-become blameless[b] and innocent,[c]

LEXICON—a. ἵνα (GEL 89.59): 'in order that' [Ln, WBC], 'so that' [GEL, Mou; NIV, NJB, NRSV, TEV], 'that' [Ea, HNTC, NTC, Pl; KJV, NASB], 'that so' [ICC], not explicit [WEC; NAB, REB]. This entire phrase is translated 'so that no one will be able to find fault with you or question your sincerity' [TNT].

b. ἄμεμπτος (GEL 88.317) (BAGD p. 45): 'blameless' [BAGD, Ea, GEL, ICC, Ln, NTC, Pl, WBC, WEC; KJV, NASB, NIV, NRSV], 'unblamable' [Mou], 'faultless' [BAGD; NJB], 'irreproachable' [HNTC], 'innocent' [GEL; NAB, REB, TEV], 'guiltless' [GEL]. This word means that no blame can be charged against them by other persons [Alf, Ea, EBC, EGT, Ln, MNTC, NIC, NTC, TNTC, WBC, WC]. It refers to the outward evidence of integrity [El, Lg, My].

c. ἀκέραιος (GEL 88.32) (BAGD p. 30): 'innocent' [BAGD, Pl; NASB, NRSV], 'untainted' [GEL], 'pure' [BAGD, Ea, GEL, HNTC, WEC; NIV, NJB, TEV], 'unmixed' [Ln], 'flawless' [WBC], 'simple' [Mou], 'harmless' [KJV], 'guileless' [ICC, NTC], 'straightforward' [NAB], 'above reproach' [REB]. This word means free from anything improper in their heart [Alf, Ea, EBC, EGT, El, Lg, Ln, MNTC, My, NIC, NTC], blameless in

God's estimation [WC]. This and the previous adjective cannot be sharply distinguished from one another [WEC].

QUESTION—What relationship is indicated by ἵνα 'in order that'?

It introduces the purpose [Lg, Ln] of what was said in 2:14 [Ea, El, MNTC, My, TH, TNTC, WBC], or of working out their salvation [EBC]: do those things in order that you may become blameless.

children of-God without-blemish[a] in-the-midst-of[b] a-generation[c] crooked[d] and perverted,[e]

LEXICON—a. ἄμωμος (GEL **88.34**) (BAGD 2.a. p. 48): 'without blemish' [NTC, Pl; NRSV], 'unblemished' [Ln], 'blameless' [BAGD, Ea, HNTC, Mou], 'without fault' [NIV], 'faultless' [GEL, WBC; REB], 'beyond reproach' [NAB], 'above reproach' [NASB], 'without reproach' [WEC], 'without rebuke' [KJV], 'unspoilt' [NJB], 'perfect' [TEV, TNT], 'true' [ICC]. It means free from evident flaws [EBC, My]. This word is connected with the preceding phrase, τέκνα θεοῦ 'children of God', not with the phrase which follows [El, ICC, Lg, MNTC, My, NTC, TH, TNTC, WBC].

b. μέσον with genitive object (GEL 83.9) (BAGD 3.b. p. 508): 'in the midst of' [BAGD, Ea, HNTC, ICC, Mou, NTC, Pl, WEC; KJV, NAB, NASB, NRSV, TNT], 'amid' [Ln], 'in' [NIV, REB, TEV], 'among' [GEL], 'surrounded by' [WBC; NJB]. This word is an adverb functioning as a preposition [EGT, ICC, Lg].

c. γενεά (GEL 11.4) (BAGD 2. p. 154): 'generation' [BAGD, Ea, GEL, Ln, NTC, Pl; NAB, NASB, NIV, REB, NRSV, TNT], 'contemporaries' [BAGD], 'those of the same time' [GEL], 'people' [WBC, WEC; TEV], 'society' [HNTC, ICC], 'race' [Mou], 'brood' [NJB], 'nation' [KJV]. Some commentators think that the reference is to people then living [Ea, ICC, TH, WBC, WEC]. Others think it refers to the successive sinful generations of mankind [Ln] as the moral offspring of Satan [EBC].

d. σκολιός (GEL 88.268) (BAGD 2. p. 756): 'crooked' [BAGD, Ea, GEL, HNTC, Ln, Mou, NTC, Pl, WBC, WEC; KJV, NASB, NIV, NRSV, REB, TNT], 'twisted' [NAB], 'unscrupulous' [BAGD, GEL], 'dishonest' [BAGD, GEL], 'deceitful' [NJB], 'corrupt' [TEV]. The phrase σκολιᾶς καὶ ἀκέραιοι 'crooked and perverted' is translated 'ungodly' [ICC]. This word refers to the wicked inner disposition [Ea, El], to the outward evil behavior [Lg].

e. perf. pass. participle of διαστρέφω (GEL 88.264) (BAGD 1.b. p. 189): 'to be perverted' [BAGD, GEL; TNT], 'to be distorted' [Ln, Mou], 'to be depraved' [BAGD; NAB, NIV, REB]. This participle is also translated as an adjective 'perverse' [Ea, HNTC, NTC, Pl, WBC, WEC; KJV, NASB, NRSV], 'underhand' [NJB], 'sinful' [TEV]. This word refers to the outward demonstration of the inner attitude [Ea], their inner distorted spiritual development [El, Lg], an improper moral condition [ICC].

QUESTION—What is this phrase connected with?

It further specifies what they may become [Ea, Ln]: in order that you may become children of God without blemish. It is in apposition with the preceding clause [Ln]. They were already children of God, but the purpose was that they should become blameless children of God [Ea, EBC, Lg].

among[a] whom you-shine[b] like[c] stars[d] in[e] (the) world,[f]

LEXICON—a. ἐν with dative object (GEL 83.9): 'among' [Ea, GEL, HNTC, Ln, Mou, NTC, WBC, WEC; all translations except NIV, NRSV, REB], 'amongst' [Pl], 'in' [ICC; NIV, NRSV, REB].

  b. pres. mid. indic. of φαίνω (GEL 14.37) (BAGD 2.a. p. 851): 'to shine' [BAGD, GEL, HNTC, Ln, NTC, WBC, WEC; all translations except NASB], 'to appear' [Ea, ICC, Mou, Pl; NASB]. The middle voice means 'to shine,' like the active voice [GNC, MNTC, WBC, WEC]; it means 'to appear' [El, Lg(H), Lt, Mou, My, NIC, Pl, TNTC]; it means 'to shine as regards yourselves' [Ln]; it means both 'to appear' and 'to shine' [EGT]. The reference is to Christians in general, not merely to the Philippians [Blm].

  c. ὡς (GEL 64.12): 'like' [GEL, HNTC, WBC, WEC; NAB, NIV, NJB, NRSV, REB, TEV, TNT], 'as' [Ea, GEL, ICC, Ln, Mou, NTC, Pl; KJV, NASB].

  d. φωστήρ (GEL 1.27) (BAGD 1. p. 872): 'star' [BAGD, GEL, HNTC, NTC, WEC; NAB, NIV, NRSV, REB, TEV, TNT], 'bright star' [NJB], 'luminary' [Ea, ICC, Ln, Mou, Pl], 'light' [WBC; KJV, NASB]. The sense is heavenly bodies [Alf, Blm, Ea, EBC, Lt, My, NIC, TH, WBC]; they are givers of light like the heavenly bodies [My, NIC]. It means a light-bearer, such as a torch [TNTC]. It means 'luminaries,' not 'light-bringers' [Ln].

  e. ἐν with dative object (GEL 83.13): 'in' [Ea, GEL, HNTC, ICC, Ln, Mou, NTC, Pl, WBC, WEC; all translations except TEV], not explicit [TEV].

  f. κόσμος (GEL 1.39; 9.23) (BAGD 2. p. 446): 'world' [Ea, GEL, HNTC, Ln, Mou, Pl, WEC; KJV, NASB, NJB, NRSV, TNT], 'dark world' [ICC; REB], 'earth' [GEL], 'universe' [BAGD, GEL, NTC; NIV], 'sky' [GEL(1.27), WBC; NAB, TEV]. It refers to the entire universe [EGT], the sky [GEL, WBC,; NAB, TEV], the physical world [My], human society [Bg, Mou], society antagonistic to God [HNTC, Lg, Ln, Lt, TNTC], the gentile world in general [WEC].

QUESTION—What is the phrase ἐν οἷς 'among whom' connected with?

Even though οἷς 'whom' is plural, it refers back to the collective noun γενεᾶς 'generation' by a construction to the sense rather than strict agreement in number [Alf, Ea, EGT, El, ICC, Lg, Ln, My]: a generation of people, among whom you shine.

QUESTION—What is the mood of the verb φαίνεσθε 'you shine'?

1. It is indicative [Alf, Bg, Blm, Ea, EBC, El, GNC, ICC, Lg, Ln, Mou, My, NIC, NTC, Pl, WEC; all translations except NJB, TEV]: you shine. They are reminded that they already shine and the challenge is to let their light be unhindered [EBC].

2. It is imperative [HNTC, TH, WBC; TEV]: you must shine.

QUESTION—What is the phrase ἐν κόσμῳ 'in the world' connected with?

1. It is connected with φωστῆρες 'stars' [Ea, EBC, El, HNTC, ICC, Lg, My, NTC, TH, WBC; NAB, NIV, TEV].

1.1 It means to give light to the world [Blm, Ea, EBC, El, GNC, HNTC, ICC, Lg, NTC, TH; TEV]: luminaries to give light to the world.

1.2 It means 'like stars in the sky' [TH, WBC; NAB].

2. It is connected with φαίνεσθε 'you shine' [Lt, My(D); TNT]: you shine in the world as stars.

2:16

holding-forth/fast[a] (the) word[b] of-life,[c] for/for-the-purpose-of[d] a-boasting[e] for-me on[f] (the) day[g] of-Christ,

LEXICON—a. pres. act. participle of ἐπέχω (GEL 31.47) (BAGD 1. p. 285): 'to hold forth' [Ea, ICC, NTC; KJV], 'to hold out' [Mou, Pl; NIV], 'to offer' [TEV, TNT], 'to proffer' [HNTC; NJB, REB], 'to hold fast' [BAGD, WEC; NASB, NRSV], 'to hold fast to' [NAB], 'to hold firm to' [WBC], 'to hold to' [GEL], 'to hold' [Ln], 'to continue to believe' [GEL].

b. λόγος (GEL 33.260) (BAGD 1.b.β. p. 478): 'word' [Ea, HNTC, Ln, Mou, NTC, WBC, WEC; all translations except TEV, TNT], 'message' [TEV, TNT], 'gospel' [GEL, Pl]. The phrase λόγον ζωῆς 'word of life' is translated 'gospel' [ICC].

c. ζωή (GEL 23.88) (BAGD 2.b.α. p. 340): 'life' [BAGD, Ea, GEL, HNTC, Ln, Mou, NTC, WEC; all translations], 'life-giving power' [Pl]. This noun is translated as an adjective 'life-giving' [WBC]. It is the eternal life which comes through faith in Christ, salvation [ICC, My, WC].

d. εἰς with accusative object (GEL 89.57; 89.48): 'for' [Ea, Ln], not explicit [NTC]. The phrase εἰς καύχημα ἐμοί 'for the purpose of a boasting for me' is translated 'in order that I may boast' [NIV], 'that I may be able to boast' [Pl], 'that I can boast' [NRSV], 'that I may rejoice' [KJV], 'so that I may have cause to glory' [NASB], 'so that I may have good reason to exult' [WBC], 'if you do so, I shall have reason to be proud of you' [TEV], 'you give me cause to boast' [NAB], 'so I shall be able to boast' [TNT], 'as a result, I will have reason to glory' [WEC], 'then I shall have reason to be proud' [NJB], 'thus I shall have good reason to boast' [ICC], 'then you will be my pride' [REB], 'that you may be my pride' [HNTC]. The sense is the (anticipated) result (the purpose [WBC]) of their good behavior [Alf, Blm, Ea, El, My].

e. καύχημα (GEL 25.203; 33.368; 33.371; 33.372) (BAGD 1. p. 426): 'a boasting' [GEL], 'a cause of boasting' [Ln], 'rejoicing' [Ea], 'exultation' [Mou], 'reason to be proud' [GEL], 'reason to glory' [WEC], 'something to be proud of' [NTC], 'what one boasts about' [GEL], 'the right to boast' [GEL], 'pride' [BAGD]. The meaning is the grounds for Paul's boasting [EBC, GNC], a proper pride produced by the Philippians' obedience to God [WBC, WC].

f. εἰς with accusative object (GEL 67.160) (BAGD 2.a.β. p. 228): 'on' [GEL, Pl; NIV, NJB, NRSV, REB, TEV, TNT], 'at' [GEL, WEC], 'in' [WBC; KJV, NASB], 'for' [BAGD, GEL, Ln], 'against' [Ea, HNTC], 'as I look to' [NAB], 'in view of' [Mou], 'with a view to' [NTC]. The phrase εἰς ἡμέραν Χριστοῦ 'on the day of Christ' is translated 'when Christ shall appear' [ICC]. The sense is boasting reserved for the day of Christ [Alf, Ea, El, ICC, Ln, MNTC, Mou, NIC, NTC, Pl, TH, WBC], although his boasting may begin now [WC].

g. ἡμέρα (GEL 67.178) (BAGD 3.b.β. p. 347): 'day' [BAGD, Ea, GEL, HNTC, Ln, Mou, NTC, Pl, WBC, WEC; all translations].

QUESTION—What is meant by ἐπέχοντες 'holding forth/fast'?

1. It means to hold the gospel forth to other people [Alf, Blm, Ea, EBC, El, GNC, ICC, Lg, Lt, Mou, My(D), NIC, NTC, TH; KJV, NJB, REB, TEV, TNT]: holding forth the gospel to help others to understand it.

2. It means to hold fast to the gospel [EGT, TNTC, WBC, WC, WEC; NAB, NASB, NRSV] to avoid yielding to the sinful world [Bg, MNTC]: holding fast to the word of life.

3. It means to possess the gospel [Ln, My]: having the word of life.

QUESTION—What relationship is indicated by the participial form ἐπέχοντες 'holding forth/fast'?

1. It is temporal [TH; NAB, NIV, TEV, TNT]: you shine as stars while you hold forth/fast the word of life.
2. It expresses the means by which they shine [Ea, Lg, WEC]: you shine by holding fast/forth the word of life.
3. It indicates the grounds for saying that they shine (2:15) [El, Ln, My]: you shine, because you are holding forth/fast the word of life.
4. It is in addition to φαίνεσθε 'you shine' in 2:15.
4.1 It is indicative like φαίνεσθε [REB]: you shine and you hold forth the word of life.
4.2 It is imperative like φαίνεσθε [WBC]: shine; hold fast to the word of life. There is a break at this verse and Paul now shifts his basis of appeal from the example of Jesus to himself and asks them to do something for his sake [WBC].
4.3 It is imperative, although φαίνεσθε 'you shine' is indicative [MNTC]: you shine; hold fast to the word of life. There is a slight break at this verse and here Paul sums up all his injunctions of 2:15 [MNTC].

QUESTION—How are the two nouns related in the genitive construction λόγον ζωῆς 'word of life'?

This phrase refers to the gospel [EGT, El, ICC, Mou, My, NTC, Pl, TH, TNTC, WC]. It is emphatic by forefronting [WBC].

1. It means the word which gives life [EBC, Ln, TH, TNTC, WBC, WC]: the word which gives life. It brings life to those who receive it by faith [EBC].
2. It means the word which is about and reveals life [Ea, El, GNC]: the word which reveals the blessing of life.
3. The word contains life and gives life [ICC, Pl]: the word which contains life and gives life. It is the genitive of contents [ICC].

QUESTION—What relationship is indicated by εἰς 'for, for the purpose of'?

1. It indicates purpose [Bg, Ea, EGT, HNTC, Lg, Ln, MNTC, Mou, Pl; KJV, NIV, NRSV]: in order that I may boast. It indicates the purpose of holding forth/fast the word of life [Bg, HNTC, MNTC].
2. It indicates result [Alf, Blm, Ea, EBC, El, ICC, My, NIC, NTC, TH, WBC, WEC; NJB, REB, TEV]: as a result I will boast. It is connected with everything from the beginning of 2:15 [ICC].
2.1 It indicates the result of obeying the injunctions in 2:14–15 [Alf, Blm, Ea, EBC, El, ICC, WEC]. Their success in working out their salvation and proclaiming the gospel will be a cause of boasting for Paul [ICC].

2.2 It indicates the result of holding forth/fast the word of life [NIC, NTC, TH, WBC].

QUESTION—How are the two nouns related in the genitive construction ἡμέραν Χριστοῦ 'day of Christ'?

The reference is to the day when Christ will return to earth [EBC, MNTC, TH, TNTC]: the day when Christ returns.

that/because[a] not in[b] vain[c] I-have-run[d] nor in[b] vain[c] I-have-toiled.[e]

LEXICON—a. ὅτι (GEL 90.21): 'that' [Ea, GEL, HNTC, ICC, Ln, NTC, Pl, WBC, WEC; KJV, NAB, NIV, NRSV, REB, TNT], 'because' [Mou; NASB], 'for' [NJB]. This entire clause is translated 'because it will show that all my effort and work have not been wasted' [TEV], 'that my labors for you have not been in vain' [ICC].

b. εἰς with accusative object (GEL 78.51) (BAGD 4.e. p. 229): 'in' [Ea, HNTC, ICC, Mou, NTC, Pl, WBC, WEC; KJV, NAB, NASB, NRSV, REB, TNT], 'to the point of' [GEL], 'for' [Ln; NIV, NJB], 'to, into' [BAGD].

c. κενός (GEL 89.53) (BAGD 2.a.β. p. 428): 'vain' [Ea, HNTC, ICC, Mou, NTC, Pl, WBC, WEC; KJV, NAB, NASB, NRSV, REB, TNT]. The two phrases εἰς κενόν 'in vain' are translated 'without result' [BAGD, GEL], '(for) nothing' [NIV, NJB], 'something empty' [Ln]. The doubled 'in vain' implies intensity and emphasis [ICC, Pl] (or his joy [My]) as do the two verbs [Ea]. 'In vain' is doubled because there are two verbs [Lg].

d. aorist act. indic. of τρέχω (GEL 41.14) (BAGD 2.a. p. 825): 'to run' [Ea, Ln, Mou, NTC, WEC; KJV, NASB, NIV, NRSV], 'to run the race' [WBC; NAB, NJB], 'to run one's race' [Pl; REB, TNT], 'to run one's course' [HNTC], 'to behave' [GEL], 'to progress' [GEL], 'to strive to advance' [BAGD]. This word refers to Paul's zealous activity [EBC, Lg], his hard work [Ln, My]. The aorist tense refers to past time from the future day of Christ [Alf, Ea, EGT, ICC, Ln, Mou, Pl, TH, WBC].

e. aorist act. indic. of κοπιάω (GEL 42.47) (BAGD 2. p. 443): 'to toil' [BAGD, GEL, Mou; NASB], 'to toil so hard' [NJB], 'to struggle and toil' [Pl], 'to labor' [Ea, GEL, HNTC, Ln, NTC, WEC; KJV, NIV, NRSV, REB, TNT], 'to work hard' [BAGD, GEL], 'to work' [NAB], 'to do one's work' [WBC]. This word refers to the aspect of exhausting work [EBC, Lg, Ln, My, NTC], of weariness from toil [El, GNC]. The aorist tense refers to past time from the future day of Christ [Alf, Ea, EGT, Ln, Mou, TH, WBC].

QUESTION—What relationship is indicated by ὅτι 'that/because'?
1. It introduces the content of the boasting [Blm, EBC, HNTC, Ln, My, NTC, Pl; NAB, NIV, NRSV, REB, TNT]: I will boast that I had not run nor toiled in vain.
2. It introduces Paul's anticipated reason for boasting [EGT, Lg, MNTC, Mou; NASB, NJB, TEV]: I will boast because I had not run nor toiled in vain. It refers to the reason which he hopes to have for boasting when Christ returns [EGT].
3. It gives the content of the understood 'knowing' [WBC, WEC]: I will boast, knowing that I had not run nor worked in vain.

QUESTION—What is meant by the two occurrences of οὐκ εἰς κενόν 'not in vain'?

They are litotes [Blm]: that my work has produced much fruit.

DISCOURSE UNIT: 2:17–30 [Lt]. The topic is Paul's plans, Timothy's proposed visit, and news concerning Epaphroditus.

DISCOURSE UNIT: 2:17–18 [EGT, WC, WEC]. The topic is rejoicing by Paul and the Philippians in service to Christ [EGT], Paul's rejoicing whether he lives or dies [WC], Paul's personal appeal [WEC].

2:17
But[a] even[b] if[c] I-am-poured-out[d] upon[e] the sacrifice[f] and service[g] of-your faith,[h]
LEXICON—a. ἀλλά (GEL 91.2): 'but' [Ea, WBC; NASB, NIV, NRSV, REB], 'yet' [GEL], 'nevertheless' [WEC], 'and' [GEL], 'yes' [ICC], 'yea' [Ln; KJV], 'nay' [Mou], 'indeed' [HNTC; NJB], 'in fact' [NTC], not explicit [GEL, Pl; NAB, TEV, TNT].
   b. καί (GEL 89.93): 'even' [BAGD, Ea, GEL, HNTC, ICC, Mou, NTC, Pl; NAB, NASB, NIV, NJB, NRSV], 'and' [KJV], 'also' [Ln], not explicit [WBC, WEC; REB]. The phrase εἰ καί 'even if' is translated 'although' [BAGD], 'perhaps' [TEV, TNT]. Καί 'even' makes σπένδομαι 'I am poured out' emphatic [Pl, WEC].
   c. εἰ (GEL 89.65) (BAGD VI.4. p. 220): 'if' [BAGD, Ea, GEL, HNTC, ICC, Ln, Mou, NTC, Pl, WBC, WEC; all translations except TEV, TNT], 'though' [BAGD].
   d. pres. pass. indic. of σπένδω (GEL 53.27) (BAGD p. 761): 'to be poured out' [Ea, GEL, ICC, Mou, NTC, Pl, WBC, WEC; all translations except KJV], 'to be poured forth' [HNTC], 'to pour oneself out' [Ln], 'to be offered' [KJV], 'to be offered up' [BAGD]. The present tense indicates that the danger was imminent [Alf, Lg, TNTC], or as in progress [Lg(H), My]; it is a futuristic present [HNTC, ICC; NAB, NJB, REB, TEV, TNT], referring to the future in a vivid way [Ln, Lt, MNTC, NTC, Pl,

WEC]. The indicative mood relates to fact [Ln]. It is to be taken as middle voice, 'I pour myself out' [Ln], or it is passive voice, and figurative since Paul is not literally offering anything [TNTC].

e. ἐπί with dative object (GEL 83.46) (BAGD II.2. p. 288): 'upon' [GEL, NTC; KJV, NASB, TNT], 'on' [Ea, Mou, Pl; NIV, TEV], 'over' [NAB, NJB, NRSV], 'at' [HNTC, ICC], 'at the time of' [BAGD], 'together with' [BAGD], 'along with' [Ln]. This preposition is translated as an infinitive: 'to complete' [REB], 'to complement' [WBC]. The phrase ἐπὶ τῇ θυσίᾳ 'upon the sacrifice' is translated 'as you offer' [BAGD]. The phrase ἐπὶ τῇ θυσίᾳ καὶ λειτουργίᾳ 'upon the sacrifice and service' is translated 'so that I will crown the sacrificial service' [WEC]. It implies 'in addition to' [ICC, NIC] in harmony with Jewish practice [El, NIC, TNTC]; it is locative, 'upon' [Ea], in harmony with pagan practice [EGT, TH, WC]; it is temporal, 'while' [My]; it refers to the circumstances of Paul's being 'poured out' [Lg].

f. θυσία (GEL 53.20) (BAGD 1, 2.b. p. 366): 'sacrifice' [BAGD, Ea, GEL, HNTC, ICC, Ln, Mou, Pl; KJV, NASB, NIV, NJB, NRSV, REB, TEV]. The phrase θυσίᾳ καὶ λειτουργίᾳ 'sacrifice and service' is translated 'sacrificial service' [WBC; NAB], 'sacrificial offering' [NTC; TNT]. This word refers to the object sacrificed [Bg, Ea, El, ICC, My]; it refers to the act of offering [Lg].

g. λειτουργία (GEL 35.22; 53.13) (BAGD 2. p. 471): 'service' [BAGD, Ea, GEL, Pl, WBC, WEC; KJV, NAB, NASB, NIV], 'priestly service' [HNTC], 'religious duty' [GEL], 'ritual' [Mou], 'public service' [Ln], 'offering' [ICC, NTC; NJB, NRSV, TNT], 'offering up' [REB]. The phrase καὶ λειτουργίᾳ τῆς πίστεως 'and service of your faith' is translated 'that your faith offers' [TEV]. This word refers to the action of offering the sacrifice [EGT, El, TH, WC]. It means priestly ministry [Ea, EBC, Lg].

h. πίστις (GEL 31.102) (BAGD 2.d.α. p. 663): 'faith' [BAGD, Ea, GEL, HNTC, ICC, Ln, Mou, NTC, Pl, WBC, WEC; all translations]. The Philippians' faith is the sacrifice [Lg]. Their faith is the source of the sacrifice [WEC]. It is their faith which offers the sacrifice [MNTC].

QUESTION—What relationship is indicated by ἀλλά 'but'?

1. It indicates contrast [Ea, WBC, WEC; NASB, NIV, NRSV, REB]: but. The contrast is to the general thought of 2:16 [Ea]; it is that he has worked hard, but even death cannot deprive him of joy [WEC].

2. It introduces an additional thought [HNTC, ICC, Ln, NTC, TH, WBC; KJV, NJB]].

QUESTION—What meaning is implied by εἰ καί 'even if' with the indicative verb σπένδομαι 'I am poured out'?

It implies a good degree of probability [Alf, EGT, El, ICC, Ln, MNTC, My, Pl, TH, TNTC, WEC]: if I am to be poured out, which may occur. This phrase introduces a concession [My]. The emphasis is on εἰ 'if' [Alf]. The indicative mood deals with the possibility as a fact [Ln].

QUESTION—What is meant by Paul's being poured out on a sacrifice?

This is a reference to the libation poured out on an offering [Bg, Ea, EGT, GNC], or at the base of the altar [Bg, GNC]. The libation was usually wine [Bg] or oil and wine [Blm].

1. Paul is referring to the possibility of his own death as a result of his ministry for his converts [all commentaries except WBC]. He is thinking of his own life's blood as the libation [Alf, Bg, MNTC, My, NTC, TH].

2. Paul is referring to his present sufferings [WBC]. His suffering and the Philippians' sacrificial gifts to him combine to form a complete sacrifice to God [WBC].

QUESTION—What is the relation between the two nouns in the phrase θυσίᾳ καὶ λειτουργίᾳ 'sacrifice and service'?

1. 'Sacrifice and service' are considered together [NAB], since the definite article with the first noun governs both nouns [Alf, EBC, HNTC, ICC, Lg, MNTC, My, NTC, TH, TNTC, WBC]: sacrificial service. Some take it to be a hendiadys [EBC, HNTC, NTC, WBC]: a sacrificial service. Others say that it is not a hendiadys [El, ICC]: a sacrifice that is ministered.

2. The two nouns have separate meanings; θυσία is the sacrifice, λειτουργία is the priestly ministry of offering the sacrifice [Ea, EGT, El].

QUESTION—How is the genitive noun τῆς πίστεως 'the faith' related to the noun phrase τῇ θυσίᾳ καὶ λειτουργίᾳ 'the sacrifice and service'?

1. Their faith is the 'sacrifice' [Alf, [Blm, Ea, EBC, El, EGT, GNC, ICC, Lg, Lt, My, Pl, WC; TNT]: your faith is the sacrifice (and service). 'Faith' is an objective genitive [Alf, Ea, El, ICC, Ln].

1.1 They offer the sacrifice of their faith to God [EBC, GNC, ICC, Lt, Pl]. Here their faith means their lives of faith [GNC], the good works which spring from their faith [Lt], or their Christian ministries that come from their faith [EBC].

1.2 Paul offers the sacrifice of the Philippians' faith to God [Alf, Blm, Ea, Lg, My, WC]. Paul considers his work for their faith as a sacrifice he offers to God [Alf].

2. Their faith is the motivation for their sacrifice [HNTC, NIC, NTC, TNTC, TH, WBC, WEC; NIV]: the sacrifice you make which is prompted by your faith.

2.1 They sacrifice themselves and all they have to God [HNTC, NIC, NTC].

2.2 Their sacrifices are the gifts they give to Paul's ministry [TH, TNTC, WBC].

2.3 Their sacrifices are the service they offer to God [WEC].

I-rejoice[a] and I-rejoice-with[b] you all;

LEXICON—a. pres. act. indic. of χαίρω (GEL 25.125) (BAGD 1. p. 874): 'to rejoice' [BAGD, Ea, GEL, HNTC, ICC, Ln, Mou, NTC, Pl, WEC; NASB, REB], 'to joy' [KJV], 'to be glad' [GEL, WBC; NAB, NIV, NJB, NRSV, TEV], 'to be happy' [TNT].

   b. pres. act. indic. of συγχαίρω (GEL 25.126) (BAGD 1., 2. p. 775): 'to rejoice with' [BAGD, GEL, NTC; KJV, NAB, NIV, NRSV], 'to rejoice jointly with' [Ln], 'to join in one's rejoicing' [NJB], 'to share one's joy with' [WEC; NASB, REB, TEV, TNT], 'to share in joy with' [HNTC], 'to give joy' [Ea], 'to share one's gladness with' [WBC], 'to congratulate' [BAGD, Mou, Pl], not explicit [ICC]. It means to cause joy [Ea], it means that he shares their joy [EGT, El, MNTC, TH], it means that they are to rejoice with him [My(D), NIC, WC].

QUESTION—Why does Paul rejoice?

He rejoices because his martyrdom would help promote the gospel and their faith [Ea, Lg(H), My(D), NIC, TH, TNTC]. He rejoices over the prospect of a martyr's death, which would crown his ministry [GNC]. Paul rejoices in his probable death as a drink offering [El, My, NTC] because he has been able to bring the Philippians to fully surrender their lives to God [NTC]. He rejoices because God has used him to bring about God's will in the Philippians' lives [EGT, WC]. Paul rejoices in the future presentation of his converts to God [Bg]. He rejoices because his sufferings for the gospel and the Philippians' gifts to him form a complete sacrifice to God [WBC]. He rejoices in the anticipation of being with Christ in heaven and of having his ministry to the Philippians seen to be successful [EBC].

QUESTION—What do they rejoice together about?

He rejoices with the Philippians in the sacrifice they have made for him [TNTC]. Paul shares the Philippians' joy over their salvation [EGT]. The Philippians are to rejoice together with Paul in the future presentation of themselves (their faith [Blm]) and other

Christians to God [Bg]. Paul rejoices with the Philippians as he
thinks about his successful ministry among them [EBC] and their
joy of salvation [NTC]. They are to rejoice with Paul over his
death, which will make their sacrifice complete [GNC]. The
meaning is 'to congratulate' [Alf, Lt]; he congratulates the
Philippians that his death will be used for their faith [My], that his
death for their faith will be an honor for them [Alf].

2:18
and^a the same-(thing)^b you also rejoice^c and rejoice-with^d me.

    LEXICON—a. δέ (GEL 89.94): 'and' [GEL, Mou, NTC, Pl, WBC;
      NASB, NJB, NRSV], 'moreover' [Ln], 'yea' [Ea], not explicit
      [HNTC, WEC; KJV, NAB, REB, TEV, TNT]. The phrase τὸ δὲ
      αὐτό 'and the same thing' is translated 'so' [NIV]. The final
      clause of 2:17 and all of 2:18 are translated 'and this will be a
      cause of joy to you no less than to me' [ICC]. The only contrast
      here is in the change from 'I' to 'you' [Alf]. Δέ introduces the
      other side of the matter [Ln].
    b. αὐτός (GEL 58.31): 'same' [GEL], not explicit [HNTC; REB,
      TNT]. The phrase τὸ αὐτό 'the same thing' is translated 'in the
      same way' [Ln, Mou, WEC; NASB, NJB, NRSV, TEV], 'in the
      same manner' [NTC], 'on the same score' [NAB], 'for the same
      cause' [KJV], 'for the same reason' [WBC], 'for the very same
      reason' [Ea]. This phrase is emphatic by forefronting [Pl]. Τὸ
      αὐτό 'the same thing' is an accusative [My] of reference [Alf,
      Ea, El] governed by χαίρετε 'you rejoice' [Alf, Ea] or by χαίρω
      'I rejoice [El]. This accusative tells how they are to rejoice; they
      are to have the same joy which Paul has [Lt]; they are to
      rejoice on the basis of Paul's death [My], to rejoice with him in
      the joy which he felt [My(D)]. Τὸ αὐτό 'the same thing' is used
      adverbially, with the meaning of 'likewise' [EGT, Ln, NIC,
      TNTC], 'in the same way' [TNTC], or 'regarding this thing I am
      speaking about' [Ln]. The meaning is 'for the same reason'
      [NIC], viz. the progress of their redemption [ICC]. It introduces
      the cause of their joy [Lg], namely his joy that his death would
      be gain for himself and for them [Lg(H)]. The Philippians are
      to be joyful just as Paul was and to be joyful about the same
      thing as Paul [Pl].
    c. pres. act. impera. of χαίρω (GEL 25.125): 'to rejoice' [GEL,
      HNTC, Ln, Mou, NTC, Pl, WEC; NASB, REB], 'to joy' [Ea;
      KJV], 'to be glad' [GEL, WBC; NAB, NIV, NJB, NRSV, TEV],
      'to be happy' [TNT]. They are to rejoice because Paul's death, if
      it occurs, is for their faith [Alf, Ea, My]. They are to rejoice as
      they work out their salvation [EBC], as they continue to work

for the gospel [WBC]. They are to rejoice because they have the blessings of salvation [NTC].

   d. pres. act. impera. of συγχαίρω (GEL 25.126): 'to rejoice with' [GEL, NTC; KJV, NAB, NIV, NRSV], 'to rejoice jointly with' [Ln], 'to join in one's rejoicing' [NJB], 'to share one's joy' [TNT], 'to share one's joy with' [WEC; NASB, REB, TEV], 'to share in joy with' [HNTC], 'to offer joy to' [Ea], 'to share one's gladness with' [WBC], 'to congratulate' [Mou, Pl]. They are to rejoice with Paul as he thinks about dying [EGT, NTC] and being with Christ and Christ's seeing his successful ministry to them [EBC]. They are to congratulate Paul because of his joy in anticipating death for their faith [Alf, Bg]; they are to congratulate him because he would be with Christ [My].

QUESTION—Why is this clause mentioned?

By this clause Paul repeats emphatically, in a reciprocal form, what he had said in the preceding verse [El]—viz., that they were indeed to rejoice in his possible death [El, GNC, Ln]. They are to rejoice in their own sacrifice [MNTC, TH] and in Paul's joy over his sacrifice [MNTC], or to rejoice together with Paul [TH]. Ὑμεῖς χαίρετε 'you rejoice' is parallel to συγχαίρω ὑμῖν 'I rejoice with you' in 2:17; συγχαίρετέ μοι 'rejoice with me' is parallel to χαίρω 'I rejoice' in 2:17 [My].

DISCOURSE UNIT: 2:19–3:1a [NJB, REB]. The topic is the mission of Timothy and Epaphroditus [NJB], Paul's plans [REB].

DISCOURSE UNIT: 2:19–30 [Alf, EBC, HNTC, Lg, Mou, NIC, NTC, Pl, TH, TNTC, WBC, WC, WEC; GNT, NAB, NASB, NIV, TEV]. The topic is information about Paul [Alf] and the mission of Timothy and Epaphroditus [Alf, Mou], information about Timothy and Epaphroditus [EBC, NIC, WBC; GNT, NASB, NIV, TEV], the conduct of Paul's helpers [Lg], Paul's helpers and his plans [NAB], Paul's plans [HNTC, TH, TNTC, WC], explanation and personal notes [Pl], resumption of Paul's missionary report [WEC], Paul as a thoughtful administrator [NTC].

DISCOURSE UNIT: 2:19–24 [EBC, EGT, ICC, Lg, Ln, MNTC, My(D), NIC, NTC, Pl, TH, TNTC, WBC, WC, WEC; NAB]. The topic is Timothy [EBC, WBC, WEC; NAB], Paul's plan to send Timothy [EGT, ICC, Lg, Ln, MNTC, NIC, NTC, Pl], Timothy's planned visit, Paul's commendation of him, and Paul's possible visit [WC], Paul's commendation of Timothy [TH, TNTC].

2:19

But/Now[a] I-hope[b] in[c] (the) Lord Jesus to-send Timothy soon[d] to-you,

LEXICON—a. δέ (GEL 89.94; 89.124): 'but' [Ea, GEL, Mou, NTC, Pl; KJV, NASB], 'but yet' [ICC], 'on the other hand' [GEL], 'now' [Ln, WBC], not explicit [HNTC, WEC; all translations except KJV, NASB].

b. pres. act. indic. of ἐλπίζω (GEL 30.54) (BAGD 2. p. 252): 'to hope' [BAGD, Ea, GEL, HNTC, ICC, Ln, Mou, NTC, Pl, WBC; all translations except KJV], 'to expect' [GEL, WEC], 'to trust' [KJV]. This verb is not as strong as the verb he uses in 2:23 of his own coming to them [WBC]. However, this word does not imply doubt; it focuses on intention [WEC].

c. ἐν with dative object (GEL 89.119; 83.13) (BAGD I.5.d. p. 259): 'in' [BAGD, Ea, GEL, HNTC, Ln, Mou, NTC, Pl; all translations except TEV, TNT], 'through' [WEC], not explicit [ICC]. The phrase ἐν κυρίου Ἰησοῦ 'in the Lord Jesus' is translated 'under the lordship of Jesus' [WBC], 'if it is the Lord's will' [TEV], 'if the Lord Jesus wills it' [TNT].

d. ταχέως (GEL 67.56) (BAGD 1.a. p. 806): 'soon' [BAGD, GEL, Ln, WEC; NIV, NJB, NRSV, REB, TEV, TNT], 'very soon' [Pl, WBC; NAB], 'without delay' [BAGD], 'shortly' [Ea, HNTC; KJV, NASB], 'promptly' [Mou], not explicit [ICC]. It means not immediately, but when the result of Paul's trial is more nearly known (2:23) [GNC, Lg].

QUESTION—What relationship is indicated by δέ 'but/now'?

1. It indicates a contrast [Ea, ICC, Lt, Mou, My, NTC, Pl, TNTC, WBC; KJV, NASB]: but/yet. Although absent, yet he hopes to send Timothy [Lt]. He is forced to remain away from the church (2:12), but in the meantime he has contingency plans to send Timothy to them [Pl, My, TNTC, WBC]. He may be put to death as a libation, yet he hopes to dispense with Timothy's service and send him to them [ICC].

2. It indicates transition [Ea, Ln, MNTC, My]: now. It indicates a change to a different matter [Ea, Ln, MNTC]. The note of concern now changes to more optimism [EBC, EGT]. Even though Paul's situation is still dangerous, he nevertheless hopes to send Timothy [My]. It indicates a transition from Paul's situation to his concern for the spiritual growth of the Philippians and his joy in it [My(D)].

QUESTION—What is meant by ἐν κυρίῳ Ἰησοῦ 'in the Lord Jesus'?

It indicates the basis of Paul's hope [Alf, Blm, Ea, EBC, EGT, El, GNC, HNTC, ICC, Lg, Lt, MNTC, Mou, My, NIC, NTC, TNTC, WBC]: I hope, based on my faith in Christ, to send Timothy. It refers to his union with Christ [EBC, GNC, HNTC, Mou, NIC].

Vital union with Christ should influence every thought and activity [EBC, GNC, NIC]. It means that his plans are subject to the Lord's approval [EBC, EGT, TH, TNTC], to the Lordship of Christ [EGT, NTC, WBC], and also that his plans are not based on man's plans for him but on God's will [TNTC], not on his own feelings or hopes [El]; he evidently is confident that the Lord will approve his plan [TH]. His hope is caused by the Lord [My].

QUESTION—What is implied by the word order Τιμόθεον ταχέως πέμψαι ὑμῖν 'Timothy soon to send to you'?

It means that the primary emphasis is on 'Timothy' [Ln, Mou] and secondary emphasis on 'soon' [Ln]: It is Timothy whom I hope to send, and I hope to send him soon.

QUESTION—What is meant by the dative case of the pronoun ὑμῖν 'you'?

It is not merely directional, 'to you' [Alf, Bg, Ea]. It is a dative of advantage [Ln]. It implies 'for your good' [Bg, Ln, MNTC, NIC, NTC] 'for your comfort' [Pl]; it focuses on the persons whom Timothy would meet [Ea, El, My]; it indicates the close relationship between Paul and the Philippians [Lg].

in-order-that[a]   I   also   may-be-encouraged[b]   knowing[c]   the-(things) concerning[d] you.

LEXICON—a. ἵνα (GEL 89.59): 'in order that' [GEL, ICC, Ln, Pl], 'so that' [GEL, HNTC, NTC, WBC, WEC; NASB, NJB, NRSV, TEV], 'that' [Ea, Mou; KJV, NAB, NIV]. The phrase ἵνα εὐψυχῶ 'in order that I may be encouraged' is translated 'it will cheer me up' [REB], 'I would like to be cheered up' [TNT].

b. pres. act. subj. of εὐψυχέω (GEL 25.146) (BAGD p. 329): 'to be encouraged' [GEL; NASB, TEV], 'to have courage' [BAGD], 'to derive courage' [NAB], 'to be heartened' [NTC], 'to be comforted' [ICC], 'to find comfort' [WEC], 'to be of good comfort' [KJV], 'to be of good spirit' [Ea], 'to be of good cheer' [Ln, Mou], 'to be cheered' [HNTC, Pl; NIV, NRSV], 'to be cheered up' [WBC; TNT], 'to cheer one up' [REB], 'to be glad' [BAGD], 'to set one's mind at rest' [NJB]. It implies that Paul is optimistic about the Philippians, even though he is somewhat anxious about them [Bg, Ea]. It implies that he expects to live until Timothy returns to him [Pl].

c. aorist act. participle of γινώσκω (GEL 27.2): 'to know' [Ea, NTC; KJV], 'to learn' [GEL, WBC, WEC; NAB, NASB], 'to find out' [GEL], 'to get to know' [Ln, Pl], 'to get knowledge' [HNTC, Mou], 'to receive news' [NIV], 'to have news' [REB, TNT], 'to hear' [ICC; NJB]. The phrase γνοὺς τὰ περὶ ὑμῶν 'knowing the things concerning you' is translated 'by news about you' [TEV], 'by news of you' [NRSV]. It implies definite

knowledge, viz. of τὰ περὶ ὑμῶν 'the things concerning you'
[Lg]. The aorist tense implies coming to know [EGT]. The
participle expresses the grounds of Paul's anticipated
encouragement, but the commentaries do not deal with this
point.

   d. περί with genitive object (GEL 90.24) (BAGD 1.i. p. 645):
   'concerning' [BAGD, GEL, Ln], 'about' [BAGD, GEL; NIV,
   TEV], 'of' [NRSV, REB, TNT]. The phrase τὰ περὶ ὑμῶν 'the
   things concerning you' is translated 'of your circumstances'
   [Mou], 'of your condition' [ICC; NASB], 'of your state' [HNTC],
   'your state' [KJV], 'your affairs' [Ea, NTC], 'how you are' [NJB],
   'how you are doing' [WEC], 'how things go with you' [NAB],
   'how things are going with you' [WBC], 'about your spiritual
   welfare' [Pl].

QUESTION—What relationship is indicated by ἵνα 'in order that'?

It introduces the purpose of Timothy's visit [Ea, Lg, MNTC,
My(D), TH, TNTC, WBC, WC, WEC]: I hope to send Timothy for
the purpose of our being mutually cheered by news concerning
each other. A second purpose is implied in 2:20: Timothy's care
for the Philippians [My(D)].

QUESTION—What relationship is indicated by κἀγώ 'I also'?

There is an ellipsis in the words following [Blm]; the meaning is
that Paul also expects to be cheered by news of the Philippians, just
as they will be cheered by news of Paul from Timothy [Alf, Bg,
Blm, Ea, EBC, EGT, El, GNC, ICC, Lg, Ln, MNTC, Mou, My,
NIC, NTC, TH, TNTC, WEC]: I also as well as you. The fact that
Paul expected the Philippians to be encouraged by Timothy's visit
[EBC, WEC] is so clear that Paul refers to it only implicitly, by
'also' [MNTC]. This expression is a complimentary implication that
the news about them will be good [My]. The ἐγώ 'I' (in κἀγώ 'I
also') is emphatic [My(D), TH, TNTC]. Paul evidently expected
Timothy to return to him soon with news about the Philippian
church [EBC].

2:20

for[a] I-have no-one like-minded,[b] who[c] genuinely[d] will-care-for[e] the-
(things) concerning[f] you;

   LEXICON—a. γάρ (GEL 89.23): 'for' [Ea, GEL, HNTC, ICC, Ln,
   Mou, NTC, Pl; KJV, NASB], 'because' [GEL, WBC, WEC], not
   explicit [all translations except KJV, NASB].

   b. ἰσόψυχος (GEL 26.5) (BAGD p. 381): 'like-minded' [Ea, ICC,
   NTC], 'of the same mind' [GEL], 'of like mind' [BAGD], 'one's
   equal in mind' [Pl], 'of like soul' [BAGD], 'equal in soul' [Ln],
   'equal-souled' [Mou], 'of kindred spirit' [NASB], 'of qualities

like (someone)' [HNTC], 'quite like one' [NAB], 'like one' [NIV, NJB, NRSV, REB], 'so close to one' [WEC]. This adjective is translated as a clause: 'who shares (my) feelings' [TEV], 'who equally shares (my) feelings' [WBC] 'shares (my) thoughts' [TNT]. Timothy is the only one who meets this qualification [Bg].

c. ὅστις (GEL 92.18) (BAGD 2.b. p. 587): 'who' [BAGD, Ea, HNTC, ICC, NTC, Pl, WBC; all translations except TNT, NAB], 'one who' [Mou], 'such as' [Ln], not explicit [WEC; TNT]. The phrase ὅστις γνησίως μεριμνήσει 'who will genuinely care for' is translated 'for genuine interest in' [NAB]. This word is qualitative, 'of the kind who' [Alf, Ea, EGT, El, Lg, Ln, Lt, My, Pl], introducing the specification of the like-mindedness [Ln, My].

d. γνησίως (GEL 73.1) (BAGD p. 163): 'genuinely' [BAGD, GEL, Ln, Mou, NTC, Pl, WBC, WEC; NASB, NRSV, TNT], 'sincerely' [BAGD, HNTC; NJB], 'really' [Ea; TEV], 'naturally' [KJV], 'with the same fatherly care' [ICC]. The phrase ὅστις γνησίως μεριμνήσει 'who genuinely will care for' is translated 'for genuine interest' [NAB], 'who takes a genuine interest' [NIV], 'who has a genuine concern' [REB]. This word gives emphasis to the thought, implying that Timothy will have no distracting thoughts for himself [Alf]; he will be sincerely concerned for the Philippians' welfare [Blm, EBC, EGT, El, Lg, Ln, Mou, My, NIC, NTC, Pl, TNTC, WC, WEC]. He will be legitimately concerned like a brother [Bg], by spiritual birth relationship [ICC], because he is Paul's legitimate spiritual son [GNC, Lt, WBC].

e. fut. act. indic. of μεριμνάω (GEL 25.225) (BAGD 2. p. 505): 'to care for' [BAGD, Ea, ICC, Ln; KJV, NJB], 'to care about' [Mou, WBC; TEV], 'to be concerned about' [BAGD, WEC; TNT], 'to be concerned for' [HNTC; NASB, NRSV], 'to have concern for' [REB], 'to be anxious about' [GEL, Pl], 'to be interested in' [NTC]. 'to take interest in' [NIV]. Timothy will be genuinely concerned to work for their best interest [Alf, Ea]; the verb indicates a legitimate concern [MNTC]. The future tense refers to the help he will give them when he visits them [Ea El, GNC, HNTC, ICC, Lg(H), Ln, My, Mou, NTC, Pl; NRSV, TNT]. The future tense actually means present time [WBC, WEC; NIV, NJB, REB, TEV].

f. περί with genitive object (GEL 89.6; 90.24): 'concerning' [GEL, Ln], 'in relation to' [GEL]. The phrase τὰ περὶ ὑμῶν 'the things concerning you' is translated 'whatever concerns you' [NAB], 'your welfare' [NTC; NASB, NIV, NRSV], 'your spiritual

welfare' [Pl], 'your well-being' [NJB], 'your affairs' [Ea, WC;
REB], 'your circumstances' [Mou], 'your state' [HNTC; KJV],
'your problems' [WEC], 'you' [ICC; TEV, TNT].

QUESTION—What relationship is indicated by γάρ 'for'?

It introduces the reason why Paul will send Timothy rather than
someone else [Alf, El, ICC, My, WBC]: the reason I will send
Timothy is because of his qualifications. It helps prevent the
Philippians from being disappointed that Paul himself was not
coming, and expresses his full confidence in Timothy's ability in the
matter [EBC, NTC, WBC]. It sets forth Timothy's qualifications
[MNTC, TNTC]. Paul is implying that he wishes to send the most
able person [My(D)]. 'Timothy' is emphatic by forefronting [Mou].

QUESTION—Who is the implied referent of ἰσόψυχον 'like-minded'?

1. It is Timothy [EBC, EGT, Lg, Ln, Lt, MNTC, Mou, NIC, NTC,
   Pl, TNTC, WC; NAB, NIV, NJB, NRSV, REB]: none of my
   other co-workers has an interest in you equal to Timothy's. If
   Paul had intended to compare Timothy with himself, he would
   doubtless have said 'any other one' [EBC, EGT, Lt, MNTC,
   Mou, TNTC]. This is clear, since the point Paul is making here
   is to explain why he is sending Timothy rather than someone
   else [Lg(H)]. The following clause fits this interpretation better
   [MNTC, WC].

2. It is Paul [Alf, Bg, Blm, Ea, El, GNC, ICC, My, TH, WBC,
   WEC; TEV, TNT]: I have no one who equally shares my mind
   as Timothy does. The only referent indicated is the subject of
   the verb ἔχω 'I have', which is Paul; and the best reason for
   sending Timothy is Timothy's like-mindedness to Paul [My],
   Timothy's good understanding of Paul's mind [WBC].

2:21

for[a] all[b] the-(persons) seek[c] the-(things) of-themselves,[d] not the-(things)
of-Jesus Christ.

LEXICON—a. γάρ (GEL 89.23): 'for' [Ea, GEL, ICC, Ln, Mou, NTC,
Pl, WBC; KJV, NASB, NIV], 'because' [GEL], not explicit
[HNTC, WEC; NAB, NJB, NRSV, REB, TEV, TNT].

b. πᾶς (GEL 59.23) (BAGD 2.b.α. p. 633): 'all' [GEL, HNTC,
ICC, Ln, NTC, WBC, WEC; KJV, NASB, NJB, NRSV, REB],
'everyone' [NAB, NIV, TEV, TNT]. The phrase οἱ πάντες 'all
the persons' is translated 'all (of them) (in contrast to a part)'
[BAGD], 'all of them' [Mou], 'one and all' [Pl], 'the whole' [Ea].

c. pres. act. indic. of ζητέω (GEL 25.9) (BAGD 2.b.α. p. 339): 'to
seek' [Ea, Ln, WEC; KJV, NAB, NRSV], 'to seek after' [NASB],
'to look out for' [NIV], 'to look after' [HNTC, NTC], 'to look to'
[TNT], 'to be concerned with' [TEV], 'to be concerned about'

[WBC], 'to be occupied with' [ICC], 'to desire' [GEL], 'to want' [NJB], 'to strive for' [BAGD], 'to be bent on' [Mou; REB], 'to pursue' [Pl].

d. ἑαυτοῦ (GEL 92.25): 'oneself' [GEL]. The phrase τὰ ἑαυτῶν 'the things of themselves' is translated 'their own' [KJV], 'their own things' [Ea, Ln], 'his own interests' [NAB, NIV, TNT], 'their own interests' [ICC, Mou, Pl, WBC, WEC; NASB, NRSV, REB], 'his own affairs' [TEV], 'their own affairs' [HNTC, NTC], 'to work for themselves' [NJB]. The reference is to their own self-interest [El, GNC]. The implication is that they are acting insincerely [Lg]. The meaning is that they are more interested in their own affairs than in the work of Christ [Ln, MNTC, NIC, WC]. The meaning is that they are interested only in their own affairs, not those of Christ [My, TH].

QUESTION—What relationship is indicated by γάρ 'for'?

This word introduces Paul's explanation for designating Timothy [Ln]. It is somewhat parenthetical, a comment about the general situation around him, not a criticism of his fellow-Christians [TNTC]. It is a strong emotional expression [EGT]. It is not possible to know exactly what Paul intended by this clause [ICC, WBC].

QUESTION—To whom does οἱ πάντες 'all the persons' refer?

This word refers to Paul's companions [Alf, Ea, My, WC], but their identity is unknown [Alf, Ea, El, Ln, My]; Paul really means 'all of them' [Alf, Bg, Ea, Lg, Lt, My, Pl], as implied by the definite article οἱ 'the' [Bg, El, ICC, Lt, Mou, Pl], corresponding to 'no one' in 2:20 [Ea]. The definite article implies the limitation to those who were available [Lg]. The reference is limited to the persons who were with Paul and who could have been considered for the mission [Ea, EBC, El, GNC, HNTC, MNTC, Mou, My, NTC, Pl], thus excluding the persons mentioned in 1:15 [Ea, Lg]. Paul actually means 'most of them' [Blm, EGT]; he uses hyperbole here [WEC]. It is not possible to explain this reference satisfactorily [ICC].

2:22

but[a] the proven-worth[b] of-him you-know,[c]

LEXICON—a. δέ (GEL 89.94; 89.124): 'but' [Ea, GEL, HNTC, ICC, Mou, NTC, Pl, WBC, WEC; KJV, NASB, NIV, NJB, NRSV, REB], 'on the other hand' [GEL], 'moreover' [Ln], 'and' [GEL; TEV], not explicit [NAB, TNT]. This word introduces the contrast between the other workers and Timothy [Bg, Ea], not between the persons but between the qualifications of the persons [My].

b. δοκιμή (GEL **65.12**) (BAGD 1. p. 202): 'proven worth' [HNTC, WBC; NASB], 'proved worth' [NTC], 'proof' [KJV], 'worth' [NRSV, TNT], 'value' [GEL], 'test' [Mou], 'testing out' [Ln], 'character' [BAGD], 'tried character' [Ea], 'qualities' [NAB], 'mettle' [WEC], 'record' [REB], 'credentials' [Pl]. This noun is also translated as a verb: 'to prove oneself' [NIV], 'to prove' [ICC]. The phrase τὴν δοκιμὴν αὐτοῦ 'his proven worth' is translated 'how he has proved his worth' [TEV], 'what sort of person he has proved himself' [NJB]. The sense is approvedness, the result of testing [ICC, MNTC, NIC], testing which results in character [EGT], tried character [El]. The Philippians knew that Timothy had been tested and had successfully passed the test [WBC].

c. pres. act. indic. of γινώσκω (GEL 28.1): 'to know' [Ea, GEL, HNTC, ICC, Ln, NTC, Pl, WBC, WEC; all translations except NAB], 'to know from experience' [NAB], 'to remember' [Mou]. This verb is indicative, not imperative [Ea, El, ICC, Lg, My, Pl, TH]. They knew from the trials he experienced when he and Paul were at Philippi (Acts 16:1, 3; 17:4) [Alf, Bg, Ea, EBC, El, GNC, HNTC, Lg, Ln, MNTC, My, TNTC, WC].

that[a] as[b] a-child[c] to-a-father he-has-served[d] with[e] me for[f] the gospel.

LEXICON—a. ὅτι (GEL 90.21): 'that' [Ea, GEL, Ln, Mou; KJV, NASB, REB], 'because' [NIV], 'how that' [WBC], 'how' [HNTC, NTC, Pl; NAB, NRSV, TEV, TNT], not explicit [WEC; NJB]. The phrase ὅτι ὡς πατρὶ τέκνον 'that as a child to a father' is translated 'with what filial devotion' [ICC].

b. ὡς (GEL 64.12) (BAGD I.2.a. p. 897): 'as' [BAGD, Ea, GEL, HNTC, Ln, Mou, NTC, Pl, WEC; KJV, NIV, TNT], 'like' [GEL, WBC; NAB, NASB, NJB, NRSV, REB, TEV].

c. τέκνον (GEL 10.36) (BAGD 1.a.β. p. 808): 'child' [Ea, GEL, Ln, Mou, NTC, WBC, WEC; NASB], 'son' [BAGD, HNTC, Pl; all translations except NASB].

d. aorist act. indic. of δουλεύω (GEL 35.27) (BAGD 2.c. p. 205): 'to serve' [BAGD, Ea, GEL, HNTC, ICC, NTC, WEC; KJV, NAB, NASB, NIV, NRSV, TNT], 'to do bondservice' [Mou], 'to slave' [Ln, Pl], 'to work' [NJB, REB, TEV], 'to work hard' [WBC]. The verb literally means to be a slave [GNC], which means doing only what one's superior wants [Ln].

e. σύν with dative object (GEL 89.107) (BAGD 2.a. p. 781): 'with' [BAGD, Ea, GEL, HNTC, Ln, Mou, NTC, Pl; KJV, NASB, NIV, NJB, NRSV, TNT], 'together with' [GEL], 'along with' [NAB], 'at the side of' [REB], 'by one's side' [WEC], 'alongside' [WBC], not explicit [ICC; TEV].

f. εἰς with accusative object (GEL 90.23; 90.41): 'for' [Ea, GEL, Mou], 'for the sake of' [NJB, TEV], 'on behalf of' [GEL], 'in the service of' [REB], 'in the cause of' [TNT], 'to advance the cause of' [WBC], 'for the promotion of' [Pl], 'in the furtherance of' [NASB], 'for the furtherance of' [WEC], 'in the propagation of' [HNTC], 'in the work of promoting' [ICC], 'in' [GEL, NTC; KJV, NIV, NRSV], 'in regard to' [Ln], 'concerning' [GEL], not explicit [NAB]. The preposition has the sense of the destination of the action [El, Lg], viz. to advance the cause of the gospel [El, Lg, Mou, NIC, TNTC]. It is almost like ἐν 'in' [EGT].

QUESTION—What relationship is indicated by ὅτι 'that'?

It introduces the specification of Timothy's approvedness [Alf, Lg, Ln]: his approvedness consists in the fact that he has served with me for the gospel.

QUESTION—What meaning is implied by the dative πατρί 'to a father'?

1. It is the predicate of the implied verb 'serves' [Alf, Ea, El, ICC, MNTC, My, Pl, WBC; NASB, REB]: as a child serves his father.

2. It is the object of the implied preposition σύν 'with' [EBC, HNTC, Mou, NTC, WC; KJV, NIV, NJB, NRSV, TEV, TNT]: as a child serves with his father. Father and son are interested in the same cause and they serve their spiritual Father [NTC]. They served Christ together [EBC, WC]. They worked together for the sake of the gospel [HNTC; TEV, TNT].

QUESTION—What is the phrase ὡς πατρὶ τέκνον 'as a child to a father' connected with?

The logical connection would be 'he served me', but Paul partially changes the figure to 'he served with me' [Alf, Ea, EGT, El, ICC, MNTC, NIC, Pl, TNTC, WBC, WC]: as a child serves his father, so he has served with me for the gospel. He realizes that Timothy's service was not primarily to him but for the gospel [Ea, EGT, ICC, NIC, TNTC]. He realizes that the verb ἐδούλευσεν, literally 'he slaved', is not appropriate for their relationship [El, MNTC]. He first thinks of Timothy as a son [EGT, TH, TNTC], then changes to think of him as a colleague [Pl, WBC, WC].

2:23

This-(one) on-the-one-hand[a] therefore[b] I-hope[c] to-send when[d] I-see[e] the-(things) concerning[f] me immediately;[g]

LEXICON—a. μέν (GEL 89.136): 'on the one hand' [GEL], 'then' [Mou], not explicit [Ea, HNTC, ICC, Ln, NTC, Pl, WBC, WEC; all translations]. This word, 'on the one hand,' is contrasted with δέ 'on the other hand' in the next verse [Ea, El, Lt, My, Pl], making a distinction between Timothy's visit and his own [EGT, Lg(H), Pl].

b. οὖν (GEL 89.50): 'therefore' [GEL, ICC, Ln, Pl; KJV, NASB, NIV, NRSV], 'then' [Ea, GEL, HNTC, NTC, WBC; NJB], 'so' [GEL, Mou, WEC; REB, TEV, TNT], not explicit [NAB].

c. pres. act. indic. of ἐλπίζω (GEL 25.59; 30.54) (BAGD 2. p. 252): 'to hope' [BAGD, Ea, GEL, HNTC, ICC, Ln, Mou, NTC, Pl, WBC; all translations except REB], 'to expect' [BAGD, GEL, WEC], 'to mean' [REB].

d. ὡς ἄν (GEL 67.45) (BAGD IV.1.c.α. p. 898): 'when' [BAGD, GEL], 'whenever' [Ea, Ln], 'as soon as' [BAGD, HNTC, ICC, NTC, WBC, WEC; all translations except KJV, NJB], 'as soon as ever' [Pl], 'so soon as' [KJV]. The phrase ὡς ἄν ἀφίδω 'when I see' is translated 'upon my getting a view of' [Mou]. The phrase ὡς ἄν ἐξαυτῆς 'when ... immediately' is translated 'immediately' [NJB]. It implies uncertainty as to the time [Alf, Ea, EGT, El].

e. aorist act. subj. of ἀφοράω (GEL 27.6) (BAGD 2. p. 127): 'to see' [BAGD, Ea, HNTC, Ln, NTC, Pl, WBC; all translations except NJB, TEV], 'to get a view of' [Mou], 'to have a clearer view of' [WEC], 'to learn' [GEL, ICC], 'to know' [TEV], 'to make out' [NJB]. This word implies to see clearly [Alf], to concentrate one's attention on one thing [EGT, El, WBC], to look at something distant [EBC, Lg]. The aorist tense implies the action of getting to see [Ln]. Only after learning the decision of his case could Paul decide whether he could in fact spare Timothy for this visit [My]; only then could Timothy take word of Paul's condemnation or release [TNTC, WC]. This explains Paul's delay in sending Timothy [WBC]. The delay is not to see what the verdict of Paul's trial will be; rather, it is because Paul needs Timothy with him for the present to help in Paul's affairs [WBC, WEC].

f. περί with accusative object (GEL 89.6) (BAGD 2.d. p. 645): 'concerning' [Ln], 'in relation to' [GEL]. The phrase τὰ περὶ ἐμέ 'the things concerning me' is translated 'my situation' [BAGD], 'my circumstances' [Mou], 'my affairs' [WEC], 'about my own affairs' [WBC], 'about my own case' [ICC], 'how I am getting along' [BAGD], 'how it will go with me' [Ea; KJV], 'how things go with me' [NAB, NASB, NIV, NRSV, REB], 'how things will go with myself' [Pl], 'what is going to happen to me' [NJB], 'how things are going to turn out for me' [TEV], 'how my affairs will turn out' [NTC], 'what the outcome of my own affairs is to be' [TNT], 'the outcome of my present situation' [HNTC].

g. ἐξαυτῆς (GEL 67.113) (BAGD p. 273): 'immediately' [BAGD, Ea, GEL, Mou; NASB], 'at once' [BAGD, GEL, HNTC, NTC], 'shortly' [ICC], 'forthwith' [Ln, Pl], 'soon thereafter' [BAGD], 'presently' [KJV], not explicit [WBC, WEC; NAB, NIV, NRSV, REB, TEV]. This word, placed in emphatic position at the end of the clause [Ln], refers to πέμψαι 'to send', emphasizing that Paul hopes to send Timothy soon [EBC, Lg], as soon as he receives the information about his case [Lg(H)]. It corresponds to τάχεως in 2:19 [Lt].

QUESTION—What relationship is indicated by οὖν 'therefore'?

This word resumes the thought in 2:19 where Paul had said that he hoped to send Timothy [Ea, El, ICC, Ln, My, NTC]. It explains the reason for the delay implied by saying he would send Timothy soon (2:19) [Lg, WBC].

QUESTION—What is implied by the position of τοῦτον 'this one'?

It is emphatic by forefronting [Ea, EBC, Ln, MNTC, Mou, Pl, TH, TNTC]: It is Timothy rather than someone else. Paul is emphasizing Timothy's qualifications [MNTC]. The emphasis is because Paul is going to speak of other persons as well [Mou, Pl].

2:24

on-the-other-hand[a] I-trust[b] in[c] (the) Lord that I-myself soon[d] will-come.

LEXICON—δέ (GEL 89.94; 89.124): 'on the other hand' [GEL], 'but' [Ea, GEL, ICC, Mou, NTC, Pl; KJV, NJB], 'and' [GEL, HNTC, Ln, WEC; NASB, NIV, NRSV, REB, TEV, TNT], 'in fact' [NAB], 'for' [WBC]. This word, 'on the other hand', is the parallel to μέν 'on the one hand' in 2:23 [Ea, Lg, Ln].

b. perf. act. indic. of πείθω (GEL 31.82) (BAGD 2.a. p. 639): 'to trust' [BAGD, Ea, GEL, ICC, NTC; KJV, NASB, NRSV, TEV], 'to be confident' [GEL, HNTC, Ln, Pl, WBC, WEC; NAB, NIV, NJB, REB], 'to be quite sure' [TNT], 'to feel sure' [Mou]. This is a strong word [TH], stronger than the word ἐλπίζω 'I hope' (2:23) [My, MNTC] which he uses of his plan to send Timothy [MNTC]; it emphatically contrasts with ἐλπίζω 'I hope' [Pl]. This verb implies 'if the Lord wills it' [TH].

c. ἐν with dative object (GEL 89.119): 'in' [Ea, GEL, HNTC, ICC, Ln, Mou, NTC, Pl, WBC, WEC; all translations except TNT], 'in union with' [GEL]. The phrase ἐν κυρίῳ 'in the Lord' is translated 'if the Lord wills' [TNT]. This preposition indicates where Paul's trust is [Ea, EBC, El, GNC, NIC, TH, WC], as in 2:19 [Alf, Ea, EBC, GNC, NIC, TH]. It means that Paul is governed by Christ's mind [EGT, NIC, TH]. This phrase indicates the basis for Paul's confidence of release, i.e., if the Lord wills it [TNTC, WBC, WC].

d. ταχέως (GEL 67.56) (BAGD 1.a. p. 806): 'soon' [BAGD, GEL, HNTC, ICC, Ln, NTC, WEC; NAB, NIV, NRSV, TEV], 'very soon' [GEL, Pl, WBC], 'without delay' [BAGD], 'shortly' [Ea; KJV, NASB], 'before long' [NJB, REB], 'not long' [TNT], 'speedily' [Mou]. It implies not long after Timothy's visit [El], and indicates Paul's expectation that he will soon be released [ICC].

QUESTION—Why is this verse mentioned?

It indicates Paul's confidence that he would be released and that it would be soon [My(D)], lest the Philippians assume that his preceding words imply that he is in imminent danger [WEC]: I am confident that I will be released and will be able to visit you soon.

QUESTION—What relationship is indicated by καί 'also'?

It emphasizes that Paul plans to come as well as to send Timothy [Alf, Ea, El, Lg, My]: I also, as well as Timothy.

DISCOURSE UNIT: 2:25–30 [EBC, EGT, ICC, Lg, Ln, MNTC, My(D), NIC, NTC, Pl, TH, TNTC, WBC, WC, WEC; NAB]. The topic is Epaphroditus [EBC, WBC, WEC; NAB], a commendation of Epaphroditus [TNTC], Epaphroditus returning to Philippi [Lg, Ln, MNTC, NTC, Pl, TH], news about Epaphroditus and his return to Philippi [NIC], information about Epaphroditus and urging that he be welcomed [EGT], the illness and recovery of Epaphroditus, his service to Paul, and his planned return to Philippi [WC].

2:25

But[a] I-considered[b] (it) necessary to-send to you

LEXICON—a. δέ (GEL 89.94; 89.124): 'but' [GEL, HNTC, Mou, NTC, Pl; NASB, NIV], 'yet' [Ea; KJV], 'still' [NRSV], 'nevertheless' [NJB], 'now' [Ln], 'meanwhile' [ICC], 'in the meantime' [WBC], 'too' [NAB], 'so' [WEC], not explicit [REB, TEV, TNT].

b. aorist mid. (deponent = act.) of ἡγέομαι (GEL 31.1) (BAGD 2. p. 343): 'to consider' [BAGD, Ln, NTC, WBC], 'to think' [BAGD, GEL, HNTC; NASB, NIV, NJB, NRSV, TEV], 'to judge' [Ea], 'to regard' [BAGD], 'to count' [Mou], 'to account' [Pl], 'to decide' [NAB, REB], 'to find' [WEC], 'to feel' [TNT], 'to suppose' [KJV], not explicit [ICC]. It is an epistolary aorist, expressing what will be past when the Philippians read the letter [Ea, EBC, EGT, El, GNC, HNTC, Ln, Lt, Mou, MNTC, My(D), NTC, Pl, TH, TNTC, WBC, WEC].

QUESTION—What relationship is indicated by δέ 'but/and'?
1. It indicates contrast [Blm, Ea, El, HNTC, ICC, Lg, MNTC, Mou, NTC, Pl; KJV, NASB, NIV, NJB]: I hope to send Timothy later, but in the meantime I will send Epahproditus.
2. It indicates transition to an additional piece of information [Ln]: now.
QUESTION—What is implied by the position of ἀναγκαῖον 'necessary'?
It is emphatic by forefronting, implying Paul's emphasis upon the importance of sending Epaphroditus [MNTC, My(D)]. Paul felt that it was necessary for him to have further news of the Philippian church [My(D)].
QUESTION—What meaning is implied by πέμψαι 'to send'?
1. It means to send him back home [Alf, El, My, NIC, NTC]: to send him home to you.
2. It does not mean to send him back home [Lg]; Epaphroditus had come to stay with Paul indefinitely [Bg, TNTC, WBC]: to send him to you.

Epaphroditus the brother[a] and fellow-worker[b] and fellow-soldier[c] of-me, and/but[d] your messenger[e] and minister[f] of my need,[g]

LEXICON—a. ἀδελφός (GEL 11.23) (BAGD 2. p. 16): 'brother' [BAGD, Ea, HNTC, ICC, Ln, Mou, NTC, WBC, WEC; all translations], 'Christian brother' [GEL], 'fellow believer' [GEL], 'one who is with me in faith' [Pl]. This word refers to their sharing of spiritual life in Christ [EBC, El, ICC, Lg, MNTC, NIC, NTC, Pl, TNTC, WBC].

b. συνεργός (GEL 42.44) (BAGD p. 787): 'fellow worker' [BAGD, GEL, HNTC, ICC, Ln, Mou, NTC, WBC; NASB, NIV, NJB, REB], 'co-worker' [WEC; NAB, NRSV], 'companion in labor' [KJV], 'one who shares my labours' [Pl], 'fellow-labourer' [Ea]. The phrase τὸν συνεργόν μου 'my fellow worker' is translated 'who has worked by my side' [TEV], 'he has worked with me' [TNT]. The reference is to their labors in the gospel [EBC, El, ICC, Lg, NIC, NTC, TNTC, WBC].

c. συστρατιώτης (GEL 34.19) (BAGD p. 795): 'fellow soldier' [BAGD, Ea, ICC, Ln, Mou, NTC, WBC, WEC; KJV, NASB, NIV, NRSV], 'comrade' [REB], 'comrade in arms' [BAGD; NAB], 'companion in arms' [HNTC; NJB], 'one who shares my conflicts' [Pl], 'fellow struggler' [GEL]. The phrase τὸν συστρατιώτην μου 'my fellow soldier' is translated 'who has fought by my side' [TEV], 'he has fought at my side' [TNT]. It refers to sharing in the dangers encountered for the gospel [EBC, Lg], to defending the gospel [El, TNTC] against hostile powers [My, NTC, WBC], against the powers of darkness [Alf, NIC, NTC] and adversaries [ICC, NIC, NTC, WBC].

d. δέ (GEL 89.94; 89.124): 'and' [GEL, Ln, NTC, WBC; TEV], 'but' [Ea, GEL, Pl; KJV], 'while' [Mou], 'who is also' [NASB, NIV], not explicit [HNTC, WEC; NAB, NJB, NRSV, REB, TNT]. The phrase ὑμῶν δὲ ἀπόστολον καὶ λειτουργὸν τῆς χρείας μου 'and your messenger and minister of my need' is translated 'and who has served as your messenger in helping me' [TEV], 'who came as the bearer of your gift to me' [ICC].

e. ἀπόστολος (GEL 33.194) (BAGD 1. p. 99): 'messenger' [BAGD, GEL, NTC; KJV, NASB, NIV, NRSV, TEV, TNT], 'special messenger' [GEL], 'emissary' [WEC], 'envoy' [WBC], 'deputy' [Ea], 'commissioner' [Ln], 'whom you sent to me' [Pl], 'missionary' [Mou]. The phrase ὑμῶν δὲ ἀπόστολον καὶ λειτουργόν 'your apostle and servant' is translated 'whom you sent' [NAB], 'since he came as your representative to look after' [NJB], 'whom you commissioned to attend to' [REB], 'whom you sent with your commission to execute your service in' [HNTC]. The meaning is not 'apostle' in the usual New Testament sense, but simply one who was sent as a commissioned messenger to carry out an assignment [Alf, Bg, Ea, EBC, HNTC, ICC, Lg, Ln, Lt, MNTC, My, NIC, NTC, Pl, TNTC, WEC], a secular relationship [El]. It is used in the special sense, presenting Epaphroditus as an apostle equal with Paul in the sense of having authority to perform a specific task [WBC], or as a commissioned person on a sacred mission [WC].

f. λειτουργός (GEL 35.23) (BAGD 3. p. 471): 'minister' [Ea, NTC, WEC; NASB, NRSV], 'servant' [BAGD, GEL], 'public servant' [Ln], 'ministrant' [Mou]. This noun is also translated as an infinitive: 'to serve' [Pl; TNT], 'to take care of' [WBC; NAB], as a phrase: 'he that ministered' [KJV]. The phrase καὶ λειτουργὸν 'and servant' is translated 'whom you sent to take care of' [NIV]. The meaning is a minister in the performance of a religious duty [Ea, EBC, EGT, GNC, HNTC, Mou, MNTC, NIC, NTC, Pl, TNTC, WBC, WC, WEC], an administrative service [El], a public service, not religious [Ln, My(D)]; its meaning is general [Lg].

g. χρεία (GEL 57.40) (BAGD 2. p. 885): 'need' [BAGD, Ea, GEL, HNTC, Ln, Mou, NTC, Pl, WBC, WEC; all translations except KJV, TEV], 'lack' [GEL], 'want' [KJV]. The gift was material or financial aid [Blm, Ea, EBC, HNTC, Lt, Mou, MNTC, My, NIC, Pl, TNTC, WBC, WC]. Paul's need was helpers, not money [Ln].

QUESTION—How are the three terms connected in the phrase describing the association between Paul and Epaphroditus?

The three terms are increasingly emphatic [Ea, El, Ln, Lt, MNTC, My, NTC, Pl], progressing from more general to more specific [Lg], and μου 'my' governs all three nouns [Lg]: my brother, my fellow worker, and my fellow soldier. All three are governed by one definite article [Ea, Lg, Pl, WBC].

QUESTION—What relationship is indicated by δέ 'but/and'?

1. It indicates contrast [Ea, Lg, Pl, WBC; KJV]: but. This word introduces ὑμῶν 'your', contrasting it with μου 'my' in the preceding clause [Lg, WBC].
2. It adds new information [Ln, NTC; NASB, NIV, TEV]: and.

QUESTION—What is ὑμῶν 'your' related to?

It is related to both ἀπόστολον 'messenger' and λειτουργόν 'servant' [Bg, Ea, El, ICC, Lg, Lt, My]: your messenger and your servant. It is emphatic by forefronting, contrasting with the preceding μου 'my' [Alf, Ea, Ln, Lt, My, Pl, WBC]. These two nouns form one idea [Lt, MNTC, TH]: your messenger to serve my need.

QUESTION—How are the two nouns related in the genitive construction λειτουργὸν τῆς χρείας μου 'servant of my need'?

Epaphroditus is a servant for the purpose of meeting Paul's need [Lg, Ln]: he serves in order to meet my need. Paul's need was the lack of things that the gift brought by Epaphroditus could supply [Ea].

2:26

because[a] he-was longing-for[b] you all and being-troubled,[c] because you-heard that he-was-sick.

TEXT—Some manuscripts add ἰδεῖν 'to see' as a predicate of ἐπιποθῶν ἦν 'he was longing for', thus reading 'he was longing to see you all'. GNT omits 'to see' with a C rating, indicating a considerable degree of doubt. 'To see' is included only by Pl (doubtfully) and by TEV (but probably stylistically rather than by accepting the textual variant).

LEXICON—a. ἐπειδή (GEL 89.32) (BAGD 2. p. 284): 'because' [BAGD, GEL, ICC, Pl, WBC, WEC; NASB, NJB], 'since' [BAGD, Ln, Mou], 'for' [HNTC, NTC; KJV, NIV, NRSV], 'forasmuch as' [Ea], not explicit [NAB, REB, TEV, TNT].
   b. pres. act. participle of ἐπιποθέω (GEL 25.18) (BAGD p. 297): 'to long for' [BAGD, GEL, HNTC, Ln, NTC, WEC; NAB, NASB, NIV, NRSV, TNT], 'to long after' [Ea; KJV], 'to yearn (for)' [Pl], 'to desire' [BAGD], 'to desire deeply' [GEL], 'to miss' [NJB, REB], 'to be homesick, longing' [ICC], 'to be very homesick for' [WBC], 'to suffer from homesickness for' [Mou],

'to be anxious' [TEV]. This word is a strong term [TH, TNTC, WBC, WEC].

   c. pres. act. participle of ἀδημονέω (GEL **25.247**) (BAGD p. 16): 'to be troubled' [BAGD, HNTC], 'to be in anxiety' [BAGD], 'to worry' [NJB], 'to be very worried' [TNT], 'to be in distress' [WEC], 'to be distressed' [BAGD, Ln, NTC; NAB, NASB, NIV, NRSV], 'to be deeply distressed' [Pl], 'to be greatly distressed' [WBC], 'to be upset' [REB], 'to be very upset' [GEL; TEV], 'to be in heaviness' [Ea], 'to be full of heaviness' [KJV], 'to suffer from distraction' [Mou]. This participle is translated as a phrase 'since he feared that you would be distressed' [ICC]. The addition of this word adds emphasis to the comment about Epaphroditus's feelings [EBC]. This is another strong word [TH, TNTC, WBC, WEC]. This participle also is connected with the preceding ἦν 'was' [ICC].

QUESTION—What relationship is indicated by ἐπειδή 'because'?

It indicates the reason Paul felt it necessary to send Epaphroditus [Alf, Ea, El, ICC, Lg, Ln, MNTC, My, NIC, NTC, TH, WBC]: I felt it necessary to send him because he was distressed. The two participles in this verse joined by καί 'and' express two reasons for sending him [Lg, Ln, NIC, WBC].

QUESTION—What does the imperfect tense of ἦν 'was' indicate?

   1. The imperfect tense of the verb is epistolary, expressing past time from the point of view of the readers [Alf, Ea, Lg, Mou, My]: when he was with me he was longing for you and was troubled.

   2. It expresses continuation of the feelings from even prior to the time when Paul wrote this letter [Ln, My(D)]: he was continuing to long for you and to be distressed while he was with me.

QUESTION—What does the use of the periphrastic form of the imperfect tense indicate?

The periphrastic imperfect tense, ἦν 'was' with the participle, intensifies the expression of the feelings of Epaphroditus [Lt, Mou]. It indicates the persistent continuance of his feelings [Ea, El, ICC, Lg, MNTC, Pl, TH, WBC]. It focuses on the state of mind of Epaphroditus [My].

QUESTION—What does the aorist tense of ἠσθένησεν 'he was sick' indicate?

   1. It refers to his whole illness as a single fact [EGT, Pl]: he had a bout of illness.

   2. It is ingressive, referring to the onset of his illness [NIC]: he became ill.

2:27
for^a indeed^b he-was-sick near^c to-death;

LEXICON—γάρ (GEL 89.23) (BAGD 1.e. p. 152): 'for' [BAGD, Ea,
   GEL, Mou, Pl; KJV, NASB], 'because' [GEL], 'and' [HNTC,
   ICC, Ln, NTC], not explicit [WBC, WEC; all translations except
   KJV, NASB].

   b. καί (GEL 89.93): 'indeed' [Ln, NTC, Pl, WBC, WEC; all
   translations except NAB], 'even' [GEL], 'in fact' [HNTC; NAB],
   'really' [Ea], not explicit [ICC, Mou].

   c. παραπλήσιος (GEL **64.9**) (BAGD p. 621): 'near' [HNTC], 'very
   near' [Ln], 'to the point of' [NAB, NASB], 'on the verge of'
   [NTC], 'nigh unto' [Ea; KJV], 'almost the same as' [GEL]. The
   phrase παραπλήσιον θανάτῳ 'near to death' is translated 'so
   much so that it seemed as though he would die' [ICC], 'so that
   he came close to death' [WEC], 'so that he nearly died'
   [BAGD; NRSV], 'and very nearly died' [Pl], 'and nearly died'
   [NJB], 'he nearly died' [WBC], 'and almost died' [NIV, TEV],
   'at death's door' [TNT], 'almost fatally' [Mou], 'dangerously'
   [REB]. This adjective is used as an adverb here [ICC, My].

QUESTION—What relationship is indicated by γάρ 'for'?

   1. It indicates a confirmation that what they had heard was
   correct [Alf, Ea, El, ICC, Lg, MNTC, My, WBC, WEC]: you
   heard correctly that he was sick, for he really was sick.

   2. The phrase καὶ γάρ 'for indeed' intensifies the previous
   statement that he was sick [EGT, GNC].

   3. The phrase καὶ γάρ 'for indeed' implies that the previous
   statement that he was sick was an understatement since he had
   nearly died [EBC, Lt].

but^a God had-mercy-on^b him, and^c not him only but me also,

LEXICON—a. ἀλλά (GEL 89.125): 'but' [Ea, GEL, HNTC, ICC, Ln,
   Mou, NTC, Pl, WBC, WEC; all translations].

   b. aorist act. indic. of ἐλεέω (GEL 88.76) (BAGD p. 249): 'to have
   mercy on' [BAGD, Ea, GEL, NTC, WEC; KJV, NASB, NIV,
   NRSV], 'to be merciful to' [GEL, ICC; REB], 'to show mercy'
   [GEL, Ln], 'to take pity on' [HNTC, WBC; NAB, NJB], 'to have
   pity on' [TEV, TNT], 'to pity' [Mou]. The phrase ἠλέησεν αὐτόν
   'had mercy on him' is translated 'in his mercy spared him' [Pl].

   c. δέ (GEL 89.94; 89.124): 'and' [Ea, GEL, HNTC, Ln, Mou,
   NTC, WBC, WEC; all translations except NAB], 'I should say'
   [NAB], not explicit [ICC, Pl]. This word introduces an
   explanatory addition [Lg].

QUESTION—In what way did God have mercy on Epaphroditus?

God had mercy on him by healing him [Bg, Blm, Ea, EBC, GNC, Lg, MNTC, NIC, TNTC, WBC], presumably through Paul's prayer but not by miracle [Ea, NTC].

in-order-that[a] not grief upon[b] grief I-might-have.[c]

LEXICON—a. ἵνα (GEL 89.59): 'in order that' [Ln], 'so that' [GEL, WBC; NRSV], 'that' [Ea, Mou, NTC]. The phrase ἵνα μή 'in order that not' is translated 'lest' [HNTC, WEC; KJV, NASB]. The phrase ἵνα μὴ σχῶ 'in order that I might not have' is translated 'to save me from having' [Pl], 'so as to spare me' [NAB], 'to spare me' [NIV, NJB, REB], 'and spared me' [ICC; TEV], 'he spared me' [TNT]. This word introduces the purpose of God's having mercy [Lg].

b. ἐπί with accusative object (GEL 89.101) (BAGD III.1.b.β. p. 289): 'upon' [BAGD, Ea, HNTC, Ln, Mou, NTC; KJV, NASB, NIV, TNT], 'added upon' [WEC], 'in addition to' [GEL], 'on top of' [NJB, REB], 'after' [WBC; NAB, NRSV]. The phrase λύπην ἐπὶ λύπην 'sorrow upon sorrow' is translated 'an even greater sorrow' [TEV], 'the additional sorrow' [ICC], 'an additional burden of sorrow' [Pl]. It indicates piling one thing on another to add to it [EGT, Mou].

c. aorist act. subj. of ἔχω (GEL 90.65) (BAGD I.2.e.β. p. 333): 'to have' [BAGD, Ea, GEL, HNTC, Ln, Mou, NTC, WBC, WEC; KJV, NASB, NRSV], 'to experience' [GEL]. The aorist tense is ingressive, pointing to the action of incurring the grief [EGT, Ln].

QUESTION—What is meant by λύπην ἐπὶ λύπην 'grief upon grief'?

1. It means adding the grief of Epaphroditus' death to the grief of Paul's imprisonment [Alf, Bg, Ea, El, ICC, Lg, Mou, My, Pl, TNTC, WC]: in order that I might not have grief over the death of Epaphroditus in addition to my grief over my imprisonment. It also includes grief over the illness of Epaphroditus [Bg], the actions of his adversaries [My, WC], and his uncertain future [WC].

2. It means adding the grief of Epaphroditus's death to the grief of Epaphroditus's illness [EBC, GNC, HNTC, Ln, NIC, NTC, TH, WBC]: in order that I might not have grief over the death of Epaphroditus in addition to my grief over his illness.

2:28

More-eagerly/quickly[a] therefore I-have-sent him,

LEXICON—a. σπουδαίως (GEL 25.75) (BAGD 1. p. 763): 'the more eagerly' [HNTC, NTC, Pl], 'all the more eagerly' [NASB], 'very eagerly' [BAGD], 'more quickly' [Ln], 'as promptly as I can'

[NJB], 'the more speedily' [Ea], 'with all the greater dispatch' [WEC], 'sooner than expected' [WBC], 'more carefully' [KJV], not explicit [ICC]. This adverb is also translated 'especially eager' [NAB], 'the more eager' [NRSV], 'all the more eager' [NIV, REB, TEV, TNT], 'with the more earnestness' [Mou]. The phrase σπουδαιοτέρως ἔπεμψα 'more diligently I have sent' is translated 'I am all the more eager to send' [GEL].

QUESTION—What relationship is indicated by οὖν 'therefore?

It introduces a further reason why Paul is sending Epaphroditus back [Lg, Ln, NTC, WBC; REB]: for this further reason I am sending him.

QUESTION—What is meant by σπουδαιοτέρως 'more eagerly/quickly'?

1. It means 'more eagerly' [El, Lt, Mou, NTC, Pl, TH, TNTC, WC; all translations except KJV, NJB].
2. It means 'more quickly' [Blm, EBC, ICC, Lg, Ln, MNTC, My, NIC, WBC, WEC; NJB].
3. It has both senses [Bg, EGT].

QUESTION—What does the aorist tense of ἔπεμψα 'I have sent' indicate?

The aorist tense is an epistolary aorist, referring to what will be past when the Philippians read the letter, since Epaphroditus will carry the letter [Ea, EBC, EGT, GNC, ICC, Ln, Lt, MNTC, Mou, NIC, Pl, TH, TNTC, WBC]: I have sent him (when you read this).

in-order-that[a] having-seen him again you-might-rejoice[b] and-I might-be less-sorrowful.[c]

LEXICON—a. ἵνα (GEL 89.59): 'in order that' [Ea, ICC, Ln, NTC, Pl, WBC; NASB, NRSV], 'so that' [GEL, HNTC, WEC; NAB, NIV, NJB, TEV], 'that' [Mou; KJV, TNT], not explicit [REB]. This word introduces Paul's purpose (his intended result [WBC]) in sending Epaphroditus [Lg, MNTC].

b. aorist act. subj. of χαίρω (GEL 25.125) (BAGD 1. p. 873): 'to rejoice' [BAGD, Ea, GEL, Ln, NTC, WEC; KJV, NASB, NRSV], 'to be glad' [BAGD, GEL, HNTC, Mou, WBC; NIV, TEV], 'to have joy' [NJB, TNT], 'to renew one's joy' [NAB], 'to regain one's joy' [Pl]. This verb is paraphrased '(I am eager) to give you happiness' [REB], '(his return) may restore your cheerfulness' [ICC].

c. ἀλυπότερος (GEL 25.278) (BAGD p. 41): 'less sorrowful' [Ea, HNTC, NTC; KJV], 'less anxious' [BAGD; NRSV], 'less concerned' [NASB], 'more relieved' [Ln], 'relieved of anxiety' [GEL, WBC, WEC]. The phrase κἀγὼ ἀλυπότερος ὦ 'and I might be less grieved' is translated 'and that I may feel less sorrow' [Mou], 'and that I may have my sorrow lessened' [Pl], 'and that my own grief may be relieved' [TNT], 'and my own anxieties may be lessened' [NAB], 'and I may have less anxiety' [NIV], 'and that will be some comfort to me in my distress' [NJB], 'that will relieve my anxiety as well' [REB], 'and the sorrow of my captivity may be mitigated' [ICC], 'and my own sorrow will disappear' [TEV]. The meaning is that Paul will have less anxiety [Alf, Bg, Ea, EBC, El, HNTC, ICC, Lg, Lt, MNTC, Mou, My, NIC, NTC, Pl, TNTC, WBC, WC; KJV, NAB, NASB, NIV, NJB, NRSV]; it means that his anxiety will be removed [GNC, TH; TEV].

QUESTION—What relationship is indicated by the participle ἰδόντες 'having seen'?

1. It is temporal [Ea, EBC, ICC, NTC; KJV, NAB, NASB, NIV, TEV]: when you have seen him you will rejoice. The aorist tense refers to the seeing as an event, but none of the commentaries mention this point.

2. It gives the reason for their anticipated joy [Alf, Ln; NJB, NRSV, REB, TNT]: you may rejoice because you see him.

QUESTION—What is πάλιν 'again' connected with?

1. It is connected with ἰδόντες αὐτόν 'having seen him' [Ln, NTC, WBC, WEC; all translations except NAB, TEV]: having seen him again.

2. It is connected with χαρῆτε 'you may rejoice' [Alf, Ea, EBC, El, HNTC, ICC, Lg, Lt, MNTC, Mou, My, NIC, Pl, TH; NAB, TEV]: you may rejoice again.

QUESTION—How would this make Paul less sorrowful?

Knowing that they are rejoicing over Epaphroditus's return would make Paul joyful and lessen his sorrows [Alf, Bg, El, MNTC, Mou, My, NIC, NTC, Pl, WC]. This is because godly men receive joy from hearing of others' joy [Bg]. One of his sorrows was sympathizing with the Philippians' anxiety [EGT, El]. He was sorry that they had heard of the illness [Ln]. He sorrowed over being an involuntary cause of their concern [GNC]. He would be relieved to know that he would no longer be responsible for Epaphroditus's well-being [WBC]. He would know that when Epaphroditus got to Philippi, this would rally them and help them resolve their differences [HNTC].

2:29

Receive/Welcome[a] him therefore[b] in[c] (the) Lord with[d] all joy and[e] hold[f] such-ones[g] honored,[h]

LEXICON—a. pres. mid. (deponent = act.) impera. of προσδέχομαι (GEL 34.53) (BAGD 1.a. p. 712): 'to receive' [Ea, GEL, ICC, Ln, Mou; KJV, NASB, TEV], 'to welcome' [BAGD, GEL,

HNTC, WBC, WEC; NAB, NIV, NJB, NRSV, REB], 'to give a welcome' [TNT], 'to give a hearty welcome' [Pl], 'to extend a welcome' [NTC], 'to accept' [GEL]. The emphasis is upon this word [Alf] by its position [Lg]; Paul is requiring an appropriate welcome [Lg].

b. οὖν (GEL 89.50) (BAGD 1.b. p. 593): 'therefore' [BAGD, Ea, GEL, HNTC, ICC, Mou, Pl; KJV, NASB], 'then' [WBC; NJB, NRSV, REB, TEV, TNT], 'accordingly' [BAGD, GEL, Ln], 'so' [BAGD, GEL, NTC, WEC], not explicit [NAB, NIV]. This word refers to Paul's purpose in the preceding verse [Alf, Ea, ICC, Lg, My].

c. ἐν with dative object (GEL 89.119) (BAGD I.5.d. p. 260): 'in' [BAGD, Ea, GEL, HNTC, ICC, Ln, Mou, NTC, Pl, WBC, WEC; all translations except REB, TNT], 'in the fellowship of' [REB]. The phrase ἐν κυρίῳ 'in the Lord' is translated 'Christian' [TNT].

d. μετά with genitive object (GEL 89.79): 'with' [Ea, GEL, HNTC, Ln, Mou, Pl, WBC, WEC; all translations except NAB, TNT]. The phrase μετὰ πάσης χαρᾶς 'with all joy' is translated 'joyously' [NAB], 'joyous' [TNT], 'most joyful' [NTC], 'joyfully' [ICC].

e. καί (GEL 89.92; 89.93): 'and' [Ea, GEL, HNTC, Ln, Mou, NTC, Pl, WEC; KJV, NAB, NASB, NIV, NRSV], 'and also' [GEL], 'in addition' [GEL], not explicit [ICC, WBC; NJB, REB, TEV, TNT].

f. pres. act. impera. of ἔχω (GEL 31.1) (BAGD I.5. p. 333): 'to hold' [BAGD, Ea, HNTC, Ln, Mou, NTC, Pl, WBC, WEC; KJV, NAB, NASB, NJB], 'to consider' [GEL], not explicit [ICC]. The phrase ἐντίμους ἔχετε 'hold honored' is translated 'show respect' [TEV], 'honor' [NIV, NRSV, REB, TNT]. The present tense implies continuing to hold [Pl].

g. τοιοῦτος (GEL 64.2; 92.31): 'such' [Ea, GEL, ICC, Ln, Mou, NTC; KJV, NRSV, TEV, TNT], 'of such a kind' [GEL], 'like that' [GEL], 'like' [HNTC, Pl, WBC, WEC; NAB, NASB, NIV, NJB, REB]. The plural used here is a generalization [EBC]; Epaphroditus is the present example, but similar treatment should be given to all such cases [EBC, El, ICC, Lg, Ln, My, NIC, NTC].

h. ἔντιμος (GEL 87.6) (BAGD 1.b. p. 269): 'honored' [GEL, ICC], 'highly honored' [BAGD], 'respected' [GEL], 'in honour' [Ea, HNTC, Ln, NTC; NJB], 'in esteem' [BAGD, WEC; NAB], 'in great esteem' [Pl], 'in high esteem' [WBC], 'in high regard' [NASB], 'in high value' [Mou], 'in reputation' [KJV]. The phrase

ἐντίμους ἔχετε 'hold honored' is translated 'show respect'
[GEL].
QUESTION—What relationship is indicated by the phrase ἐν κυρίῳ
'in the Lord'?
1. It expresses the sphere of the reception [Ea, EBC, El, Lg,
MNTC, Mou, My, Pl]: receive him in a warm Christian manner.
They should receive him as Christians should [EBC, MNTC], in
the manner appropriate to their common share in Christ [Mou].
2. It implies Epaphroditus's membership in the Christian
community [GNC]: receive him as a fellow Christian.
3. It means in gratitude to the Lord because the Lord had restored
Epaphroditus to them [NIC]: receive him with thanks to the
Lord.

2:30

because[a] on-account-of[b] the work[c] of-Christ he-came-near[d] to-the-point-
of[e] death having-risked[f] the life,[g]
TEXT—Instead of παραβολευσάμενος 'having risked', some
manuscripts read παραβουλευσάμενος 'not having regarded'. GNT
does not deal with this variant. Only Bg, Blm, and KJV read 'not
having regarded'.
TEXT—Instead of τὸ ἔργον Χριστοῦ 'the work of Christ', some
manuscripts read τὸ ἔργον κυρίου 'the work of the Lord' and one
manuscript reads simply τὸ ἔργον 'the work'. GNT reads 'the work of
Christ' with a C rating, indicating a considerable degree of doubt. 'The
work' is read by Alf, EGT, Lg, Lt, My, and Pl.
LEXICON—a. ὅτι (GEL 89.33): 'because' [GEL, Ln, Mou, NTC, Pl,
WEC; KJV, NASB, NIV, NJB, NRSV, TEV], 'because that'
[Ea], 'for' [HNTC, ICC, WBC; NAB], not explicit [REB, TNT].
b. διά with accusative object (GEL 89.26): 'on account of' [GEL,
Ln, Mou], 'because of' [GEL], 'for' [Ea, NTC, WBC, WEC;
KJV, NASB, NIV, NJB, NRSV], 'for the sake of' [HNTC; NAB,
TEV], 'through his zeal for' [ICC], 'through his devotion to' [Pl].
The phrase διὰ τὸ ἔργον Χριστοῦ 'on account of the work of
Christ' is translated 'in Christ's cause' [REB], 'in Christ's
service' [TNT]. This phrase is emphatic by forefronting [Ea,
My].
c. ἔργον (GEL 42.42) (BAGD 2. p. 308): 'work' [BAGD, Ea,
GEL, HNTC, ICC, Ln, Mou, NTC, Pl, WEC; all translations
except REB, TNT], 'service' [TNT], 'cause' [WBC; REB]. The
work here is service given to Paul [Ea, El, HNTC, ICC, My(D)]
and the difficulties of the journey to him [ICC]; it is his
carrying the gift to Paul and his zealous performance [Lg].

(Omitting Χριστοῦ 'of Christ',) 'the work' refers to the gospel [My].

d. aorist act. indic. of ἐγγίζω (GEL 15.75) (BAGD 4. p. 213): 'to come near' [Ea, GEL, Ln; NAB, NJB, REB], 'to come close' [BAGD; NASB, NRSV], 'to draw near' [GEL], 'to approach' [GEL], 'to be nigh' [KJV]. The phrase μέχρι θανάτου ἤγγισεν 'he came near to the point of death' is translated 'he came to the brink of death' [NTC], 'he came near death' [HNTC, WEC], 'he narrowly escaped death' [TNT], 'he was at death's very door' [Mou], 'he almost died' [NIV], 'he nearly died' [WBC; TEV], 'he very nearly died' [Pl], 'he well nigh died' [ICC]. This phrase repeats (more emphatically [Ea]) the similar thought in 2:27 and refers to the same thing [Ea, El, Lg]. It indicates the seriousness of his illness [El].

e. μέχρι with genitive object (GEL 78.51) (BAGD 1.c. p. 515): 'to the point of' [BAGD, GEL], 'up to' [GEL], 'even to' [Ea], 'to' [Ln; NAB, NASB, NJB, NRSV, REB], 'unto' [KJV]. The prepositional phrase μέχρι θανάτου 'to the point of death' is emphatic by forefronting, but none of the commentaries mention this point.

f. aorist mid. (deponent = act.) participle of παραβολεύομαι (GEL 21.7) (BAGD p. 612): 'to risk' [BAGD, GEL, HNTC, NTC, WBC, WEC; all translations except KJV], 'to hazard' [Ea, ICC, Pl], 'to venture' [Ln], 'to play the gambler' [Mou]; reading a different text, 'not to regard one's life' [KJV].

g. ψυχή (GEL 23.88) (BAGD 1.a.β. p. 893): 'life' [Ea, GEL, HNTC, ICC, Ln, Mou, NTC, Pl, WBC, WEC; all translations], 'earthly life' [BAGD].

QUESTION—What relationship is indicated by ὅτι 'because'?

It indicates the reason for Paul's commendation of Epaphroditus [Ea, NTC] or the reason he should be given a welcome and held in honor [Alf, EBC, GNC, Lg].

QUESTION—How are the two nouns related in the genitive construction ἔργον Χριστοῦ 'work of Christ'?

1. The genitive expresses the beneficiary [Ea, El, HNTC, WBC; NAB, TEV]: work which is done for the sake of Christ. It is work for the apostle and thus for Christ [El]. It is service for Christ [WBC].

2. The genitive expresses the source [HNTC, TH]: the work which Christ gave him to do.

3. The genitive is possessive [Ln, Mou; NAB, NJB, REB, TNT]: Christ's work.

QUESTION—What relationship is indicated by the use of the participle παραβολευσάμενος 'having risked'?

1. The aorist tense indicates the same action as ἤγγισεν 'he came near', but none of the commentaries mention this point.

1.1 The participle repeats the thought of 'he came near', but none of the commentaries mention this point): he came near to death; that is, he risked his life.

1.2 The participle expresses means [Ea, Lg, WBC]: he came near to death by risking his life.

2. The aorist tense indicates an action prior to ἤγγισεν 'he came near,' and the participle expresses the reason why he came near to death, but none of the commentaries mention this point: he came near to death because he had risked his life.

in-order-that he-might-make-up-for[a] your lack[b] of-the service[c] to[d] me.

LEXICON—a. aorist act. subj. of ἀναπληρόω (GEL 57.79) (BAGD 3. p. 59): 'to make up for' [GEL; NIV, NRSV], 'to provide what is lacking' [GEL], 'to fulfil' [HNTC, Pl], 'to fill' [Ln], 'to complete' [NASB], 'to bring to completion' [WEC], 'to supply' [Ea, Mou, NTC; KJV], 'to fill a gap' [BAGD], 'to take one's place' [TNT], 'to render' [ICC; NAB, REB], 'to give' [WBC; TEV], 'to do' [NJB]. This verb is emphatic by forefronting [Lg]. The aorist tense implies completion of the making up [Ln].

b. ὑστέρημα (GEL 57.38) (BAGD 1. p. 849): 'lack' [Mou; KJV], 'what is lacking' [GEL, NTC], 'deficiency' [Ea], 'what is deficient' [NASB], 'what is needed' [GEL], 'absence' [BAGD, Ln]. The phrase τὸ ὑμῶν ὑστέρημα 'your lack' is translated 'what you could not fulfil' [HNTC], 'that you yourselves could not give' [TEV], 'that you yourselves were not able to give' [WBC], 'which you could not do yourselves' [NJB], 'what you could not have done' [WEC], 'which you were unable to render in person' [Pl], 'which you would gladly have performed in your own persons' [ICC], 'you could not render' [NAB], 'you could not give' [NIV, NRSV, REB], 'you were not there' [TNT].

c. λειτουργία (GEL 35.22) (BAGD 2. p. 471): 'service' [BAGD, Ea, GEL, HNTC, NTC, Pl; KJV, NAB, NASB, NRSV, REB], 'ministry' [WEC], 'sacrificial service of love' [ICC], 'ministration' [Mou], 'public service' [Ln], 'help' [WBC; NIV, TEV], 'duty' [NJB]. This noun is translated as a verb 'to help' [TNT].

d. πρός with accusative object (GEL 90.58): 'to' [Ea, GEL, ICC, NTC, WEC; NASB, NJB], 'toward' [Ln, Pl; KJV], 'for' [HNTC, Mou], not explicit [WBC; NAB, NIV, NRSV, REB, TEV, TNT].

QUESTION—What relationship is indicated by ἵνα 'in order that'?

1. It indicates the purpose of παραβολευσάμενος 'having risked' [Ea, HNTC, ICC, Lg, Ln, MNTC, My, NTC, Pl, WBC, WEC;

all translations except KJV, TEV]: he risked his life in order
that he might make up for your lack.
2. It indicates the purpose of ἤγγισεν 'he came near' [TEV]: he
came near to death in order that he might make up for your
lack. This alternative agrees with Bruce Hollenbach's hypothesis
concerning subordination.

QUESTION—How are the two nouns and the pronoun related in the
genitive construction ὑμῶν ὑστέρημα τῆς λειτουργίας 'your lack of
ministry'?

Ὑμῶν 'your' tells whose lack is referred to [Ea, El, ICC, Ln, My];
λειτουργίας 'service', tells what the lack consisted of [Ea, El, Ln,
My]: what you lacked was service. Ὑμῶν 'your' is connected with
ὑστέρημα 'lack' [Ea, El, ICC, Lg, Ln, My].

QUESTION—What was their lack of service to Paul?

Their lack was their absence which prevented them from personally
ministering the gift [Alf, Ea, Ln, WEC] or ministering personal care
to Paul [EBC, EGT, El, HNTC, Lt, NIC, TH, TNTC]. This
deficiency was felt more by the Philippians, because of their love
for Paul, than by Paul himself [Bg]. This service was their gift of
money to Paul [Alf, GNC, ICC, Lg, My, Pl]; this service was a
religious service [Ea, HNTC, ICC, MNTC, My, NIC, WEC],
including also personal care, which the Philippians could not give
[GNC, HNTC].

DISCOURSE UNIT: 3:1–4:9 [TEV]. The topic is true righteousness.

DISCOURSE UNIT: 3:1, 4:2–9 [Lt]. The topic is final exhortations. After
beginning the final injunctions at 3:1, Paul breaks off and doesn't resume
them until 4:2 [Lt].

DISCOURSE UNIT: 3:1–4:1 [Alf, Lg, WEC]. The topic is warning
against Judaizers and against immoral persons (wicked deceivers [Lg])
[Alf, Lg], arguments about doctrines [WEC].

DISCOURSE UNIT: 3:1–21 [EBC, NIC, NTC, TH, TNTC, WBC; NAB,
NASB]. The topic is a major digression [TNTC], warnings and an example
[TH], warnings concerning false teachers and exhortation to follow Paul's
example [WBC], warnings concerning Judaizing teachers [NIC], warning
against Judaizing and antinomian teachers [EBC], Paul as an untiring
idealist [NTC], Christian dedication [NAB], the goal of life [NASB].

DISCOURSE UNIT: 3:1–16 [EBC, Lg, Ln; NAB]. The topic is the
danger of Judaistic teachings [EBC], the character of the false teachers
contrasted with Paul's character [Lg, Ln], breaking with the past [NAB].

DISCOURSE UNIT: 3:1-11 [Mou, TH; GNT, NIV, TEV]. The topic is joy in the Lord and how it can keep them [Mou], the true righteousness [TH; GNT, TEV], putting no confidence in the flesh [NIV].

DISCOURSE UNIT: 3:1-6 [WEC]. The topic is the Judaizers.

DISCOURSE UNIT: 3:1-3 [EGT, ICC, NIC, NTC, TNTC, WBC, WEC]. The topic is a greeting which becomes a warning [EGT], a warning against false teachers [ICC], a warning against the Judaizing teachers [NIC, NTC], a warning and a claim [TNTC], a warning against submitting to circumcision and against pride in personal accomplishments [WBC], Paul taking the offensive [WEC].

DISCOURSE UNIT: 3:1 [HNTC, My(D), Pl]. The topic is a call for the Philippians to rejoice [Pl], the beginning of the conclusion and postscript [HNTC].

DISCOURSE UNIT: 3:1a, 20-21, 4:1 [MNTC]. The topic is joy and being steadfast in the Lord.

DISCOURSE UNIT: 3:1a [WC]. The topic is a renewed call to rejoice.

3:1
(For) the rest,[a] my brothers,[b] rejoice[c] in[d] (the) Lord.
> LEXICON—a. λοιπόν (GEL 61.14; 67.134): 'for the rest' [Mou, NTC, Pl; NAB], 'as for the rest' [ICC], 'finally' [Ea, GEL, HNTC, WEC; KJV, NASB, NIV, NJB, NRSV], 'in conclusion' [TEV], 'from now on' [GEL], 'and now' [REB, TNT], 'furthermore' [Ln], 'well then' [WBC].
> b. ἀδελφός (GEL 11.23): 'brother' [Ea, HNTC, ICC, Ln, Mou, NTC, Pl, WBC, WEC; all translations except NRSV, REB], 'brother and sister' [NRSV], 'fellow believer' [GEL], 'friend' [REB]. See this word at 1:12, 14; 3:13, 17; 4:8, 21.
> c. pres. act. impera. of χαίρω (GEL 25.125) (BAGD 2.a. pp. 873, 874): 'to rejoice' [BAGD, Ea, GEL, ICC, Ln, NTC, Pl, WBC, WEC; KJV, NAB, NASB, NIV, NRSV], 'to be joyful' [TEV], 'to be glad' [Mou], 'to wish (one) joy' [NJB, REB], 'to bid (one) farewell' [HNTC]. This verb is translated 'farewell' [BAGD; TNT]. This phrase is emphatic [Lg].
> d. ἐν with dative object (GEL 89.119; 89.26) (BAGD I.5.d. p. 260): 'in' [BAGD, Ea, HNTC, ICC, Ln, Mou, NTC, WBC, WEC; all translations except TEV, TNT], 'in union with' [GEL; TEV], 'because of' [GEL], not explicit [TNT]. The phrase ἐν κυρίῳ 'in the Lord' is translated 'as all Christians should' [Pl].

QUESTION—What relationship is indicated by τὸ λοιπόν 'for the rest'?

1. It indicates that Paul was intending to close the epistle [Alf, Ea, El, GNC, HNTC, Lt, My, NIC, Pl]: finally, my brothers. He had completed dealing with his principal object in writing, and what follows is supplementary [Ea] (the concluding portion [El]). Something prompted Paul to add what follows instead of concluding immediately [GNC, HNTC, Lt, My, Pl].

2. It indicates a transition in the discourse to a new subject [Bg, Blm, EBC, ICC, Ln, Mou, WBC, WC], possibly a concluding comment [TH] which he wishes to emphasize [NTC]: furthermore, my brothers.

QUESTION—What is meant by his command to rejoice?

1. It is to be taken with what follows [EBC, Ln], urging them to rejoice even in the face of some unpleasant matters which he is about to mention [EBC]: rejoice in the Lord in spite of the following dangers. The phrase ἐν κυρίῳ 'in the Lord' shows that he is not merely telling the Philippians to rejoice on the basis of what he has mentioned in the preceding verses [Ea].

2. It means to rejoice in general and is not limited to the immediate context [ICC]: rejoice in the Lord as a regular practice.

3. It is a parting greeting meaning 'farewell' [BAGD, HNTC]. He is commencing his conclusion here, but interrupts himself to appeal to two women in the church [HNTC].

QUESTION—What is meant by rejoicing ἐν κυρίῳ 'in the Lord'?

It indicates the area or the nature of the rejoicing [Ea, ICC]; it is a joy based on the Lord [El, WBC]; it is a joy based on understanding the love of Christ [Blm]. They are to rejoice in union with him [NTC], or in connection with him [Ln]. Christ is the object of their joy [GNC]. Joy comes from him [Lg, TH], by being in fellowship with him and having the assurance of his control over their lives [NIV]. It refers to Christian joy [My]. It indicates the area within which it operates [WBC].

DISCOURSE UNIT: 3:1b-4:9 [REB]. The topic is the goal of Christians.

DISCOURSE UNIT: 3:1b, 4:1 [NJB]. The topic is the true path of salvation.

DISCOURSE UNIT: 3:1b-21 [WC]. The topic is warnings against two groups of adversaries.

DISCOURSE UNIT: 3:1b-11 [WC]. The topic is a warning against Jews.

DISCOURSE UNIT: 3:1b–7 [MNTC]. The topic is a warning and a new set of values.

DISCOURSE UNIT: 3:1b–6 [WC]. The topic is a protest against Jewish pride and exclusive spirit.

3:1b
To-write the same-(things) to-you for-me on-the-one-hand (is) not troublesome,[a] on-the-other-hand for-you (it is) safe.[b]

LEXICON—a. ὀκνηρός (GEL 22.8) (BAGD 2. p. 563): 'troublesome' [BAGD, WEC; NRSV], 'grievous' [Ea; KJV], 'irksome' [Mou, Pl], 'wearisome' [WBC], 'sluggish' [Ln]. This adjective is also translated as a noun: 'trouble' [NTC; NASB, NIV, NJB, REB], 'a bother' [GEL], 'a burden' [NAB]. The phrase ἐμοὶ οὐκ ὀκνηρόν 'for me is not troublesome' is translated 'I don't mind' [TEV], 'need not cause me trepidation' [HNTC], 'I am not backward about' [ICC], 'I do not mind' [GEL]. This phrase is a litotes, meaning that Paul is very diligent in this matter [Ln]. This word implies that such a repetition might have been tiresome to him if it were not for their benefit [Ea, Lg]. It is not tiresome, since his purpose is to guard them from wrong teaching [EBC]. It means that they can be sure that what he says is profitable for them [ICC].

b. ἀσφαλής (GEL 21.10) (BAGD 2. p. 119): 'safe' [BAGD, Ea, HNTC, Ln, Mou; KJV]. This adjective is also translated as a noun: 'a safeguard' [NTC, WEC; NAB, NASB, NIV, NRSV, REB], 'a protection' [NJB], and as a phrase: 'a matter of safety' [GEL], 'a safe course to follow' [WBC]. The phrase ὑμῖν ἀσφαλές 'for you it is safe' is translated 'you will be safer' [TEV], 'it may save you from mistakes' [Pl], 'I am moved by anxiety for your safety' [ICC].

QUESTION—What does the phrase τὰ αὐτά 'the same things' refer to and why is it safe for them?

1. It refers to his previous counsels and warnings of danger to the Philippian church [Blm, Ea, EBC, EGT, ICC, Lg, Ln, Mou, My, NIC, NTC, TH, WC, WEC] and to their unity in Christ [NTC]: to write to you again about dangers to you and the importance of your unity in Christ. For Paul to repeat in this way is for their safety [Blm, Ln, MNTC, Mou, My, NTC]. It refers to matters which Paul had previously mentioned to them and which he is about to mention again [WC, WEC]. He had mentioned these matters in person [Blm, Lg(H)]. He had written these things in a previous letter or letters [Ea, ICC, Lg, My, NIC, TH]. He had written these things earlier in this letter

[EBC, EGT, Ln, Lt]. The reference is to 1:27–30 [EBC, Ln]. The reference is to dissensions in the church [Lt]. He had mentioned these matters orally earlier and then in this and possibly a previous letter [NTC].

2. It refers to their rejoicing in the Lord [Alf, Bg, El, GNC, Mou, WBC]: to write the same things, that is, urging you to rejoice in the Lord. To rejoice in the Lord produces safety from error [Bg, WBC]: to rejoice in the Lord produces safety for you. Their rejoicing will guard them from the problems which beset the church [WBC].

DISCOURSE UNIT: 3:2–4:9 [Pl]. The topic is warnings and exhortations.

DISCOURSE UNIT: 3:2–4:1 [Lt]. The topic is a warning against two errors.

DISCOURSE UNIT: 3:2–21 [HNTC]. This is a fragment of another letter.

DISCOURSE UNIT: 3:2–16 [HNTC]. The topic is a warning against Jewish arguments, and Paul's rejection of Judaism and his dedication to Christ.

DISCOURSE UNIT: 3:2–11 [Pl]. The topic is a warning against Judaism.

3:2
Beware-of/Observe[a] the dogs,[b] beware-of/observe[a] the evil workers, beware-of/observe[a] the mutilation.[c]

LEXICON—a. pres. act. impera. of βλέπω (GEL 27.58) (BAGD 6. p. 143): 'to beware of' [BAGD, HNTC, ICC, Ln, Mou, NTC; KJV, NAB, NASB, NJB, NRSV], 'to watch out for' [GEL; NAB, NIV, TEV], 'to keep one's watch for' [WEC], 'to be on guard against' [NAB], 'to be on one's guard against' [REB, TNT], 'to be on one's guard about' [Pl], 'to look to' [Ea], 'to observe' [WBC]. The present tense implies continued watching [WEC]. This verb is repeated three times for emphasis [Ea, EGT, Lg, Ln, MNTC, My, NIC, NTC, TH, TNTC, WBC, WC, WEC].

b. κύων (GEL **88.122**; 88.282) (BAGD 2. p. 461): 'dog' [BAGD, Ea, GEL, HNTC, ICC, Ln, Mou, NTC, WBC, WEC; all translations except NAB], 'unclean dog' [Pl], 'unbelieving dog' [NAB], 'wicked person' [GEL]. This word always implies reproach [EBC, EGT, ICC, MNTC, My, NIC, Pl, TH, TNTC, WC]. This phrase describes the character of the false teachers [Ea, EBC, Lg, My]. The reference is to persons who are profane and impure [Alf, El]. It refers to false apostles and other persons who are slaves to sinful desires [Bg]. It refers to those who would excommunicate Christians who did not agree with their Judaistic teachings [Mou].

c. κατατομή (GEL **19.22**) (BAGD p. 419): 'mutilation' [BAGD, GEL, Ln, WEC], 'physical mutilation' [ICC], 'self-mutilation' [Pl], 'concision' [Ea, Mou, NTC; KJV], 'incision' [HNTC], 'false circumcision' [NASB]. This noun is translated so as to refer to the persons: 'mutilator' [WBC], 'self-mutilator' [NJB], 'one who mutilates' [NAB], 'one who mutilates the flesh' [NIV, NRSV], 'one who practices mutilation' [GEL], 'one who insists on mutilation' [REB], 'one who insists on physical mutilation' [TNT], 'one who insists on cutting the body' [TEV]. It refers to the persons who promote circumcision (to persons who are circumcised [Lg]), not the action [Blm, Ea, EBC, GNC, Lg, Ln, MNTC, TH, WC, WEC; NAB, NIV, NJB, NRSV, REB], with emphasis on their teachings [Ea, EBC]. It refers to the action of circumcision [Pl, TNTC]. It is the apostle's derogatory wordplay on circumcision when it has no spiritual significance [Ea, EBC, EGT, El, GNC, HNTC, ICC, Ln, My, NIC, NTC, Pl, TH, TNTC, WC, WEC]; this word also links it to pagan mutilations of the flesh [GNC].

QUESTION—What is the meaning of βλέπετε 'beware of, observe'?

1. The meaning is to beware of them [EGT, GNC, Ln, Lt, TH, WEC].

2. The meaning is to observe them [Alf, Bg, El, ICC, Lg, MNTC, My, NIC, WBC], which will cause the Philippians to avoid their teachings [Alf, Bg, Ea, ICC, Lg, MNTC, My, NIC, WBC].

QUESTION—Who are the persons referred to in this verse?

All three phrases refer to the same persons [NIV, REB]. The definite article with each indicates that a well-known group is referred to [Pl].

1. They are the Judaizers, who taught that circumcision is necessary in addition to faith in Christ [Ea, EBC, EGT, GNC, ICC, Lg, Ln, Lt, MNTC, My, NIC, NTC, Pl, TH, TNTC, WEC]. The first term refers to their character, the second to their conduct, and the third to their teachings [Ea, EBC, Lg].

2. They are unconverted Jews who were attempting to win Gentile converts to Judaism [Bg, HNTC, WBC, WC].

QUESTION—What is implied by the term κακοὺς ἐργάτας 'evil workers'?

1. It refers to persons who professed to work for the gospel, but whose works were evil [Alf, Ea, El, Lg, Ln, Lt, NTC, TH]: beware of those who do evil things in the name of the gospel. It refers to persons who do not serve God [Bg].

2. It refers to those who insisted on works for salvation.
2.1 They were Judaizers [Ea, EBC, EGT, ICC, Lg, MNTC, My, NIC, Pl, TNTC, WEC]: those Judaizers who insist on works for salvation. The evil was their false aim [EGT].
2.2 They were Jews [WBC]: those Jews who insist on works for salvation. The meaning is not that their deeds were evil but rather that reliance on works for salvation was harmful [WBC].

3:3
For[a] we are the circumcision,[b] the-(ones) worshiping[c] by-(the)-Spirit/ spirit[d] of-God and boasting[e] in[f] Christ Jesus and not trusting[g] in[h] flesh,[i]

TEXT: Instead of the genitive case θεοῦ 'of God', some manuscripts read the dative θεῷ, which changes the translation of the phrase from 'worshiping by the Spirit of God' to 'worshiping God in/by spirit/the Spirit'. GNT reads the genitive case with a C rating, indicating a considerable degree of doubt. The genitive case is read by Alf, Ea, EBC, El, GNC, HNTC, ICC, Lg, Ln, Lt, Mou, My, NIC, NTC, Pl, TNTC, WBC, WC, WEC, and by all translations except KJV and possibly TEV. The dative case is read by Bg, Blm, EGT, and KJV.
LEXICON—a. γάρ (GEL 89.23): 'for' [Ea, GEL, HNTC, Ln, Mou, NTC, Pl, WBC, WEC; KJV, NASB, NIV, NRSV], 'because' [GEL], not explicit [ICC; NAB, NJB, REB, TEV, TNT].
  b. περιτομή (GEL 53.51) (BAGD 4.b. p. 653): 'circumcision' [BAGD, Ea, GEL, HNTC, Ln, Mou, NTC, WBC; KJV, NAB, NIV, NJB, NRSV, REB], 'true circumcision' [ICC, Pl; NASB], 'true people of the circumcision' [NJB]. This noun is translated as a participle: 'circumcised' [WEC]; and as a phrase: 'the truly circumcised' [TNT]. The phrase ἐσμεν ἡ περιτομή 'we are the circumcision' is translated '(we) who have received the true circumcision' [TEV]. The reference is to spiritual circumcision [Blm, Lt, NIC, TH, TNTC], whether or not physical circumcision has taken place [Alf, Ea, EBC, Lg, My, NTC]. The reference is to the circumcised persons, not to the rite itself [Bg, Ea, GNC, HNTC, Ln, TNTC; NJB, TEV].
  c. pres. act. participle of λατρεύω (GEL 53.14) (BAGD p. 467): 'to worship' [GEL, HNTC, Ln, Mou, NTC, WBC, WEC; all translations except TNT], 'to offer worship' [Pl], 'to serve' [Ea]. The phrase οἱ πνεύματι θεοῦ λατρεύοντες 'the ones worshiping by the Spirit of God' is translated 'the Spirit of God directs our worship' [TNT], 'whose service is prompted by the Spirit of God' [ICC]. The meaning is religious service [Ea] by people in general [Alf, ICC, Ln, Lt, Mou, WBC, WC] and obedience to

God [Alf]. This verb is used here of the worship of God but without an expressed object [Ea, El, Lg, Lt, My]. The present participle is used as a noun to identify a class of people [EGT].

d. πνεῦμα (GEL 12.18; 26.9) (BAGD 5.a. p. 676): 'Spirit' [BAGD, Ea, GEL, HNTC, ICC, Ln, Mou, NTC, Pl, WBC, WEC; all translations except KJV, NAB], 'spirit' [GEL; KJV, NAB]. The phrase πνεύματι θεοῦ 'by the Spirit of God' is emphatic by word order [Alf].

e. pres. mid. (deponent = act.) participle of καυχάομαι (GEL 33.368) (BAGD 1. p. 425): 'to boast' [BAGD, GEL, Ln, WBC; NRSV], 'to make one's boast' [Ea; NJB], 'to place one's boast' [WEC], 'to have one's boast' [Pl], 'to pride oneself' [BAGD], 'to take pride' [HNTC], 'to rejoice' [KJV, TEV], 'to glory' [BAGD, NTC; NAB, NASB, NIV], 'to exult' [Mou]. The phrase οἱ καυχώμενοι 'the ones boasting' is translated 'whose rejoicing is' [ICC], 'whose pride is' [REB], 'our pride is' [TNT]. The present tense indicates continuing boasting or further identifies a class of people, but none of the commentaries mention this point.

f. ἐν with dative object (GEL 89.5; 89.119; 90.23): 'in' [Ea, GEL, HNTC, ICC, Ln, Mou, NTC, Pl, WBC, WEC; all translations except NJB, TEV], 'with regard to' [GEL], 'in union with' [GEL; TEV], not explicit [NJB].

g. perf. act. participle of πείθω (GEL 31.82) (BAGD 2.a. p. 639): 'to trust' [BAGD, GEL, ICC], 'to have trust' [Ea], 'to put trust' [TEV], 'to put one's trust' [NAB], 'to rely' [GEL, NJB], 'to depend' [BAGD, GEL], 'to have confidence' [GEL; KJV, NRSV], 'to place confidence' [WEC; TNT], 'to put confidence' [NTC, Pl, WBC; NASB, NIV, REB], 'to put one's confidence' [BAGD, HNTC], 'to rest confidence' [Ln], 'to be confident' [Mou]. The perfect tense indicates a state of boasting continuing from past boasting [Ln].

h. ἐν with dative object (GEL 90.23): 'in' [Ea, GEL, HNTC, Ln, Mou, NTC, Pl, WBC, WEC; all translations except NJB], 'on' [NJB], not explicit [ICC].

i. σάρξ (GEL 8.63; 9.12) (BAGD 6. p. 744): 'flesh' [Ea, GEL, HNTC, ICC, Ln, Mou, NTC, WEC; KJV, NAB, NASB, NIV, NRSV], 'earthly things' [BAGD], 'external things' [TNT], 'external ceremonies' [TEV], 'external privileges' [Pl], 'physical nature' [GEL], 'physical advantages' [BAGD], 'physical qualifications' [NJB], 'ourselves' [WBC]. This noun is translated as an adjective: 'physical' [REB]. The phrase ἐν σαρκί 'in flesh' is emphatic by word order [Alf].

QUESTION—What relationship is indicated by γάρ 'for'?

 1. It indicates the reason why Paul used the word κατατομή 'mutilation' in the preceding sentence [Bg, Blm, Ea, EBC, El, ICC, Lg(H), MNTC, My, Pl, TH, WBC]: I do not call it circumcision, for we, not they, are the true circumcision.

 2. It indicates the reason why they should beware of the false teachers [Ln, NTC]: beware of them, for we, not they, are the true circumcision. Since the Philippian Christians are different from the false teachers, they should have nothing to do with these teachers [Ln].

QUESTION—What is the significance of the overt pronoun ἡμεῖς 'we'?

 It is emphatic, contrasting Paul and the Philippian Christians with those whose circumcision was only physical [Blm, EGT, ICC, Lg, Ln, MNTC, Mou, My, Pl, TH, WEC]: we, in contrast with them. It includes all true Christians [Ln, MNTC, Mou, My, Pl, WEC].

QUESTION—Why are the three participial phrases mentioned?

 They give the content of the true spiritual circumcision [EBC, El, Lg, Ln, MNTC, My, NIC, NTC, TH, TNTC, WBC, WC, WEC]: this is how true circumcision is identified. The three phrases under one definite article show that they all describe one group [MNTC, My]. The second and third phrases describe the same thing, first positively and then negatively [My, NTC, TH, WBC]. However, the third is not the same as the second [TH] (since it is introduced by καί 'and' [My]), but rather repudiates the basis for the Judaizers' boasting [ICC].

QUESTION—What is meant by the phrase οἱ πνεύματι θεοῦ λατρεύοντες 'the ones worshiping by the Spirit of God'?

 1. For those who accept the genitive θεοῦ 'of God'.

 1.1 This refers to the Holy Spirit and means the ones who worship by the agency of God's Spirit [Alf, Ea, EBC, El, ICC, Lg, Lt, Mou, My, NIC, NTC, Pl, TH, TNTC, WBC, WC, WEC]. The Spirit inspires them to worship [TH, TNTC, WBC]. They worship under the impulse and direction of the Spirit [ICC, TH]. The Spirit prompts and accompanies their worship [Ea]. The presence of the Spirit enables them to offer true worship to God [WC, WEC].

 1.2 This refers to the Holy Spirit and means the ones who worship God's Spirit [Ln].

 1.3 This refers to the human spirit and means the ones who worship in spirit [HNTC].

 2. For those who accept the dative θεῷ 'God', it refers to human spirit and means the ones who worship God in spirit, not in the

letter or rules [Bg, Blm, EGT]. They worship God with the spiritual service that Christ spoke about in John 4:23 [Blm].

QUESTION—What is implied by the phrase ἐν Χριστῷ Ἰησοῦ 'in Christ Jesus'?

Christ is the object of their boasting [GNC]. It implies that the basis of their boasting is Christ, rather than ceremonies and status [Blm, Ea, EBC, ICC, Ln, NTC, WBC]: Christ Jesus is the basis of our boasting. They recognize that their hope is found in Christ alone [EBC]. They rejoice in Christ as the only source of righteousness [ICC]. Their exultation stems from and is based on Christ's finished work [TNTC]. They rejoice because of their life in union with Christ [TH].

QUESTION—What is meant by the flesh?

The reference is to circumcision [NIC, WBC, WC, WEC] and other physical and external ceremonies and things as opposed to things internal and non-tangible [Blm, El, Lt, My, NIC, NTC, Pl, TH], to external status such as ancestry and privilege [Ea, HNTC, Lt, My, NTC, WC], to anything on which unredeemed human nature depends for salvation [MNTC, NIC, TNTC, WC, WEC]. It refers to human nature apart from Christ [EBC, GNC, ICC, Mou, WBC], to the 'self' [EGT, Mou, NTC].

DISCOURSE UNIT: 3:4–16 [NTC]. The topic is Paul as an example in contrast with the Judaizers.

DISCOURSE UNIT: 3:4–14 [TNTC]. The topic is Paul's description of his life.

DISCOURSE UNIT: 3:4–11 [My(D), NIC, WBC]. The topic is Paul's abandonment of human privileges in order to gain Christ [NIC], Paul's example as a refutation to Judaism [WBC].

DISCOURSE UNIT: 3:4–7 [ICC]. No topic is given.

DISCOURSE UNIT: 3:4–6 [EGT, NIC, TNTC, WEC]. The topic is Paul's basis for confidence in the flesh [EGT, NIC, NTC], Paul's inheritance as a Jew [TNTC], Paul boasts mockingly [WEC].

3:4

although[a] I having confidence[b] even[c] in[d] flesh[e].

LEXICON—a. καίπερ (GEL 89.71) (BAGD p. 394): 'although' [BAGD, GEL, Ln, Pl, WBC; NASB, NJB], 'even though' [GEL, HNTC; NRSV], 'though' [Ea, Mou, NTC; KJV, NAB, NIV], 'of course' [TEV], not explicit [ICC, WEC; TNT]. The phrase καίπερ ἐγὼ ἔχων 'although I having' is translated 'it is not that I am myself without' [REB]. The περ strengthens the meaning, 'although indeed' [El].

b. πεποίθησις (GEL 31.82) (BAGD 1. p. 643): 'confidence' [Ea, GEL, Ln, Mou, Pl, WEC; KJV, NASB], 'reason for confidence' [NTC; NIV, NRSV], 'good reasons for putting confidence' [WBC], 'grounds for putting confidence' [HNTC], 'grounds for confidence' [REB], 'trust' [BAGD, GEL; TEV], 'nothing to fear' [TNT], not explicit [ICC]. The phrase ἔχων πεποίθησιν 'having confidence' is translated 'can be confident' [NAB], 'could rely' [NJB], 'could put trust' [GEL]. This word means grounds for confidence [EBC, NIC, NTC]. It means actual present confidence, not merely grounds for confidence [Alf, Ea, Lg, My].

c. καί (GEL 89.93): 'even' [GEL, Ln, Mou, NTC, Pl; NAB, NASB], 'also' [GEL; KJV, TNT], 'too' [Ea; NJB], not explicit [HNTC, WBC, WEC; NIV, NRSV, REB, TEV, TNT]. This word implies confidence in the flesh (although he rejects it) in addition to his confidence in Christ [Alf, ICC, Lg, Lt, My].

d. ἐν with dative object: 'in'. See this word at 3:3.

e. σάρξ: 'flesh'. See this word at 3:3.

QUESTION—What relationship is indicated by καίπερ 'although'?

1. It indicates concession and qualifies or limits the preceding statement [Ea, El, My, WEC]: I am among those who have no confidence in flesh, although I have those qualifications.

2. It indicates concession and is linked to an implied statement, such as "but I will not do so" [WBC]: although I have grounds to put confidence in the flesh, I will not do so.

QUESTION—What is the significance of the overt pronoun ἐγώ 'I'?

It is emphatic [GNC, Ln, Pl, TH]; it singles him out from the ἡμεῖς 'we' of the preceding sentence [ICC, Lg, Lt, MNTC, My].

1. It indicates Paul alone in contrast with the Philippians as the one with the following qualifications [Alf, Bg, Ln, Lt, Pl], since most of the Philippian Christians were Gentiles [Bg, Pl]: I refer to my own qualifications in contrast with most of you.

2. It indicates Paul in contrast with the Judaizers [ICC, Lg, NIC, NTC]: I refer to my own qualifications in contrast with those of the Judaizers.

QUESTION—What is meant by ἔχων 'having'?

The implication is that it is not because he does not possess these qualifications that he disparages them [Blm, Ea, EBC, El, ICC, MNTC, My, NTC, WBC]; rather, he has renounced them [El, ICC, MNTC, WBC]. He temporarily adopts the Judaizers' point of view for the sake of argument [EBC, ICC, Lt, MNTC, My, WBC, WC];

if Jewish advantages are the ground for confidence, he has a stronger reason for confidence than even the Judaizers do [ICC, WC, WEC].

1. It implies that Paul actually does have grounds for confidence in the flesh, although he does not rely on it [Alf, Bg, Ea, El, ICC, Lg, Ln, Lt, MNTC, Pl, WBC]: I have confidence in the flesh, but I do not rely on it.
2. It means that he has the qualifications but does not accept the fact that they are grounds for confidence [Blm, NTC]: I have the qualifications, but they are not true grounds for confidence.

If any other-person thinks[a] to-have-confidence[b] in flesh, I (have) more:

LEXICON—a. pres. act. indic. of δοκέω (GEL 31.29) (BAGD 1.a. p. 201): 'to think' [BAGD, Ea, GEL, ICC, Ln, Mou, Pl, WBC, WEC; KJV, NAB, NIV, TEV], 'to believe' [BAGD], 'to suppose' [BAGD, GEL, HNTC], 'to consider' [BAGD], 'to imagine' [GEL, NTC], 'to claim' [NJB], 'to make claims' [REB], 'to have a mind' [NASB], 'to have reason' [NRSV], not explicit [TNT]. It refers to a person's own opinion of his situation [Alf, Ea, El], but implies that such an opinion is false [EGT, El].

b. perf. act. infin. of πείθω (GEL 31.82): 'to have confidence' [Ea, GEL], 'to put confidence' [HNTC; NASB], 'to place confidence' [Pl], 'to rest confidence' [Ln], 'to have reason for confidence' [NTC, WBC], 'to have reasons to put confidence' [NIV], 'to have reason to place confidence' [WEC], 'to be confident' [NRSV], 'to confide' [Mou], 'to rely' [GEL; NJB, TNT], 'to trust' [GEL; TEV], 'to depend' [GEL], 'to have whereof to trust' [KJV], 'to have a right to put one's trust' [NAB], 'to be warranted in trusting' [ICC], not explicit [REB]. It implies that such thinking is presumptuous [My].

QUESTION—What role does this clause have?

Paul is showing that it is not because he does not have these Jewish privileges that he is disparaging them [Blm, HNTC, NTC], and it gives a basis for his argument that these privileges have no saving power [NTC]: I have these privileges, but they cannot save.

QUESTION—Who is referred to by τις ἄλλος 'any other person'?

1. It means any of the Judaizers [EBC, Ln, MNTC, NTC, Pl, TNTC, WBC, WC]: any other person, that is, any of the Judaizers.
2. It means any other Jew [ICC, WBC]: any other person, that is, any Jew.
3. It has a general reference, which Paul leaves to the Philippians to apply to the Judaizers [Lg, My]: any other person.

QUESTION—Why is the phrase ἐν σαρχί 'in flesh' repeated?
It adds emphasis, pointing to the inadequacy of such a grounds for
confidence [Ln]: in such an inadequate thing as human privileges.
QUESTION—What is the meaning of ἐγὼ μᾶλλον 'I more'?
It means that Paul has (thinks he has [ICC, Lg, Ln, Lt, My]) more
grounds for confidence than τις ἄλλος 'any other person' [Bg, Blm,
ICC, Lg, Ln, Lt, My, WBC, WC]: I (think I) have more grounds for
confidence in the flesh than anyone else.

3:5

QUESTION—How are verses 3:5-6 related to their context?
They give the justification for Paul's confidence in the flesh [Alf,
Blm, EBC, GNC, HNTC, ICC, Lg, MNTC, My, TH, TNTC, WBC,
WEC]: I more than they, namely by the following factors. The first
four phrases of 3:5 refer to his pure Jewish heritage [Alf, ICC, Lt,
MNTC, TNTC, WBC, WC, WEC], the final phrase to his position
and legal exactitude [Alf]. The first phrase expresses his first
advantage; the second, third, and fourth belong together as a
second advantage [Lg].
in-respect-to-circumcision (it was on the) eighth day,[a]
LEXICON—a. ὀκταήμερος (GEL **67.182**) (BAGD p. 563): 'the eighth
day' [KJV, NASB], 'on the eighth day' [BAGD, GEL, HNTC,
NTC, WEC; NAB, NIV, NRSV, TNT], 'an eighth day one' [Ea,
Ln], 'an eight-day child' [Mou], 'on (my) eighth day' [REB], 'on
the eighth day of (my) life' [WBC; NJB], 'the eighth day after
birth' [Pl], 'when eight days old' [ICC], 'when (I was) a week
old' [TEV]. This word shows his Jewish parentage in contrast
with his being a proselyte, who would have been circumcised
later in life [Alf, Ea, MNTC].
QUESTION—Why does Paul bring up this point?
It is a ritualistic point [El] and shows that he had been circumcised
on the prescribed day according to the law [HNTC, Lg, Ln, Lt,
NIC, NTC, Pl, TH, TNTC, WBC, WC, WEC] and not later in life
as a proselyte would have been [Ea, El, GNC, HNTC, Lg, Ln, Lt,
MNTC, Mou, My, Pl, TH, TNTC, WBC, WC, WEC] or an
Ishmaelite [ICC, Lt, MNTC, Pl, TNTC, WBC]. It shows that his
parents were careful to fulfill their religious duties [TH, TNTC,
WBC]. Περιτομῇ is a dative of reference, in respect to circumcision
[Blm, Ea, EGT, El, ICC, Lg, Ln, Mou, WBC]. Paul mentions this
because it was so important to the Judaizers [EBC, ICC, Ln,
MNTC, NTC].

(I am) from[a] (the) race[b] of-Israel, of-(the)-tribe[c] of-Benjamin, a-Hebrew from[d] Hebrews,[e]

LEXICON—a. ἐκ with genitive object: (GEL 89.3) (BAGD 3.b. p. 235): 'from' [BAGD, GEL, Mou, Pl], 'of' [Ea, HNTC, NTC; KJV, NAB, NASB, NIV, NJB, NRSV], 'out of' [Ln], 'by' [REB]. The phrase ἐκ γένους Ἰσραήλ 'from the race of Israel' is translated 'an Israelite by birth' [WBC; TEV], 'an Israelite by race' [TNT], 'of direct Israelitish descent' [ICC], 'a pure Israelite' [WEC].

   b. γένος (GEL 10.1) (BAGD 3. p. 156): 'race' [Ea, GEL, HNTC, Mou; NJB, REB, TNT], 'nation' [BAGD, GEL; NASB], 'people' [BAGD, NTC; NIV, NRSV], 'stock' [Ln, Pl; KJV, NAB].

   c. φυλή (GEL 10.2) (BAGD 1. p. 868): 'tribe' [BAGD, Ea, GEL, HNTC, ICC, Ln, Mou, NTC, Pl, WBC, WEC; all translations].

   d. ἐκ with genitive object (GEL 89.3) (BAGD 3.b. p. 235): 'from' [GEL], 'of' [Ea, NTC, WEC; KJV, NAB, NASB, NIV], 'out of' [Ln], 'born of' [HNTC, WBC; NJB, NRSV], 'son of' [BAGD, Pl; TNT], 'offspring of' [Mou]. The phrase Ἑβραῖος ἐξ Ἑβραίων 'a Hebrew from Hebrews' is translated 'a Hebrew born and bred' [REB], 'a pure-blooded Hebrew' [TEV], 'a child of Hebrew ancestors' [ICC]. This word means here 'descended from' [MNTC].

   e. Ἑβραῖος (GEL 93.105) (BAGD 1. p. 213): 'Hebrew' [BAGD, Ea, GEL, Ln, NTC, WEC; KJV, NASB, NIV, NRSV]. The plural is translated 'Hebrew origins' [NAB], 'Hebrew ancestors' [ICC, Mou], 'Hebrew parents' [HNTC, Pl, WBC; NJB, TNT]. The plural indicates that both of his parents were Hebrews [Alf, Bg, Blm, Lg, My] or that all his ancestors were Hebrews [TH].

QUESTION—What is meant by the phrase ἐκ γένους Ἰσραήλ 'from the race of Israel'?

It indicates that he was of Israelite heritage, not a proselyte [Ea, EBC, GNC, ICC, Lt, MNTC, Mou, NIC, NTC, WBC, WEC] nor of proselyte parents [Ea, El, Lt, MNTC]. He was a descendent of Jacob [Ea, ICC, Mou, My]. He therefore had all the privileges of the race of Israel [Ea, GNC, HNTC, TH, WBC]. Ἰσραήλ 'of Israel' is a genitive of apposition; the race was Israel [El, ICC, WBC]. 'Israel' refers to the race as a whole [El, ICC, WBC]; it refers specifically to Jacob [NTC].

QUESTION—What is meant by the phrase φυλῆς Βενιαμίν 'from the tribe of Benjamin'?

It indicates that he, unlike many Jews, knew to which tribe he belonged [MNTC, Pl]. It means that he was descended from the tribe which bore special honors [Ea, EGT, El, ICC, Lg, Lt, MNTC,

Mou, NIC, Pl, TH, TNTC, WBC, WC], or perhaps simply to stress further his Jewish ancestry [EBC, Ln], or because Benjamin was the most strongly Israelitish [NTC], or simply expressing his natural pride in his own tribe [HNTC]. He apparently considers this point to be important [GNC].

QUESTION—What is meant by the phrase Ἑβραῖος ἐξ Ἑβραίων 'a Hebrew from Hebrews'?

1. It refers to the purity of his heritage, with no Gentile blood among his ancestors [Ea, EBC, EGT, El, Ln, NTC, WC].

2. It means that he and his parents normally spoke Aramaic and retained Hebrew customs [GNC, HNTC, ICC, Lt, Mou, TNTC].

3. It includes both of the above interpretations [MNTC, NIC, Pl, TH, WBC, WEC].

with-regard-to[a] (the) law[b] a-Pharisee,

LEXICON—a. κατά with accusative object (GEL 89.4) (BAGD p. 407): 'with regard to' [GEL, WBC, WEC], 'in regard to' [NIV], 'as regards' [Pl], 'with respect to' [BAGD], 'in respect of' [Mou], 'in relation to' [BAGD, GEL], 'in the matter of' [HNTC; NJB], 'in observing' [TNT], 'as to' [NTC; NASB, NRSV], 'as touching' [Ln; KJV], 'touching' [Ea], 'in (my) practice of' [REB], not explicit [ICC]. The phrase κατὰ νόμον 'with regard to the law' is translated 'in legal observance' [NAB], 'as far as keeping the Jewish law is concerned' [TEV].

b. νόμος (GEL 33.55; 33.56) (BAGD p. 542): 'the law' [BAGD, Ea, Pl, WEC; KJV, NIV, NRSV, REB], 'the Law' [GEL, HNTC, Mou; NASB, NJB, TNT], 'the Jewish Law' [WBC; TEV], 'law' [Ln, NTC], not explicit [ICC]. It refers to the Mosaic law [ICC, MNTC, My]. It refers to the Jewish law [Pl, WBC], which included the scribes' interpretations as well as the law of Moses [TH, WBC, WEC].

QUESTION—Why does Paul bring up this point?

It refers to his own choice to be a Pharisee [Ea, EBC, Lt, MNTC, NTC, Pl, TH, TNTC, WBC, WC, WEC], the party known for strict devotion to the law in all its details [Bg, Ea, EBC, GNC, HNTC, ICC, Lg, Ln, Lt, MNTC, Mou, My, NIC, NTC, Pl, TH, TNTC, WBC, WC, WEC]. It implies his previous high degree of dedication to obedience to God's law [HNTC, TH]. This is Paul's third advantage [Lg]. It is the first of three points of boasting based on his personal choice [Lt, MNTC, My, TH, TNTC, WBC, WC].

3:6

with-regard-to[a] zeal[b] persecuting[c] the church,

LEXICON—a. κατά with accusative object (GEL 89.4; 89.8) (BAGD II.5.b.β., 6. p. 407): 'with regard to' [GEL, WBC], 'as regards'

[Pl], 'in relation to' [GEL], 'in respect of' [Mou], 'in accordance with' [BAGD, GEL], 'concerning' [KJV], 'as to' [Ea, NTC; NASB, NRSV], 'as for' [NIV, NJB], 'as touching' [Ln], 'in' [REB], 'in the matter of' [HNTC], not explicit [TNT]. The phrase κατὰ ζῆλος 'with regard to zeal' is translated 'so zealous' [NAB, TEV], 'I was zealous' [ICC], 'I proved my zeal' [WEC].

b. ζῆλος (GEL 25.46) (BAGD 1. p. 337): 'zeal' [BAGD, Ea, HNTC, Ln, Mou, NTC, Pl, WBC, WEC; KJV, NASB, NIV, NRSV, REB, TNT], 'earnest concern' [GEL], 'religious fervor' [NJB].

c. pres. act. participle of διώκω (GEL 39.45) (BAGD 2. p. 201): 'to persecute' [BAGD, Ea, GEL, ICC, Mou, NTC, Pl, WEC; KJV, NAB, NIV, TEV, TNT]. This present participle is also translated as a noun: 'a persecutor' [HNTC, Ln, WBC; NASB, NJB, NRSV, REB].

QUESTION—What is meant by the phrase κατὰ ζῆλος 'with regard to zeal'?

It means that the following phrase tells how his zeal was attested [Blm]: my zeal was attested in the following way. The phrase is highly ironic [TH]; Paul is condemning himself while seeming to praise himself [Lt, MNTC, Pl, WEC].

QUESTION—What is the meaning of the present participle διώκων 'persecuting'?

1. It has the participial meaning [Ea, El, ICC], since it refers to his actions when he was trusting in the flesh [Ea, TNTC]: (I was) repeatedly persecuting the church.

2. It has the meaning of a substantive [HNTC, Ln, My, WBC; NJB, NRSV, REB]: I was a persecutor.

with-regard-to[a] righteousness[b] the-(one) in[c] law,[d] having-become[e] blameless.[f]

LEXICON—a. κατά with accusative object (GEL 89.4; 89.8) (BAGD 6. p. 407): 'with regard to' [GEL, WBC, WEC], 'as regards' [Ea, Pl], 'with respect to' [BAGD], 'in respect of' [Mou], 'in relation to' [BAGD, GEL], 'in the matter of' [HNTC], 'touching' [KJV], 'as touching' [Ln], 'as to' [NTC; NASB, NRSV], 'as for' [NIV, NJB], 'as far as' [TEV], 'when it came to' [NAB], 'by the standard of' [REB], not explicit [TNT]. The phrase κατὰ δικαιοσύνην τὴν ἐν νόμῳ 'with regard to the righteousness in the law' is translated 'in my legal righteousness' [ICC].

b. δικαιοσύνη (GEL 88.13) (BAGD 2.a. p. 196): 'righteousness' [BAGD, Ea, GEL, HNTC, ICC, Ln, Mou, NTC, Pl, WBC, WEC; KJV, NASB, NIV, NRSV, REB], 'justice' [NAB], 'uprightness' [NJB], 'doing what God requires' [GEL], 'exact requirements of the Law' [TNT]. The phrase κατὰ δικαιοσύνην 'with regard to righteousness' is translated 'as far as a person can be righteous' [TEV]. It means justification before God which was obtainable through the Law [Blm, Ea, EGT, TH]. It means judged righteous by men by the standard of the Law [EBC, HNTC, Lg, Ln]. It refers to the righteousness required by the law [GNC, MNTC, NIC], obedience to external rules [Alf, ICC, Lt, NIC, WBC], righteousness which resides in the law [El, ICC, Mou, My].

c. ἐν with dative object (GEL 83.13; 89.76): 'in' [Ea, GEL, Mou, Pl; KJV, NASB, NJB], 'by' [GEL], 'in connection with' [Ln], 'under' [NRSV], not explicit [REB]. The phrase τὴν ἐν νόμῳ 'the one which is in law' is translated 'which rests on the Law' [HNTC], 'based on the Law' [WBC], 'set forth in our Jewish law' [WEC], 'by obeying the commands of the law' [TEV], 'legalistic' [NTC; NIV].

d. νόμος (GEL 33.55; 33.333) (BAGD 3. p. 542): 'law' [GEL, Ln], 'the law' [Ea, Pl; KJV, NAB, NRSV, REB], 'the Law' [BAGD, GEL, HNTC, Mou, WBC; NASB, NJB, TEV, TNT], '(the) Jewish law' [WEC]. It refers to the Jewish law [My(D), Pl].

e. aorist mid. (deponent = act.) participle of γίνομαι (GEL 13.3; 13.48): 'to be' [Ea, GEL, ICC, WBC; NAB, NJB, TEV, TNT], 'to become' [GEL, NTC], 'to be found' [Mou, WEC; NASB], 'to be proven' [HNTC], 'to come to be' [Ln], 'to show oneself' [Pl], not explicit [KJV, NIV, NRSV, REB].

f. ἄμεμπτος (GEL 88.317) (BAGD p. 45): 'blameless' [BAGD, Ea, GEL, HNTC, ICC, Ln, Mou, NTC, Pl, WBC; KJV, NASB, NRSV], 'without blame' [GEL], 'without fault' [REB, TEV], 'faultless' [BAGD; NIV, NJB], 'guiltless' [GEL], 'above reproach' [NAB], 'beyond criticism' [TNT], 'never at fault' [WEC]. The meaning is not absolute blamelessness, but blameless in the judgment of other people [El, ICC, My, NIC, NTC]. It refers to scrupulous fulfillment of the law's requirements [EBC, NTC, Pl, TH, TNTC, WBC, WC, WEC].

QUESTION—What is the participle γενόμενος 'having become' connected with?

It is connected with ἄμεμπτος 'blameless' [Alf, Ea, ICC, Lg, Ln, Lt, Mou, My, Pl, WBC, WEC]: having become blameless.

DISCOURSE UNIT: 3:7–14 [TNTC]. The topic is what Paul has given up, and what are his intentions and his hope.

DISCOURSE UNIT: 3:7–11 [NIC, WC, WEC]. The topic is considering everything as loss for Christ's sake [NIC], a summary of Paul's theology [WEC].

DISCOURSE UNIT: 3:7–9 [EGT]. The topic is considering earthly achievements as loss in order to gain Christ.

DISCOURSE UNIT: 3:7–8 [WEC]. The topic is Paul's spiritual bankruptcy.

3:7
But[a] whatever[b] (things) were gains[c] for-me, these-(things) I-have-considered[d] loss[e] on-account-of[f] the Christ.

> LEXICON—a. ἀλλά (GEL 91.2): 'but' [Ea, HNTC, ICC, Ln, Mou, Pl, WBC; all translations except NRSV, TNT], 'yet' [GEL; NRSV, TNT], 'nevertheless' [NTC, WEC]. This word introduces a strong contrast with the preceding [Ea, My(D), TH], contrasting Paul's situation with the Judaizers' position [Lg].
>
> b. ὅστις (GEL 92.18): 'whatever' [Ea, GEL, WEC; NASB, NIV, NRSV], 'what' [Ln, WBC; KJV, NJB], 'the kind which' [Mou], 'such' [HNTC, NTC, Pl], not explicit [ICC; NAB, TEV]. The phrase ἅτινα ἦν μοι κέρδη 'whatever things were gain for me' is translated 'all such assets' [REB], 'all such advantages' [TNT]. This pronoun has a qualitative sense, implying the *kind* of things as those he mentions [EGT, El, ICC, Ln, Lt, My, Pl]. This word is emphatic [Alf, Ea, Lg, My] as the ταῦτα 'these things' which follows shows [Lg, My]; it refers to the things he has mentioned [Bg, Ea, EBC, WC] and any other things which previously were gain to him [Alf, Blm, EBC, Lg, Ln].
>
> c. κέρδος (GEL 57.192): 'gain' [Ea, GEL, HNTC, Ln, Mou, NTC, Pl, WBC; KJV, NAB, NASB, NRSV], 'profit' [GEL; TEV], 'to (one's) profit' [NIV], 'asset' [WEC; NJB, REB], 'advantage' [ICC; TNT]. The plural is used here, implying various kinds of gain [Alf, Ea, EBC, El, ICC, Lg, Lt, MNTC, Mou, My, NTC, TNTC, WBC], a comprehensive sense [Bg].
>
> d. perf. mid. (deponent = act.) indic. of ἡγέομαι (GEL 31.1) (BAGD 2. p. 343): 'to consider' [BAGD, GEL, Ln, Mou, WEC; NIV], 'to regard' [GEL; NRSV], 'to count' [HNTC, ICC, NTC, WBC; KJV, NASB, NJB], 'to reckon' [Ea; TEV, TNT], 'to set down' [Pl], 'to reappraise' [NAB]. The phrase ἥγημαι ζημίαν 'I have considered loss' is translated 'I have written off' [REB]. The perfect tense means that he drew this conclusion in the past (at his conversion [My, WC]) and is still of that opinion [Ea, EBC, EGT, El, Lg, Ln, My, NIC, NTC, Pl, TH, TNTC, WEC].
>
> e. ζημία (GEL 57.69) (BAGD p. 338): 'loss' [BAGD, Ea, GEL, HNTC, ICC, Ln, Mou, NTC, Pl, WBC, WEC; all translations except REB]. The singular here implies one overall loss, in

contrast with the preceding plural gains [Alf, Ea, ICC, Lg, Lt, MNTC, Mou, My, NTC, TNTC, WBC]. Paul means that those things did not bring him to Christ [Ea, EBC, GNC, Pl] or actually kept him from Christ [Ea, GNC, HNTC, MNTC, My, NIC, TNTC, WBC, WC].

    f. διά with accusative object (GEL 90.44): 'on account of' [GEL], 'because of' [GEL, Ln, Mou, WBC; NRSV, REB, TNT], 'for' [Ea, NTC; KJV], 'for the sake of' [HNTC, ICC, WEC; NASB, NIV, TEV], 'in the light of' [NAB], 'in order to win' [Pl], 'through' [NJB].

QUESTION—What is the meaning of ἦν 'were'?

    1. It means that the things he mentions actually were gain to him [Ea, EBC, EGT, El, HNTC, ICC, Lg, Ln, My, NIC, NTC, TNTC, WBC, WEC; KJV, NASB, NIV, NJB, NRSV]: whatever things were gain for me.

    2. It means that he considered them to be gain [Mou, Pl; NAB]: whatever things I formerly considered to be gain.

QUESTION—To what does ταῦτα 'these things' refer?

    It is emphatic [Ea, ICC, Lg, My, WEC] and defines the preceding pronoun ἅτινα 'whatever things' [ICC, WEC], referring to the things he has mentioned [Bg, Ea]: these very things which I have mentioned.

QUESTION—What is meant by διὰ τὸν Χριστόν 'on account of Christ'?

    It means for the sake of gaining Christ [Bg, GNC, Lt, TH, Pl, TNTC, WEC], as he states in the following verse [Bg, Lt, WEC]: in order that I might gain Christ. It is a general reference whose more specific meaning, given in the following verses, should not be anticipated here [My]. It means because of the fact of his encounter with Christ [WBC].

DISCOURSE UNIT: 3:8–14 [ICC]. The topic is Paul's present standard and his striving to reach it.

DISCOURSE UNIT: 3:8–11 [MNTC]. The topic is loss and gain.

3:8

But[a] indeed[b] also[c] I-consider[d] all-(things) to-be loss[e] because-of[f] the being-of-surpassing-value[g] (thing) of-the knowledge[h] of-Christ Jesus my Lord,

    LEXICON—a. ἀλλά (GEL 89.96; 91.11) (BAGD 3. p. 38): 'but' [BAGD, Ea, HNTC], 'and' [GEL, WBC], 'certainly' [GEL], 'yea' [Ln; KJV], 'aye' [Mou], 'yes' [NTC; NJB], 'nay' [Pl], not explicit [ICC; NAB]. The phrase ἀλλὰ μενοῦνγε 'but indeed' is translated 'more than that' [BAGD; NASB, NRSV, REB, TNT], 'what is more' [NIV], 'not only those things' [TEV], 'let me be clearer' [WEC]. This word contrasts Paul's previous action of considering things as loss with his present continuation of that decision [Ea, EBC, EGT, El, Lg]. It introduces an expansion or intensification of the preceding [My, NIC, Pl].

b. μενοῦνγε (GEL 89.128) (BAGD p. 503): 'indeed, therefore' [Ea], 'moreover' [Pl], 'I will go further' [NJB], 'what is more' [NTC, WBC], 'not only that' [HNTC], 'more' [Mou], 'on the other hand' [GEL], 'doubtless' [KJV], not explicit [ICC, Ln; NAB]. This word amplifies the previous statement [Bg, Lt]. The sense is something like 'indeed, more than that, I therefore affirm at least even this' [NTC], adding to and reinforcing what he has just said [MNTC, TH, TNTC]. With the καί 'also' following, it strongly emphasizes the shift from the preceding 'I have considered' to the following 'I continue to consider' [WBC]. The μέν confirms the following ἡγοῦμαι 'I consider' [ICC, Lg, My]. The μέν is emphatic [EBC, EGT], the οὖν extends what has already been said, and γε implies a coverage beyond what was implied in ἅτινα 'whatever things' in the preceding verse [EBC, EGT]. Οὖν γε indicates that Paul's past decision is his present conviction as well [ICC].

c. καί (GEL 89.93): 'also' [Ea, GEL, Ln], 'even' [GEL, Pl], 'and' [KJV], 'certainly' [NTC], 'actually' [Mou], not explicit [HNTC, ICC, WBC, WEC; all translations except KJV]. This word means 'even' ('also' [El]) and intensifies the present tense of the verb ἡγοῦμαι 'I consider' [Bg, El], expanding what he said previously [My]. It connects 'I consider' with the preceding 'I have considered' [Lg, Ln].

d. pres. mid. (deponent = act.) of ἡγέομαι: 'to consider'. See this word at 3:7. The shift from the perfect tense in the previous verse to the present tense here is significant, implying that his previous decision must be continually supported [WBC]. What Paul previously concluded, he still maintains [Lg(H), Ln, NTC, Pl, WBC, WC, WEC], and his present position is the point here [TNTC]. This present tense, 'I continue to consider', is in contrast with the perfect tense in the preceding verse [Alf]. Another view is that it does not contrast with the preceding perfect tense, since the perfect tense includes his present conviction [EGT, My]; it expands and extends the idea of the perfect tense [Lt].

e. ζημία: 'loss'. See this word at 3:7.

f. διά with accusative object (GEL 89.26): 'because of' [GEL, Ln, Mou, NTC, WBC; NJB, NRSV], 'on account of' [Ea, GEL], 'by

reason of' [GEL], 'for the sake of' [HNTC, WEC; TEV], 'for'
[KJV], 'in the light of' [NAB], 'in view of' [NASB], 'far
outweighed by' [REB], 'compared to' [NIV], 'as compared with'
[ICC], 'when compared with' [Pl]. The phrase διὰ τὸ ὑπερέχον
τῆς γνώσεως Χριστοῦ 'because of the surpassing thing of the
knowledge of Christ' is translated 'because knowing Christ far
outweighs everything else' [TNT].

g. pres. act. participle of ὑπερέχω (GEL 65.4) (BAGD 2.c.
   p. 841): 'to be of surpassing value' [GEL]. This participle is also
   translated as a noun: [EGT] 'excellency' [Ea; KJV], 'gain'
   [REB], 'surpassingness' [Ln, Mou]; as a noun phrase:
   'surpassing greatness' [BAGD; NIV], 'surpassing value' [NASB,
   NRSV], 'surpassing worth' [ICC], 'all-surpassing excellence'
   [NTC], 'supreme advantage' [NJB], 'supreme value' [Pl, WBC],
   'incomparable value' [WEC], 'what is so much more valuable'
   [TEV], 'supreme good' [HNTC]. The phrase τὸ ὑπερέχον τῆς
   γνώσεως 'the surpassing thing of the knowledge' is translated
   'the surpassing knowledge' [NAB]. The sense is not 'the
   excellent knowledge' but rather points out the excellence of the
   knowledge [Ea, El, ICC]. It is this 'supreme value' for which
   Paul abandoned those other values [WBC].

h. γνῶσις (GEL 28.1) (BAGD 2. p. 164): 'knowledge' [Ea, HNTC,
   ICC, Ln, Mou; KJV, NAB, TEV], 'personal knowledge' [WBC],
   'acquaintance' [GEL], 'personal acquaintance' [BAGD],
   'knowing' [NTC, Pl, WEC; NASB, NIV, NJB, NRSV, REB,
   TNT]. It includes loving Christ and being loved by him [GNC].
   It includes knowing Christ Jesus as a person and as Lord [Lg]
   in personal appropriation and communion [TH, WBC], his
   entire Christian experience [WC].

QUESTION—What is meant by πάντα 'all things'?

1. It refers to everything in general which might keep him from
   trusting Christ solely for salvation [Bg, Blm, EBC, EGT, GNC,
   Ln, Lt, Mou, My, NIC, NTC, Pl, TH, TNTC, WBC, WC; all
   translations except NAB]: I consider everything as loss.
2. It refers only to the things which he has just mentioned [Alf,
   Ea, El, HNTC, ICC, Lg]: I consider them all as loss.

QUESTION—What relationship is indicated by διά 'because of'?

1. It indicates the reason why Paul considers these things as loss
   [Bg, Ea, ICC, Lg, My]: I consider them thus on account of the
   excellency of knowing Christ. It explains more fully the
   preceding διὰ τὸν Χριστόν 'on account of Christ' in 3:7 [ICC,
   Ln, WEC].
2. This word implies a comparison of the excellency of knowing
   Christ with the value of the things he considers as loss [Blm,

Ea, MNTC, NTC, Pl]: I consider them as loss in comparison with the supreme value of knowing Christ.

QUESTION—How are the participle and the noun related in the genitive construction τὸ ὑπερέχον τῆς γνώσεως 'the surpassing value of the knowledge'?

1. 'Surpassing value' expresses the quality of the 'knowledge' [Ea, El]: the excellent quality of the knowledge.

2. The surpassing value, or supreme advantage, consists of knowing Christ [EGT, HNTC, TH, WBC; TEV]: the supreme advantage, namely, to know Christ.

QUESTION—How are the two parts of the genitive construction τῆς γνώσεως Χριστοῦ Ἰησοῦ 'the knowledge of Christ Jesus' related?

Christ Jesus is the one who is known [Ea, EGT, GNC, ICC, MNTC, NTC, Pl, TH, WBC, WEC; NASB, NIV, NJB, NRSV, REB, TNT]: knowing Christ Jesus.

QUESTION—What is implied by the pronoun μου 'my'?

It implies a personal surrender to Christ and a personal appropriation of him [MNTC, NIC, TH, TNTC], his own experience of Christ [Pl, TH, WC].

because-of[a] whom I-have-lost[b] the everything, and I-consider (it) rubbish,[c]

LEXICON—a. διά with accusative object (GEL 89.26): 'because of' [GEL, Ln, Mou], 'on account of' [GEL], 'for the sake of' [WEC], 'for (his/whose) sake' [HNTC; NAB, NIV, NRSV, REB, TEV, TNT], 'for' [Ea, NTC, WBC; KJV, NASB, NJB]. The phrase δι᾽ ὅν 'because of whom' is translated 'to win him' [Pl]. This word is a more general reference which is explained by the clause at the end of this verse [Alf].

b. aorist pass. indic. of ζημιόω (GEL 57.69) (BAGD 1. p. 338): 'to lose' [WBC; NIV], 'to accept loss' [NJB], 'to sustain loss' [WEC], 'to suffer loss' [Ea, GEL, Ln, NTC, Pl; KJV, NASB, NRSV], 'to suffer deprivation' [Mou], 'to forfeit' [BAGD, HNTC; NAB, REB], 'to throw away' [TEV], 'to let go' [TNT], not explicit [ICC]. The meaning is that Paul rejected these things [Bg, TH, TNTC, WBC], that they have fallen away [ICC], that he has been deprived of them [El, GNC, Ln, Lt], that he not only considers these things as loss but that he has in fact undergone the loss of everything [MNTC, WBC]. This occurred at his conversion [MNTC, My, NIC, TH, TNTC].

c. σκύβαλον (GEL 6.225) (BAGD p. 758): 'rubbish' [BAGD, GEL, HNTC; NAB, NASB, NIV, NRSV, REB], 'worthless rubbish' [TNT], 'garbage' [TEV], 'refuse' [Ea, ICC, Mou, NTC], 'utter refuse' [Pl], 'filth' [NJB], 'unspeakable filth' [WBC], 'dung'

[BAGD, Ln, WEC; KJV]. This word is an amplification of the preceding word ζημία 'loss' [Bg].

QUESTION—What is meant by τὰ πάντα 'the everything'?

1. It is general [Alf, GNC, ICC, MNTC] and is emphatic (by forefronting) [Alf, WBC]: I have lost everything. With the article the phrase implies the whole as a unit [EGT, MNTC].
2. It refers only to the things previously referred to [Ea, EBC, El, Lg, Ln, NTC]: I have lost all those things. The article refers back to the previous πάντα 'all things' [Lg, Ln].

QUESTION—What is the phrase καὶ ἡγοῦμαι σκύβαλα 'and I consider them as refuse' connected with?

1. It is connected with the immediately preceding clause introduced by δι' ὄν 'on account of whom' [My]: on account of Christ I have lost everything and consider them as refuse.
2. It is connected with the following clause introduced by ἵνα 'in order that' and is parallel to ἡγοῦμαι earlier in this verse [My(D)]: I consider all things as loss; and I consider them as refuse in order that I may gain Christ.

in-order-that[a] Christ I-might-gain[b]

LEXICON—a. ἵνα (GEL 89.59) (BAGD I.1.a. p. 376): 'in order that' [BAGD, NTC, Pl; NASB, NRSV], 'in order to' [GEL], 'for the purpose of' [GEL], 'so that' [WEC; NAB, TEV], 'that' [Ea, HNTC, Ln, Mou; KJV, NIV], 'for the sake of' [REB], 'for the goal of' [WBC], not explicit [ICC; NJB, TNT].

b. aorist act. subj. of κερδαίνω (GEL 57.189) (BAGD 1.b. p. 429): 'to gain' [BAGD, Ea, GEL, HNTC, Ln, Mou, NTC, Pl, WBC, WEC; NASB, NIV, NJB, NRSV, REB, TEV], 'to win' [KJV], 'to have as a reward' [TNT], 'to make (someone) one's own' [BAGD, ICC]. The phrase Χριστὸν κερδήσω 'Christ I might gain' is translated 'Christ may be my wealth' [NAB]. The meaning is to obtain what Christ's sacrificial death has made possible [Blm, WBC], to belong to Christ [El, TH, WBC], to have him as Savior and the ground of his justification [TNTC, WBC].

QUESTION—What relationship is indicated by ἵνα 'in order that'?

It indicates Paul's purpose in considering those things as loss and refuse [Alf, Ea, EBC, El, Lg, MNTC, Mou, My, TH, TNTC, WBC], or the purpose of his conversion [WEC]: I do/did this for the purpose of gaining Christ.

1. It refers to his past decision and is the purpose of his loss [Ln, Mou]: my purpose in losing those things (and I still consider them as rubbish) was to gain Christ. It expands the sense of διὰ τὸν Χριστὸν ζημίαν 'loss on account of Christ' in 3:7 [Ln].

2. It is presented as something present and future, anticipating fuller possession in the future [EGT, Lg, My, WBC], not as an act in the past; and implies the necessity of continuing to consider earthly things as loss [EGT].

DISCOURSE UNIT: 3:9–11 [WEC]. The topic is spiritual wealth.

3:9

and I-might-be-found[a] in[b] him,

> LEXICON—a. aorist pass. subj. of εὑρίσκω (GEL 27.27) (BAGD 1.b. p. 325): 'to find' [BAGD, Ea, GEL, HNTC, ICC, Ln, Mou, NTC, Pl, WBC, WEC; KJV, NASB, NIV, NRSV, REB, TNT], 'to give a place' [NJB], 'to be' [NAB, TEV]. It is emphatic by word order [My]. It is parallel to 'gaining Christ' in 3:8 [WC]. It means to be found in Christ (to be found 'being in Christ' [Bg]) by God [El, Mou, Pl], by people [El, ICC] at his death [MNTC, WBC], at the final judgment [MNTC, Pl, TNTC, WBC], now and always [Alf, HNTC, ICC, My, TH, WC], especially when Christ comes again [Alf, Blm, EBC, GNC]. It means simply to be in Christ [EGT, HNTC].
>
> b. ἐν with dative object (GEL 89.119) (BAGD I.5.d. p. 259): 'in' [BAGD, Ea, GEL, HNTC, ICC, Mou, NTC, WBC; KJV, NAB, NASB, NIV, NJB, NRSV], 'in union with' [GEL, WEC; REB], 'completely united with' [TEV], 'one with' [TNT], 'in connection with' [Ln]. The phrase ἐν αὐτῷ 'in him' is translated 'a member of his body' [Pl]. It means living in Christ [Alf, TH] as a member of his spiritual body [Lt, Pl] in an intimate spiritual union [Blm, Ea, HNTC, WBC], identification with Christ for salvation [ICC].

> QUESTION—What relationship is indicated by καί 'and'?
>
> 1. It introduces the second part of the purpose clause introduced by ἵνα 'in order that' in 3:8 [ICC, WBC; all translations]: in order that I might gain Christ and also be found in him.
> 2. It explains what is meant by gaining Christ and suggests the means by which Christ is gained [Blm, Ln, WEC]: in order that I might gain Christ—that is, that I might be found in him.
> 3. It expresses the result of gaining Christ [Ea]: to gain Christ and as a result to be found in him.

not having my righteousness[a] the-(one) from[b] law[c] but the-(one) through[d] faith[e] of-Christ,

> LEXICON: a. δικαιοσύνη (GEL 34.46; 88.13) (BAGD 3. p. 197): 'righteousness' [BAGD, Ea, GEL, HNTC, ICC, Ln, Mou, NTC, Pl, WBC, WEC; all translations except NAB, NJB], 'justice' [NAB], 'uprightness' [NJB]. The rest of this verse from this

point is translated 'I want to be found, not as one who has some legal form of righteousness of his own, but as one who believes in Christ and whom God, for that very reason, has made right with himself' [TNT]. The absence of the definite article emphasizes righteousness as a quality [EGT]. The meaning is a right relationship with God [EGT] and forgiveness of sins [HNTC]. As related to ἐμήν 'my', it implies (by the absence of the definite article [ICC, Lt]) a hypothetical attainment which cannot be a reality [El, ICC, Ln, Lt, Mou, My]; as related to ἐκ νόμου 'from law', it implies the fulfillment of the law's claims [El].

b. ἐκ with genitive object (GEL 89.3; 90.16) (BAGD 3.c. p. 235): 'from' [BAGD, GEL, HNTC; NJB], 'derived from' [Mou; NASB], 'comes from' [Pl, WEC; NIV, NRSV], 'by' [BAGD, GEL; TEV], 'based on' [NAB, REB] 'of' [Ea, ICC; KJV], 'out of' [Ln], 'by keeping' [WBC]. The phrase τὴν ἐκ νόμου 'the one from law' is translated 'legal' [NTC; TNT]. It expresses origin [Ea]. This prepositional phrase defines ἐμὴν δικαιοσύνην 'my righteousness' [ICC].

c. νόμος (GEL 33.55; 33.333) (BAGD 3. p. 542): 'the Law' [BAGD, GEL, Mou, WBC; NASB, NJB, TEV], 'Law' [HNTC], 'the law' [Ea, GEL, ICC, Pl, WEC; KJV, NAB, NIV, NRSV, REB], 'law' [Ln].

d. διά with genitive object (GEL 90.4): 'through' [Ea, GEL, HNTC, ICC, Mou, NTC, Pl, WBC, WEC; all translations except REB, TNT], 'by' [GEL], 'by means of' [Ln], 'from' [REB]. It expresses the instrument of faith [Ea], the means [NIC]. The reason for this preposition is expressed by ἐπί 'on the basis of' which follows [Ea].

e. πίστις (GEL 31.85) (BAGD 2.b.β. p. 663): 'faith' [BAGD, Ea, GEL, HNTC, ICC, Ln, Mou, NTC, Pl, WBC, WEC; all translations except TNT].

QUESTION—What relationship is indicated by the participial phrase μὴ ἔχων 'not having'?

1. It gives the circumstance of being found in Christ [Alf]: found in Christ, in the circumstance of not having my righteousness.

2. It gives the means of being found in Christ [Blm, El, ICC]: found in Christ, not by means of my own righteousness but rather by means of justification by faith.

3. It gives the result of being found in Christ [Ea, My]: found in Christ, resulting in not having my own righteousness. It refers to possession, not to holding firmly [Ea, My].

QUESTION—What relationship is indicated by ἐμήν 'my'?

It is emphatic [EBC, Lg, Ln, Pl]: my own.

1. It contrasts with the following emphatic ἐκ θεοῦ 'from God' [Bg, Ea, EBC, Lt, Pl, TH]: righteousness—not my own, but instead the one which is from God.
2. It contrasts with ἐπὶ τῇ πίστει 'on the basis of faith' [WEC]: righteousness—not my own but that which is on the basis of faith.
3. It contrasts with τὴν διὰ πίστεως Χριστοῦ 'the (righteousness) which is through faith in Christ' [My]: righteousness—not my own but instead the one which is through faith in Christ.

QUESTION—What relationship is indicated by the emphatic (by word order) ἐκ νόμου 'from law'?

1. It is contrasted with the emphatic (by word order) διὰ πίστεως 'through faith' [Bg, Lt, NIC, Pl, TH]: not from law but rather through faith. This is the second part of a chiasmus [TH].
2. It is contrasted with ἐκ θεοῦ 'from God' [Ea, My, WEC]: not from law but rather from God. It is the other part of a chiasmus [WEC].

QUESTION—What relationship is indicated by ἀλλά 'but'?

It expresses a strong contrast [EBC, Lg]: not my own; on the contrary, through faith.

QUESTION—How are the two nouns related in the genitive construction πίστεως Χριστοῦ 'faith of Christ'?

1. Christ is the object of the faith [Bg, Ea, GNC, HNTC, ICC, Ln, MNTC, Mou, NIC, NTC, Pl, TH, WBC, WC, WEC; all translations except KJV]: faith in Christ.
2. Christ is the author or source of the faith [EGT]: faith which Christ produces in me.

the righteousness[a] from[b] God on-the-basis-of[c] the faith,

LEXICON—a. δικαιοσύνη: 'righteousness'. See this word above. Here it includes being put right with God [EGT, Ln, MNTC, NIC, WC] and the righteous conduct which results from being put right with God [EGT, WC].

b. ἐκ with genitive object (GEL 89.3; 90.16) (BAGD 3.c. p. 235): 'from' [BAGD, GEL, HNTC, ICC, Ln, Mou, NTC; NJB, NRSV], 'comes from' [NASB, NIV, TEV], 'by' [BAGD, GEL], 'given by' [WBC; REB], 'of' [Ea; KJV], 'has its origin in' [NAB]. The phrase τὴν ἐκ θεοῦ δικαιοσύνη 'the righteousness from God' is translated 'God's own righteousness' [WEC]. This word expresses the origin [Ea, WBC].

c. ἐπί with dative object (GEL 89.13; 90.9) (BAGD II.1.b.γ. p. 287): 'on the basis of' [BAGD, GEL, Ln; NASB], 'based on' [WEC; NAB, NJB, NRSV, TEV], 'based upon' [ICC], 'on condition of' [Pl], 'rests on' [NTC], 'on' [Ea], 'by' [GEL; KJV, NIV], 'by means of' [GEL], 'obtained through' [WBC], 'in

response to' [REB], 'accorded to' [HNTC], 'on terms of' [Mou].
It expresses the basis of the justification [Ea], the condition of
the justification [Blm], and gives the reason for the preceding
διά 'through' [Ea].
QUESTION—What is the function of this phrase?
It explains (and clarifies [WBC]) the preceding phrase τὴν διὰ
πίστεως Χριστοῦ 'the righteousness which is through faith in Christ'
[Blm, Ea, ICC, WBC]: that is, the justification which is from God
on the basis of faith.
QUESTION—What is ἐπὶ τῇ πίστει 'on the basis of faith' connected
with?
    1. It is connected with the immediately preceding δικαιοσύνη
    'righteousness' [Alf, El]: righteousness which is based on faith.
    2. It is connected with ἔχων 'having' [My]: having this righteous-
    ness based on faith.

DISCOURSE UNIT: 3:10–11 [EGT]. The topic is being conformed to the
death and resurrection of Christ.

3:10
the to-know[a] him
    LEXICON—a. aorist act. infin. of γινώσκω (GEL 27.18; 28.1; 32.16):
    'to know' [Ea, GEL, Mou, NTC, Pl, WBC, WEC; all
    translations except NJB], 'to get to know' [Ln], 'to come to
    know' [HNTC; NJB], 'to become acquainted with' [GEL], 'to
    come to understand' [GEL], 'to comprehend' [GEL]. This
    infinitive is also translated as a noun: 'knowledge' [ICC]. The
    reference is to coming to full knowledge experienced by union
    with Christ [Alf, Ea, EGT, HNTC, ICC, My, NIC, TH, WBC].
    The aorist tense indicates completion of an action, not
    continuation [HNTC, TH], and therefore does not refer to a
    gradual increase of knowledge, but to the final attainment at the
    resurrection of the dead [HNTC].
QUESTION—What relationship is indicated by the use of the
infinitive γνῶναι 'to know'?
    1. It indicates purpose [Alf, Ea, EGT, El, HNTC, ICC, Lg, Mou,
    My, NTC, TH, WBC, WEC].
    1.1 It gives the purpose of the righteousness based on faith [Alf,
    ICC, Lg, My]: having the righteousness of faith in order that I
    may know Christ.
    1.2 It indicates the purpose of all of 3:8–9 [Ea, EGT, HNTC,
    NIC]: to be found in Christ, and to be justified by faith—and
    all this in order to know Christ. The goal of Paul's whole life

is to come to know Christ and the power of his resurrection and the fellowship of his sufferings [HNTC].

1.3 It indicates the purpose of the excellence of knowing Christ (3:8) [My].

1.4 It indicates the purpose of having the righteousness which is by faith [NTC].

1.5 It indicates the purpose of being found in Christ [El]: to be found in Christ, in order that I may know him.

1.6 It indicates a third goal [WBC]: I consider all things as refuse in order that I may gain Christ, in order that I may be found in him, and in order that I may know him.

2. It explains ἵνα Χριστὸν κερδήσω καὶ εὑρεθῶ ἐν αὐτῷ 'in order that I might gain Christ and be found in him' in 3:8-9 [Ln, MNTC]: to know him and be found in him in the following aspects.

3. It more fully explains the noun γνώσεως 'knowledge' in 3:8 [Bg, Blm, EBC].

QUESTION—What is meant by 'knowing Christ'?

It is personal, intimate knowledge gained by personal experience [HNTC, NIC], which is gained by being in union with him [Ea, NIC]. It is explained by the two following phrases [EGT, El, ICC, Lg, Ln, Lt, My(D), TH, TNTC, WBC, WC, WEC]: that I may know him—i.e., know the power of his resurrection and the fellowship of his sufferings. The καί 'and' introduces an explanation of αὐτόν 'him' [ICC, Ln, My, TH, WBC, WEC]. Only those who are righteous by faith possess this knowledge [Lg, My].

and the power[a] of-his resurrection[b]

LEXICON—a. δύναμις (GEL 76.1; 76.7): 'power' [Ea, GEL, HNTC, ICC, Ln, Mou, NTC, Pl, WBC, WEC; all translations].

b. ἀνάστασις (GEL 23.93) (BAGD 2.a., b. p. 60): 'resurrection' [BAGD, Ea, GEL, HNTC, Ln, Mou, NTC, Pl, WBC, WEC; all translations], '(his) risen life' [ICC].

QUESTION—What relationship is indicated by καί 'and'?

1. It indicates an additional thing to be known [Alf, GNC]: I want to know Christ and to know the power of his resurrection.

2. It indicates a fuller explanation of what is involved in knowing Christ [EGT, El, ICC, Lg, Ln, Lt, MNTC, My(D), NTC, Pl, TH, TNTC, WBC, WC, WEC]: I want to know Christ; that is, I want to know the power of his resurrection, and the fellowship of his sufferings.

QUESTION—How are the two nouns related in the genitive construction τὴν δύναμιν τῆς ἀναστάσεως αὐτοῦ 'the power of his resurrection'?

1. It means the power which resurrected him [GNC, HNTC, WC]:
   I want to experience God's power, the same power that
   resurrected Christ. The power God manifested in raising Christ,
   God now manifests in the new life of the believer [HNTC]. God
   empowers believers to overcome temptation and to lead holy
   lives [TH].
2. It means the power that Christ received at his resurrection [Ln,
   MNTC, NTC, TH, TNTC, WBC]: I want to experience Christ's
   power that became his at his resurrection. At his resurrection,
   Christ was made both Lord and Christ [Ln]. It is the power of
   the resurrected Christ at work in Paul's life [TH]. He wants to
   know Christ and to experience the power Christ wields as a
   result of his resurrection [MNTC, WBC]. Christ's power
   destroys sin in one's life [NTC]. The two following phrases are
   aspects of knowing the power of Christ's resurrection [TH].
3. It means the powerful influence of his resurrection [Alf, Blm,
   Ea, EGT, El, ICC, Lg, Mou, My, NIC, Pl]: I want to experience
   the mighty effects of the fact of Christ's resurrection. The fact
   of Christ's resurrection confirms Paul's faith in Christ and his
   hope of salvation through Christ [Blm]; it assures him of his
   justification [Alf, El], and secures our final justification [El]. It
   refers to all that his resurrection implies and effects [Pl]. His
   resurrection is a powerful guarantee of our justification and
   salvation [My].

QUESTION—How would the power affect him?
1. It is the power to give new life and enable Christians to live the
   new life in Christ [EBC, EGT, HNTC, NIC, TH, TNTC, WBC,
   WC], to make personal holiness possible [GNC, ICC, Lt, Mou,
   NTC], and to energize the whole spiritual body [Lt].
2. It is the effectiveness of the resurrection of Christ in assuring
   believers of their salvation [Alf, Blm, Ea, El, ICC, Lt, Mou, Ln,
   My, NTC, Pl] and their resurrection and glory [El, ICC, Lt,
   Mou, My, NTC, Pl] by demonstrating that Christ's saving work
   was successful [Ea].

and the fellowship[a] of-his sufferings,[b]

TEXT—Some manuscripts omit the article τήν 'the' before κοινωνίαν
'fellowship'. GNT brackets this article, indicating a considerable
degree of doubt of doubt about including it. The absence of the article
tends to unite ἀναστάσεως 'resurrection' and κοινωνίαν 'fellowship' as
one unit. The inclusion of the article tends to make them two distinct
entities. This article is omitted by EBC, EGT, HNTC, ICC, Ln, Lt,
MNTC, NTC, Pl, TH, and WBC; it is included by Alf, Bg, Blm, Ea,
El, Lg, and My; others are unclear.

LEXICON—a. κοινωνία (GEL 34.5) (BAGD 4. p. 439): 'fellowship'
[Ea, GEL, HNTC, Ln, NTC, Pl, WBC; KJV, NASB], 'fellowship
of sharing' [NIV], 'sharing' [BAGD; NRSV], 'partnership'
[Mou], 'how to share' [NAB], not explicit [ICC]. This noun is
also translated as a verb: 'to share' [REB, TEV, TNT], 'to
partake of' [NJB], 'to participate' [WEC].

b. πάθημα (GEL 24.78) (BAGD 1. p. 602): 'suffering' [BAGD, Ea,
GEL, HNTC, ICC, Ln, Mou, NTC, Pl, WBC, WEC; all
translations].

QUESTION—How are the two nouns related in the genitive
construction τὴν κοινωνίαν τῶν παθημάτων αὐτοῦ 'the fellowship of
his sufferings'?

1. It refers to physical sufferings [Alf, Blm, Ea, EBC, El, GNC,
HNTC, ICC, Lg, Lt, Mou, My, NIC, NTC, TNTC].

1.1 It means to participate in the sufferings which Christ endured
in his earthly life [Alf, El, GNC, HNTC, ICC, Lt] in the sense
that Christ's sufferings are continued in the Church [Alf, Ea,
EBC, HNTC, NTC]: to participate in Christ's sufferings. This
is a necessary condition in order to come under the power of
Christ's resurrection [Alf, Blm, El]. They are the means by
which Paul is becoming conformed to the death of Christ
[HNTC].

1.2 It means to suffer for Christ [GNC, Lg, My, TNTC]. To do
this is to suffer with him [GNC, Lg, My].

2. It refers to an inward mystical experience [EGT, MNTC, TH,
WBC, WC, WEC].

2.1 It refers to the mystical experience of dying to Paul's old life
[MNTC, WBC, WEC]. Since knowing the power of Christ's
resurrection is an inward experience, this closely related
phrase must also refer to an inward experience [WBC].

2.2 It refers to the mystical experience of sharing in all of Christ's
experiences [WC].

3. It refers both to dying to sin and to suffering for Christ [NIC].

4. It refers to suffering from persecutors and Paul's internal
struggle with temptation [Pl].

being-conformed[a] to-his death,

LEXICON—a. pres. pass. participle of συμμορφίζω (GEL 58.6)
(BAGD p. 778): 'to be conformed' [Ln, Pl; NASB], 'to become
conformed' [NTC], 'to conform oneself' [HNTC, WBC], 'to be
made conformable' [KJV], 'to grow into conformity' [Mou], 'to
come to be similar in form' [GEL], 'to invest with the same
form' [BAGD], 'to be formed into the pattern of' [NAB], 'to be
moulded to the pattern of' [NJB], 'to be molded in accordance
with' [WEC], 'to become like him' [NIV, NRSV, TEV, TNT],

not explicit [ICC]. This participle is also translated as a noun: 'conformity' [REB]. The subject is Paul, the implied subject of the infinitive τοῦ γνῶναι 'to know' [Alf, ICC, Lg, My, TH], or of the following verb καταντήσω 'I may attain' [Bg]. The present tense implies continuation [Ea, El, ICC, Ln, Mou, TH, WC], or development [My]. It is passive voice, 'being conformed' [ICC, Ln], or it is middle voice, 'conforming myself' [HNTC, WBC]. This word implies deep and inward resemblance [Ln].

QUESTION—What relationship is indicated by the use of the participial form συμμορφιζόμενος 'being conformed'?

1. It indicates an accompanying circumstance of 'knowing' [Ea El]: in order to know him and the power of his resurrection and the fellowship of his sufferings while, at the same time, being conformed to his death.
2. It explains the phrase τὴν κοινωνίαν τῶν παθημάτων αὐτοῦ 'the fellowship of his sufferings' [EBC, WC]: to know the fellowship of his sufferings, which means being conformed to his death. Sharing Christ's sufferings means identification with Christ, which amounts to death to the former life [EBC].
3. It is one aspect of experiencing the power of Christ's resurrection [TH].

QUESTION—What is meant by 'being conformed to his death'?

It means to become dead to sin [EGT, MNTC, NTC, TNTC, WEC] and alive in Christ [EGT], to strive continually to put one's sinful nature to death [TH], to strive to make one's death to sin in Christ's death a daily reality [WBC], and whatever physical suffering may be encountered [WBC, WEC]. Paul is describing his threatened martyrdom as, in a sense, similar to the death of Christ [My, Pl]. Christ's death was a sacrifice and Paul contemplates his own death in the same light [Ea].

3:11

if[a] somehow[b] I-may-attain[c] into[d] the resurrection[e] the-(one) from[f] (the) dead.

TEXT—Instead of τὴν ἐκ νεκρῶν 'the one from (the) dead', some manuscripts have τῶν νεκρῶν 'of the dead'. GNT does not deal with this variant. Only Blm and KJV clearly read 'of the dead'.

LEXICON—a. εἰ (GEL 89.65; 90.26) (BAGD VI. 1.2.b. p. 220): 'if' [Ea, GEL, HNTC, Ln, Mou, NTC, Pl; KJV, NRSV], 'whether' [BAGD, GEL], 'and so' [NIV], 'in hope of' [REB]. The phrase εἴ πως 'if somehow' is translated 'if this may be' [ICC], 'thus do I hope that' [NAB], 'in the hope that' [TEV], 'in the hope of' [WBC], 'if I dare hope for it' [TNT], 'hoping that' [WEC], 'in order that' [NASB]. The phrase εἴ πως καταντήσω 'if somehow I may attain' is translated 'striving toward the goal' [NJB].

b. πως (GEL not listed): 'somehow' [Ln, Mou; NIV, NRSV, REB], 'by any means' [KJV], 'anyhow' [Ea], 'only' [HNTC, NTC], 'so be' [Pl]. This word implies Paul's humility, not doubt [Blm, Ea, El, ICC, Lg, My, NIC, NTC, Pl, TH, WBC, WC] and modest hope or self-confidence [Lt, NIC, TH], opening the way for what he says in the following verse [Blm, WEC]. Any implied doubt is distrust of himself, not of God (the absence of absolute moral certainty [Lg, My]) [EGT, ICC, MNTC, WC, WEC], emphasizing the need of constant vigilance [EGT, ICC, MNTC, NIC]. He has no uncertainty of his salvation [TNTC].

c. aorist act. subj. of καταντάω (GEL 13.16) (BAGD 2.a. p. 415): 'to attain' [BAGD, Ea, GEL, HNTC, NTC, Pl, WBC; KJV, NASB, NIV, NRSV, REB], 'to arrive' [BAGD, Mou; NAB], 'to get to arrive' [Ln], 'to reach' [WEC]. The phrase καταντήσω εἰς τὴν ἐξανάστασιν 'I may attain to the resurrection' is translated 'I may be raised from the dead' [ICC], 'I myself will be raised from death to life' [TEV], 'I want to be raised again from death' [TNT]. It implies obtaining a much-desired result [Ea].

d. εἰς with accusative object (GEL 84.22; 78.51): 'into' [GEL], 'to' [Ea, HNTC, NTC, Pl; NASB, NIV], 'unto' [KJV], 'to the point of' [GEL], 'at' [Ln, Mou; NAB], not explicit [WBC, WEC; NJB, NRSV, REB].

e. ἐξανάστασις (GEL 23.93) (BAGD p. 272): 'resurrection' [BAGD, Ea, GEL, HNTC, Mou, NTC, WBC, WEC; all translations except TEV, TNT], 'rising up' [Ln], 'rising again' [Pl]. The prefixed preposition ἐξ- adds the thought of rising 'up' [Alf, Ea, My] or 'out from among' the dead persons and emphasizes the concept of a literal resurrection [GNC]; it distinguishes Paul's resurrection from Christ's [Ln]. It refers to Christ's resurrection, with our resurrection identified with it [Bg]. It refers to the resurrection of the righteous [Alf, Blm, EBC, EGT, El, GNC, HNTC, ICC, Lg, Lt, Mou, NIC, TH, TNTC, WC] at Christ's return [Alf, HNTC, TH]. It refers to Paul's desire to be raised above sin in this life [NTC].

f. ἐκ with genitive object (GEL 84.4): 'from' [Ea, GEL, HNTC, ICC, Ln, NTC, Pl, WEC; all translations except KJV], 'from among' [WBC], 'out from' [GEL, Mou], 'out of' [GEL]. The resurrection ἐκ νεκρῶν 'from the dead' refers to the resurrection of believers [NIC, Pl], the literal resurrection, not a mystical experience [WBC, WEC].

QUESTION—What is this clause connected with?
1. It is connected with the final phrase of 3:10 [My, TH, WEC]: being conformed to Christ's death if somehow I may attain the resurrection. It is Paul's aim to experience likeness to Christ's death [My].
2. It is connected with all of 3:10 [Lg, MNTC]: I desire all of those things if somehow I may attain the resurrection. It is the result Paul hopes will follow his experiencing all that is mentioned in the preceding verse [MNTC].

QUESTION—What is meant by εἴ πως 'if somehow'?
1. It implies a goal but with the possibility of failure implied [Alf, Bg, GNC, ICC], since the attainment is, in part, beyond Paul's power [GNC]: if somehow, but it is not absolutely certain.
2. It implies doubt as to whether he will be resurrected from death or will be alive at Christ's return [EBC, GNC]: if somehow, either by resurrection from death or by being alive at Christ's return.
3. It implies doubt as to the kind of death he will have [Ln]: if somehow, by whatever kind of death.
4. It implies doubt concerning the outcome of his trial [TNTC]: if somehow, whether by the death penalty or otherwise.
5. It implies purpose [Blm, My]: in order that by any means.
6. It is equivalent to an indirect question [EGT, Ln, MNTC]: I desire these things, so as to see whether I may attain the resurrection. It implies expectation [Ln].

DISCOURSE UNIT: 3:12–4:1 [GNT, NIV]. The topic is pressing toward the goal [GNT, NIV].

DISCOURSE UNIT: 3:12–21 [Pl, TH, WC; TEV]. The topic is a warning against antinomianism [Pl], pressing toward the goal [TH; TEV], a warning against the two groups who claimed to be spiritual [WC].

DISCOURSE UNIT: 3:12–16 [EGT, MNTC, Mou, My(D), NIC, NTC, WBC, WC, WEC]. The topic is pressing forward as a sign of maturity [EGT], advancing to perfection in Christ [NTC], the conditions for progress as a Christian [MNTC], the Christian's status and progress [Mou], pressing toward the high calling in Christ Jesus [NIC], warning against claiming perfection now [WBC], warning against those who presumptuously claimed perfection [WC], practical theology [WEC].

DISCOURSE UNIT: 3:12–14 [WEC]. The topic is Paul's frustration and his hope.

3:12

Not that already I-have-received[a] (it) or already am-perfected,[b]

LEXICON—a. aorist act. indic. of λαμβάνω (GEL 18.1; 57.55; 57.125) (BAGD 1.g. p. 465): 'to receive' [GEL, Mou], 'to grasp' [GEL, WBC], 'to acquire' [GEL], 'to obtain' [GEL; NASB, NIV, NRSV], 'to attain' [Ea, WEC; KJV], 'to secure' [NJB], 'to achieve' [REB], 'to reach' [Pl; NAB], 'to win' [HNTC], 'to take hold of' [GEL], 'to get hold of' [Ln], 'to get hold' [NTC], 'to succeed' [TEV], 'to make one's own' [BAGD], 'to be one's (own)' [TNT], not specific [ICC]. The aorist tense refers to a single event [El]. It sums up Paul's experience thus far, considering it as a single fact [EGT, ICC, WBC]. It implies Paul's certainty of attaining it in the future [My].

b. perf. pass. indic. of τελειόω (GEL 53.50; **68.31**; 68.22; 88.38) (BAGD 3. p. 810): 'to be perfected' [Ea, GEL, Mou, WEC], 'to be made perfect' [GEL, NTC, Pl; NIV, TNT], 'to be perfect' [KJV], 'to become perfect' [WBC; NASB, TEV], 'to reach perfection' [REB], 'to attain perfection' [HNTC], 'to be consecrated' [BAGD], 'to be completely successful' [GEL], 'to complete' [GEL], 'to be made complete' [Ln], 'to finish' [GEL], 'to finish one's course' [NAB], 'to reach one's goal' [NJB], 'to reach the goal' [NRSV], 'to realize one's ideal' [ICC], 'to become an initiate' [GEL]. It refers to spiritual (and moral [ICC]) perfection [Alf, ICC]. It explains the preceding figurative ἔλαβον 'I have received' more fully [ICC, Lg, Ln] and without figurative expression [My]. The perfect tense brings the action down to the present time [Ea, EBC, ICC, Lt]. The passive voice implies that God is the actor [Ln].

QUESTION—What is implied in οὐχ ὅτι 'not that'?

The meaning is 'I do not mean to say that I have received' [Alf, Blm, Ea, EGT, El, ICC, Lg, Lt, MNTC, My, NIC, NTC, Pl, TH, WBC; TEV, TNT]. This is added to avoid misunderstanding about what he said about himself [El, MNTC, NTC].

QUESTION—What is the implied object of ἔλαβον 'I have received'?

1. He had not received the resurrection from the dead (3:11) [NOT 4(4), WEC]: not that I have already received the resurrection from the dead.

2. He had not received τὸ βραβεῖον 'the prize' (3:14) [Bg, Ea, El, GNC, HNTC, Mou, My]: not that I have already received the prize. See 3:14 for the meaning of prize. This is already in Paul's mind in his preceding comments [Ea, My].

3. He had not received the fulfillment of his goals listed in 3:8–11 [Alf, EBC, EGT, ICC, MNTC, NIC]: not that I have accomplished all that I want to be and do. Some specify his

goal to be gaining Christ [Alf], accomplishing all that is involved in winning Christ and knowing him [EGT], or simply all that he longs for [EBC].

4. He had not attained to the purpose for which Christ appeared to him [TNTC].
5. He had not fully grasped the meaning of Christ [Lg, WBC]: not that I fully know Christ.
6. He had not received the certainty of salvation [Blm].
7. He had not received spiritual perfection [NTC, TH]. The following clause defines the meaning of this clause [TH].

QUESTION—What is meant by οὐχ τετελείωμαι 'I am not perfected'?

1. It means that he has not completed his life's work and died, as in Lk. 13:32 and Heb. 12:23 [Adam Clarke's Commentary, NOT 4(4), Wesleyan Bible Commentary]: I have not completed my work and died.
2. It means he has not reached his goal [NJB, NRSV], finished his course [Bg; NAB], and received the prize [Blm]: I have not yet reached my goal and received the prize.
3. It means he has not yet attained spiritual perfection [Alf, EGT, EBC, EGT, El, GNC, ICC, Lg, Mou, My, NIC, NTC, TH, TNTC, WC]: I have not reached perfection. It means to become what God intended him to become [My]. It is the state of perfection in heaven [Mou, TNTC], that is attained after the resurrection [TH]. It refers to both moral and spiritual perfection [ICC].
4. On the analogy of the mystery religions, it means he has not attained the highest level of Christian life [HNTC].
5. It means he does not have perfect knowledge of Christ [WBC].
6. It means he is not blameless for the Day of Christ [WEC].

but I-pursue[a] if[b] even I-may-take-hold-of[c] (the-thing) on-the-basis-of[d] which I-was-taken-hold-of[e] also by[f] Christ Jesus.

TEXT—Some manuscripts omit Ἰησοῦ 'Jesus'. GNT brackets Ἰησοῦ, indicating a considerable degree of doubt about including it. Ἰησοῦ is bracketed by WEC and NAB; it is omitted by Ea, El, Lt, My, Pl, and REB.

LEXICON—a. pres. act. indic. of διώκω (GEL 15.158; 15.223; 68.66): 'to pursue' [GEL, WEC; NJB], 'to continue pursuit' [Ln], 'to press forward' [GEL, Pl], 'to press on' [Ea, GEL, ICC, Mou, NTC, WBC; NASB, NIV, NRSV, REB, TNT], 'to strive' [TEV], 'to persist' [GEL], 'to follow after' [KJV], 'to race' [NAB], 'to speed on' [HNTC]. The present tense implies Paul's continuing pursuit of the goal [EBC].

b. εἰ (GEL 89.65; 90.26) (BAGD V.2.b. p. 219): 'if' [Ea, GEL, Ln, Mou, NTC, Pl], 'if that' [KJV], 'in the hope that' [HNTC], 'whether' [BAGD, GEL, WBC], 'in order that' [NASB], not specific [ICC]. The phrase εἰ καὶ καταλάβω 'if I may even take hold of' is translated 'to grasp if possible' [NAB], 'to win' [TEV], 'to take hold of' [NIV], 'in the attempt to take hold of' [NJB], 'and trying to lay hold of it' [TNT], 'hoping to take hold of' [REB], 'with the hope of reaching it' [WEC], 'to make it my own' [NRSV]. Εἰ here is synonymous with ὅτι 'that' [Blm], with a hint of modesty [Lg], modest doubt of success [Blm], or self-distrust [WEC]. It means 'whether', in an indirect deliberative question [EGT, My, WBC]. Εἰ καί implies expectation [Ln; TH]. It here introduces the purpose of Paul's striving [GNC].

c. aorist act. subj. of καταλαμβάνω (GEL 57.56) (BAGD 1.a. p. 413): 'to take hold of' [NTC; NIV, NJB, REB], 'to lay hold of' [NASB, TNT], 'to grasp' [Pl; NAB], 'to acquire' [GEL], 'to obtain' [GEL], 'to attain' [BAGD, GEL], 'to apprehend' [WBC; KJV], 'to reach' [WEC], 'to win' [BAGD, HNTC; TEV], 'to capture' [Ln], 'to make one's own' [BAGD; NRSV], 'to seize' [Ea, Mou], not specific [ICC]. It is the subjunctive mood in an indirect deliberative question [EGT] and refers to a future point of time [Ln]. This compound verb is stronger than λαμβάνω 'to take' [Ea] and implies being in full possession of the object [Bg], to overtake and seize something [ICC].

d. ἐπί with dative object (GEL 89.13; 89.27; 89.60) (BAGD II.1.b.γ. p. 287): 'on the basis of' [GEL], 'in view of' [GEL], 'with a view to' [Mou], 'for' [Ea, NTC; KJV, NASB, NIV, NJB, REB, TEV], 'for the sake of' [GEL], 'because of' [GEL], 'for the purpose of' [GEL], 'for this reason' [BAGD], 'just as' [HNTC], 'since' [Ln], not specific [ICC]. The phrase ἐφ' ᾧ is translated 'because' [BAGD, Pl; NRSV, TNT], 'since' [NAB], 'inasmuch as' [WBC], 'after all' [WEC].

e. aorist pass. indic. of καταλαμβάνω (GEL 57.56) (BAGD 1.a. p. 413): 'to take hold of' [NIV, NJB, REB], 'to lay hold of' [NASB, TNT], 'to grasp' [Pl; NAB], 'to seize' [BAGD, Ea, Mou], 'to capture' [Ln], 'to acquire' [GEL], 'to obtain' [GEL], 'to apprehend' [WBC; KJV], 'to win' [BAGD, HNTC; TEV], 'to make one's own' [BAGD], 'to reach' [WEC], 'to lay hold on' [NTC], not specific [ICC]. The phrase κατελήμφθην ὑπὸ Χριστοῦ Ἰησοῦ 'I was grasped by Christ Jesus' is translated 'Christ Jesus took hold of me' [NIV, NJB], 'Christ once took hold of me' [REB], 'Christ Jesus himself laid hold of me' [TNT], 'Christ Jesus has made me his own' [NRSV], 'Christ Jesus has already won me to himself' [TEV]. The aorist tense refers to Paul's conversion [Alf, Blm, GNC, ICC, Ln, My, NIC, TNTC]. He was grasped by a heavenly calling [Bg]. This compound verb is stronger than λαμβάνω 'to take' [Ea] and implies being in full possession of the object [Bg].

f. ὑπό with genitive object (GEL 90.1) (BAGD 1.a.α. p. 843): 'by' [BAGD, Ea, GEL, HNTC, Ln, Mou, NTC, Pl, WBC, WEC; NAB, NASB], 'of' [KJV], not specific [ICC].

QUESTION—What relationship is indicated by δέ 'but'?

It indicates a contrast with the preceding clause but not a negation of it [Ea, El, My]: I am not perfected; however, I press on for the prize. It further implies that Paul cannot yet claim the condition he has just described. It points out Paul's determination [WBC].

QUESTION—What is the implied object of διώκω 'I pursue'?

1. It is τὸ βραβεῖον 'the prize' in 3:14 below [Alf, My]: I pursue the prize.
2. It is his goal, the resurrection [NJB]: I am pursuing the goal, namely, the resurrection.
3. It is the righteousness of faith, which is the thing for which Christ laid hold on him [ICC].
4. It is used intransitively, with no object implied [My(D); NAB, NASB, NIV, NRSV, TEV].

QUESTION—What relationship is indicated by καί 'even' before καταλάβω 'I may grasp'?

1. It is intensive [Bg]: if I may go so far as to grasp.
2. It adds to the preceding thought [Ea, ICC]: if in addition to pressing on I may also grasp the prize.
3. It emphasizes the correspondence of καταλάβω 'I may grasp' with the following verb κατελήμφθην 'I have been grasped' [EGT]: I may grasp that for which/because I was grasped.
4. It contrasts καταλάβω 'I may grasp' with διώκω 'I pursue' [El]: I pursue if I may even grasp.
5. It contrasts καταλάβω 'I may grasp' with the preceding ἔλαβον 'I have grasped' [Lg]: I have not received, but I pursue if I may seize.

QUESTION—What is the object of καταλάβω 'I may grasp'?

1. When the following phrase ἐφ' ᾧ is translated 'on the basis of which' or 'for which' [Alf, Blm, Ea, El, GNC, ICC, Mou, My(D), NTC, TH; NASB, NIV, NJB, REB, TEV]. The object of καταλάβω 'I may grasp' is the understood antecedent of the following relative pronoun ᾧ 'which' [Alf, Blm, Ea, El, GNC, ICC, Mou, My(D), TH; NASB, REB, TEV].
1.1 It is an as yet unspecified idea [Alf, Blm, El, GNC, ICC, My(D), NTC; NASB, NIV, REB]: if I may even grasp that for which I was grasped by Christ Jesus.

1.2 It is the understood τὸ βραβεῖον 'the prize' [Ea, Mou, TH; NJB, TEV]: if I may also grasp the prize, to grasp which Christ Jesus grasped me.

2. When the following phrase ἐφ' ᾧ is translated 'since/because' [Bg, Lg, Ln, MNTC, My, NIC, Pl, WBC, WEC; NAB, NRSV, TNT].

2.1 The object of καταλάβω 'I may grasp' is 'it' understood [WEC; NRSV, TNT]: if I may even grasp it, because I was grasped by Christ Jesus. Perceiving Christ's power thus influences the Christian [Bg].

2.2 Its object is τὸ βραβεῖον 'the prize' [My, Pl; NAB]: I am racing to grasp the prize, because I have been grasped by Christ Jesus.

2.3 It is perfect holiness [NIC], in preparation for heaven [MNTC]: I am racing to grasp perfect holiness.

2.4 It is full understanding of Jesus [WBC]: I am racing to grasp full understanding of Jesus.

QUESTION—What is the area of meaning of καί 'also' following ᾧ 'which'?

1. It is intensive [Bg, Mou]: I was actually grasped by Christ Jesus.

2. It is additive [ICC]: if I may not only strive for it, but it is also the thing for which also I was grasped.

3. It points out that his seeking to grasp the prize is in harmony with Christ's grasping him [Ea, My, WEC]: I am seeking to grasp the prize, just as Christ grasped me. Christ's grasping Paul is the basis for Paul's hope [WEC].

4. It relates to and specifies the relative pronoun ᾧ 'which' [El]: for which object I was grasped by Christ.

3:13

Brothers,[a] I do-not consider[b] myself to-have-taken-hold-of[c] (it);

TEXT—Instead of οὐ 'not', some manuscripts have οὔπω 'not yet'. GNT reads 'not' with a C rating, indicating a considerable degree of doubt. 'Not' is read by Alf, Bg, Blm, Ea, EGT, El, GNC, HNTC, Lg, Lt, Pl, MNTC, TH, TNTC, WBC, WEC, KJV, NAB, NJB, NRSV, and TEV. 'Not yet' is read by Ln, ICC, NIC, NTC, WC, NASB, NIV, REB, and TNT.

LEXICON—a. ἀδελφός: 'brother'. See this word at 3:1, 17.

b. pres. mid. (deponent = act.) indic. of λογίζομαι (GEL 31.1) (BAGD 3. p. 476): 'to consider' [BAGD, GEL; NIV, NRSV], 'to regard' [GEL; NASB], 'to reckon' [Ea, HNTC, Ln, WBC, WEC; NJB], 'to account' [Mou, Pl], 'to think' [TEV], 'to claim' [REB], 'to have an opinion' [GEL], 'to think of oneself' [NAB], 'to count' [NTC; KJV], 'to know' [TNT], not explicit [ICC]. It implies drawing a calm conclusion following a discussion [EGT, ICC, MNTC, NIC, TH]. The perfect tense implies taking hold of and keeping hold [Lg].

c. perf. act. infin. of καταλάμβανω (GEL 57.56) (BAGD 1.a. p. 413): 'to take hold of' [NIV, NJB], 'to obtain' [GEL], 'to acquire' [GEL], 'to seize' [BAGD, Mou], 'to grasp' [Pl], 'to lay hold' [Ea, NTC], 'to lay hold of' [NASB, TNT], 'to have hold of' [REB], 'to capture' [Ln], 'to attain' [BAGD, Ea, GEL, ICC], 'to make one's own' [BAGD; NRSV], 'to apprehend' [KJV], 'to apprehend fully' [WBC], 'to win' [BAGD, HNTC; TEV], 'to reach' [WEC; NAB]. The perfect tense implies a present possession following having received it [Ln].

QUESTION—What is implied by ἀδελφοί 'brothers'?

1. It implies affection [Alf, Ea, EBC, Lg, My, NTC], the intention to lessen the sense of severity [MNTC], familiarity [Bg], earnestness [El, My, NTC], and emphasis [Alf, El].
2. It implies the seriousness of the matter [EGT, Pl].
3. It is used to focus his readers' attention [Lt].
4. It is an appeal to those who claimed special spirituality [WC].
5. By this word and the following emphatic ἐγὼ ἐμαυτόν 'I myself' Paul is preparing for a new exhortation [My(D)].

QUESTION—What is implied by the use of ἐγώ 'I' and ἐμαυτόν 'myself'?

They are both emphatic [Alf, Ea, EBC, EGT, El, ICC, Lg, Ln, Lt, Mou, My, Pl, TH].

1. They imply that Paul is giving his own opinion concerning himself [ICC, My]: I, for my own part.
2. These words disclaim an unduly high opinion which some of the Philippians might have concerning him [ICC, Ln]: I, in contrast with the opinion which some might have concerning me.
3. It contrasts Paul's estimate of himself with the opinion of some persons who claimed that they had grasped the prize already [EGT, Lt, MNTC, Mou, WBC], who had developed antinomian tendencies [Lt]: I, in contrast with the opinion of some others concerning their own state.
4. It includes the possible opinion of others about themselves or about Paul [NIC, Pl]: whatever others may think about themselves or about me, I for myself do not consider that I have taken hold of it.

but[a] one-(thing) (I do), on-the-one-hand the-(things) behind[b] (me)
forgetting[c] and[d] (on the other hand) to-the-(things) in-front[e] reaching-
out,[f]

LEXICON—a. δε (GEL 89.124): 'but' [Ea, GEL, HNTC, ICC, NTC,
WBC, WEC; KJV, NASB, NIV, NRSV], 'no' [Mou], 'yes' [Ln],
not explicit [Pl; NAB]. The phrase ἒν δέ 'but one thing' is
translated 'I can only say that' [NJB], 'what I do say is this'
[REB], 'the one thing I do, however' [TEV], 'only one thing
matters to me' [TNT].

b. ὀπίσω (GEL 83.40) (BAGD 1.a. p. 575): 'behind' [BAGD, Ea,
GEL, HNTC, Ln, Mou, NTC, Pl, WBC, WEC; all translations],
'in back of' [GEL], 'past' [ICC]. It refers to the time from
writing these words back to his conversion [Ea].

c. pres. mid. (deponent = act.) of ἐπιλανθάνομαι (GEL 29.14)
(BAGD 1. p. 295): 'to forget' [BAGD, Ea, GEL, HNTC, Ln,
Mou, NTC, Pl, WBC, WEC; all translations except NAB], 'to
give no thought to' [NAB], 'not to be encouraged to self-
satisfaction or relaxation of effort' [ICC]. The prefixed ἐπι
'upon' has no real significance [ICC]; it intensifies the meaning
of the verb [Ea, El]. The present tense implies continuing to
forget [TH, TNTC]. It implies intentional forgetting [My]. He is
not merely leaving the things which are behind, he is forgetting
them [NTC]. He valued the memory of his previous service but
did not rest on their memory [Ea, EBC, ICC]. His past has no
bearing on his present conduct [TNTC].

d. δέ (GEL 89.94): 'and' [GEL, HNTC, Ln, Mou, NTC, Pl, WBC,
WEC; all translations except NAB], 'but' [Ea; NAB], not
explicit [ICC].

e. ἔμπροσθεν (GEL 83.33) (BAGD 1.a. p. 257): 'in front' [Ln,
Mou, Pl; NJB], 'in front of' [BAGD, GEL], 'before' [Ea, GEL,
WBC; KJV], 'ahead' [BAGD, HNTC, NTC, WEC; all
translations except KJV, NJB], not explicit [ICC].

f. pres. mid. (deponent = act.) of ἐπεκτείνομαι (GEL 13.20;
16.20) (BAGD p. 284): 'to reach out' [GEL; TNT], 'to reach
forth' [KJV], 'to reach forward' [NASB], 'to stretch toward'
[GEL], 'to stretch forward' [ICC], 'to stretch forth' [Ea], 'to
stretch out' [BAGD, Ln, WBC], 'to stretch out and onward'
[Mou], 'to strain toward' [BAGD; NIV, REB], 'to strain eagerly
towards' [HNTC], 'to strain forward' [NJB, NRSV], 'to strain
forward eagerly' [NTC], 'to strain after' [Pl], 'to push on' [NAB],
'to do one's best to attain' [GEL], 'to do one's best to reach'
[TEV], 'to seek strongly' [GEL], 'to try hard' [GEL], 'to exert
oneself' [WEC]. This verb implies not merely looking ahead but
stretching forward to reach the goal [Blm, Ea, MNTC, Mou].

The prefixed ἐκ 'out' implies the racer's body stretching out [Ea, El], and the prefixed ἐπί 'at' implies motion toward the goal [Ea, El, My].

QUESTION—What is the implied content of ἕν 'one thing'?

It implies concentration on a single aim [MNTC]: I concentrate on one single aim. It refers to the two following participles [Ln]: this one thing—namely, forgetting and reaching out. Or it refers to the entire following sentence [Lg, My]: this one thing—namely, forgetting and reaching out, I pursue along the course.

QUESTION—What is the implied verb for ἕν 'one thing'?

1. It is 'I do' [Alf, Bg, Ea, El, ICC, My(D), NTC, TH, WBC; KJV, NASB, NIV, NRSV, TEV]: one thing I do.
2. Since the 'one thing' is in opposition to the following 'things', διώκω 'I pursue' or a similar verb must be supplied [Blm]: one thing I pursue.
3. It is λέγω 'I say' or the repetition of λογίζομαι κατειληφέναι 'I consider to have grasped' [Lg], or simply λογίζομαι 'I consider' [My]: but one thing I say/consider to have grasped.
4. It is 'matters to me' [TNT]: only one thing matters to me.
5. It is 'is certain' [WEC]: one thing is certain.

QUESTION—What is implied by τὰ ὀπίσω 'the things behind'?

The implied object is 'me' [Alf, HNTC, NTC, Pl, WBC, WEC; NJB, TEV]. It refers to the part of his Christian life which he has completed [Bg, El, GNC, HNTC, ICC, Lt, MNTC, My, TH, WC], his previous work, problems, and accomplishments for Christ [Blm, Ea, Lg, WBC], his previous life both before and after becoming a Christian [NIC, NTC], his Jewish advantages [Ln, TNTC]: forgetting the things I have done previously.

QUESTION—What relationship is indicated by the use of the two participles ἐπιλανθανόμενος 'forgetting' and ἐπεκτεινόμενος 'stretching forward'?

1. They define more specifically the following verb διώκω 'I pursue' (3:14) [Lg, MNTC] as participles of manner [WBC]: by forgetting the things behind and reaching out to the things ahead, I pursue along the course.
2. They are temporal [WBC]: while forgetting and stretching out, I pursue along the course.

QUESTION—What does τοῖς ἔμπροσθεν 'to the things in front' refer to?

1. It refers to the things which lie between him now and his goal [Ea, El, Lg, Ln], the higher spiritual attainments [ICC]: the things which are ahead of me before I reach the goal.

2. It refers to the perfection which he has not yet reached [Alf], the progress still to be made [Ea]: I press forward to the perfection which I have not yet reached.
3. It refers to full knowledge of Christ [WBC]: I press forward to full knowledge of Christ.
4. It refers to the final judgment and the resurrection [NOT 4(4), TNTC].

3:14

I-press[a] toward[b] (the) goal[c] for[d] the prize[e] of-the upward[f] calling[g] of-God in[h] Christ Jesus.

LEXICON—a. pres. act. indic. of διώκω (GEL 15.158; **15.223**; 68.66; **89.56**) (BAGD 1. p. 201): 'to press' [GEL; KJV, REB], 'to press on' [BAGD, Ea, Mou, NTC; NASB, NIV, NRSV, TNT], 'to press forward' [Pl], 'to run' [BAGD, WBC], 'to run straight' [**GEL**; TEV], 'to race' [NJB], 'to speed on' [HNTC], 'to pursue' [GEL, WEC], 'to continue pursuit' [Ln], 'to strive' [**GEL**], 'to hasten' [BAGD], 'to stretch forward' [ICC]. The phrase κατὰ σκοπὸν διώκω 'I press toward the goal' is translated 'my entire attention is on the finish line' [NAB]. The present tense emphasizes the need of constantly pursuing the goal [WBC].

b. κατά with accusative object (GEL **83.45**; 84.30; **89.56**) (BAGD II.1.6. p. 406): 'toward' [BAGD, Ea, **GEL**, ICC, NTC; KJV, NASB, NIV, NRSV, TEV], 'towards' [HNTC, Pl, WBC; NJB, REB], 'to' [TEV], not specific [WEC]. The phrase κατὰ σκοπόν 'toward the goal' is translated 'goalward' [Ln, Mou]. It indicates the direction of the pursuit [EGT, El].

c. σκοπός (GEL **84.28**; **89.56**) (BAGD p. 756): 'goal' [BAGD, GEL, ICC, NTC, Pl, WEC; NASB, NIV, NRSV, TEV, TNT], 'goal-marker' [WBC], 'mark' [Ea; KJV], 'finish line' [HNTC; NAB], 'finishing line' [REB], 'finishing-point' [NJB]. It means the goal [NIC, Pl, TH]. It refers to the goal-marker, but its meaning is not specifically identified [WBC]. It means a point to aim at, not the goal itself [MNTC]. The goal is full knowledge of Christ [EBC], perfection in Christ [NTC].

d. εἰς with accusative object (GEL **89.56**; 89.57): 'for' [Ea, **GEL**, Ln, NTC, WBC; KJV, NASB, NRSV], 'for the purpose of' [GEL], 'to' [TNT], 'unto' [Mou], 'toward' [ICC; NAB], 'to win' [HNTC, Pl; NIV, NJB, REB], 'in order to win' [WEC; TEV]. This preposition expresses the purpose of pressing forward [Alf, EBC, Lg].

e. βραβεῖον (GEL **57.120**; **89.56**) (BAGD 2. p. 146): 'prize' [BAGD, Ea, **GEL**, HNTC, Ln, Mou, NTC, Pl, WBC, WEC; all

translations], 'reward' [GEL], 'destiny' [ICC]. It is the object of
the pursuit [El].

f. ἄνω (GEL 83.48; 84.25) (BAGD 2. p. 77): 'upward' [BAGD,
NTC; NASB], 'upwards' [GEL], 'up' [GEL], 'above' [GEL],
'high' [Ea, HNTC, ICC, Mou; KJV], 'lofty' [Ln], 'heavenly'
[WEC; NJB, NRSV, REB, TNT], 'heavenward' [NIV], not
specific [Pl]. The phrase τῆς ἄνω κλήσεως τοῦ θεοῦ 'of the
upward calling of God' is translated 'to which God calls me up'
[WBC], 'to which God calls me—life on high' [NAB], 'for which
God has called me heavenward' [NIV], 'which is God's call to
the life above' [TEV], 'of the heavenly life to which God calls
me' [TNT]. This word describes the call [Ea, El]. It implies that
the call originated in heaven [Alf, Ea, Mou] from God [My],
that the goal of the calling is life in heaven [EGT, Ln, Mou,
TH, WC; NIV, TEV, TNT], life with God [MNTC, TNTC], that
it calls to heavenly things [HNTC, Lg].

g. κλήσις (GEL 33.312; 33.313) (BAGD 1. p. 435): 'calling' [Ea,
GEL, Ln; KJV], 'call' [BAGD, Mou, NTC, WEC; NASB, NJB,
NRSV, TEV], 'vocation' [HNTC], 'invitation' [Pl]. The phrase
κλήσεως τοῦ θεοῦ 'calling of God' is translated 'to which God
has called me' [REB], 'to which God is ever summoning me'
[ICC]. This word refers to God's act of calling [Alf, Ea, EBC,
EGT, ICC, My]. It refers to God's call to people in general, not
merely to Paul [ICC, My, WC]. It is a call to holiness of one's
life [NTC].

h. ἐν with dative object (GEL 83.13; 89.119): 'in' [Ea, GEL,
HNTC, ICC, Ln, Mou, NTC, Pl, WBC; all translations except
TEV, TNT], 'through' [WEC; TEV, TNT], 'one with' [GEL],
'joined closely to' [GEL], 'in union with' [GEL], 'by virtue of my
union with' [WEC]. This word indicates the means or area
through which God made the call [Ea, Lg].

QUESTION—What is the prize?

The prize consists of the resurrection [Ln, NOT 4(4)], the crown of
life [Bg], gaining Christ [GNC, HNTC], knowing Christ fully
[WBC], salvation defined further as 'the high calling of God' [My],
final salvation [WEC], life in heaven [My(D); NAB], eternal glory
[NIC], the blessings accompanying everlasting life [NTC]. It is
eternal perfection and blessedness, received at the goal [Ea]. The
prize is not identified [TNTC].

QUESTION—How is the noun σκοπόν 'goal' related to βραβεῖον
'prize'?

They are essentially the same [EBC, EGT, MNTC, NTC], both
indicating perfection in Christ [NTC], both referring to final bliss
[MNTC]. Both words focus on the fellowship with Christ in heaven

which Christ's resurrection makes possible [EGT]. There are distinctions made between the two words. 'Goal' focuses on the race [EBC, NTC]; 'prize' focuses on the glory which follows the successful completion of the race [EBC, NTC], and on perfection as God's gift [NTC]. 'Goal' refers to the vision of the mark which keeps him on the right track; 'prize' refers to what he hopes to receive at the end of life [MNTC].

QUESTION—How are the two nouns related in the genitive construction τὸ βραβεῖον τῆς ἄνω κλήσεως 'the prize of the high calling'?

1. 'Calling' is in apposition with 'prize' [EGT, GNC, TH, WC; TEV]: the prize which is the calling.
2. The 'calling' looks forward to (or is the subject of [Ea]) the 'prize' [El, ICC, Lg, MNTC, My, WBC, WEC; NAB, NIV, REB]: the prize which is the aim of the calling. It is a call to come and receive the prize, as in the Olympian games [GNC, WBC].

QUESTION—How are the two nouns related in the genitive construction κλήσεως τοῦ θεοῦ 'calling of God'?

God is the one who calls [Alf, Ea, El, Lg, Ln, My, TH, WBC; TEV, TNT]: the call which God made.

QUESTION—What is the prepositional phrase ἐν Χριστῷ Ἰησοῦ 'in Christ Jesus' connected with?

1. It is connected with τῆς κλήσεως τοῦ θεοῦ 'the calling of God' [Alf, Ea, EBC, EGT, El, ICC, Lg, Ln, MNTC, Mou, My(D), NTC, Pl, TH, WC; NIV, REB, TEV, TNT]: God calls in/through Christ. Only in connection with Christ does the calling have real meaning [EGT, NTC]. Christ is God's agent in the calling [TH].
2. It is connected with διώκω 'I press' [My]: in Christ Jesus I press on. This phrase is placed at the end of the clause for emphasis [My].

DISCOURSE UNIT: 3:15–21 [ICC].

DISCOURSE UNIT: 3:15–17 [TNTC]. The topic is Paul's exhortation that the Philippians be united in their convictions and behavior.

DISCOURSE UNIT: 3:15–16 [WEC]. The topic is spiritual development through obedience [WEC].

3:15
As-many-as[a] therefore[b] (are) perfect/mature,[c] let-us-set-our-minds-on[d] this;

LEXICON—a. ὅσος (GEL 59.7): 'as many as' [Ea, GEL, Ln, NTC; KJV, NASB], 'all' [HNTC, Mou, WBC; NAB, NIV, NJB, TEV, TNT], 'any' [WEC], 'those' [Pl; NRSV], 'we' [REB], 'who' [ICC].

b. οὖν (GEL 89.50): 'therefore' [Ea, GEL, ICC, Pl, WEC; KJV, NASB], 'then' [GEL; NRSV], 'so then' [GEL], 'so' [GEL, Mou, WBC; NJB], 'accordingly' [GEL, Ln, NTC], not explicit [HNTC; NAB, NIV, REB, TEV, TNT]. It introduces an exhortation arising from the preceding comments [Ea, El, Lg, Ln, My].

c. τέλειος (GEL **11.18**; 88.36; 88.100) (BAGD 2.b. p. 809): 'perfect' [Ea, GEL, Mou, Pl, WBC, WEC; KJV, NASB], 'mature' [GEL, Ln, NTC; NIV, NJB, NRSV, REB], 'spiritually mature' [NAB, TEV], 'mature Christians' [TNT], 'initiated' [GEL], 'an initiate' [BAGD], 'committed to this high Christian ideal of perfection' [ICC].

d. pres. act. subj. of φρονέω (GEL 26.16; 31.1) (BAGD 1. p. 866): 'to set one's mind on' [NTC], 'to be minded' [Pl; KJV], 'to mind' [Ln], 'to be of a (certain) mind' [Mou; NRSV], 'to have a (certain) frame of mind' [WEC], 'to think' [BAGD, Ea; NJB, TNT], 'to think in a particular manner' [GEL], 'to keep to a (certain) way of thinking' [REB], 'to hold a view' [GEL], 'to take a (certain) view' [NIV], 'to have a (certain) attitude' [GEL, WBC; NAB, NASB, TEV], 'to be disposed' [HNTC], 'to consider' [GEL], 'to cherish a (certain) spirit' [ICC]. This hortatory subjunctive includes both thought and conduct [Ln]; Paul's gentle approach is indicated by including himself in the verb [NTC, WBC].

QUESTION—What relationship is indicated by the phrase ὅσοι τέλειοι 'as many as are perfect/mature'?

It identifies the subject 'we' of the verb φρονῶμεν 'let us set our minds on' [Ln]: let us, as many as are perfect/mature, set our minds on this.

QUESTION—What is the meaning of τέλειοι 'perfect/mature'?

1. It means a relative perfection, not an absolute perfection that Paul denied having reached in 3:12 [Blm, Ea, El, HNTC, ICC, Lg, NIC]. This is a relative perfection of one who is still striving for the goal of final perfection [Ea]. It is a comparative perfection obtained by those who have advanced in religious knowledge and Christian virtue [Blm]. It is perfection in principle, not the ethical perfection he denied in 3:12 [NIC]. The extent of perfection is indicated in 3:9–10 [Lg].

2. Close to the preceding meaning of relative perfection is the meaning 'maturity' [Alf, EBC, EGT, GNC, Ln, MNTC, Mou, My, NOT 4(4), NTC, TH, TNTC; NAB, NIV, NJB, NRSV, REB, TEV, TNT]. It refers to spiritual growth and stability [EBC, Mou]. It means reaching a certain point of completeness [EGT]. It means all that one should be at a particular stage and implies the absence of significant defects [NOT 4(4)].

3. It means the same as the perfection Paul denied having reached in 3:12 and is to be taken as an ironic statement [Lt, Pl, WBC, WC, WEC]. The statement means 'as many of us as suppose we have reached perfection' [WBC], 'as many of us who boast of our "perfection" ' [WC], 'listen to me, any of you who consider yourselves perfect' [WEC]. Some in Philippi thought that they had reached the kind of perfection that Paul denied having reached and Paul exhorts them to have the same attitude he described in 3:12 [WBC, WC, WEC].

QUESTION—To what does τοῦτο 'this' refer?

It refers to the attitude which Paul has claimed for himself in the preceding thoughts [Alf, Bg, Ea, EBC, El, ICC, Ln, My, TH, WEC]: have the attitude which I have just described. It refers especially to pressing along the course for the prize (3:14) [Bg, Ea], to 3:13–14 [ICC, My], to 3:12–14 [Ea, El], to 3:7–14 [Alf, El], to 3:2–14 [Ln]. It means acknowledging being still far from the final goal [EGT]. It refers to forgetting the past and pressing on forward [Lt, My, NIC] in humility [My].

and if anything[a] differently[b] you-are-setting-your-mind-on,[c] even/also[d] this God will-reveal[e] to-you;

LEXICON—a. τις (GEL 92.12): 'anything' [GEL, Mou; KJV, NASB, NRSV], 'things' [HNTC], 'any way' [NJB], 'any respect' [Ea], 'any particular' [ICC, Pl], 'any point' [REB, TNT], 'some point' [Ln; NIV], 'some particular point' [WEC], 'some minor point' [NTC], not explicit [TEV]. The phrase καὶ εἴ τι ἑτέρως φρονεῖτε 'and if anything differently you are setting your mind on' is translated 'but since you have a somewhat different attitude' [WBC]. This is an accusative of reference [Alf, Ea] or object [My], referring to points of truth or Christian experience which Paul has been discussing [Ea, My].

b. ἑτέρως (GEL **58.36**) (BAGD p. 315): 'differently' [BAGD, GEL, HNTC, Ln, NTC, Pl; NIV, NJB, NRSV, REB, TNT], 'otherwise' [BAGD, Ea; KJV], 'another way' [NAB], 'diversely' [Mou]. The phrase ἑτέρως φρονεῖτε 'differently you are setting your mind on' is translated 'you have a different attitude' [NASB, TEV], 'you have the wrong frame of mind' [WEC], 'your ideal differs' [ICC]. It implies a different and incorrect view [Alf, El, Lg, My,

Pl], too much presumption concerning Christian perfection
[Alf]. It means if anyone was otherwise than τέλειος
'perfect/mature' [Bg]. It refers to prejudices of weak Christians
and misconceptions of others [Blm, Ea]. It concerns minor
points in the views of the Christians [ICC, Lg, Ln, Mou, My].

    c. pres. act. indic. of φρονέω (GEL 26.16; 31.1): 'to set one's mind
on', 'to be minded' [Ln, Mou, NTC, Pl; KJV], 'to have a
(certain) attitude' [GEL, WBC; NASB, TEV], 'to have a
(certain) frame of mind' [WEC], 'to think' [Ea; NIV, NJB,
NRSV, REB, TNT], 'to think in a particular manner' [GEL], 'to
hold a view' [GEL], 'to consider' [GEL], 'to look on' [HNTC],
not explicit [ICC]. The phrase τι φρονεῖτε 'anything you are
setting your mind on' is translated 'you see it' [NAB]. Although
the verb here is changed from first person plural to second
person plural, the same persons are addressed except that Paul
himself is now excluded [Ea, MNTC, My]. It is those who are
not τέλειος 'perfect/mature' who are now addressed [Bg].

    d. καί (GEL 89.93): 'even' [GEL, WBC, WEC; KJV], 'also' [GEL,
Mou, Pl; NASB, REB], 'too' [HNTC, Ln, NTC; NIV, NRSV],
'yea' [Ea], not explicit [NJB, TEV, TNT]. The phrase καὶ τοῦτο
ἀποκαλύψει 'even this (he) will reveal' is translated '(he) will
clarify the difficulty' [NAB].

    e. fut. act. indic. of ἀποκαλύπτω (GEL 28.38) (BAGD 2. p. 92): 'to
reveal' [BAGD, Ea, GEL, HNTC, Ln, Pl, WBC, WEC; KJV,
NASB, NRSV], 'to disclose' [GEL], 'to make clear' [NIV, NJB,
TEV], 'to make plain' [NTC; REB], 'to unveil' [Mou], 'to
enlighten' [TNT], 'to correct' [ICC]. The implication is that God
will reveal this to them [Ea, ICC] even if Paul does not state it
in writing [Bg], through the operation of the Holy Spirit on their
understanding [Blm, El, ICC, Lg, My] or through teaching or
other means [ICC]. The future tense expresses a prediction or
promise [Ea, El], hope [El, Lg], wish [El].

QUESTION—What is the meaning of καί 'even/also'?

    1. It means 'even' [Bg, Ea, WBC, WC, WEC; KJV]. Even in the
matter in which they are mistaken, God will reveal the truth
[Ea].

    2. It means 'also' [Alf, EGT, GNC, HNTC, ICC, Lg, Ln, Mou, My,
NTC, Pl, TH; NASB, NIV, NRSV, REB]. God will reveal this
in addition to what he has already revealed [Alf, El, ICC, Lg,
Ln, My].

QUESTION—What is implied by the clause καὶ εἴ τι ἑτέρως φρονεῖτε
'and if anything differently you are setting your mind on'?

1. It expresses a condition, implying that there may be some who are differently minded [Ea, El, ICC, TH]: if any of you are differently minded, as may be the case.
2. It means if any of them supposed that they were τέλειος 'perfect' [EGT]: if you think that you are perfect. The clause, a condition of fact, suggests that Paul knew that some of the Philippians had mistaken views of perfection [EGT].
3. The καί 'and' before εἰ 'if' implies that this is a very unlikely possibility, since the Philippians were mature Christians [Ln]: and if, which I think is unlikely.

QUESTION—To what does τοῦτο 'this' refer?

It refers to the preceding τι 'anything', meaning whatever wrong view anyone of them may have [Alf, Ea, EBC, El, ICC, My, MNTC, NIC, Pl]: God will reveal your error to you. It means that God will reveal to them what they should be setting their minds on, as described in 3:14 [Bg]: God will reveal to you that you should be setting your mind on pursuing the prize. God will show them that what Paul has stated about true perfection is correct [TNTC]. God will show them the attitude on this matter which they should have [EGT].

3:16

nevertheless[a] to[b] that-which we-have-attained,[c] by-the same-(thing) to-behave.[d]

TEXT—Instead of τῷ αὐτῷ στοιχεῖν 'by the same thing to behave', some manuscripts read τῷ αὐτῷ στοιχεῖν κανόνι, τὸ αὐτὸ φρονεῖν 'by the same rule to behave, on the same thing to set our mind'. GNT reads the shorter text with a B rating, indicating some degree of doubt. The longer text is read by only Bg, Blm, and KJV.

LEXICON—a. πλήν (GEL 89.130) (BAGD 1.c. p. 669): 'nevertheless' [GEL; KJV], 'but' [BAGD, GEL; TNT], 'in any case' [BAGD, WBC], 'however' [BAGD, WEC; NASB, TEV], 'howbeit' [Ea], 'only' [HNTC, Ln, Mou, NTC, Pl; NIV, NRSV, REB], 'but only' [ICC], 'meanwhile' [NJB], 'it is important that' [NAB].
   b. εἰς with accusative object (GEL 78.51; 84.16; 84.22): 'to' [GEL, Ln, WEC; NASB, NIV, NRSV], 'as to' [Mou], 'into' [GEL], 'to the extent of' [GEL], 'at' [HNTC], not explicit [ICC, NTC, Pl, WBC; NAB, NJB, REB, TEV, TNT]. The phrase εἰς ὅ 'to that which' is translated 'whereto' [Ea; KJV].
   c. aorist act. indic. of φθάνω (GEL 13.16) (BAGD p. 857): 'to attain' [BAGD, Ea, GEL, Ln, NTC, WBC; KJV, NASB, NIV, NJB, NRSV, REB], 'to achieve' [GEL; TNT], 'to reach' [BAGD, HNTC, Pl; NAB], 'to succeed in reaching' [Mou], 'to

follow until now' [TEV], not explicit [ICC]. This verb is
translated as a phrase: 'God has brought us' [WEC].

d. pres. act. infin. of στοιχέω (GEL 41.12) (BAGD p. 769): 'to
behave' [GEL], 'to live' [GEL; NASB], 'to live up to' [WBC;
NIV], 'to go on living' [TNT], 'to act up to' [ICC], 'to keep in
line with' [Ln], 'to conduct oneself' [WEC], 'to hold on to'
[BAGD], 'to hold fast to' [NRSV], 'to walk' [Ea; KJV], 'to go
forward' [NJB, TEV], 'to direct one's steps' [Pl], 'to continue on
(one's) course' [NAB], 'to stand in line' [HNTC], 'to step in (a
path)' [Mou]. The phrase τῷ αὐτῷ στοιχεῖν 'by the same thing
to behave' is translated 'let our conduct be consistent' [NTC;
REB].

QUESTION—What relationship is indicated by πλήν 'nevertheless'?

It expresses an exhortation and a caution following the promise of
3:15 [Ea, EBC, El, MNTC, My, NIC, TH]: God will reveal this to
you; but in the meantime go forward in what you already know.
This is parenthetical [EGT]. It emphasizes what Paul has just said
[NTC], calling the readers to accept what he has said [TNTC]. It
points up the contrast between the past attainment and the future
revelations [El]. It introduces the condition for attaining the hope
just mentioned [Lg, MNTC, My]. It serves to break off the
preceding discussion in order to emphasize the important point
[WBC]. It implies a preceding phrase, 'whatever progress you may
have made' [Blm], 'although some are otherwise minded' [Ea],
'although you will still need additional revelation' [El, ICC], 'even if
you are otherwise minded in some points' [My], 'whatever
differences of opinion there may be' [NIC].

QUESTION—What is meant by the phrase εἰς ὃ ἐφθάσαμεν 'to that
which we have attained'?

It means the extent to which each person has progressed in his
spiritual life [Alf, Ea, EBC, My, NIC, NTC, Pl, WC], knowledge
[Ea, HNTC, MNTC, WBC], revelation [ICC, TNTC], progress
toward the goal [EGT], the rule of faith instead of works [Lt].

QUESTION—What relationship is indicated by the infinitive phrase
τῷ αὐτῷ στοιχεῖν 'by the same thing to behave'?

This phrase is used for an imperative [Alf, Bg, Ea, EBC, EGT, El,
HNTC, ICC, Lg, Ln, Lt, My, NIC, NTC, Pl, TH, WBC] in the
second person plural [Alf, Ea, El] or first person plural exhortation
[Mou; all translations]: you should walk, or let us walk, by the
same rule. It is not connected with either 3:15 or what follows [Lg].
The use of the infinitive leaves the command general [Ln, NIC]. It
is emphatic [Lt, Pl, WBC]; it is mild [Bg].

QUESTION—To what does τῷ αὐτῷ 'by the same thing' refer?
It refers back to εἰς ὅ 'to that which' and means that they should
walk according to their present attainments [Alf, Ea, EBC, EGT,
El, GNC, HNTC, ICC, Lg, Ln, Lt, MNTC, Mou, NTC, Pl, WBC,
WC, WEC; all translations]: walk according to your attainments.

DISCOURSE UNIT: 3:17–4:1 [HNTC, Lg, Ln]. The topic is a warning
against self-indulgence [HNTC], the final destiny of false Christians and
true Christians contrasted [Lg], a personal appeal by Paul and a reference
to the glory of the resurrection to emphasize his warning [Ln].

DISCOURSE UNIT: 3:17–21 [EBC, Mou, My(D), NTC; NAB]. The topic
is the danger of antinomianism [EBC], a warning against sensual-minded
persons and a reference to the heavenly home [NTC], the Christian's hope
and the power of it [Mou], Christ the Christian's goal [NAB].

DISCOURSE UNIT: 3:17–19 [EGT, MNTC, NIC, WC, WEC]. The topic
is a warning against sensual-mindedness [EGT], Paul's exhortation to the
Philippians to imitate him [MNTC], enemies of the cross of Christ [NIC],
warning against those who fell into immorality through despising the
human emotions [WC], a reference to types of behavior [WEC].

DISCOURSE UNIT: 3:17 [GNC, WBC]. The topic is Paul as a pattern to
imitate [GNC, WBC].

3:17

Become joint-imitators[a] of-me, brothers,

LEXICON—a. συμμιμητής (GEL **41.46**) (BAGD p. 778): 'joint
imitator' [GEL, Ln], 'fellow-imitator' [BAGD], 'united imitator'
[Mou], 'imitator' [NAB], 'follower together' [KJV]. The phrase
συμμιμηταί μου γίνεσθε 'become joint imitators of me' is
translated 'join in imitating me' [HNTC; NRSV], 'join in being
my imitators' [GEL], 'join in being imitators of me' [NTC],
'continue to join with one another in imitating me' [WBC], 'join
in following my example' [NASB], 'join together in following my
example' [REB], 'join with others in following my example'
[NIV], 'be together imitators of me' [Ea], 'unite in imitating me'
[ICC], 'be united in imitating me' [WEC; NJB], 'be united in
becoming imitators of me' [Pl], 'keep on imitating me' [TEV],
'try to be like me' [TNT]. They are to join with one another in
imitating Paul [Alf]. This word is emphatic by position [Alf].
The prefixed preposition συμ- implies the urging of common
action by all together [El, ICC, Ln, WBC]; it refers to Paul's
associates whom they are to join in imitating Paul [Lg].

QUESTION—How are the noun and pronoun related in the phrase συμμιμηταί μου 'joint imitators of me'?

1. Μου 'of me' is the objective genitive of συμμιμηταί 'joint imitators' [Alf, Blm, Ea, EBC, EGT, El, GNC, HNTC, ICC, Lg, Ln, Lt, MNTC, Mou, My, NIC, NTC, Pl, TH, TNTC, WBC, WC, WEC; all translations].

1.1 It means that they should unitedly imitate Paul [Alf, Blm, Ea, EGT, GNC, HNTC, ICC, Lg(H), Ln, Lt, MNTC, Mou, My(D), NIC, NTC, Pl, TH, WBC, WC, WEC; NJB]: jointly imitate me.

1.2 It means that they should join with others who imitate Paul [EBC, El, Lg, My; NIV]: join with others in imitating me.

2. Μου 'of me' is the object of the prefixed preposition συμ- in συμμιμηταί 'joint imitators' [Bg]: you should join with me in imitating Christ.

QUESTION—Why does Paul again use the vocative ἀδελφοί 'brothers'?

It is a term indicating endearment [NIC, NTC, WEC] and unity [NIC, WEC]. It indicates earnestness [Lg]. It adds to the appeal [Ln]. It presents Paul as their spiritual brother [Ln, WBC]. It is intended to avoid any resentment of his exhortation to imitate him [MNTC, WBC].

and pay-attention-to[a] the-(ones) walking[b] thus just-as[c] you-have us (as)-an-example.[d]

LEXICON—a. pres. act. impera. of σκοπέω (GEL 24.32) (BAGD p. 756): 'to pay attention to' [TEV], 'to observe' [Ea; NASB, NRSV], 'to observe carefully' [ICC], 'to regard carefully' [Pl], 'to notice' [BAGD], 'to notice carefully' [GEL], 'to take note' [NIV], 'to take careful note' [TNT], 'to regard closely' [GEL], 'to watch closely' [NTC], 'to watch' [GEL, Ln, WEC], 'to keep one's eyes on' [BAGD, WBC], 'to keep one's eyes fixed on' [HNTC; NJB], 'to mark' [Mou; KJV], 'to take as one's guide' [NAB], 'to imitate' [REB]. They are to observe Paul and those like him in order to imitate them [Alf, Blm, Ea, EBC, El, GNC, Ln, Lt, MNTC, Mou, TH, WBC].

b. pres. act. participle of περιπατέω (GEL 41.11) (BAGD 2.a.γ. p. 649): 'to walk' [Ea, Ln, Mou, NTC; KJV, NASB], 'to walk around' [BAGD], 'to go about' [BAGD], 'to live' [GEL, HNTC, WBC; NIV, NRSV], 'to behave' [GEL; TNT], 'to follow (one's example)' [NAB, TEV], 'to act' [NJB]. The phrase τοὺς περιπατοῦντας 'the ones walking' is translated 'those whose way of life' [REB], 'those whose walk in life' [Pl]. The phrase τοὺς περιπατοῦντας καθὼς ἔχετε τύπον ἡμᾶς 'the ones walking just as you have us as an example' is translated 'those whose

conduct resembles mine' [ICC], 'those whose conduct conforms
to the pattern you have in us' [WEC]. The present tense implies
continuous behavior [WBC].

c. καθώς (GEL 64.14): 'just as' [GEL], 'as' [Ea, HNTC, Ln, Mou;
KJV, TNT], 'according to' [NTC, WBC; NASB, NIV, NJB,
NRSV], not explicit [Pl; NAB, REB, TEV]. It expresses the
manner of the behavior implied in οὕτω 'thus' [Ea, El, ICC,
My(D)].

d. τύπος (GEL 58.59) (BAGD 5.b. p. 830): 'example' [BAGD, Ea,
GEL, Ln, NTC; NAB, NJB, NRSV, TEV], 'ensample' [KJV],
'pattern' [BAGD, Pl, WBC, WEC; NASB, NIV], 'model' [GEL,
Mou; REB], not explicit [TNT]. The phrase ἔχετε τύπον ἡμᾶς
'you have us as an example' is translated 'you see exemplified in
us' [HNTC]. The singular indicates that they all present the
same example [Alf, Ea, Lg, Pl]; it is singular because the
reference is to Paul alone [WBC]. It is emphatic by word order
[My].

QUESTION—To what does οὕτω 'thus' refer?

It refers back to μου 'of me' [EGT]: those who walk thus—that is,
as I walk.

QUESTION—To whom does τοὺς οὕτω περιπατοῦντας 'the ones
walking thus' refer?

1. It refers to Paul and his close associates in ministry [GNC, Lg,
NIC, NTC, TNTC]: me and my close associates. It refers to
Christians other than the Philippians [My].

2. It refers to Paul and any among the Philippians who live thus
[Ea, El, HNTC, Ln].

3. It refers to persons among them whose conduct is exemplary
[Mou, WBC], their pastors [Pl], including Epaphroditus [WBC].

QUESTION—To whom does ἡμᾶς 'us' refer?

1. It refers to Paul and his close associates in ministry, probably
including Timothy and Epaphroditus (or others not identified
[MNTC]) [Alf, Ea, EBC, GNC, ICC, Lt, Mou, My(D), NIC,
NTC, Pl, TH, TNTC]: me and my close associates. It refers to
Paul and τοὺς οὕτω περιπατοῦντας 'the ones walking thus' [My].
Ἡμᾶς 'us' is emphatic by word order [GNC].

2. It refers to Paul alone [El, ICC, WBC, WEC]: as you have me
as an example.

3. It refers to Paul and those whose conduct is like his [Lg].

DISCOURSE UNIT: 3:18-19 [GNC, TNTC, WBC]. The topic is a
warning against enemies of the gospel [GNC], a comment about false
teachers [TNTC], a warning not to imitate other teachers [WBC].

3:18

For[a] many (persons) walk[b]

  LEXICON—a. γάρ (GEL 89.23): 'for' [Ea, GEL, HNTC, ICC, Ln, Mou, NTC, Pl, WBC; KJV, NASB, NIV, NJB, NRSV, TNT], 'because' [GEL, WEC], 'unfortunately' [NAB], not explicit [REB, TEV].

  b. pres. act. indic. of περιπατέω: 'to walk'. See this word at 3:17. This word is emphatic [Ea].

  QUESTION—What relationship is indicated by γάρ 'for'?

  It introduces the reason for the Philippians to observe those whose conduct is proper and a warning against those whose conduct is not right (or the reason why Paul's warning is needed [WEC]) [Alf, Ea, El, Lg, MNTC, My, Pl, WBC]: you should observe those whose conduct is right, because there are many whose conduct is wrong. The fact that there were many whose example they should avoid (and so few whom they should imitate [WBC]) is an added reason for imitating Paul and others of right conduct [Lg(H), WBC].

  QUESTION—What is πολλοί 'many persons' connected with?

  It is connected with the following phrase οὓς πολλάκις ἔλεγον ὑμῖν 'whom many times I was saying to you' [Alf]: there are many people, whom I was telling you about many times.

whom many-times I-was-saying to-you, and now even weeping[a] I-say,

  LEXICON—a. pres. act. participle of κλαίω (GEL 25.138) (BAGD 1. p. 433): 'to weep' [BAGD, Ea, GEL, ICC, Ln, NTC, WBC; KJV, NASB], 'to cry' [BAGD]. This participle is translated as a phrase: 'with tears' [HNTC, Pl; NAB, NIV, NRSV, REB, TEV], 'with cries and tears' [Mou], 'with tears in my eyes' [WEC; NJB], 'with eyes full of tears' [TNT]. The participle expresses manner [WBC].

  QUESTION—What is implied by πολλάκις 'many times'?

  It implies that the problem had existed for a long time [MNTC, Pl], that it was widespread and serious [Pl]. There were probably not many in this group; πολλοί 'many' is probably rhetorical [WEC].

  QUESTION—Why did Paul weep?

  Paul wept in grief [EGT, MNTC, My, Pl, TH, WBC] over the condition and destiny of these persons [ICC, My, Pl, WBC] and his own suffering because of it [Pl], over the false view of the gospel which their conduct gave [Ea, ICC], over the extent of the evil [El, NIC], over the attempt of these persons to lead the Philippian church astray [NTC], over their possible influence in disturbing the church [Ln, MNTC, My]. He now weeps because the evil had become more serious [Lg, Lt, Mou, My].

(they are) the enemies[a] of-the cross[b] of-the Christ,

LEXICON—a. ἐχθρός (GEL 39.11) (BAGD 2.b.γ. p. 331): 'enemy'
[BAGD, Ea, HNTC, ICC, Ln, Mou, NTC, Pl, WBC, WEC; all
translations], 'being an enemy' [GEL], 'in opposition to' [GEL].
It is in the accusative case by attraction to the preceding οὕς
'whom' [EGT, ICC, Lg, Ln, Lt, My]. The article with this noun
treats these persons as a class [Alf, Ea, El, ICC, Mou, My] or
adds prominence [Ea, NIC].

b. σταυρός (GEL 6.27) (BAGD 3. p. 765): 'cross' [BAGD, Ea,
GEL, HNTC, ICC, Ln, Mou, NTC, Pl, WBC; all translations
except TEV], 'death on the cross' [TEV], 'what the cross stands
for' [WEC].

QUESTION—Who were these enemies?

Many commentaries think that the enemies were professing
Christians [Ea, EBC, EGT, El, HNTC, Lg, Ln, MNTC, My, NTC,
TH, TNTC, WC], who were in the Philippian church [MNTC], or
at least some of whom were in the Philippian church [My(D)], or
they were all from other churches [EBC, EGT, HNTC, Pl]. Another
view is that they were antinomians (probably Gentiles [MNTC]),
who perverted Christian liberty into licentiousness [Lt, MNTC, My,
TH, WC]. Or they were Judaizers [Ln, NIC] who were not yet
working in Philippi [Ln]. Still another view is that they were non-
Christian Jews who were seeking to win converts, probably not yet
active in Philippi [WBC]; their lives were not morally evil, but their
dependence on the Mosaic Law made them opponents of salvation
by faith in Christ [WBC]. Their enmity consisted in their continuing
practice of sin [Alf, EGT, El, Lg, Lt, NTC, WC], in their failure to
understand that the cross was intended to provide sanctification,
and their consequent failure to forsake sin [Ea].

QUESTION—How are the two nouns related in the genitive
construction τοῦ σταυροῦ τοῦ Χριστοῦ 'of the cross of Christ'?

It means the cross upon which Christ died [TEV]. It refers to
Christ's death on the cross [GNC, TH, WBC]. These enemies were
probably professed Christians whose lives disavowed the
significance of Christ's death [GNC, TH], that is of all that the
cross stands for [NIC, WEC, WC]. They did not realize its purpose
of securing sanctification for them [Ea]. The Judaizers opposed the
gospel about the cross [NIC].

3:19

of-whom the destiny[a] (is) destruction,[b]

LEXICON—a. τέλος (GEL 67.66; 89.40) (BAGD 1.c. p. 811): 'destiny'
[BAGD; NIV], 'destination' [WEC], 'outcome' [BAGD, GEL],
'goal' [BAGD], 'end' [BAGD, Ea, GEL, HNTC, ICC, Ln, Mou,

NTC, Pl, WBC; KJV, NASB, NRSV]. The phrase τὸ τέλος
ἀπώλεια 'the destiny is destruction' is translated 'are heading
for destruction' [REB], 'are doomed to destruction' [TNT], 'will
end in disaster' [NAB], 'destined to be lost' [NJB], 'are going to
end up in hell' [TEV].

  b. ἀπώλεια (GEL 20.31) (BAGD 2. p. 103): 'destruction' [BAGD,
    Ea, GEL, ICC, NTC, WBC, WEC; KJV, NASB, NIV, NRSV,
    REB, TNT], 'ruin' [BAGD], 'perdition' [HNTC, Ln, Mou, Pl],
    'hell' [TEV], 'disaster' [NAB]. It relates to their eternal lostness
    [Blm, Ea, EBC, El, Ln, Mou, NTC, WC] when Christ returns
    [Alf], if they continue in their evil ways [Blm]. It means eternal
    condemnation and punishment [My, NTC, TH, WBC], physical,
    moral, and spiritual ruin [NIC]. It is the opposite of salvation
    [MNTC, TH, WBC].

QUESTION—Why is this verse mentioned?

It is a further and more detailed description of the persons referred
to [El, MNTC, My, NIC]. Paul describes the fate and the character
of those enemies mentioned in 3:18 [TH].

QUESTION—What is meant by τέλος 'destiny'?

This word refers to their fixed and certain end [Alf, El, MNTC]. It
is the inevitable result of their conduct [TH, WBC, WC]. Their
destiny is stated first in order to add an aspect of horror to the
statements that follow [Bg, My].

**of-whom the god (is) the stomach[a] and the glory[b] (is) in the shame[c] of-
them,**

  LEXICON—a. κοιλία (GEL 8.67; 25.28) (BAGD 1. p. 437): 'stomach'
    [BAGD; NIV, NJB], 'belly' [Ea, GEL, HNTC, ICC, Ln, Mou,
    NTC; KJV, NAB, NRSV], 'physical desires' [GEL], 'bodily
    desires' [TEV], 'desires of the body' [GEL], 'visceral impulses'
    [WEC], 'appetite' [NASB, REB, TNT], 'sensual indulgence' [Pl],
    'observance of food laws' [WBC].

  b. δόξα (GEL 25.205; 33.357): 'glory' [Ea, HNTC, Ln, Mou, NTC,
    Pl; KJV, NAB, NASB, NIV, NRSV], 'glorying' [WBC], 'pride'
    [GEL], 'praise' [GEL]. This noun is translated as a verb 'they
    glory' [ICC, WEC; NJB], 'they take pride' [REB], 'they are
    proud of' [TEV], 'they boast' [TNT]. This glory is subjective,
    meaning glory in the opinion of these persons [Alf, El, My].
    Since this word is parallel to ὁ θεός 'God' in the preceding
    clause, it implies glorying concerning a god [Bg].

  c. αἰσχύνη (GEL 25.191; 88.149) (BAGD 2. p. 25): 'shame' [Ea,
    HNTC, Ln, Mou, NTC; KJV, NAB, NASB, NIV, NRSV],
    'shameful deed' [GEL], 'that which is their shame' [ICC], 'what
    is really their shame' [Pl], 'what they should be ashamed of'
    [GEL; TEV], 'what they should think shameful' [NJB], 'what

should bring shame' [REB], 'what should fill them with shame' [TNT], 'that which causes shame' [GEL], 'that which causes them shame' [BAGD], 'disgrace' [WEC], 'circumcision' [WBC]. It is shame objectively, according to reality [Alf, El, My]. It refers to the disgrace that comes with God's judgment upon them [WEC]. It refers to boasting in their circumcision [Bg, NIC, WBC], which is now shameful [Bg].

QUESTION—What is meant by the phrase ὁ θεὸς ἡ κοιλία 'god is their stomach'?

It is as though they worship their stomachs [NTC]. They obey their stomachs as they would obey God [Ln]. It is their highest concern [Lg].

QUESTION—What is meant by κοιλία 'stomach'?

1. It is a metonymy for sensual desires [EGT, GNC, Lg, Ln, MNTC, Mou, NTC, Pl, TH, WC, WEC; TEV]. 'Stomach' is figurative for the lowest nature [Ln]. They worshipped their sensual desires [NTC]. Their ultimate concern was their bodily desires [GNC]. It was a general attitude which was opposed to the spiritual aspect of life [WEC].

2. It is a metonymy for what they eat and drink [Alf, HNTC, My, NIC, WBC]. There are very different opinions about what this refers to. One commentator thinks that this refers to obsession with food on the part of gluttons or gourmets [HNTC]. Others think that it refers to having as their highest goals the conforming to strict food laws [NIC, WBC].

QUESTION—What is meant by 'the glory is their shame'?

1. They glory in things of which they ought to be ashamed [Blm, EBC, El, HNTC, MNTC, NTC, TH, WC; NJB, REB, TEV, TNT]: they are proud about things they should be ashamed of.

2. They glory in things which really bring shame on them [Ea, EGT, ICC, Lg, Ln, My, Pl]: they are proud about things that bring shame upon them.

3. They glory in their private parts, that is, the circumcised part of their bodies [NIC, WBC]. They boast of their circumcision [NIC, WBC].

the-ones setting-their-minds-on[a] the earthly[b] (things).

LEXICON—a. pres. act. participle of φρονέω (GEL 26.16) (BAGD 2. p. 866): 'to set one's mind on' [BAGD, NTC; NASB], 'to mind' [Ea, Ln; KJV], 'to be intent on' [BAGD], 'to be set upon' [NAB], 'to think' [GEL; TEV]. The phrase οἱ φρονοῦντες 'the ones setting their minds on' is translated 'their mind is on' [NIV], 'their minds are set on' [WBC; NJB, NRSV, REB, TNT], 'their minds are set upon' [ICC], 'whose mind is for' [Mou], 'their hearts are set on' [HNTC], 'their frame of mind is molded by' [WEC], 'whose minds grovel in' [Pl]. It refers to the concentration of all the thoughts and interests [Alf, El, TH].

b. ἐπίγειος (GEL 1.41) (BAGD 2.a. p. 290): 'earthly' [BAGD, Ea, HNTC, ICC, Ln, NTC, Pl, WBC, WEC; all translations except NAB, TEV], 'on earth' [Mou], 'on the earth' [GEL], 'in the world' [GEL], 'of this world' [NAB], 'that belongs to this world' [TEV]. Their entire attention is toward things of earth [MNTC, My]. The word refers to Judaistic piety, which focuses on earthly things [NIC].

QUESTION—How is the phrase οἱ τὰ ἐπίγεια φρονοῦντες 'the ones setting their minds on the earthly things' related to the two preceding relative clauses introduced by ὧν 'of whom'?

It refers to the same persons as the relative clauses [Alf]: these same persons set their minds on earthly things. The nominative case here agrees with the case of the implied subject of the relative clauses [Alf, Bg], it agrees with πολλοί 'many' in 3:18 [EBC, EGT, El], it is used to add emphasis [El, My], it is a loose apposition with the preceding relative clauses [ICC, TH], it is related to the logical subject of what precedes [Lg, My]. This phrase begins a contrast of these persons with those described in the following verse [ICC, My(D), Pl]. It means that these persons exhibit a selfish spirit and an attitude of superiority [WEC].

DISCOURSE UNIT: 3:20–4:1 [WEC]. The topic is citizenship in heaven.

DISCOURSE UNIT: 3:20–21 [EGT, GNC, NIC, TNTC, WBC, WC]. The topic is the result of being heavenly-minded [EGT], citizenship in heaven and its hope [GNC], the believer's blessed hope [NIC], the believer's inheritance [TNTC], Paul's hope for the yet unseen future [WBC], the contrast of the earthly-minded life with the Christian's hope of glory [WC].

3:20

For[a] our citizenship/homeland[b] is[c] in[d] heaven,

LEXICON—a. γάρ (GEL 89.23): 'for' [Ea, GEL, HNTC, Ln, Mou, NTC, Pl, WBC; KJV, NASB], 'because' [GEL, WEC], 'as you well know' [NAB], 'but' [NIV, NJB, NRSV], 'however' [TEV]. This entire phrase is translated 'but we are citizens of heaven' [TNT], 'we, by contrast, are citizens of heaven' [REB], 'we, however, are citizens of heaven' [TEV], 'we, on the other hand, are citizens of a commonwealth which is in heaven' [ICC].

b. πολίτευμα (GEL 11.71) (BAGD p. 686): 'citizenship' [WBC; NAB, NASB, NIV, NRSV], 'homeland' [HNTC, NTC; NJB], 'place of citizenship' [GEL], 'commonwealth' [BAGD, GEL,

ICC, Ln, WEC], 'country' [Ea], 'state' [BAGD, GEL], 'real home and country' [Pl], 'city-home' [Mou], 'conversation' [KJV]. It refers to a place, a country [Alf, Bg, Blm, Ea, EBC, EGT, El, HNTC, ICC, Ln, Lt, Mou, My, NIC, NTC, Pl, TNTC, WBC, WC; NJB, REB]; it refers to citizenship [Lg, MNTC; NAB, NASB, NIV, NRSV].

c. pres. act. indic. of ὑπάρχω (GEL 13.5; 13.77) (BAGD 1. p. 838): 'to be' [BAGD, Ea, GEL, HNTC, NTC, Pl, WBC, WEC; KJV, NASB, NIV, NJB, NRSV], 'to exist' [BAGD, Ea, GEL, Ln], 'to subsist' [Mou]. The phrase ἡμῶν τὸ πολίτευμα ὑπάρχει 'our citizenship/homeland is' is translated 'we have our citizenship' [NAB]. The present tense indicates that they are now citizens of heaven [ICC]. It stresses the idea of real existence [Bg, EGT, El, MNTC, Pl]; it means that it exists already [GNC, Lt, Mou, WC].

d. ἐν with dative object (GEL 83.13): 'in' [Ea, GEL, HNTC, ICC, Ln, Mou, NTC, Pl, WBC, WEC; KJV, NAB, NASB, NIV, NJB, NRSV].

QUESTION—What relationship is indicated by γάρ 'for'?

1. It indicates the reason why they should not imitate the persons described in 3:18–19 [Alf, El, HNTC, ICC, My, NIC, NTC, Pl, WC]: don't imitate these earthly-minded persons, for our citizenship/homeland is in heaven.

2. It indicates the reason why they should imitate Paul and others like him (3:17) [Bg, Blm, Ea, Lg, Ln, WEC]: you should imitate us, for our citizenship/homeland is in heaven. It also highlights the contrast between the two groups of persons mentioned [Ea].

3. It indicates the grounds for urging them to rejoice in the Lord (3:1), assuming that 3:1b–19 were not a genuine part of this epistle [MNTC]: rejoice in the Lord, for our citizenship is in heaven.

4. It is not a natural connective with the preceding verse [TH] and should be translated 'however', introducing a contrast [TH, TNTC; NIV, NJB, NRSV, REB, TEV, TNT].

4. It introduces a hymn of the early church which Paul quotes here, and therefore the γάρ 'for' has no meaning for the present context [WBC].

QUESTION—What relationship is indicated by ἡμῶν 'our'?

It is emphatic by word order [MNTC], and contrasts 'our' situation with that of the earthly-minded persons [Alf, EBC, El, ICC, Lg(H), Ln, Lt, My, NIC, NTC, Pl, TH, TNTC, WBC, WEC]: our citizenship/homeland in contrast with theirs.

QUESTION—What is the phrase ἐν οὐρανοῖς 'in heaven' connected with?

1. It tells where the citizenship/homeland is located [Alf, Ea, EBC, El, HNTC, ICC, Ln, MNTC, Mou, My, NTC, Pl, TH, WBC; all translations]: it is located in heaven.
2. It describes the character of the πολίτευμα 'citizenship' [Lg]: our citizenship in heaven exists.

from[a] which also[b] (a/as) Savior[c] we-await[d] Lord Jesus Christ,

LEXICON—a. ἐκ with genitive object (GEL 84.4; 90.16): 'from' [GEL, HNTC, Ln, NTC, Pl, WBC, WEC; all translations], 'out of' [GEL, Mou], 'out from' [GEL]. The phrase ἐξ οὗ 'from which' is translated 'whence' [Ea, ICC].

b. καί (GEL 89.93): 'also' [Ea, GEL, Ln, NTC, Pl, WEC; KJV, NASB], 'even' [GEL], 'actually' [Mou], not explicit [HNTC, ICC, WBC; all translations except KJV, NASB].

c. σωτήρ (GEL 21.31) (BAGD 2. p. 801): 'Savior' [BAGD, Ea, GEL, HNTC, ICC, Ln, Mou, NTC, Pl, WBC, WEC; all translations except REB, TNT], 'deliverer' [REB]. This noun is also translated as a phrase: 'to save us' [TNT]. It is emphatic by word order [Alf, Ea, ICC, MNTC, My, Pl, TH, WC]. Without the definite article it is descriptive, not a title, referring to his work [TH, TNTC, WBC].

d. pres. act. indic. of ἀπεκδέχομαι (GEL 25.63) (BAGD p. 83): 'to await' [Ea, HNTC], 'to wait for' [Mou; TNT], 'to wait for eagerly' [WBC; NASB, TEV], 'to await eagerly' [BAGD, NTC, WEC; NAB, NIV], 'to await the appearing of' [ICC], 'to await expectantly' [GEL], 'to expect' [Ln; NJB, NRSV, REB], 'to look forward eagerly' [GEL], 'to look for' [KJV], 'to look for confidently' [Pl]. It means to expect him [Alf, GNC] eagerly [Lt, MNTC, NIC, NTC, WBC, WC], earnestly [Ea, ICC, MNTC, TH], anxiously [Blm], longingly [NIC]. The idea of eager longing is expressed by the compounded prepositions ἀπό [EGT, Pl] and ἐκ [EGT].

QUESTION—What is οὗ 'which' connected with?

1. It refers back to οὐρανοῖς 'heaven' (οὗ is adverbial, 'where' [Alf, El, ICC, Lg, MNTC, My, NIC, TH]) [Alf, Blm, Ea, EBC, El, HNTC, ICC, Lg, Lt, MNTC, My, NIC, NTC, Pl, TH, WBC; NAB, NIV, NJB, NRSV, TEV, TNT], since the plural word οὐρανοῖς 'heaven' has a singular sense [NIC, NTC]: from which/where, namely heaven. The clause tells why we should direct our attention to heavenly things [Blm].
2. Its antecedent is πολίτευμα 'homeland' [Bg, EGT, Ln, Mou, TNTC, WC], since it is singular and the alternative οὐρανοῖς

'heaven' is plural in the Greek [Ln, Mou]: from which, namely our homeland.

QUESTION—What relationship is indicated by καί 'also'?

1. It introduces a point in addition to the fact that heaven is their homeland [Alf, El, ICC]: in addition, we are awaiting a Savior.
2. It points to the reasonableness of expecting the Savior to come from heaven [EGT, My]: our homeland is heaven, so it is reasonable that the Savior should come from there. It indicates the agreement between this and the preceding thought [Ea].
3. It indicates that he is expected not only as κύριος 'Lord' but also as σωτήρ 'Savior' [Lg].
4. It adds emphasis to the thought [Mou]: we are actually awaiting him.

QUESTION—How are the noun σωτῆρα 'Savior' and the noun phrase κύριον Ἰησοῦν Χριστόν 'Lord Jesus Christ' related to one another?

1. The predicate of the verb is 'Savior' and 'Lord Jesus Christ' is in apposition with it [Alf, Blm, EBC, HNTC, WC; all translations except TNT]: we await the Savior, namely the Lord Jesus Christ.
2. The predicate of the verb is 'Lord Jesus Christ' and 'Savior' is in apposition with it [Ea, El, ICC, Ln, Lt, Mou, My, NIC, NTC; TNT]: we await the Lord Jesus Christ as Savior.

QUESTION—Why is the full phrase κύριον Ἰησοῦν Χριστόν 'Lord Jesus Christ' used?

It is for emphasis [Pl], implying his coming in the fullness of his power [WC]. Paul uses the full title to include the fact that he is now exalted Lord, still the human Jesus, and still God's anointed Messiah, Christ [Ea].

3:21

who will-transform[a] the body of-the humble-state[b] of-us (so as to be) conformed[c] to-the body of-the glory[d] of-him

TEXT—Some manuscripts add the phrase εἰς τὸ γενέσθαι αὐτό 'in order that it may become' before σύμμορφον 'conformed'. GNT does not discuss this variant. The meaning of this phrase is implied even without being in the text, which is doubtless why scribes added it. In the case of some versions, therefore, it is not possible to be certain whether they include this phrase, and it is immaterial for our purpose. The addition is, however, specifically rejected by Blm, Ea, EGT, El, ICC, Lg, Lt, My, WBC, WEC.

LEXICON—a. fut. act. indic. of μετασχηματίζω (GEL 58.18) (BAGD p. 513): 'to transform' [Ea, WBC, WEC; NASB, NIV, NRSV, TNT], 'to transfigure' [Mou; NJB, REB], 'to change' [BAGD, GEL; KJV, TEV], 'to change the fashion of' [Ln], 'to change the passing fashion of' [Pl], 'to refashion' [HNTC, ICC, NTC], 'to give a new form to' [NAB]. It means to change the form of the body [Blm, EBC, ICC] to a spiritual one [El]. Salvation will include glory [Bg].

b. ταπείνωσις (GEL 87.60) (BAGD 2. p. 805): 'humble state' [NASB], 'humble station' [BAGD], 'humble condition' [TNT], 'humiliation' [BAGD, Ea, ICC, Mou, Pl; NRSV], 'humility' [BAGD, GEL], 'low estate' [GEL], 'low status' [GEL], 'lowliness' [HNTC, Ln]. This noun is also translated as an adjective: 'humble' [BAGD, WEC; REB], 'lowly' [NTC, WBC; NAB, NIV], 'weak' [TEV], 'wretched' [NJB], 'vile' [KJV].

c. σύμμορφος (GEL 58.5) (BAGD p. 778): 'conformed to' [Ea, Mou; NRSV], 'conform to' [Ln], 'in conformity with' [WEC], 'into conformity with' [NASB], 'having the same form' [BAGD], 'to share' [Pl], 'to share the form' [HNTC], 'of the same form' [GEL], 'similar in form' [BAGD], 'a form like' [NTC; REB], 'likeness' [ICC], 'like' [WBC; TEV, TNT], 'to be like' [NIV], 'into the mould of' [NJB], 'fashioned like unto' [KJV], 'according to the pattern of' [NAB]. It means having the same form and nature as Christ's body [Blm] as a result of the transformation [Alf, Blm, Ea, EBC, ICC, Lg, Lt, My]. The compounded preposition σύν implies the complete conformation to Christ's body [EGT].

d. δόξα (GEL 79.18) (BAGD 1.a. p. 203): 'glory' [Ea, GEL, HNTC, ICC, Ln, Mou, Pl; NASB, NRSV, TNT], 'splendor' [BAGD, GEL], 'radiance' [BAGD]. This noun is also translated as an adjective: 'glorious' [BAGD, NTC, WBC, WEC; KJV, NIV, NJB, REB, TEV], 'glorified' [NAB], 'radiant' [BAGD]. It refers to the outward manifestation of the spiritual life [EGT].

QUESTION—Why is this clause mentioned?

It tells what Christ will do at his coming [Ea, EBC, El, HNTC, Ln, MNTC, My, TH, WBC]: he will transform our bodies at his coming. It tells how Jesus will act as our Savior [Alf, Lg, Ln]: he will be our Savior by transforming our bodies. It tells what will be the first of the rewards Christ will give [Blm]: as Savior he will first transform our bodies. This will complete our salvation [MNTC]. It is the purpose of Christ's return [TH, TNTC]. It implies a contrast with what is said in 3:19 [TH].

QUESTION—How are the two nouns related in the genitive construction τὸ σῶμα τῆς ταπεινώσεως 'the body of the humble state'?

The body has the attribute of humbleness [NTC, WBC, WEC; KJV, NAB, NIV, REB, NJB, TEV]: he will transform our humble bodies. The body is in a humble state [Alf, El, ICC, My]. It belongs to our humble state [Ea, Lt, MNTC, Mou]. The reference is to this

humble body in contrast with the Lord's glorified body [ICC], and
also implies being weak and susceptible to physical [My] and moral
ills [EBC, El, ICC, Lt, MNTC, NIC, NTC, TH, TNTC, WBC, WC],
being unfit for the fulfillment of the spiritual life [EGT]. It refers
especially to the sinful aspect of human nature [Lg].
QUESTION—What is the pronoun ἡμῶν 'of us' connected with?
    1. It is connected with σῶμα 'body' [WEC; all translations except
       NASB, NRSV]: our body.
    2. It is connected with ταπεινώσεως 'humble state' [Alf, El, ICC,
       Ln, Lt, MNTC, Mou, My; NASB, NRSV]: the body of our
       humble state.
QUESTION—How are the two nouns related in the genitive
construction τὸ σῶμα τῆς δόξης 'the body of glory'?
    1. It is the body in which Christ's glory has taken place [Alf, El,
       GNC, ICC, Lg(H), Lt, NIC; NAB]: his glorified body.
    2. It is the body which contains or possesses Christ's glory [Ea,
       MNTC, Mou, My, NTC, WBC, WEC; KJV, NIV, NJB, REB,
       TEV]: his glorious body. It is the body in which his glory is
       shown [Alf, Lg(H), Mou, My].
QUESTION—What is the pronoun αὐτοῦ 'of him' connected with?
    1. It is connected with σώματι 'body' [WEC: all translations except
       NASB, NRSV]: his body.
    2. It is connected with δόξης 'glory' [Alf, El, ICC, Lg(H), Ln, Lt,
       MNTC, Mou, My; NASB, NRSV]: the body of his glory.
according-to[a] the operation[b] of-the his being-able[c] even/also[d] to-subject[e]
to-himself the every(thing).[f]
    TEXT—Instead of αὐτῷ (commonly 'him'), some manuscripts have
ἑαυτῷ 'himself'. However, αὐτῷ sometimes has the reflexive sense
'himself'. It may therefore not be possible to determine which form a
version accepts, and it is immaterial for our purpose, except when it is
translated 'him' (e.g., Alf).
    LEXICON—a. κατά with accusative object (GEL 89.8): 'according to'
      [Ea, Mou; KJV], 'in accord with' [Ln], 'in accordance with'
      [GEL], 'in keeping with' [HNTC], 'by' [ICC, NTC, Pl, WBC,
      WEC; NAB, NASB, NIV, NRSV, REB], 'through' [NJB], 'using'
      [TEV, TNT]. It implies a comparison [Alf, MNTC], a norm or
      measure [Ea].
    b. ἐνέργεια (GEL 42.3) (BAGD 1. p. 265): 'operation' [BAGD],
      'effectual action' [HNTC], 'working' [BAGD, GEL, Ln, Pl; KJV,
      NJB], 'inworking' [Ea], 'out-working' [WBC], 'exertion' [NASB],
      'power' [BAGD, ICC, WEC; NIV, TEV, TNT], 'forth-putting'
      [Mou]. The phrase τὴν ἐνέργειαν τοῦ δύνασθαι αὐτόν 'the
      operation of his being able' is translated 'his power' [NAB], 'the
      power that enables him' [NRSV], 'that power which enables

him' [NTC; REB]. It means power in operation [Bg, ICC, Lt, NIC, TNTC, WBC]. It is always a supernatural power [EBC, EGT, ICC, MNTC, NIC, Pl, TH, WBC, WC]. It is the unlimited power of the Father [GNC]. It is Christ's power in action [NTC].

c. pres. mid. (deponent = act.) infin. of δύναμαι (GEL 74.5): 'to be able' [GEL, Ln; KJV, TEV]. The phrase τοῦ δύνασθαι αὐτόν 'of his being able' is translated 'of his ability' [Ea, Mou, WBC], 'of his power' [HNTC], 'of the power that he has' [NASB], 'of the power which he has' [NJB], 'of the Divine power which enables him' [Pl], 'that enables him' [NIV], 'which enables him' [ICC; TNT], 'with which he is able' [WEC]. It refers to ability [TH]. This word states Christ's ability to subject everything to himself, not whether he will in fact do so [Ea].

d. καί (GEL 89.93): 'even' [Ea, GEL, HNTC, NTC, Pl, WEC; KJV, NASB, NJB], 'also' [GEL, Ln; NRSV], 'actually' [Mou], not explicit [ICC, WBC; NAB, NIV, REB, TEV, TNT]. It is emphatic [Ea] and indicates the unlimited extent of his power, namely the power to subject everything to himself in addition to his power to transform our bodies [Alf, Bg, Ea, El, ICC, Lg, Lt, NTC], since it connects μετασχηματίσει 'he will transform' with ὑποτάξαι 'to subject' [Lg]. It means that if he can do the greater thing he can do the lesser thing [Lg, My]. It introduces the general category of which his power to transform our bodies is a specific [My].

e. aorist act. infin. of ὑποτάσσω (GEL 37.31) (BAGD p. 848): 'to subject' [BAGD, GEL, ICC, Ln, NTC, WBC; NAB, NASB], 'to make subject' [NRSV, REB], 'to bring into subjection' [HNTC, Pl], 'to subdue' [Ea, Mou, WEC; KJV], 'to subordinate' [BAGD], 'to bring under one's control' [NIV], 'to bring under one's mastery' [NJB], 'to bring under one's rule' [TEV], 'to serve one's purpose' [TNT]. This infinitive is governed by the preceding infinitive phrase τοῦ δύνασθαι αὐτόν 'his being able' and tells what Christ is able to do [Ea, WBC].

f. πᾶς (GEL 59.23; 63.2) (BAGD 2.b.β. p. 633): 'every' [GEL], 'all' [GEL, Ln], 'whole' [GEL]. The phrase τὰ πάντα is translated 'everything' [WBC; NAB, NIV], 'all things' [BAGD, Ea, HNTC, ICC, NTC, Pl, WEC; all translations except NAB, NIV], 'all things that are' [Mou], 'the universe' [BAGD]. The phrase 'all things' is collective [ICC, My], including all created things without exception [My, Pl], and is emphatic by word order [Pl]. The article strengthens the sense [Lg(H)]. This phrase refers to the universe [Alf, TH, WBC].

QUESTION—What is the function of this phrase?

It is connected with μετασχηματίσει 'he will transform' [Bg, ICC, MNTC]: he will transform our bodies in accordance with his infinite power. It gives the basis for Paul's confidence in Christ's power to transform our bodies [ICC, NIC]. It supports the statement that Christ will transform our bodies, since he can even subject the whole universe to himself [Blm, My, TNTC, WEC]. It tells how Christ is able to transform our bodies [Ln, NIC, TH, TNTC, WBC].

QUESTION—How are the noun and the infinitive phrase related in the genitive construction τὴν ἐνέργειαν τοῦ δύνασθαι αὐτόν 'the operation of his being able'?

1. The ἐνέργειαν 'operation' is the means by which he is able to subject everything to himself [GNC, Ln, NTC; KJV, TEV, TNT]: the operation by which he is able.
2. The 'operation' is the power in which the 'being able' is manifested [ICC]: his ability is manifested in his operation.
3. The infinitive phrase is a possessive genitive [El]: the operation which belongs to his being able.

QUESTION—To whom does αὐτῷ 'himself/him' refer?

1. It refers to Christ in a reflexive sense [El, EBC, EGT, GNC, HNTC, ICC, Ln, Lt, Mou, My, NIC, NTC, Pl, TNTC, WBC, WC, WEC; all translations] as implied by the preceding ὅς 'who' [Lt, Pl], and is therefore to be translated 'himself' [Ea].
2. It refers to Christ from the point of view of the writer and is to be translated 'him' [Alf].

DISCOURSE UNIT: 4:1–23 [TNTC; NAB]. The topic is thanksgiving, personal greetings, and words of encouragement [TNTC], exhortations to live virtuously [NAB].

DISCOURSE UNIT: 4:1–20 [TH]. The topic is instructions and thanksgiving.

DISCOURSE UNIT: 4:1–9 [EBC, ICC, Mou, NIC, NTC, Pl, TH, WBC, WC; NASB, TEV]. The topic is additional exhortations [EBC, ICC, Pl, TH], instructions [TEV], exhortation to be pure and peaceable [Mou], exhortation to live virtuously [NIC], exhortation to live in harmony and to be joyful and mentally sound [WBC], exhortation to set their minds on excellence [NASB], tactful exhortations [NTC].

DISCOURSE UNIT: 4:1–3 [EBC, EGT, My(D), NIC, NTC, TNTC, WC; NAB]. The topic is various exhortations [NTC], an exhortation to be steadfast and united [EBC, NIC, TNTC, WC] and expressions of appreciation [TNTC], exhortation to live in harmony [NAB], advice to individuals [EGT].

4:1
Therefore,[a] brothers[b] of-me beloved[c] and longed-for,[d] joy and crown[e] of-me,

LEXICON—a. ὥστε (GEL 89.52) (BAGD 1.b. p. 900): 'therefore' [BAGD, GEL, HNTC, WEC; KJV, NASB, NIV, NRSV], 'wherefore' [Ea], 'for this reason' [BAGD], 'for these reasons' [NAB], 'so then' [GEL, NTC, Pl; NJB, TEV], 'so' [BAGD, GEL, Mou], 'and so' [Ln], 'as a result' [GEL], 'well then' [WBC], not explicit [REB]. This word is also translated as a phrase: 'because of all that Christ can do for you' [TNT], 'in view of this glorious future' [ICC].

b. ἀδελφός: 'brother'. See this word at 1:12, 14; 3:1, 13, 17; 4:8, 21.

c. ἀγαπητός (GEL 25.45) (BAGD 2. p. 6): 'beloved' [BAGD, GEL, HNTC, ICC, Ln, Mou, NTC, WEC; NASB], 'dearly beloved' [KJV], 'loved' [Ea], 'dear' [BAGD, GEL], 'dear friend' [NJB]. This word is also translated as a phrase: 'whom I love' [Pl, WBC; NIV, NRSV, REB], 'whom I so love' [NAB], 'I love you' [TNT], 'how dear you are to me' [TEV]. It indicates loving spiritual affection [Bg, Ea, EBC, El, Lg, WBC].

d. ἐπιπόθητος (GEL 25.48) (BAGD p. 298): 'longed for' [BAGD, Ea, HNTC, Ln, Mou, NTC, WEC; KJV], 'very dear' [GEL], 'desired' [BAGD], not explicit [ICC]. This word is also translated as a phrase: 'whom I long for' [GEL, WBC; NAB, NIV, NRSV, REB], 'whom I long to see' [NASB], 'whom I long to see again' [Pl], 'whom I miss so much' [NJB], 'I long for you' [TNT], 'how I miss you' [TEV]. This word implies Paul's absence from them [Bg] and his desire to see them [El, Lg, WBC]. It is stronger than ἀγαπητός 'beloved' [Blm]; it indicates special affection for them [Ea, EBC].

e. στέφανος (GEL 6.192; 42.19) (BAGD 2.b. p. 767): 'crown' [Ea, GEL, HNTC, Ln, Mou, NTC, Pl, WBC; all translations except TEV, TNT], 'wreath' [GEL], 'adornment' [BAGD], 'pride' [BAGD], 'symbol of success' [GEL], 'sign of accomplishment' [GEL], 'source of my boasting' [WEC], not explicit [ICC]. This word is also translated as a phrase: 'how proud I am of you' [TEV], 'you are the sign of my victory' [TNT]. It refers to the wreath of victory [EBC, GNC, Lg(H), Ln, Lt, MNTC, Mou, My, NIC, Pl, TNTC, WBC, WC] or celebration [EBC, MNTC, NTC, WBC]. Their spiritual condition was like a victor's garland for Paul [Ea].

QUESTION—What relationship is indicated by ὥστε 'therefore'?

It indicates an exhortation based on the preceding context [Bg, Blm, Ea, Lt, My, NTC, WBC]. It is based on 3:20–21 [Lg(H)], 3:18–21 [NIC], 3:17–21 [Alf, EGT, El, My], all of chapter 3 [Ea, ICC, Lg, Ln, My(D)], the earlier part of the letter [WC], the letter as a whole [WEC]. It is also a transition to what follows [EBC, Mou, Pl, TH, WBC, WEC].

QUESTION—What do χαρὰ καὶ στέφανος 'joy and crown' refer to?

The Philippian Christians are a cause of joy and glory for Paul [Blm].

1. The words joy and crown refer to his reward at the final judgment [Alf, EGT, Lt, TNTC, WC]: my joy and crown at the judgment day.

2. They refer to his present joy in them [Ea, ICC, My, NIC, WBC]: my present joy and crown. They are the subject and the cause of Paul's joy [ICC, WBC].

3. They refer both to the time of the Lord's return and also to the present [El, MNTC, NTC]: my present and future joy and crown.

4. They refer to his present joy and to his crown when Christ returns [EBC, Lg, Pl]. The joy is personal, the crown relates to his apostleship [Lg].

thus[a] stand[b] in[c] (the) Lord, beloved.[d]

LEXICON—a. οὕτως (GEL 61.9; 61.10): 'thus' [GEL, Ln, Mou, WEC], 'so' [Ea, GEL, NTC; KJV, NASB], 'in this way' [GEL, HNTC; NRSV], 'as follows' [GEL], 'that is how' [NIV], 'this is how' [WBC; TEV], 'for all these reasons' [Pl], not explicit [ICC; NAB, NJB, REB, TNT].

b. pres. act. impera. of στήκω (GEL 13.30) (BAGD 2. p. 768): 'to stand' [Ea, GEL], 'to stand firm' [BAGD, HNTC, Ln, Mou, WBC, WEC; all translations except KJV, NJB], 'to hold firm' [NJB], 'to stand fast' [NTC, Pl; KJV], 'to be steadfast' [BAGD], 'to continue steadfast' [ICC], 'to continue to be' [GEL].

c. ἐν with dative object (GEL 83.13; 89.119) (BAGD I.5.d. p. 259): 'in' [BAGD, Ea, GEL, HNTC, ICC, Ln, Mou, NTC, Pl, WBC, WEC; all translations except TEV, TNT], 'inside' [GEL], 'in union with' [GEL], 'in your life in' [TEV]. The phrase ἐν κυρίῳ 'in the Lord' is translated 'as Christians' [TNT].

d. ἀγαπητός (GEL 25.45) (BAGD 2. p. 6): 'beloved' [BAGD, Ea, GEL, HNTC, Ln, NTC, WEC; NASB, NRSV], 'beloved one' [Mou, Pl], 'dearly beloved' [KJV], 'dear' [BAGD, GEL], 'dear one' [NAB], 'dear brother' [TEV], 'dear friend' [NIV, NJB, TNT], 'Christian friend' [WBC], not explicit [ICC; REB].

QUESTION—What does οὕτως 'thus' refer to?
 1. It refers to what preceeds and means to stand in the way he has
    been describing and exhorting [Alf, El, ICC, Lg, Lt, My, NIC,
    Pl], as Christians should [El, ICC], as indicated by his example
    [Lg, Lt, My(D)] in chapter 3 [Lg, Ln], in 3:17-21 [EGT], in
    3:20-21 [Ea], in 1:27 [WC], or as they are now standing [Bg]. It
    means to stand fast by rejoicing in the Lord [MNTC], to stand
    fast because they have such a hope [Mou].
 2. It refers to what follows and means to stand in the way he is
    about to tell them in 4:2-9 [WBC].
QUESTION—What is meant by standing ἐν κυρίῳ 'in the Lord'?
 It describes the area or the element in which their steadfastness
 should occur [Alf, Ea, El, ICC, Ln, My, NIC, TNTC]: stand firm in
 your union and fellowship with the Lord.
QUESTION—Why is ἀγαπητοί 'beloved' repeated at the close of this
verse?
 It indicates Paul's affection for his readers [Alf, Ea, Lg, WEC],
 emphatically repeated [El, ICC, Lg, WEC]: you whom I dearly
 love. This word is repeated to indicate affection [Alf, Bg] and to
 strengthen Paul's exhortation [Bg].

DISCOURSE UNIT: 4:2-23 [WEC]. The topic is Paul's final concerns.

DISCOURSE UNIT: 4:2-20 [Lg]. The topic is exhortations for their
cooperation with Paul.

DISCOURSE UNIT: 4:2-9 [Alf, HNTC (plus 3:1b), WEC; GNT, NIV,
NJB]. The topic is Paul's concluding exhortations [Alf, WEC; GNT, NIV,
NJB] and greetings [HNTC].

DISCOURSE UNIT: 4:2-3 [Lg, Ln, Lt, MNTC, Pl, WEC]. The topic is an
exhortation for unity [Lg, Pl, WEC], the matter of Euodia and Syntyche
[Ln, MNTC].

4:2
**Euodia I-urge[a] and Syntyche I-urge[a] to-set-their-mind-on[b] the same-
thing in[c] (the) Lord.**
 LEXICON—a. pres. act. indic. of παρακαλέω (GEL 33.168) (BAGD 2.
    p. 617): 'to urge' [BAGD; NASB, NJB, NRSV], 'to beseech'
    [ICC, WEC; KJV], 'to entreat' [NTC], 'to plead with' [NAB,
    NIV], 'to appeal to' [GEL, Mou], 'to implore' [HNTC], 'to ask
    for earnestly' [GEL], 'to request' [GEL], 'to appeal to' [BAGD,
    GEL; REB], 'to plead for' [GEL], 'to beg' [WBC; TEV], 'to

exhort' [BAGD, Ea, Pl], 'to admonish' [Ln], 'to have a special plea for' [TNT].

b. pres. act. infin. of φρονέω (GEL 26.16; 31.1) (BAGD 1. p. 866): 'to set one's mind on', 'to mind' [Ln], 'to think' [BAGD], 'to have an attitude' [GEL], 'to hold a view' [GEL], 'to think in a particular manner' [GEL]. The phrase τὸ αὐτὸ φρονεῖν 'to set their mind on the same thing' is translated 'to be of the same mind' [Mou, NTC, Pl; KJV, NRSV], 'to be of one mind' [Ea], 'to adopt the same frame of mind' [WEC], 'to agree' [REB, TEV], 'to agree with each other' [WBC; NIV], 'to come to agreement with each other' [NJB], 'to come to some mutual understanding' [NAB], 'that they settle their differences' [TNT], 'to be reconciled' [ICC], 'to live in harmony' [NASB], 'to be united' [HNTC]. The present tense implies that they should then continue their agreement [Ea, Ln].

c. ἐν with dative object (GEL 83.13; 89.119) (BAGD I.5.d. p. 259): 'in' [BAGD, Ea, GEL, HNTC, Ln, Mou, NTC, Pl, WBC; all translations except TNT], 'in union with' [GEL], 'joined closely to' [GEL], not explicit [ICC]. This word is also translated as a phrase: 'by virtue of their union with' [WEC]. The phrase ἐν κυρίῳ 'in the Lord' is translated 'as the Lord's followers' [TNT].

QUESTION—What is implied by the repeated παρακαλῶ 'I urge'?

The repetition adds emphasis to his urging [WBC, WC, WEC] and shows Paul's eagerness that they resolve their problem [TH]. It indicates that there was a separation between the two women [Alf], and that he was impartially urging each of them to seek accord with the other [Bg, Ea, EGT, El, GNC, HNTC, ICC, Ln, MNTC, NTC, Pl, WBC, WC, WEC]. It implies that both were at fault [El, Lg, MNTC, Pl]. The repetition may indicate that the disagreement was serious [EBC].

QUESTION—What is implied by the phrase ἐν κυρίῳ 'in the Lord'?

They must come to agreement because they are sisters in Christ [Pl], and because they are both in union with the Lord [Mou, WC, WEC]. They should do this as the Lord's followers should [TNTC; TNT], in a submissive attitude to the Lord [TH], or as is proper for those who are under Christ's lordship [WBC]. Their agreement was to be shown in the sphere of the Lord [Ea, El], in realization of their common relationship to the Lord [MNTC], or in their attachment to the Lord [NIC].

4:3

Yes,[a] I-ask you also, genuine[b] yokefellow/Syzygus,[c] join-in-helping[d] them,

TEXT—Instead of ναί 'yes', a very few manuscripts read καί 'and'. GEL does not deal with this variant, nor does Nestle. Καί is read by

KJV, but the few others who read 'and' here probably do so on stylistic, and not textual, grounds.

LEXICON—a. ναί (GEL 69.1) (BAGD 3. p. 533): 'yes' [GEL, HNTC, Ln, NTC, Pl, WBC; NAB, NIV, NRSV, REB, TNT], 'yea' [Ea], 'indeed' [GEL; NASB], 'yes, indeed' [BAGD], 'and' [ICC, Mou; KJV, NJB, TEV], 'moreover' [WEC]. This word implies that the previous request will be granted [Alf]; it carries the matter further [Alf, Ln]. It confirms the plea [El, Pl]. It is emphatic [NIC], emphasizing the preceding exhortation [ICC]. It is an affectionate comment [Bg, Lt, MNTC] implying urgency as well [MNTC, My].

b. γνήσιος (GEL 73.1) (BAGD 1. p. 163): 'genuine' [GEL, Ln, Mou], 'genuine and faithful' [Pl], 'faithful' [TEV], 'dependable' [NAB], 'loyal' [WBC, WEC; NIV, NRSV, REB], 'true' [BAGD, Ea, HNTC; KJV, NASB, TNT], 'real' [GEL], 'in deed as well as in name' [NTC], 'who are justly so named' [ICC]. This adjective is also translated as an adverb: 'really' [NJB]. It means true in contrast with counterfeit [Alf].

c. σύζυγος (GEL 42.45) (BAGD p. 776): 'yokefellow' [BAGD, Ea, Mou, Pl; KJV, NIV], 'fellow worker' [GEL; NAB], 'partner' [TEV], 'comrade' [BAGD, HNTC; NASB, REB, TNT], 'companion' [NRSV], 'Syzygus' [Ln, NTC; NJB], 'Synzygus' [ICC]. This singular noun is intentionally translated as a plural: 'yoke-fellows' [WBC], 'friends' [WEC]. It is a stronger term than συνεργός 'fellow worker' [Blm, Lg].

d. pres. mid. indic. of συλλαμβάνω (GEL 35.5) (BAGD 2.b. p. 777): 'to join in helping' [GEL], 'to help' [BAGD, Ea, HNTC, Mou, WBC; all translations except NAB], 'to assist' [BAGD], 'to be of assistance to' [Ln, WEC], 'to come to the aid of' [BAGD], 'to go to one's aid' [NAB], 'to lend a hand' [NTC], 'to give a helping hand' [Pl], 'to use one's influence' [ICC]. They are to help by bringing about a reconciliation between the two women [Alf, Bg, Ea, EBC, EGT, El, GNC, HNTC, ICC, Lg, MNTC, My, NIC, NTC, Pl, TH, TNTC, WBC], this appeal indicating that harmony between the two women was important [Ea]. This imperative verb form implies urgency [WBC].

QUESTION—What is meant by καὶ σέ 'you also'?

It implies that others in addition to this faithful yokefellow may be able to help [Ln]: you as well as any others.

QUESTION—What is meant by σύζυγοι 'yokefellow/Syzygus'?

1. This describes a member of the congregation as a yokefellow [Bg, Blm, Ea, EBC, El, GNC, HNTC, Lg, Lt, Mou, Pl, TH, WC; all translations except NJB].

2. This refers to the entire Philippian church, which Paul here addresses as though it were a single individual, describing him as 'a yokefellow' [WBC, WEC].

3. This refers to a man in the congregation, whose name is Syzygus [EGT, ICC, Ln, My, NIC, NTC; NJB].

(women) who[a] in[b] the gospel struggled-along-with[c] me together-with[d] both/also[e] Clement and my remaining[f] fellow-workers,[g]

LEXICON—a. ὅστις (GEL 92.18): 'women who' [Mou, WBC], 'who are such as' [Ln], 'as being persons who' [Ea], 'who' [GEL; NASB, NIV, REB], 'which' [KJV], 'these women' [WEC; NJB], 'those women' [ICC], 'they' [HNTC, NTC, Pl; NAB, NRSV, TEV, TNT]. This relative pronoun introduces the classification of these two women [ICC, Lt, NIC]; it is qualitative and causal [Ln].

b. ἐν with dative object (GEL 89.5): 'in' [Ea, GEL, NTC; KJV], 'in the cause of' [HNTC, Mou; NASB, NIV, REB, TNT], 'in the work of' [ICC, WEC; NRSV], 'in the spread of' [WBC], 'in promoting' [NAB], 'on behalf of' [Pl], 'with regard to' [GEL], 'for' [NJB], 'to spread' [TEV], not explicit [Ln]. It indicates the area in which the struggle took place [Ea, El, ICC, Lg, MNTC, My].

c. aorist act. indic. of συναθλέω (GEL 42.50) (BAGD p. 783): 'to struggle along with' [BAGD], 'to struggle with' [WEC], 'to struggle at one's side' [NAB], 'to share one's struggles' [REB, TNT], 'to struggle beside (someone)' [NRSV], 'to struggle hard' [NJB], 'to share one's struggle' [NASB], 'to strive with' [Ln], 'to strive side by side with' [NTC], 'to strive along with' [Ea], 'to contend along with' [BAGD], 'to contend at one's side' [HNTC; NIV], 'to wrestle along with' [Mou], 'to fight at one's side' [BAGD, WBC], 'to fight side by side with' [Pl], 'to labor with' [GEL; KJV], 'to labor alongside of' [GEL], 'to toil with' [GEL], 'to work hard with' [TEV]. This verb is also translated as a phrase: 'were helpers' [ICC]. It implies danger [Bg], opposition [ICC, MNTC], suffering [ICC], or struggle [MNTC, WC].

d. μετά with genitive object (GEL 89.108): 'together with' [GEL; NASB, NRSV, TEV], 'along with' [Ea, HNTC, ICC, NTC, Pl, WBC, WEC; NAB, NIV, NJB], 'with' [GEL, Ln, Mou; KJV, REB], 'as have' [TNT].

e. καί (GEL 89.93; 89.102) (BAGD II.7. p. 393): 'both', 'also' [BAGD, GEL, Ln, Pl; KJV, TNT], 'too' [Ea, HNTC, Mou], not explicit [ICC, NTC, WBC, WEC; all translations except KJV, TNT]. The double καί . . . καί is translated 'both . . . and' [GEL] in a correlative sense [El]. The first καί 'both' (the double καί . . . καί [El]) indicates that the preposition μετά 'with' governs 'the rest of my coworkers' as well as 'Clement' [El, ICC]. It means 'Clement as well as the genuine yokefellow' [Lt]. It means Clement in addition to Paul [My].

f. λοιπός (GEL 63.21) (BAGD 2.a. p. 479): 'remaining' [BAGD, GEL], 'rest' [GEL, HNTC, NTC, Pl, WBC, WEC; NASB, NIV, NRSV, TNT], 'other' [BAGD, GEL, ICC, Ln, Mou; KJV, NAB, NJB, REB, TEV], not explicit [Ea].

g. συνεργός (GEL 42.44) (BAGD p. 787): 'fellow worker' [BAGD, GEL, HNTC, Ln, Mou, NTC, Pl; NASB, NIV, NJB, REB, TEV, TNT], 'co-worker' [WBC, WEC; NRSV], 'fellow laborer' [Ea; KJV], 'faithful laborer' [ICC]. This word is also translated as a phrase: 'who have labored with' [NAB].

QUESTION—What relationship is indicated by αἵτινες 'who'?

1. It gives the reason why these women should be helped [Alf, EGT, El, HNTC, ICC, Lg, Ln, Lt, My, NTC, Pl, TH, WBC, WC, WEC; NRSV, TEV, TNT]: help them, for they are women who have worked in the gospel with me.

2. It comments on these women's work [GNC, Mou, NIC; NAB, NJB, REB]: help them; they are women who have helped me.

3. It introduces a restrictive relative clause indicating which women he is referring to [KJV, NASB, NIV]: help these women who have helped me.

QUESTION—What is the phrase introduced by μετά 'along with Clement and the rest of my fellow workers' connected with?

1. It is connected with συνήθλησαν 'struggled along with' [Alf, Bg, Ea, EBC, EGT, El, GNC, HNTC, ICC, Lg, Ln, MNTC, My, NIC, NTC, Pl, TH, WC, WEC; NAB, NJB, NRSV, TEV, TNT]: they have struggled along with Clement and the others.

2. It is connected with συλλαμβάνου αὐταῖς 'help them' [Lt, Mou]: I request Clement and the other fellow workers to join in helping in the reconciliation.

of-whom the names (are) in[a] (the) book of-life.

LEXICON—a. ἐν with dative object (GEL 83.13): 'in' [Ea, GEL, HNTC, Ln, Mou, NTC, Pl, WBC, WEC; all translations], not explicit [ICC].

QUESTION—What is ὧν 'of whom' connected with?

1. It refers to the unnamed others of Paul's fellow workers [Alf, Bg, Ea, EBC, El, ICC, Lg, Ln, Lt, My, NIC, NTC, Pl, TNTC]: the names of these other fellow workers. The reference is to living persons [Alf, El, Pl], or to persons who were now dead [Bg, HNTC], or it is not certain whether they were living or dead [EBC, Lg(H), Ln, My].

2. It refers to all the persons mentioned in this verse [TH, WBC, WEC]: the names of all those I have mentioned.

QUESTION—How are the two nouns related in the genitive construction βίβλῳ ζωῆς 'book of life'?

Ζωῆς 'of life' evidently is a genitive of general relationship with βίβλῳ 'book', but none of the commentaries discuss this point: the book which has to do with life. The phrase refers to God's record of Christians [Blm, EBC, GNC, ICC, Lg(H), My, TH, TNTC, WBC, WC]: the book which contains the names of the persons who have eternal life. It may imply also that their service for the gospel is recorded as well [GNC].

DISCOURSE UNIT: 4:4-9 [EBC, EGT, Ln, Lt, My(D), NIC, TNTC; NAB]. The topic is an exhortation to persist in Christian qualities of life [EBC, NIC], an exhortation to live with the proper attitude and in proper conduct [EGT], an exhortation to live joyfully, in freedom from anxiety, and in following after good goals [Lt], an exhortation to pray and to live nobly [TNTC], an exhortation to have joy and peace [NAB], a summary of Christian attitudes and life [Ln].

DISCOURSE UNIT: 4:4-7 [Lg, MNTC, NTC, Pl, WC, WEC]. The topic is the secret for achieving real blessedness [NTC], an exhortation to have Christian joy [Lg, Pl], an exhortation to manifest joy, consideration for others, and trust in God, followed by a benediction [WC], joyfulness and peace [MNTC], joyfulness and an anxious spirit [WEC].

DISCOURSE UNIT: 4:4-5 [NIC]. The topic is joyfulness and forbearance.

4:4

Rejoice[a] in[b] (the) Lord always; again I will say, "Rejoice!"[a]

LEXICON—a. pres. act. impera. of χαίρω (GEL 25.125) (BAGD 1. pp. 873, 874): 'to rejoice' [BAGD, Ea, GEL, ICC, Ln, Mou, NTC, WBC, WEC; KJV, NAB, NASB, NIV, NRSV, TNT], 'to be joyful' [NJB], 'to have joy' [Pl], 'to be glad' [BAGD, GEL]. This repeated verb is translated 'I wish you joy . . . all joy be yours' [REB], 'may you always be joyful . . . rejoice' [TEV], 'I bid you farewell . . . fare you well' [HNTC]. The present tense indicates that they are to rejoice continually [Ea]. This verb implies joy and exultation [Ea]. It implies both a farewell and an exhortation to rejoice [Lt]. Another view is that it refers only to rejoicing [Ea, GNC, Pl, TH, WC], since Paul would hardly repeat a farewell with emphasis [TH], and πάντοτε 'always' does not fit well with 'farewell' [GNC, TH].

b. ἐν with dative object (GEL 89.26; 89.119) (BAGD I.5.d. p. 260): 'in' [BAGD, Ea, HNTC, ICC, Ln, Mou, NTC, WBC, WEC; all

translations except TEV, TNT], 'because of' [GEL], 'in union
with' [GEL], 'in your union with' [TEV]. The phrase ἐν κυρίῳ
'in the Lord' is translated 'as Christians' [TNT], 'as all
Christians should' [Pl].

QUESTION—Why is this verse mentioned?

The entire verse is a repetition of the similar exhortation in 3:1
[Blm, GNC, Mou, TH, WBC]: as I said in 3:1, so I urge you now
to rejoice. He repeats the exhortation here because of his strong
feelings [Blm]. It is an exhortation to all the Philippians [Alf, EBC,
El, MNTC, My, TNTC]. It picks up his topic of 3:1 [Ea, Lg, My];
it is not directly connected with 4:3 [Ea]. Rejoicing is a key theme
of this epistle [Alf, EGT, El, ICC, Lg, My, NIC, Pl, TH, WC,
WEC].

QUESTION—How are the two parts of this verse related?

1. The second part of the verse is a repetition of the first part, for
   emphasis [GNC, Lg, Ln, MNTC, TH, WBC], indicating that
   even in spite of their difficulties they should rejoice in the Lord
   [EBC, EGT, El, ICC, MNTC, NIC, NTC, TNTC, WEC]: I will
   repeat what I have just said: "Rejoice!" The future tense ἐρῶ 'I
   will say' is used for the present tense 'I say' [Bg, EGT; KJV,
   NAB, NJB, REB, TEV]. It is a proper future tense [Ea, El,
   GNC, ICC, Lg(H), Ln, Lt, MNTC, My, NTC, Pl; NASB, NIV,
   NRSV, TNT] indicating that Paul has given serious thought to
   this matter [My].
2. The phrase πάλιν ἐρῶ, χαίρετε 'again I will say, "Rejoice!"' is
   simply a restatement of the first 'rejoice', and the πάλιν 'again'
   refers back to 3:1 [Alf]: rejoice in the Lord; I will say again
   what I said in 3:1, "Rejoice!"

QUESTION—To whom does κυρίῳ 'Lord' refer?

It refers to Christ [Ea, MNTC, NTC]: rejoice in Christ.

QUESTION—What relationship is indicated by ἐν 'in'?

1. It indicates the object of their rejoicing [Ea, GNC, MNTC]:
   rejoice about the Lord. They are to rejoice that the one who is
   loving, gracious, and powerful fellowships with them and he is
   their benefactor [Ea]. They are to rejoice that their freedom and
   redemption was won by him [MNTC].
2. It indicates the circumstance in which they are to rejoice [NTC,
   Pl, TH]: rejoice as you live in union with the Lord. Only as they
   are one with Christ can they be completely happy [TH].
3. It indicates the grounds for exhorting them to rejoice [TNTC,
   WBC, WEC]: rejoice because of the Lord. It is their faith in the
   Lord that make it possible to rejoice in the midst of suffering
   [TNTC, WBC].

QUESTION—What is the word πάντοτε 'always' connected with?
1. It is connected with the first χαίρετε 'rejoice' [Blm, Ea, EBC, El, ICC, Lg, Ln, MNTC, Mou, My, NTC, TH, WBC; all translations]: rejoice always. It means that they should rejoice regardless of their circumstances [Ln].
2. It is connected with the second χαίρετε 'rejoice' [Bg]: again I will say, always rejoice!

4:5
The gentle[a] (thing) of-you let-it-be-known[b] to-all persons.[c]
　　LEXICON—a. ἐπιεικής (GEL 88.63) (BAGD p. 292): 'gentle' [GEL], 'gracious' [GEL], 'forbearing (spirit)' [BAGD, GEL, ICC, Pl; NASB], 'unselfish' [NAB]. The phrase τὸ ἐπιεικές 'the gentle thing' is translated 'gentleness' [WEC; NIV, NRSV, TEV, TNT], 'kindliness' [HNTC], 'forbearance' [Ea], 'yieldingness' [Ln, Mou], 'magnanimity' [WBC], 'big-heartedness' [NTC], 'consideration of others' [REB], 'good sense' [NJB], 'moderation' [KJV]. The sense is having consideration for one another [Alf], not insisting on one's rights [Ea, EBC, EGT, El, GNC, ICC, Ln, Lt, My(D), NTC, Pl, TH, WBC, WC, WEC], nor on rigid exactitude [Ea, El, ICC, NTC, Pl, WBC], not being contentious nor self-seeking [Lt], refraining from retaliation [MNTC, TH, TNTC].
　　b. aorist pass. impera. of γινώσκω (GEL 28.1): 'to be known' [Ea, GEL, Ln, Mou, NTC, WBC; KJV, NASB, NRSV, REB], 'to become known' [Pl], 'to be perceived' [HNTC], 'to be apparent' [WEC], 'to be evident' [NIV], 'to be obvious' [NJB]. The phrase γνωσθήτω πᾶσιν ἀνθρώποις 'let (it) be known to all persons' is translated 'everyone should see' [NAB], 'show toward everyone' [TEV], 'let all men see' [ICC], 'let it be that all men know you' [TNT]. Their gentleness must not be merely their attitude but must be made known openly [Alf, Bg, Blm, Ea, El, HNTC, Lg, Ln, MNTC, Mou, My, NIC, Pl, WBC].
　　c. ἄνθρωπος (GEL 9.1): 'person' [GEL], 'man' [Ea, HNTC, ICC, Ln, Mou, Pl; KJV, NASB, TNT], 'human being' [GEL], 'individual' [GEL]. The plural is translated 'everyone' [WEC; NAB, NRSV, REB, TEV], 'everybody' [NTC, WBC; NJB], 'all' [NIV]. 'All persons' here means everyone, including opponents as well as fellow-believers [Alf, Bg, Blm, EBC, El, HNTC, Lg, Ln, MNTC, Mou, My, NIC, NTC], non-Christians rather than Christians [TNTC].
QUESTION—What is this clause connected with?
　　It is connected with the preceding exhortation to rejoice [Lg, Ln, WEC]: rejoice in the Lord and let your gentleness be known.

The Lord (is) near.[a]
LEXICON—a. ἐγγύς (GEL 67.61) (BAGD 2.a. p. 214): 'near' [BAGD,
   Ea, GEL, HNTC, Ln, Mou, WBC, WEC; NAB, NASB, NIV,
   NJB, NRSV, REB], 'near you' [TNT], 'at hand' [ICC, NTC, Pl;
   KJV], 'coming soon' [TEV].
QUESTION—To whom does ὁ κύριος 'the Lord' refer?
   It refers to Jesus [Alf, Bg, Blm, Ea, El, EBC, EGT, HNTC, ICC,
   Lg, Ln, Lt, MNTC, NIC, NTC, Pl, TH, TNTC, WC, WEC; TEV]:
   Jesus is near.
QUESTION—What is the meaning of the phrase ὁ κύριος ἐγγύς 'the
Lord is near'?
   1. It is a temporal reference to the nearness of Christ's return [Alf,
      Bg, Blm, Ea, EBC, EGT, El, HNTC, ICC, Lg, Ln, Lt, MNTC,
      My, NIC, NTC, Pl, TH, TNTC, WEC; TEV]: the time of the
      Lord's return is near. If a person dies before the Lord returns,
      he will meet the Lord then [Blm, NTC].
      1.1 This gives the grounds for exhorting them to be gentle [EBC,
          HNTC, Lg, Ln, Lt, MNTC, My, NIC, TH, WEC]: let your
          gentleness be known to all, because the Lord is coming soon.
          The Lord will come to judge and settle all differences [EBC,
          EGT], and he will avenge his people [MNTC, TNTC]. When
          the Lord comes, these differences will be seen to be
          inconsequential [EBC, EGT]. We can afford to be gentle when
          living in the expectation of the Lord's coming and our
          resurrection and glorification [Ln].
      1.2 This gives the grounds for exhorting them not to be anxious
          [El, NTC, Pl]: the Lord is coming soon, so don't be anxious.
      1.3 This gives the grounds for both of the above [Alf, Ea, ICC].
          His coming enforces the command to be gentle and also leads
          to the duty of avoiding anxiety [Alf]. This clause is a link in
          the train of thought [Ea].
   2. It is a place reference, referring to the nearness of the Lord's
      indwelling presence [GNC, Mou; TNT]: the Lord is near to us.
      It is the grounds for the exhortation not to be anxious [GNC,
      Mou]. He is near to calm his people [Mou].
   3. It refers both to Christ's return and to his constant presence
      [WBC]: Christ is always with you and will return to earth soon.

DISCOURSE UNIT: 4:6–7 [NIC]. The topic is freedom from an anxious
spirit.

4:6

(For) nothing be-anxious,[a]

> LEXICON—a. pres. act. impera. of μεριμνάω (GEL 25.225) (BAGD 1.
> p. 505): 'to be anxious' [ICC, Mou, NTC; NASB, NIV, REB],
> 'to be anxious about' [GEL], 'to have anxiety' [BAGD], 'to
> worry' [Ln, WBC, WEC; NJB, NRSV, TEV, TNT], 'to be
> worried about' [GEL], 'to be fretful' [HNTC], 'to be careful'
> [Ea; KJV], 'to spoil one's life with needless anxieties' [Pl]. The
> phrase μηδὲν μεριμνᾶτε 'be anxious for nothing' is translated
> 'dismiss all anxiety from your minds' [NAB]. This refers, not to
> a proper concern, but to undue anxiety [Blm, Ea, EBC, My(D),
> Pl, WBC]; it is any concern at all which is short of full
> confidence in God [My]. The present tense implies a habitual
> attitude, but none of the commentaries mention this point.
> QUESTION—What is the significance of μηδέν 'nothing' occurring
> first in the sentence?
> It is the object of μεριμνᾶτε 'be anxious' and is emphatic by word
> order [Alf, Ea, El, Lg, My]: for *nothing* be anxious.

but in[a] **everything by-means-of-the prayer**[b] **and the petition**[c] **with**[d]
thanksgiving[e] **let-be-made-known**[f] **the requests**[g] **of-you to**[h] **the God.**

> LEXICON—a. ἐν with dative object (GEL 89.5): 'in' [Ea, GEL, ICC,
> Ln, Mou, NTC, Pl, WBC, WEC; all translations except NJB,
> TNT], 'about' [GEL], 'in the case of' [GEL], 'with regard to'
> [GEL], 'by' [HNTC]. The phrase ἐν παντὶ 'in everything' is
> translated 'whatever the matter' [TNT]. The phrase ἐν παντὶ τὰ
> αἰτήματα ὑμῶν γνωριζέσθω πρὸς τὸν θεόν 'in everything let
> your requests be made known to God' is translated 'tell God all
> your desires of every kind' [NJB].
> b. προσευχή (GEL 33.178) (BAGD 1. p. 713): 'prayer' [BAGD,
> Ea, GEL, HNTC, Ln, Mou, NTC, Pl, WBC, WEC; all
> translations except TEV]. The phrase τῇ προσευχῇ καὶ τῇ
> δεήσει 'by prayer and petition' is translated 'in prayer' [ICC], 'in
> prayers' [TEV]. This word refers to prayer with a worshipful
> attitude and feeling [Ea, EBC, EGT, Mou, NIC]; it is the
> general term for prayer to God [GNC, Lt, My, NIC, NTC,
> TNTC].
> c. δέησις (GEL 33.171) (BAGD p. 172): 'petition' [Ln, WBC;
> NAB, NIV, NJB, REB, TNT], 'request' [GEL], 'plea' [GEL],
> 'entreaty' [BAGD, WEC], 'supplication' [Ea, HNTC, Mou, NTC,
> Pl; KJV, NASB, NRSV], 'prayer' [BAGD, GEL]. This word
> refers to petition for what is needed [Ea, EBC, EGT, GNC, Lt,
> Mou, My, NIC, NTC, TNTC]. Some mention that this noun and
> the preceding one are not different in meaning [TH, WEC].

d. μετά with genitive object (GEL 89.78; 89.79; 89.108; 89.123) (BAGD A.III.1. p. 509): 'with' [BAGD, GEL, HNTC, ICC, Mou, NTC, WBC; KJV, NASB, NIV, NRSV, REB, TEV], 'together with' [GEL, Ln], 'along with' [Ea, WEC], 'combined with' [GEL, Pl], 'shot through with' [NJB], 'full of' [NAB], 'by means of' [GEL], 'through' [GEL], not explicit [TNT].

e. εὐχαριστία (GEL 33.349) (BAGD 2. p. 328): 'thanksgiving' [BAGD, Ea, GEL, HNTC, Ln, Mou, NTC, Pl, WBC, WEC; KJV, NASB, NIV, NRSV, REB, TNT], 'gratitude' [NAB, NJB]. This noun is also translated as a phrase: 'thankful hearts' [ICC], 'a thankful heart' [TEV]. The absence of the article focuses on thanksgiving as a quality, but none of the commentaries mention this point.

f. pres. pass. impera. of γνωρίζω (GEL 28.26) (BAGD 1. p. 163): 'to be made known' [BAGD, Ea, GEL, HNTC, Ln, Mou, NTC, Pl; KJV, NASB, NRSV]. The phrase τὰ αἰτήματα ὑμῶν γνωριζέσθω 'let your requests be made known' is translated 'present your needs' [NAB], 'present your requests' [NIV], 'make your requests known' [WBC; REB]. The phrase τὰ αἰτήματα ὑμῶν γνωριζέσθω πρὸς τὸν θεόν 'let your requests be made known to God' is translated 'ask God for what you need' [TEV], 'let God know what you want' [TNT], 'let God know what your requests are' [WEC], 'commit every matter to God' [ICC].

g. αἴτημα (GEL 33.164) (BAGD p. 26): 'request' [BAGD, Ea, GEL, HNTC, Mou, Pl, WBC, WEC; KJV, NASB, NIV, NRSV, REB], 'asking' [Ln], 'petition' [NTC], 'desire' [NJB], 'need' [NAB], 'what was being asked for' [GEL], 'what you need' [TEV], 'what you want' [TNT]. The implication is that the requests are for things which are desired [Ea]. The plural implies the various things which are requested [Lt].

h. πρός with accusative object (GEL 90.58) (BAGD III.1.f. p. 710): 'to' [BAGD, Ea, GEL, HNTC, ICC, Ln, WBC; NAB, NASB, NIV, NRSV, REB], 'unto' [KJV], 'towards' [Mou], 'before' [NTC, Pl]. It implies fellowship as well as the direction [ICC].

QUESTION—What relationship is indicated by the dative phrase τῇ προσευχῇ καὶ τῇ δεήσει 'by prayer and petition'?

It indicates the means by which the requests are to be made known to God [Alf, Ea, El, ICC, Lg, Ln, Mou, My, NIC, Pl, TNTC, WEC; all translations]: let your requests be made known to God by means of prayer and petition. The repeated article implies the prayer or supplication for each need [Alf, El, ICC, Lg, My] and emphasizes each noun [Ea, El, Lg, My]. The articles imply 'your' [Ln]. This is to be done in an attitude of reverence and devotion [NTC].

QUESTION— How is the phrase ἐν παντί 'in everything' related to its context?

1. It modifies the verb 'be made known' [Alf, Ea, El, ICC, Lg, Ln, Mou, My, NIC, Pl, TNTC, WEC; all translations except NAB, TEV]: in everything let your requests be made known to God by means of prayer and supplication. The phrase emphasizes the comprehensiveness of the exhortation [Ea, ICC, Lg, Mou, My, NTC, Pl].
2. It modifies the following dative phrase [HNTC, TH; NAB, TEV] and means 'all' [TEV], 'every form of' [NAB], or continual' [HNTC].
2.1 Both nouns in the dative phrase are modified [HNTC, TH; TEV]: in every prayer and petition let your requests be made known to God.
2.2 Only προσευχῇ 'prayer' is modified [NAB]: in every form of prayer, and in petitions let your requests be made known to God.

QUESTION—What is the phrase μετὰ εὐχαριστίας 'with thanksgiving' connected with?

1. It is connected with what precedes [Ea, El, EBC, EGT, GNC, HNTC, Ln, Pl, WBC; NASB, NJB, REB, TNT].
1.1 It is connected with both words for prayer [Ea, HNTC, Ln, Pl, WBC; NASB, NJB, REB, TNT]: prayer and supplication with thanksgiving.
1.2 It is connected with only δεήσει 'petition' [NAB]: in petitions filled with thanksgiving.
2. It is connected with what follows, stating how they should make their requests known to God [Lg, My, NTC, WEC; TEV]: with thanksgiving let your requests be made known to God.

QUESTION—What is meant by μετὰ εὐχαριστίας 'with thanksgiving'?
It describes the attitude which should accompany the prayers [Alf, Ea, EBC, EGT, El, GNC, HNTC, ICC, Lg, Ln, My, NIC, Pl, TH, TNTC] (or the attitude in making them known to God [NTC]): prayer and petition accompanied by a thankful spirit. It refers to thankfulness for what God grants [Blm, EBC, ICC, My, TH], for past blessings [EBC, EGT, GNC, HNTC Ln, Lt, My, NIC, TH, TNTC], blessings past, present, and future [NIC, NTC], for the privilege of access to God [Mou]; it implies acceptance of what he withholds [Blm], recognizing that what he gives is for our good [EBC, ICC]; it includes many things [Ea].

4:7

and the peace of-the God the-(one) surpassing[a] all understanding[b] will-guard[c] the hearts[d] of-you and the minds[e] of-you in[f] Christ Jesus.

> LEXICON—a. pres. act. participle of ὑπερέχω (GEL 65.4) (BAGD 2.b. p. 841): 'to surpass' [BAGD, HNTC, NTC, WEC; NASB, NRSV], 'to surpass in value' [GEL], 'to pass' [Ea; KJV], 'to transcend' [Mou; NIV], 'to exceed' [Ln], 'to be better' [GEL], 'to excel' [WBC], 'to be beyond' [NAB, NJB, REB], 'to be far beyond' [TEV], not explicit [ICC, Pl]. The phrase ἡ ὑπερέχουσα πάντα νοῦν 'which surpasses all understanding' is translated 'which is more than we can ever understand' [TNT]. The meaning is absolute uniqueness, not merely superiority [TNTC].
>
> b. νοῦς (GEL 26.14) (BAGD 1. p. 544): 'understanding' [BAGD, Ea, Ln, NTC, WEC; all translations except NASB, TNT], 'comprehension' [NASB], 'mind' [BAGD, GEL, Mou], 'power of thought' [BAGD], 'imagination' [HNTC], 'human planning' [WBC], not explicit [ICC, Pl]. It is the intelligence, the power to perceive [Alf, Ea, ICC, Lg, NIC], the aspect of thinking [TH].
>
> c. fut. act. indic. of φρουρέω (GEL 37.119) (BAGD 2. p. 867): 'to guard' [BAGD, Ea, GEL, HNTC, ICC, Ln; NASB, NIV, NJB, NRSV, REB], 'to safeguard' [Mou], 'to stand guard over' [WBC, WEC; NAB], 'to keep guard over' [NTC, Pl; TNT], 'to protect [BAGD], 'to watch over' [GEL], 'to keep' [BAGD; KJV], 'to keep safe' [TEV], 'to keep under watch' [GEL]. The future tense makes this verb a declaration of what will result when the preceding admonitions are carried out [Alf, Ea, El, ICC, Lg, Mou, My, Pl] and implies continuation [Lg]. The promise includes every possible situation [ICC].
>
> d. καρδία (GEL 26.3): 'heart' [Ea, GEL, HNTC, ICC, Ln, Mou, NTC, Pl, WEC; all translations], 'inner self' [GEL], 'mind' [GEL], 'thought' [WBC]. It is the source of one's thoughts [Alf, Bg, ICC, Lg(H), Lt, My, TH] and intentions [Ea], the feelings [EGT, El, ICC, Lg(H), Lt, TH, WBC] and the will [EGT, El, ICC, Mou, My, TH], the intellect [Blm], the center of personality [Ln], the source of mental and spiritual powers [EBC].
>
> e. νόημα (GEL 26.14) (BAGD 1. p. 540): 'mind' [BAGD, GEL, Pl; all translations except NJB, REB], 'thought' [BAGD, Ea, HNTC, ICC, Ln, Mou, NTC, WEC; NJB, REB], 'feeling' [WBC]. It is the mind [TH], the affections and feelings [Blm], the product of the νοῦς 'mind' [Ea, EBC, EGT, Ln, WBC], of the καρδία 'heart' [ICC, Lg(H), Lt, Mou], the result of thinking and willing [El].

f. ἐν with dative object (GEL 89.119; 90.6): 'in' [Ea, GEL, HNTC, ICC, Ln, Mou, NTC, Pl, WBC; NAB, NASB, NIV, NJB, NRSV, REB], 'in union with' [GEL; TEV], 'in your union with' [TNT], 'by virtue of your union with' [WEC], 'by' [GEL], 'through' [KJV].

QUESTION—How is this verse related to the preceding verse?

It expresses the result of the preceding verse [Alf, Blm, Ea, EBC, EGT, El, GNC, ICC, Ln, Lt, MNTC, Mou, My, NIC, NTC, Pl, My, TH, WBC, WC; NAB, NJB, REB, TNT]: make your requests known to God, then God's peace will guard your hearts.

QUESTION—What is meant by εἰρήνη 'peace'?

It means the absence of troubled and anxious thoughts [Alf, Bg, Blm, Ea, Lg, Ln, My, WC], and the presence of harmonious relations [EGT]. It is the tranquil peace of one who rests fully on God [El, ICC, Mou, My, TH, WBC].

QUESTION—How are the two nouns related in the genitive construction ἡ εἰρήνη τοῦ θεοῦ 'the peace of God'?

God imparts peace to those who pray to him [Alf, El, GNC, HNTC, Ln, MNTC, Mou, My, NIC, NTC, Pl, TH, NTC,, TNTC WBC]: the peace that God gives. He is its source [Ea, El, Ln, TH, TNTC, WC], its author [Lg.] Some commentators add that the peace that God gives is also the peace that God himself has as a part of his nature [Alf, Ea, HNTC, MNTC].

QUESTION—What is meant by ἡ ὑπερέχουσα πάντα νοῦν 'which surpasses all understanding'?

1. It means that this peace is greater than our minds are able to understand [Alf, Ea, EBC, EGT, El, Lg, Mou, My(D), NTC, TH, TNTC, WEC]. It is beyond our understanding [Ln].

2. It means that this peace is greater than the human mind can plan [GNC, ICC, Lt, My, NIC, Pl, WBC, WC]. The peace that God gives is not attainable by human planning or effort [NIC, WBC].

QUESTION—What is the significance of the repeated article and the repeated pronoun in the phrase τὰς καρδίας ὑμῶν καὶ τὰ νοήματα ὑμῶν 'the hearts of you and the minds of you'?

They place separate emphasis on each of the two nouns [Lg, WBC].

QUESTION—What is meant by guarding hearts and minds?

The verb is a military term used metaphorically [EBC, EGT, GNC, HNTC, ICC, Ln, Lt, MNTC, Mou, NIC, NTC, Pl, TH, TNTC, WBC, WC]. Peace is like a soldier on guard duty. It protects the emotions and thoughts from anxiety [EBC, EGT, GNC, ICC, NIC, NTC, TH], worry [TH], doubts [EBC], despair [EBC], fear [ICC], and temptations [EGT, NIC, WC]. It mounts guard at the door of one's heart and mind to prevent anxiety from entering [NTC].

QUESTION—What is meant by ἐν Χριστῷ Ἰησοῦ 'in Christ Jesus'?
It indicates the circumstance in which the guarding takes place
[Alf, Ea, EGT, El, GNC, ICC, Lg, Ln, MNTC, Mou, My, NIC, Pl,
TH, WBC, WEC; NAB, TEV, TNT]: it is in union with Christ that
the peace of God will guard your hearts. Being in Christ is
necessary to experience this peace [Alf, Ea, ICC, Lg, MNTC, NIC,
WBC]. This implies that it is because they are in Christ that they
can experience it [TH, WEC].

DISCOURSE UNIT: 4:8–9 [Lg, MNTC, NIC, NTC, Pl, WC, WEC]. The
topic is a summary of Christian duty [NTC], progress in the Christian life
[Lg], exhortation to noble behavior [Pl, WC], Christian truth compared
with pagan morality [MNTC], various virtues [NIC], a discussion of
obedience and peace [WEC].

4:8
The final[a] (thing), brothers,
> LEXICON—a. λοιπός (GEL 61.14) (BAGD 3.b. p. 480): 'final'. The
> phrase τὸ λοιπόν 'the final thing' is translated 'finally' [BAGD,
> GEL, HNTC, ICC, Mou, WEC; all translations except REB,
> TEV], 'last of all' [WBC], 'in conclusion' [TEV], 'in fine' [Ea],
> 'for the rest' [NTC, Pl], 'as for the rest' [Ln], 'and now' [REB].
> This phrase indicates Paul's intention of closing his letter [Alf,
> EGT, El, HNTC, ICC, Lg, Lt, MNTC, Pl, TH], as he had done
> in 3:1 [Lg(H), Lt, Pl] but had remembered other matters he
> wished to say [Alf] or indicating his reluctance to bid a final
> farewell [Lg(H)]. It concludes his exhortations concerning all of
> their duties [Bg, Ea, WBC]. It is closely connected to 4:4–7
> [Ln]. It has no reference to the same phrase in 3:1 [My].

QUESTION—Why is this verse mentioned?
This and the following verse are a general exhortation concerning
additional qualities of Christian conduct [Alf, Blm, ICC, My, TH]:
do these additional things. It makes clear that a faithful Christian
life requires fulfillment of all of the Christian virtues, not merely
one [Blm]. There is a close connection with the preceding thought
[EGT], telling how God's peace will come to them [Lg]. This
summary is emphatic and comprehensive [El].

QUESTION—Why is ἀδελφοί 'brothers' mentioned?
It is added to give emphasis to the following exhortation [Ea],
indicating the depth of his feelings toward them [Lg].

as-many-things-as[a] are true,[b] as-many-things-as (are) noble,[c] as-many-things-as (are) righteous,[d] as-many-things-as (are) pure,[e] as-many-things-as (are) pleasing,[f] as-many-things-as (are) commendable,[g]

LEXICON—a. ὅσος (GEL 59.7) (BAGD 2. p. 586): 'as many as' [BAGD, GEL], 'whatever' [HNTC, Ln, NTC, WBC; NASB, NIV, NRSV], 'whatsoever' [Ea, Pl; KJV], 'that which' [WEC], 'all' [Mou; NAB, REB, TNT], 'everything' [ICC; NJB], 'things' [TEV]. This word indicates a generalization or universal reference [Bg, Ea, Lg, Ln, My]. The six repetitions of this word add great emphasis [Alf, El, Lg, My, WEC], a dignified impressiveness [MNTC, TH]. All six phrases refer to the same things [Ln]. By using this word Paul is referring to specific things, not to abstractions [Ea]. These six clauses give the content of ταῦτα 'these things' at the end of this verse and are stated first for emphasis [WBC].

b. ἀληθής (GEL 72.1) (BAGD 2. p. 36): 'true' [BAGD, Ea, GEL, HNTC, Ln, Mou, NTC, Pl, WEC; all translations], 'truthful' [WBC], not explicit [ICC]. The sense is moral truthfulness [Ea, GNC, Lg, My], in reference to ethical qualities [Alf], spiritually true [Ln], that which corresponds to God's nature [ICC], true in words [Bg], truly virtuous [Blm], valid and honest [EBC].

c. σεμνός (GEL 88.47) (BAGD 2. p. 747): 'noble' [NIV, REB, TEV, TNT], 'honest' [KJV], 'honorable' [BAGD, GEL, Mou, NTC, WEC; NASB, NJB, NRSV], 'worthy' [BAGD], 'worthy of respect' [GEL], 'deserves respect' [NAB], 'worthy of reverence' [HNTC], 'revered' [Ln], 'venerable' [ICC], 'grave' [Ea], 'decorous' [Ea], 'grand' [Pl], 'majestic and awe-inspiring' [WBC]. It means worthy of respect [Ea, EBC, El, GEL, Lg(H), My], fitting for a Christian [Ea], having serious and dignified motives and behavior [NTC], moral dignity which elicits reverence [ICC, Ln], and things that lift the mind to what is noble [WBC].

d. δίκαιος (GEL 88.12) (BAGD 5. p. 196): 'righteous' [GEL, Ln, Mou, Pl, WEC], 'right' [BAGD, Ea; NASB, NIV, TEV, TNT], 'just' [GEL, ICC, NTC, WBC; KJV, NRSV, REB], 'upright' [HNTC; NJB], 'honest' [NAB]. The sense is what is right or righteous in God's sight and man's [Alf, NTC], worthy of God's approval [EBC, Ln], meeting all obligations to God and man [ICC], what is just toward other persons [Bg, WC], in harmony with the law [Lg].

e. ἁγνός (GEL 88.28) (BAGD 2. p. 12): 'pure' [BAGD, Ea, GEL, HNTC, ICC, Ln, Mou, NTC, Pl, WBC, WEC; all translations]. It means pure in respect to themselves [Bg], things which do not stain the conscience nor the person [Ea], morally pure [EBC], free from error or sin [Ln].

f. προσφιλής (GEL **25.97**) (BAGD p. 720): 'pleasing' [BAGD, **GEL**, NRSV], 'lovely' [BAGD, Ea, GEL, HNTC, ICC, Ln, NTC, Pl, WEC; KJV, NASB, NIV, TEV], 'lovable' [REB, TNT], 'calls forth love' [WBC], 'admirable' [NAB], 'amiable' [Mou]. The phrase ὅσα προσφιλῆ, ὅσα εὔφημα 'as many things as are pleasing, as many things as are commendable' is translated 'everything that we love and admire' [NJB]. It combines love and respect [Blm], love and nobility [El], love and admiration [Pl]; things which express love [NTC] and inspire it [ICC, NTC, TH, WBC], things harmonious with the spirit of Christian love [Ea], things which are worthy of love [My]; it refers to things which are attractive and agreeable [EBC, GNC, Ln, MNTC], valuable and precious to people [Lg]; it relates especially to one's attitude toward other persons [EGT].

g. εὔφημος (GEL **33.360**) (BAGD p. 327): 'commendable' [NRSV], 'praiseworthy' [BAGD], 'worthy of praise' [GEL], 'worthy of approval' [GEL], 'respectable' [WEC], 'admirable' [NIV], 'esteemed' [HNTC], 'honorable' [TEV], 'attractive' [REB, TNT], 'winsome' [Pl, WBC], 'sweet to speak of' [Mou], 'of good report' [Ea, ICC, Ln, NTC; KJV], 'of good repute' [NASB], 'decent' [NAB]. It refers to actions which rightly have a good reputation [GNC], which are properly complimented or indicate admirable qualities in the person who does them [Ea, Lg], what one hears with pleasure [TH], what is kind and will attract people [Pl, WBC], what is in accord with the highest standards [EBC], truths in relation to God and man which sound well [NTC] and elicit belief [El] and imply worthiness [ICC].

if (there is) any virtue[a] and if (there is) any praise,[b] consider[c] these (things);

LEXICON—a. ἀρετή (GEL **88.11**) (BAGD 1. p. 105): 'virtue' [BAGD, Ea, GEL, HNTC, ICC, Mou, NTC, Pl, WEC; KJV], 'excellence' [Ln; NASB, NRSV], 'moral excellence' [BAGD, GEL, WBC], 'outstanding goodness' [GEL]. This noun is also translated as an adjective: 'virtuous' [NAB], 'morally excellent' [TNT], 'excellent' [NIV, REB], 'good' [NJB]. The phrase εἴ τις ἀρετή 'if there is any virtue' is translated 'things that are good' [TEV]. It refers to moral excellence [Ea, WBC], moral uprightness which elicits praise [Lg].

b. ἔπαινος (GEL **33.355**) (BAGD 2. p. 281): 'praise' [Ea, HNTC, ICC, Ln, Mou, NTC, Pl; KJV], 'something worthy of praise' [GEL], 'a thing worthy of praise' [BAGD]. This noun is also translated as an adjective: 'admirable' [REB], 'praiseworthy' [BAGD, GEL; NIV, NJB], as a phrase: 'worthy of praise' [BAGD, WBC, WEC; NAB, NASB, NRSV, TNT]. The phrase εἴ τις ἔπαινος 'if there is any praise' is translated 'things that deserve praise' [TEV]. It implies being worthy of praise [Lg, TH, TNTC, WBC, WEC], things which are universally praised [Pl].

c. pres. mid. (deponent = act.) impera. of λογίζομαι (GEL 30.9) (BAGD 2. p. 476): 'to consider' [BAGD], 'to think about' [BAGD, GEL, NTC; NIV, NRSV], 'to think on' [KJV], 'to think upon' [Ea], 'to think out' [Mou], 'to ponder' [BAGD, GEL], 'to take account of' [ICC], 'to take into account' [Pl], 'to reckon with' [Ln], 'to let one's mind dwell on' [BAGD, HNTC; NASB], 'to let one's mind be filled with' [NJB], 'to fill one's mind with' [TEV], 'to keep one's mind on' [WEC], 'to focus one's mind on' [WBC], 'to fill one's thoughts with' [REB], 'to keep in one's thoughts' [TNT], 'to direct one's thoughts wholly to' [NAB]. The meaning is to take these things into account in making their decisions [HNTC, Lg, MNTC, My, TH, TNTC, WBC], to consider thoughtfully the value of the things referred to [ICC]. The present tense implies continually considering them [EBC, Ln, NTC, Pl, TH, WBC].

QUESTION—What is meant by introducing the two clauses with εἰ 'if'?

By these two conditional clauses, Paul places on the reader the responsibility to choose things of these qualities [EBC]: if you see that there are these qualities in certain things, consider them.

1. They summarize the qualities just mentioned [Ea, El, ICC, Lg, My, TH]: in other words, if there is any virtue or grounds for praise in these things.
2. They add further generalizations [Blm, Lt, MNTC, TNTC, WEC]: whatever other things there may be of virtue or praise.
3. They summarize the qualities just mentioned and add further generalizations [Alf]: if there is any virtue or grounds for praise in these or any other things.

QUESTION—What verb is to be supplied in the two 'if' clauses?

The verb 'is' is to be supplied [Alf, Ea, El]: if there is any virtue and if there is any grounds for praise. It is assumed that there are such things [Alf, Ea, El, WBC].

QUESTION—What does ταῦτα 'these things' refer to?

It refers to all of the things mentioned in this verse [Alf]: consider all of these kinds of things.

4:9

(the things) which also/both you-learned[a] and received[b] and heard[c] and saw[d] in[e] me, these (things) be-doing;[f]

LEXICON—a. aorist act. indic. of μανθάνω (GEL 27.12) (BAGD 1. p. 490): 'to learn' [BAGD, Ea, GEL, HNTC, ICC, Ln, Mou, NTC, Pl, WBC, WEC; all translations except REB, TNT], 'to be instructed' [GEL], 'to be taught' [GEL]. The phrase ἃ ἐμάθετε 'the things which you learned' is translated 'the lessons I taught you' [REB], 'the lessons you have learnt' [TNT]. The reference is to instruction [Ea].

b. aorist act. indic. of παραλαμβάνω (GEL 27.13; 33.238) (BAGD 3.b. p. 619): 'to receive' [Ea, HNTC, Ln, Mou, NTC, Pl; KJV, NASB, NIV, NRSV, TEV], 'to receive instruction from' [GEL], 'to accept' [BAGD, WEC; NAB], to learn from someone' [GEL], 'to be taught by' [GEL], 'to be told by' [NJB]. The phrase ἃ παρελάβετε 'the things you received' is translated 'the tradition I have passed on' [REB], 'the traditions that I passed on to you' [WBC], 'the traditions you have received from me' [TNT], not explicit [ICC]. The verb refers to receiving a tradition [GNC, TNTC] in order to pass it on to others [WBC]; it means that they accepted the instruction given [Ea]. They received by Paul's instructions [Blm, TH] and from other teachers [Pl].

c. aorist act. indic. of ἀκούω (GEL 24.52): 'to hear' [Ea, GEL, HNTC, Ln, Mou, NTC, Pl, WBC, WEC; all translations except TEV], not explicit [ICC]. This verb is translated 'from my words' [TEV]. The reference is not to preaching but to what they heard about his character from other persons [Alf, Ea, El, Lg, MNTC, My, NTC, WBC] when he was absent [Pl].

d. aorist act. indic. of ὁράω (GEL 24.1) (BAGD 1.a. p. 220): 'to see' [BAGD, Ea, GEL, HNTC, Ln, Mou, NTC, Pl, WBC, WEC; all translations except TEV], 'to perceive' [BAGD], not explicit [ICC]. This verb is translated 'from my actions' [TEV]. It refers to what they had seen concerning Paul's character and behavior [Ea, NTC].

e. ἐν with dative object (GEL 83.13): 'in' [Ea, GEL, HNTC, Ln, Mou, NTC, WBC; KJV, NASB, NIV, NRSV], 'exemplified in' [WEC], not explicit [ICC, Pl; NAB, NJB, REB, TEV, TNT].

f. pres. act. impera. of πράσσω (GEL 42.8) (BAGD 1.a. p. 698): 'to do' [BAGD, Ea, GEL; KJV, NJB, NRSV], 'to put into practice' [NTC, WBC; NIV, REB, TEV, TNT], 'to put in practice' [HNTC], 'to put to practice' [WEC], 'to practice' [Ea, ICC, Ln, Mou, Pl; NASB], 'to carry out' [GEL], 'to accomplish' [BAGD], 'to live according to' [NAB]. They are to put into practice what they were told to consider in the preceding verse [El, Lg, Ln, MNTC, My, NTC]. The present tense implies continuous action [Blm, TH, WBC].

QUESTION—Why is this clause mentioned?

It turns from general references to specific things [Bg, WBC].

QUESTION—What is ἅ '(the things) which' connected with?

1. It refers to specific examples of the kinds of things he described in the preceding verse [Alf, Ea, El, Ln, NIC, My, Pl]: you have learned from me the kinds of things I have mentioned; put them into practice.

2. It does not refer specifically to the preceding verse [EGT, MNTC, TH, WC]: practice the things in general which you learned from me.

QUESTION—What relationship is indicated by the first καί 'also/both'?

1. It means 'also', introducing a further comment about the things he has just mentioned [Alf, Bg, Ea, El, Lg(H), My, Pl]: these things I have mentioned, which you also learned from me. This word makes it clear that the things he is now referring to are the kinds of things he referred to in the preceding verse [Alf].

2. It is parallel to the same word preceding ἠκούσατε 'you heard', with the sense of 'both . . . and' [Lt]: you both learned and received, and you heard and saw.

QUESTION—What relationship is indicated by the aorist tense of the four verbs following ἅ 'which'?

They indicate that they refer to the time when Paul was with them in person [Alf, ICC]: things which you learned, etc., from me when I was with you.

QUESTION—What is the content of these four verbs?

1. They refer to ethical matters [Alf, GNC].

2. They refer both to doctrinal and practical matters [Blm].

3. The first two refer to doctrine and the last two to Paul's example [El, My].

QUESTION—What is the relationship between the four verbs in this series?

1. Each of the four verbs has its distinct meaning and form a series of increasing definiteness [Ea].

2. The verbs fall into two pairs, the first two and the last two [EBC, EGT, El, HNTC, ICC, Lg, Ln, Lt, MNTC, My, NIC, NTC, Pl; NAB, TEV, TNT]. The first two verbs refer to instructions given by Paul, the last two to what the Philippians had observed concerning him [EBC, EGT, El, ICC, Lg, Ln, Lt, MNTC, My, NTC; TNT]. The first two refer to Paul's instruction and their acceptance of it; the third and fourth refer

to Paul's preaching to them and their observance of his manner
of life [NIC].

3. The first three go together since they are heard from him and
the fourth is another category since they saw this in him [NIV].

QUESTION—What is the phrase ἐν ἐμοί 'in me' connected with?

Paul is the source of all four kinds of information [Alf, Blm, Ea,
EGT, El, ICC, Lg, Ln, Lt, MNTC, My, NIC, TH, TNTC, WBC;
NIV, NJB, NRSV, REB, TEV, TNT]: the things which you learned,
received, and heard from me, and saw in me. However, this phrase
is related formally only to the last two verbs [Ea, El, ICC, Lg, Ln,
Lt, My, TH] or the last verb [NIC, WBC; NIV], and from this
phrase, the phrase 'from me' should be understood for the first two
verbs [Lt, MNTC], or the first three verbs [NIV].

and the God of-the peace will-be with[a] you.

LEXICON—a. μετά with genitive object (GEL 89.108; 90.60) (BAGD
A.II.1.c.γ. p. 509): 'with' [BAGD, Ea, GEL, HNTC, ICC, Ln,
Mou, NTC, Pl, WBC, WEC; all translations].

QUESTION—What relationship is indicated by καί 'and'?

It introduces the result which will follow if they put these matters
into practice in their lives [Alf, Ea, El, GNC, ICC, Lg, Ln, MNTC,
NTC, Pl, TH, WBC, WC; NAB, NJB, TNT]: practice these things,
and the result will be that the God of peace will be with you.

QUESTION—How are the two nouns related in the genitive
construction ὁ θεὸς τῆς εἰρήνης 'the God of peace'?

The focus is on the fact that God himself will be with them [Bg,
Ln, NIC, NTC, Pl, TH, WBC, WC, WEC].

1. It means that peace is given by God [Ln, Pl, MNTC, My, TH,
TNTC, WC; TEV]: the God who gives peace.

2. It means that peace characterizes God [El]: God who is
characterized by peace.

3. It means that peace is both given by God and characterizes
God [Ea, GNC]: God who gives peace and is characterized by
peace.

4. It means that God both gives the peace and is its source [ICC,
Mou, NIC]: God who is the source and the giver of peace.

QUESTION—What is indicated by the definite article with εἰρήνης 'of
peace'?

The article refers back to 'the peace' mentioned in 4:7 [EBC, Ln]:
the God of the peace which I mentioned previously.

DISCOURSE UNIT: 4:10–23 [Mou, NTC; NASB, REB]. The topic is
Paul's grateful reception of gifts [NTC], their gift to Paul, and his farewell
[Mou], God's provisions [NASB], thanksgivings and greetings [REB].

DISCOURSE UNIT: 4:10-20 [Alf, EBC, HNTC, ICC, Lg, Ln, MNTC, NIC, Pl, TH, TNTC, WBC, WC, WEC; GNT, NAB, NIV, NJB, TEV]. The topic is the gift from the Philippians [EBC], an expression of thanks [WEC], thanks for their gift [Alf, Lg, Ln, NIC, TH, TNTC, WBC, WC; NIV, NJB, TEV], acknowledgment of their gift [GNT], Paul's joy over the Philippians' generosity [HNTC], generosity [NAB], Paul's thankfulness and his self-sufficiency [MNTC], historical and personal comments [Pl].

DISCOURSE UNIT: 4:10-19 [Lt, My(D)].

DISCOURSE UNIT: 4:10-18 [Pl]. The topic is thankfulness for the gift from the Philippians [Pl].

DISCOURSE UNIT: 4:10-14 [EBC, EGT, WEC]. The topic is the recent gift [EBC], a gentle expression of thanks for the gift [EGT], Paul's need and his contentment [WEC].

DISCOURSE UNIT: 4:10-13 [NIC, NTC, WC]. The topic is the beginning of the expression of thanks, and the declaration of the secret Paul has learned [NTC], Paul's contentment whatever the circumstances [NIC], recognition of the Philippians' care for him and his testimony of his contentment whatever the circumstances [WC].

4:10
Now[a] I-rejoiced[b] in[c] (the) Lord greatly that/because[d] already[e] at-some-time[f] you-revived[g] the on-behalf-of[h] me to-be-minded,[i]

LEXICON—a. δέ (GEL 89.94): 'now' [Ln, NTC], 'and' [GEL, WBC], 'but' [Ea, Mou, Pl; KJV, NASB], not explicit [HNTC, WEC; all translations except KJV, NASB]. This word marks the transition to a different subject [Alf, Ln, MNTC, TH], to more personal matters [Alf, Ea, EGT, El, Lg, TNTC], to something which Paul feels he must not forget [EGT, Lt, My(D), Pl, WBC].

b. aorist pass. indic. of χαίρω (GEL 25.125) (BAGD 1. p. 873): 'to rejoice' [BAGD, Ea, GEL, ICC, Ln, Mou, NTC, WBC, WEC; KJV, NASB, NIV, NRSV], 'to be glad' [BAGD, GEL], 'to be delighted' [TNT], 'to be full of joy' [NJB]. This verb is translated 'it is a joy to me' [REB, TEV], 'it was a joy to me' [HNTC, Pl], 'it gave me joy' [NAB]. It is emphatic by word order [TH].

c. ἐν with dative object (GEL 89.119) (BAGD I.5.d. p. 260): 'in' [BAGD, Ea, GEL, HNTC, ICC, Ln, Mou, NTC, Pl, WBC, WEC; all translations except TEV, TNT], 'in union with' [GEL], 'in (one's) life in union with' [TEV], 'as one who belongs to' [TNT].

d. ὅτι (GEL 89.33; 90.21): 'that' [Ea, GEL, HNTC, Ln, Mou, NTC, Pl; all translations], 'because' [GEL, ICC, WBC, WEC], 'since' [GEL], 'in view of the fact that [GEL], 'the fact that' [GEL]. This word introduces the basis for Paul's joy [Lg, Ln, TH, WBC].

e. ἤδη (GEL 67.20) (BAGD 1.c. p. 344): 'already' [GEL, Pl], not explicit [ICC]. The phrase ἤδη ποτέ 'already at some time' is translated 'already now' [GEL], 'at last' [WEC; NIV], 'now at last' [BAGD, GEL, Ln, WBC; KJV, NASB, NJB, NRSV], 'now at length' [BAGD, Ea, GEL, HNTC, Mou, NTC], 'after so long' [REB], 'after so long a time' [TEV, TNT], 'once more' [NAB]. No reproof is implied by this phrase [Alf, Ea, EBC, GNC, HNTC, Lg, My, TH, TNTC]. The implication of ἤδη 'already' is 'not too late' [Bg], the immediate present [Ln]; the phrase implies that it was at an appropriate time [Bg], that it had been some time since they had helped Paul [Ea], that the gift was unexpected [EGT], that something in process or expected has now been completed [ICC].

f. ποτέ (GEL 67.9) (BAGD 1. p. 695): 'at some time' [GEL], 'at some time or other' [BAGD], 'ever' [GEL], 'once more' [Pl], not explicit [ICC]. This word makes an indefinite past of the period of the preceding ἤδη [Alf, Ea, ICC, Ln, Pl]. The implication is 'not too soon' [Bg].

g. aorist act. indic. of ἀναθάλλω (GEL 13.23) (BAGD 2. p. 54): 'to revive' [BAGD, Pl; NASB, NRSV, REB], 'to renew' [NIV], 'to begin again' [TNT], 'to give effect to' [HNTC], 'to flourish' [Ea; KJV], 'to cause to flourish' [WEC], 'to cause to bloom' [NTC], 'to let bloom' [Ln], 'to blossom' [WBC, NJB], 'to blossom out' [Mou], 'to bear fruit' [NAB], 'to be again in a position to' [GEL], 'to be as one was formerly' [GEL], 'to have the chance of showing' [TEV], not explicit [ICC]. It suggests the idea that their care had now blossomed, although it had existed previously [Alf]. No censure is implied [El, Lg, Ln, WBC] but rather joyful surprise [WBC].

h. ὑπέρ with genitive object (GEL 90.36): 'on behalf of' [GEL, Mou], 'for' [Ea, GEL, HNTC, ICC, NTC, Pl, WEC; all translations except KJV], 'for the sake of' [GEL], 'for the benefit of' [Ln], 'of' [WBC; KJV].

i. pres. act. infin. of φρονέω (GEL 26.16; 31.1) (BAGD 1. p. 866): 'to be minded' [Ln], 'to show concern' [TNT], 'to think (of someone)' [BAGD], 'to have an attitude' [GEL], 'to think in a particular manner' [GEL], 'to hold a view' [GEL]. The phrase τὸ φρονεῖν 'the being minded' is translated 'your concern' [HNTC, NTC, WEC; NAB, NASB, NIV, NRSV], 'your care'

[KJV, REB], 'your thoughtful care' [WBC], 'your consideration' [NJB], 'your kind thought' [ICC], 'in mindfulness' [Ea], 'in your thought' [Pl], 'into thought' [Mou], 'that you care' [TEV]. It implies having a vital interest in someone's affairs [WBC]. The subject of this infinitive is the same as for the preceding verb, 'you' [Ln]. The present tense implies that they had been caring about him all along [Ln].

QUESTION—Why is this verse mentioned?

1. It introduces one of Paul's principal purposes in writing this letter [Ea, EGT, GNC, ICC, NTC, TH]; this expression of thankfulness is reserved to the last part of the letter to make it prominent [GNC].

2. It is not a principal reason for writing the letter [Ln]; Paul had sent his thanks earlier [MNTC] when the men who had come with Epaphroditus had returned to Philippi, and he is now telling what the gift means to him [Ln]. Placing this passage near the close of the letter suggests that it is not his first expression of thanks for the gift [MNTC]. The Philippians had evidently complained that Paul had not fully appreciated their gift; he is now gently rebuking them for this misinterpretation of what he had said [MNTC].

3. This passage (4:10–20) is part of a different letter, which Paul sent to the Philippians as soon as their gift was brought to him by Epaphroditus several months earlier [HNTC]. (There is absolutely no manuscript evidence to support this view [WEC].)

QUESTION—What relationship is indicated by the aorist tense of ἐχάρην 'I rejoiced'?

1. It refers to the moment when he received the gift [Ea, GNC, HNTC, Ln, MNTC, WEC]: I rejoiced when I received the gift.

2. It is an epistolary aorist, referring to his feeling of joy as he writes the letter [ICC, Mou, TH, WBC; NIV, NRSV]: I rejoice as I write.

QUESTION—What relationship is indicated by the phrase ἐν κυρίῳ 'in the Lord'?

1. It means 'in reference to the Lord' [Alf].

2. It identifies the nature of his joy as Christian joy [Ea, El, Pl].

3. It means 'in my/our union with the Lord' [ICC, Mou, NTC, TH].

4. It is both Christian joy and joy which comes from his union with Christ [WBC].

5. It refers to the element in which his joy occurred [Lg].

QUESTION—What is meant by ἀνεθάλετε 'you revived'?

1. It is transitive [EGT, HNTC, ICC, NTC, TH, WEC; NIV, NRSV, REB, TNT]: you have revived/caused to revive your caring for me. The phrase τὸ ὑπὲρ ἐμοῦ φρονεῖν 'the in behalf

of me to be minded' (i.e., 'your care for me') is the predicate of
ἀνεθάλετε 'you revived' [EGT, ICC, WEC].

2. It is intransitive [Alf, Bg, Blm, Ea, El, Lg, My]: you have
revived again in caring for me.

QUESTION—What relationship is indicated by the phrase τὸ ὑπὲρ
ἐμοῦ φρονεῖν 'the in behalf of me to be minded'?

The prepositional phrase ὑπέρ ἐμοῦ 'in behalf of me' is the
predicate of the infinitive φρονεῖν 'to be minded' [Bg, Ea, My]: the
being minded for me.

1. The article τό 'the' is connected with the infinitive φρονεῖν 'to
be minded' [Lt], forming the articular infinitive 'the being
minded' [Ln]: the being minded in behalf of me.

2. The article is connected with the prepositional phrase [Alf, Bg,
Ea, Lg, My]: to be minded, which mindedness is in behalf of
me.

for[a] which even/also[b] you-were-being-minded,[c] but you-were-lacking-
opportunity[d].

LEXICON—a. ἐπί with dative object (GEL 89.60; 90.40) (BAGD
II.1.b.γ. p. 287): 'for' [BAGD, Ea, GEL], 'with reference to'
[NTC], 'with a view to' [Mou, Pl], 'for the purpose of' [GEL],
'for the sake of' [GEL], not explicit [WEC]. The phrase ἐφ' ᾧ
'for which' is translated 'since' [Ln], 'wherein' [KJV], 'in that'
[HNTC], 'a thought which' [ICC], 'indeed' [BAGD, WBC;
NASB, NIV, NRSV]. The phrase ἐφ' ᾧ καὶ ἐφρονεῖτε 'for which
you were even being minded' is translated 'I know you always
cared' [REB], 'I know that your concern never ceased' [TNT], 'I
don't mean that you had stopped caring for me' [TEV], 'you
really did have consideration before' [NJB], 'you had been
concerned all along, of course' [NAB].

b. καί (GEL 89.93): 'even' [GEL], 'also' [GEL; KJV], 'indeed'
[ICC, Ln, NTC], 'really' [Pl; NJB], 'I know' [Mou], not explicit
[Ea, HNTC, WBC, WEC; NASB, NIV, NRSV]. This word adds
emphasis to the following verb [El, ICC, Pl], indicating that it is
an addition to the preceding mention of their present caring
[My].

c. imperf. act. indic. of φρονέω (GEL 26.16; 31.1) (BAGD 1.
p. 866): 'to mind' [Ln], 'to take thought' [Mou, Pl], 'to think (of
someone)' [BAGD], 'to be concerned' [HNTC, NTC; NAB,
NASB, NIV, NRSV], 'to have a concern' [WEC], 'to care'
[WBC; REB, TEV], 'to have consideration' [NJB], 'to have an
attitude' [GEL], 'to think in a particular manner' [GEL], 'to
hold a view' [GEL], 'to entertain (a thought)' [ICC], 'to be
careful' [KJV], not explicit [Ea]. The imperfect tense implies
continued concern in the past [Alf, El, ICC, Ln, My, Pl, TH,

WBC], thus stating overtly what was implied by the preceding φρονεῖν 'to be minded' [Ln] and additionally removing any suggestion of reproach [ICC, Lt].

   d. imperf. mid. (deponent = act.) indic. of ἀκαιρέομαι (GEL **67.7**) (BAGD p. 29): 'to lack opportunity' [Ea, GEL, NTC, Pl; KJV, NAB, NASB, REB], 'to have no opportunity' [BAGD, **GEL**, ICC, Ln, WEC; NIV, NJB, NRSV], 'not to have the opportunity' [WBC], 'to be at a loss for opportunity' [Mou], 'to have no chance to' [GEL; TEV, TNT], 'to be unable to find occasion' [HNTC]. The imperfect tense implies a continuing lack of opportunity while they were taking thought [ICC, WBC].

QUESTION—Why is this clause mentioned?

   It is intended to make additionally clear that he does not intend any reproach by what he had just said [Lt, NTC, WEC].

QUESTION—What is the area of meaning of the phrase ἐφ' ᾧ 'for which'?

   1. It refers to a neuter antecedent, not to a person [Alf, Bg, Ea, El, ICC, Lg, Ln, Lt, Mou, My, NTC, Pl, TH; KJV], as Paul always uses it [Alf, Ea, Lg, My].

   1.1 It refers back to ἀνεθάλετε 'you revived' [Alf, Ln].

   1.1.1 It refers to the fact of the reviving of their care [Alf]: with reference to which, namely the purpose of reviving your care, you were mindful.

   1.1.2 It is a causal reference [Ln]: your care revived because you were mindful all along.

   1.2 It refers back to τὸ ὑπὲρ ἐμοῦ 'which is in behalf of me' [Ea, Lg, My, TH], meaning Paul's welfare [Ea, ICC, Lg, Lt, Mou, My, NTC, TH]: with reference to which, namely my interests, you were mindful. This phrase is related to both of the two following verbs [My].

   2. It refers back to ἐμοῦ 'me' [EGT]: with reference to me you were mindful.

4:11

Not that in-accordance-with[a] lack[b] I-am-speaking,

   LEXICON—a. κατά with accusative object (GEL 89.4; 89.8) (BAGD II.5.a.δ. p. 407): 'in accordance with' [GEL], 'with regard to' [GEL, Ln], 'in relation to' [GEL], 'in respect of' [KJV], 'in the tone of' [Mou], 'because of' [BAGD, NTC], 'on account of' [Ea], 'as a result of' [BAGD], 'on the basis of' [BAGD], 'as if complaining of' [HNTC], 'from' [NASB]. This entire phrase is translated 'I do not say this because I am in want' [NAB], 'I do not say this because I have lacked anything' [NJB], 'I am not saying this because I am in need' [NIV], 'I am not saying this because I am in need of anything' [TNT], 'I am not saying this because of any need I had' [WBC], 'I am not saying this because I feel neglected' [TEV], 'I do not speak as though I had been in want' [ICC], 'I do not mean that I was actually in want' [Pl], 'It is not out of a sense of deprivation that I speak' [WEC], 'Not that I am referring to being in need' [NRSV], 'Not that I am speaking of want' [REB]. The sense is causal [El, TH, WBC].

b. ὑστέρησις (GEL 57.37) (BAGD p. 849): 'lack' [BAGD, GEL, Ln], 'need' [BAGD, Mou, WBC; NIV, NRSV, TNT], 'want' [BAGD, Ea, HNTC, ICC, NTC, Pl; KJV, NAB, NASB, REB], 'deprivation' [WEC].

QUESTION—Why is this verse mentioned?

It is added as an explanation [Blm, Ea, EBC, El, Ln, WBC], to avoid a misunderstanding of Paul's meaning in the preceding verse [Alf, Blm, El, Lg, MNTC, My, NTC, TH, TNTC, WEC]: I was not implying that I was in need. He did have needs, but his expression is based on higher motives [Ea, EBC, ICC, TH], namely his joy over the Philippians' generous spirit [Blm, Ln, WBC].

for I have-learned[a] (in the things) in[b] which I-am to-be content.[c]

LEXICON—a. aorist act. indic. of μανθάνω (GEL 27.12; 27.15) (BAGD 4. p. 490): 'to learn' [BAGD, Ea, GEL, HNTC, ICC, Ln, Mou, NTC, Pl, WBC, WEC; all translations], 'to come to realize' [GEL], 'to be taught' [GEL]. The aorist tense refers to his varied experiences considered as a single fact [EGT, ICC, WBC] or to the result of these experiences [TH], to what he learned at the moment of his conversion and his experiences [NTC], at his conversion only, not through long experience [TNTC]. It refers to his learning by experiences [Alf, Ea, El, My, WBC], not taught directly by God [Ea, El], or to being taught by God [Bg].

b. ἐν with dative object (GEL 13.8; 83.13): 'in' [Ea, GEL, HNTC, ICC, Ln, Mou, NTC, Pl, WBC; KJV, NAB, NASB], 'with' [GEL], 'within' [GEL]. The phrase ἐν οἷς εἰμι 'in the things in which I am' is translated 'whatever the circumstances' [NIV], 'whatever my circumstances' [WEC; REB], 'with whatever I have' [NJB, NRSV], 'with what I have' [TEV]. The phrase ἐν οἷς εἰμι αὐτάρκης εἶναι 'in the things in which I am to be content' is translated 'to be independent of my circumstances' [TNT].

c. αὐτάρκης (GEL 25.84) (BAGD p. 122): 'content' [BAGD, Ea, GEL, Ln, NTC, Pl, WEC; KJV, NASB, NIV, NRSV], 'satisfied' [TEV], 'self-sufficient' [BAGD, ICC, WBC; NAB, REB], 'self-sufficing' [Mou], 'sufficient to myself' [HNTC]. The phrase αὐτάρκης εἶναι 'to be content' is translated 'to manage' [NJB]. The self-sufficiency is from God (from Christ [EBC, ICC, NTC, TNTC, WEC]), not from himself [Blm, Ea, EBC, GNC, Ln, TH, TNTC, WBC, WC, WEC].

QUESTION—Why is this clause mentioned?

It introduces the reason why Paul was not speaking on the basis of his needs [Blm, Ea, Lg, Ln, MNTC, WBC]: I was not speaking in reference to my lacks, for I have learned to be self-sufficient.

QUESTION—What is implied by the emphatic ἐγώ 'I'?

1. It means that, whatever may be the experience of others, he has learned to be content [Alf, Ea, EGT, El, ICC, Lg, MNTC, Mou, My, WBC]; it focuses on his many adversities [Bg].
2. It emphasizes his comment that he is not speaking in reference to his lacks [Ln]: I am not speaking in reference to my lacks, for I myself have learned to be self-sufficient.

QUESTION—What relationship is indicated by the phrase ἐν οἷς 'in which'?

1. It refers to his actual circumstances at any time, not to generalized possibilities [Alf, Ea, EGT, El, Lg, MNTC, My, TNTC]: in the circumstances in which I actually am at any given time.
2. It refers to his present circumstances [Bg, EBC, ICC, WC]: in the circumstances in which I actually am now.
3. It refers to his present possessions [TH; NJB, NRSV, TEV]: with the possessions which I have.

4:12

I-know[a] even/both[b] to-be-humbled,[c] I-know[a] also to abound;[d]

LEXICON—a. perf. (with pres. meaning) act. indic. of the irregular verb οἶδα; (GEL 28.1; 28.7) (BAGD 3. p. 556): 'to know' [Ea, GEL, Ln, Mou, NTC, Pl, WBC, WEC; all translations except NAB], 'to know how' [BAGD], 'to understand how' [BAGD], 'to know how to' [GEL], 'to be able to' [BAGD], 'to be experienced . . . to know' [NAB], 'to be schooled' [HNTC]; this entire verse, not explicit [ICC]. The sense is to know how to do something [El, ICC, Lg, Ln, MNTC, My, NIC, WBC], further explaining the preceding clause [El, WBC]. This knowledge is the result of having learned [ICC, Lg, My, NIC, TH, WC], the result of divine instruction [Mou], the source of his learning mentioned in the preceding verse [Ea]. The repetition of this verb indicates emphasis [Ea, ICC, MNTC, TH, TNTC, WBC], indicating that he was as well acquainted with abundance as with lack [MNTC].

b. καί (GEL 89.93; 89.102) (BAGD I.6. p. 393): 'even' [GEL]. The combination καὶ... καί is translated 'both... and' [BAGD, GEL, Mou; KJV, TNT], 'both... as well' [Ln], 'not only... but also' [BAGD], 'also... 'also' [Ea, Pl], not explicit... 'also' [HNTC, NTC; NASB], not explicit... 'too' [NJB], not explicit [WBC, WEC; NAB, NIV, NRSV, REB, TEV]. These two instances of καί add emphasis to the verbs which follow them [Alf]. The first occurrence, 'also', introduces the specific instances; the second occurrence, 'and', implies a contrast by what follows [Ea].

c. pres. pass. infin. of ταπεινόω (GEL 87.62; **87.63**; 88.56) (BAGD 2.c. p. 805): 'to be humbled' [BAGD, GEL, WBC], 'to make humble' [BAGD, GEL], 'to be made lowly' [Ln], 'to be brought low' [GEL; NAB], 'to run low' [Mou], 'to be abased' [Ea; KJV], 'to be in need' [NIV, TEV], 'to have little' [NRSV], 'to be reduced to penury' [Pl], 'to have nothing' [REB], 'to live modestly' [NJB], 'to live in humble circumstances' [GEL], 'to live in straitened circumstances' [NTC], 'to live in humble conditions' [TNT], 'to get along with humble means' [NASB]. This verb is also translated as a noun: 'dearth' [WEC], 'indigence' [HNTC].

d. pres. act. infin. of περισσεύω (GEL 57.24): 'to abound' [Ea, Ln, WBC; KJV], 'to have plenty' [NTC; NIV, NRSV, REB], 'to be in abundance' [Pl], 'to have an abundance' [NAB], 'to have an overabundance' [GEL], 'to have more than enough' [GEL; TEV], 'to run over' [Mou], 'to live in prosperity' [NASB], 'to live in prosperous conditions' [TNT], 'to live luxuriously' [NJB]. This verb is also translated as a noun: 'abundance' [WEC; HNTC].

QUESTION—Why is this verse mentioned?

It specifies how Paul is self-sufficient or contented [Lg, TH, WBC]: I am contented because I know these things. It expands on the preceding thought [Lg, TH. WBC].

QUESTION—What relationship is indicated by the two instances of καί 'both/even'?

1. The sense is 'both... and' in spite of the insertion of the repeated οἶδα 'I know' [EBC, Ln, Lt; KJV, TNT]: I know both to be humbled and I know to abound. The repetition of 'I know' gives emphasis [Ln, Lt] and adds balance to the two phrases [Ln].

2. The first occurrence connects the preceding general statement to the following infinitive [El, ICC, Lg, My], the second connects and contrasts the two infinitives [El, Lg, My]: I have learned to be content; that is, also to be humbled and (in contrast) to abound.

in[a] everything and in[a] all-things I-have-learned-the-secret[b] both to-be-well-fed[c] and to-be-hungry[d] and to-have-plenty[e] and to-lack;[f]

LEXICON—a. ἐν with dative object (GEL 13.8; 83.13): 'in' [Ea, GEL, HNTC, Ln, Mou]. The phrase ἐν παντὶ καὶ ἐν πᾶσιν 'in everything and in all things' is translated 'in any and all circumstances' [NTC; NRSV], 'in every and all circumstances' [WBC], 'in any and every circumstance' [NASB], 'in each and all circumstances of life' [Pl], 'whatever my circumstances' [TNT], 'with every circumstance' [NAB], 'in any and every situation' [NIV], 'with each and every situation' [WEC], 'everywhere and in all things' [KJV], 'anywhere, at any time' [TEV], 'in every way . . . all conditions' [NJB], 'thoroughly' [REB]. This phrase emphasizes the comprehensiveness of the reference [Alf].

b. perf. pass. indic. of μυέω (GEL 27.14) (BAGD p. 529): 'to learn the secret' [BAGD, GEL, NTC, WBC; NASB, NIV, NRSV, TEV], 'to be let into the secret' [Mou], 'to master the secret' [NJB], 'to be given the secret' [TNT], 'to be initiated into the secret' [Pl], 'to be initiated' [BAGD, Ea, Ln, Pl; REB], 'to be taught' [WEC], 'to be instructed' [KJV], 'to become adept' [HNTC], 'to learn how to cope' [NAB]. It is parallel to the preceding οἶδα 'I know' [WBC]. It implies thorough knowledge from experience [Blm, Ea, El, TH, WBC] involving difficulties [EGT, MNTC, WBC]. The sense is general, not technical [Alf, EBC, EGT, El, Ln, MNTC, TH, WC]. It means trained in a secret [Lt, My] not known to everyone [Bg, Mou, My]. The perfect tense implies the continuance of the results of the instruction [Lg, Ln]. This verb is the climax of the two preceding verbs referring to knowledge [Lg, My].

c. pres. pass. infin. of χορτάζω (GEL 23.16) (BAGD 2.a. p. 884): 'to be well-fed' [WBC; NIV, NRSV], 'to be full fed' [HNTC, Mou], 'to eat one's fill' [BAGD; TNT], 'to be satisfied with food' [GEL], 'to feed' [BAGD], 'to eat well' [NAB], 'to fill' [BAGD], 'to be filled' [Ea, Ln, NTC; NASB], 'to be full' [WEC; KJV, TEV], 'to satisfy' [BAGD], 'to be satisfied' [BAGD], 'to have plenty' [Pl]. This verb is also translated 'fullness' [REB], 'full stomach' [NJB].

d. pres. act. infin. of πεινάω (GEL 23.29) (BAGD 1. p. 640): 'to be hungry' [BAGD, GEL, Ln, Mou, NTC, WEC; KJV, NIV, TEV], 'to hunger' [BAGD], 'to have hunger' [GEL], 'to go hungry' [HNTC, WBC; NAB, NASB, NRSV, TNT], 'to be famished' [Ea, Pl]. This verb is also translated 'hunger' [REB], 'empty stomach' [NJB].

e. pres. act. infin. of περισσεύω (GEL 57.24): (see d. above in the first clause). The following translate this occurrence differently than the preceding occurrence: 'to have plenty' [NRSV], 'to live in plenty' [NIV], 'to experience plenty' [WEC], 'to be well provided for' [NAB], 'to be amply supplied' [HNTC], 'to have abundance' [Pl; NASB], 'to prosper' [TNT], 'to have more than enough' [WBC], 'to have too much' [TEV]. This verb is also translated as a noun: 'plenty' [NJB, REB].

f. pres. pass. infin. of ὑστερέω (GEL 57.37) (BAGD 2. p. 849): 'to lack' [BAGD, GEL, Ln], 'to come short' [Mou], 'to experience shortage' [WEC], 'to be in want' [Ea, GEL, HNTC, NTC, Pl], 'to live in want' [NIV], 'to be in need' [NRSV, TNT], 'to be in need of' [GEL], 'to suffer need' [KJV, NASB], 'to go without' [BAGD], 'to do without' [NAB], 'to have too little' [WBC; TEV]. This verb is also translated as a noun: 'poverty' [NJB, REB].

QUESTION—What is the meaning of the two phrases ἐν παντί 'in every' and ἐν πᾶσιν 'in all'?

1. Both phrases refer to circumstances [Alf, Ea, EBC, EGT, El, ICC, Lg, Lt, MNTC, Mou, My, Pl, WC; NAB, NASB, NIV, NRSV, TNT]. They relate to ἐν οἷς 'the things in which' in the preceding clause [Lg, My]. These two prepositional phrases are emphatic by forefronting [My].

1.1 The first refers to specific occasions, the second refers to circumstances in general [Alf, Ea, El, EBC, ICC, Lt, Mou, WC; NRSV]: in every individual situation and in all things in general.

1.2 Both phrases together form a general expression [EGT, MNTC, My, Pl; NAB, NASB, NIV, REB, TNT]: in all sorts of situations.

2. The first refers to circumstances, the second to ways or respects [Ln]: in everything and in all ways.

3. The first refers to ways or respects, the second to circumstances [NIC; NJB]: in every way and in all conditions.

4. The first refers to places, the second to circumstances [KJV]: in every place and in all things.

5. The first refers to place, the second to time [TEV]: anywhere, at any time.

6. The first refers to circumstances, the second refers to persons [Bg]: in everything and in reference to all people.

QUESTION—What is the verb μεμύημαι 'I am instructed' connected with?

1. It is connected with the two preceding phrases [Ea, El, My, WBC, NIV]: in everything and in all things I have learned the secret. The preceding phrases indicate the universality of his instruction [Ea].

2. It is connected with the four following infinitives [Alf, EGT, Lg]: I have learned the secret of having much or little. The preceding phrases describe the conditions in which this instruction is revealed [Lg].

3. It is connected with the preceding phrases and the following infinitives [ICC; KJV, NAB, NASB, NRSV]: in everything and in all things I have learned the secret both to have much or little.

QUESTION—What relationship is indicated by the chiastic word order, with verbs implying "little/much" in the first clause and "much/little" in the second?

It is intended for emphasis on the expressed contrast [Bg].

QUESTION—What is the area of meaning of the four infinitives in this clause, χορτάζεσθαι καὶ πεινᾶν καὶ περισσεύειν καὶ ὑστερεῖσθαι 'to be well-fed and to be hungry and to have plenty and to lack'?

They fall into two pairs [Bg, Blm, Ea, Ln, Pl, TH, WBC; all translations], the four occurrences of καί being 'both . . . and, both . . . and' [Ea, Ln; KJV]. They refer to varied and changing circumstances, not to one continuing condition [Ea].

1. The first two infinitives refer to food, the second two to needs in general [Ea, Ln, TH; all translations]: both to have plenty of food and to be hungry, both to have what I need in general and to lack what I need.

2. The second pair repeat the sense of the first pair for further explanation [Pl, WBC]: 'both to be well-fed and to be hungry; that is, both to have plenty and to lack'.

3. The first two, 'both to be well-fed and to be hungry', refer to a short time; the second two, 'both to have plenty and to lack', refer to longer times [Bg].

4. The four refer to the preceding infinitives ταπεινοῦσθαι καὶ περισσεύειν 'to be humbled and to abound', the first two of these latter four making the sense of the preceding pair plainer, while the last two give a stronger sense of being utterly lacking in needed things [Blm].

4:13

(for/in-regard-to) all-things I-have-strength[a] in[b] the-(one) enabling[c] me.

TEXT—Some manuscripts add Χριστῷ 'Christ' at the end of this verse, giving the translation 'in Christ who enables me'. GNT does not deal with this variant. Only KJV, TEV, and TNT read 'Christ' (although TEV and TNT probably do not accept this addition but read 'Christ' only for clarity) and Blm indicates uncertainty concerning including or omitting it.

LEXICON—a. pres. act. indic. of ἰσχύω (GEL **74.9**) (BAGD 2.a.
p. 383): 'to have strength' [HNTC, Pl; NAB, TEV], 'to have the
strength to' [GEL], 'to be strong' [Ln, Mou], 'to be strong
enough' [WEC; TNT], 'to have power' [BAGD], 'to have the
power' [WBC], 'to be able' [BAGD, **GEL**; REB]. This verb is
translated 'I can' [Ea, ICC, NTC; KJV, NASB, NIV, NRSV].
The phrase πάντα ἰσχύω 'I have strength for all things' is
translated 'there is nothing I cannot do' [NJB], 'I am able to
face all conditions' [GEL]. The present tense of the indicative
mood here indicates a general or timeless state, or a continuing
state, meaning that he always has this strength from Christ
[Mou, WBC]. The active voice of the verb focuses on Paul's
sufficiency [WBC].
  b. ἐν with dative object (GEL 89.119; 90.6): 'in' [Ea, GEL, HNTC,
ICC, Mou; NAB, NJB], 'in union with' [GEL, WBC], 'when
united with' [Pl], 'in connection with' [Ln], 'through' [NTC,
WEC; KJV, NASB, NIV, NRSV, REB, TNT], 'by' [GEL; TEV].
This word indicates the source of Paul's strength [Blm]. The
meaning is by virtue of his spiritual union with Christ [Alf, Ea,
El, HNTC, MNTC, My, NTC, Pl, TNTC]. Christ gives him this
ability [TH].
  c. pres. act. participle of ἐνδυναμόω (GEL **74.6**) (BAGD 1.
p. 263): 'to enable' [GEL], 'to make (one) able' [**GEL**, Mou], 'to
empower' [GEL, Ln, WEC], 'to give power' [Pl; TNT], 'to make
strong' [HNTC], 'to strengthen' [BAGD, Ea, ICC; KJV, NASB,
NJB, NRSV], 'to give strength' [NIV, REB], 'to infuse strength
into' [NTC], 'to infuse with strength' [WBC]. The participial
phrase τῷ ἐνδυναμοῦντί με 'the one enabling me' is translated
'him who is the source of my strength' [NAB], 'the power that
Christ gives me' [TEV]. The present participle indicates a
continual strengthening, but none of the commentaries deal with
this point.
QUESTION—Why is this clause mentioned?
  1. It further expands what he has been saying, making it universal
[Alf, Ea, El, ICC, Lg, MNTC, My, NIC, NTC, WC]: not only in
the areas I have mentioned, but in everything. Πάντα
'everything' is the accusative of measure or extent [Ea, El, Lg]
or reference [EBC, Ln]. The meaning is not limited to the
preceding areas [Alf, Ea, MNTC, WC], but does refer
principally to his Christian duties [Blm, Ea, My(D), NTC], to
what the Lord may send to him [Ln, Mou]. 'To do all things'
means to face all conditions [GEL, TH, TNTC; TEV], to face
anything [TNT], to meet any circumstance of life [NIC, WC].

2. It summarizes only the aspects mentioned in 4:11–12 [TNTC, WBC]: I have strength for all of the situations I have mentioned.

QUESTION—Who is the one who strengthens Paul?

It is Christ [Alf, Blm, Ea, EBC, El, GNC, HNTC, Lt, MNTC, Mou, My, NIC, NTC, Pl, TH, TNTC, WBC, WEC; KJV, TEV, TNT]: Christ who strengthens me.

DISCOURSE UNIT: 4:14–19 [WC]. The topic is an acknowledgment of the Philippians' kindness and a prayer for God's blessings on them.

DISCOURSE UNIT: 4:14–18 [NIC, NTC]. The topic is the completion of the expression of thanks [NTC], an expression of appreciation for their help [NIC].

4:14

Nevertheless,[a] you-did[b] well[c] having-shared[d] my affliction.[e]

LEXICON—a. πλήν (GEL 89.130) (BAGD 1.c. p. 669): 'nevertheless' [GEL, HNTC, NTC, Pl; NASB], 'nonetheless' [NAB], 'yet' [Mou, WBC; NIV], 'but' [GEL; TEV, TNT], 'however' [BAGD], 'all the same' [NJB, REB], 'in any case' [BAGD; NRSV], 'only' [Ln] 'notwithstanding' [KJV], 'howbeit' [Ea], 'of course' [WEC], not explicit [ICC].

b. aorist act. indic. of ποιέω (GEL 90.45) (BAGD I.2.a.γ. p. 682): 'to do' [BAGD, Ea, GEL, HNTC, Ln, Mou, NTC, Pl, WEC; KJV, NASB], 'to act' [BAGD]. The phrase καλῶς ἐποιήσατε 'well having shared' is translated 'it was kind of you' [BAGD; NAB, NRSV, REB, TNT], 'it was good of you' [WBC; NIV, NJB], 'it was very good of you' [TEV], 'it was a beautiful thing for you' [ICC]. This phrase in the past tense implies 'thank you' [GNC, WBC].

c. καλῶς (GEL 65.23) (BAGD 4.a. p. 401): 'well' [BAGD, Ea, GEL, Mou, WEC; KJV, NASB], 'rightly' [BAGD], 'correctly' [BAGD], 'nobly' [Ln, NTC]. This word is also translated as a phrase: 'what is right' [BAGD], 'what was right' [HNTC], 'a noble thing' [Pl]. The word implies that it was a beautiful [ICC, WC] or noble deed [Ln, MNTC, WC].

d. aorist act. participle of συγκοινωνέω (GEL 34.4) (BAGD 1. p. 774): 'to share' [NTC, WEC; all translations except KJV, TEV], 'to participate with' [BAGD, GEL], 'to join together in participating' [Mou], 'to be in partnership with' [GEL], 'to become partners with' [WBC], 'to make (oneself) (someone's) partner' [HNTC], 'to put (oneself) in fellowship with' [ICC], 'to have fellowship with' [Ea, Pl], 'to fellowship jointly' [Ln], 'to associate with' [GEL], 'to help' [TEV], 'to communicate' [KJV]. The compounded preposition συν- indicates that a number of persons had joined together in sharing with him [Bg, Ln]. The action of the aorist participle is simultaneous with the action of the verb ἐποιήσατε 'you did' [El, My] (actually, it refers to the *same action* as that of the verb). Paul considers the gift not merely as financial help [TH] but especially as an act of sympathy [Alf, El, GNC, Ln, Lt, MNTC, Mou, My, NIC, Pl, WBC]; their sympathy was expressed in sending Epaphroditus [TH, WBC].

e. θλῖψις (GEL 22.2) (BAGD 1. p. 362): 'affliction' [BAGD, Ea, HNTC, ICC, Ln, NTC, Pl, WEC; KJV, NASB], 'hardships' [WBC; NAB, NJB], 'troubles' [NIV, REB, TEV, TNT], 'distress' [BAGD; NRSV], 'tribulation' [BAGD, Mou], 'trouble and suffering' [GEL], 'suffering' [GEL], 'persecution' [GEL]. The reference is to his hardships in general, not merely his financial needs [Alf, El, Lg, MNTC, My, WBC].

QUESTION—What relationship is indicated by πλήν 'nevertheless'?

It adds a comment to avoid any implication that he did not appreciate their gift [Blm, Ea, EBC, El, GNC, HNTC, ICC, MNTC, NIC, NTC, WBC]: in spite of my contentment in any situation, I am thankful that you sent the gift. It turns attention from Paul's situation to the Philippians and their gift [Lg, MNTC, TH, WBC].

QUESTION—What relationship is indicated by the use of the participle συγκοινωνήσαντες 'having shared'?

1. It specifies what it was that they had done well [Blm, Ea, El, HNTC, ICC, Lg]: you did well in sharing with me.
2. It tells why he said that they had done well [Bg]: you did well because you shared with me.

QUESTION—What relationship is indicated by μου 'my'?

1. It is connected with θλίψει 'affliction' [Ea, EGT, El, ICC, Lg, Ln, MNTC, Mou; KJV, NAB, NASB, NIV, NRSV, REB]: you shared in my afflictions. It is forefronted, emphasizing the Philippians' relationship with Paul [EGT].
2. It is connected with the participle [My]: you shared with me in the afflictions.
3. It is connected with both the preceding participle and the following noun [Blm]: you shared with me in my afflictions.

DISCOURSE UNIT: 4:15–20 [EBC, WEC]. The topic is the previous gifts [EBC], the theological implications of giving [WEC].

DISCOURSE UNIT: 4:15–19 [EGT]. The topic is the Philippians' generosity and its reward from God.

4:15

Now/But[a] you-know even/also you, Philippians,

> LEXICON—a. δέ (GEL 89.94): 'now' [WBC; KJV], 'but' [Ea, Mou, Pl, WEC], 'moreover' [Ln, NTC; NIV], 'indeed' [NRSV], 'and' [GEL, HNTC; NASB], not explicit [ICC; NAB, NJB, REB, TEV, TNT].
>
> QUESTION—What relationship is indicated by δέ 'now/but'?
>
> This word introduces the transition from their earlier help to the present help [Alf, Ea, EGT, El, ICC, Lg, Ln, My, WBC], to show his willingness to receive their gifts by reminding them that he had accepted their help previously [Lt].
>
> QUESTION—What is meant by καὶ ὑμεῖς 'you also'?
>
> It emphasizes the fact that the Philippians as well as Paul knew [Alf, Ea, EGT, El, ICC, Lg, Ln, Lt, My, NTC, Pl, WBC]: you also as well as I. The ὑμεῖς 'you' is emphatic [TH].
>
> QUESTION—What is indicated by Paul's calling them by name, Φιλιππήσιοι 'Philippians'?
>
> It further emphasizes the fact that they were the ones who had helped Paul [Alf, El], and it indicates affection [El, GNC, ICC, Lg, Pl, TH, WC].
>
> > 1. It is used as a noun of direct address [Ea, El, GNC, HNTC, Lg, Lt, MNTC, Mou, Pl, WEC; NAB, NASB]: you know, Philippians.
> >
> > 2. It is in apposition with the subject of οἴδατε 'you know' [Ln, NTC, WBC; all translations except NAB, NASB]: you Philippians know.

that in[a] (the) beginning of-the gospel, when I-went-out from[b] Macedonia,

> LEXICON—a. ἐν with dative object (GEL 67.136): 'in' [HNTC, ICC, Ln, Mou, NTC, Pl, WBC; all translations except NAB, NASB], 'at' [Ea; NAB, NASB], 'during' [GEL], 'in the course of' [GEL]. The phrase ἐν ἀρχῇ τοῦ εὐαγγελίου 'in the beginning of the gospel' is translated 'when the gospel first came to you' [WEC].
>
> > b. ἀπό with genitive object (GEL 90.15): 'from' [Ea, GEL, HNTC, Ln, NTC, Pl, WBC; KJV, NASB, NIV, REB]. The phrase ἐξῆλθον ἀπό 'I went out from' is translated 'I left' [Mou, WEC; NAB, NJB, NRSV, TEV, TNT], 'I was leaving' [ICC].
>
> QUESTION—What is meant by the phrase ἐν ἀρχῇ τοῦ εὐαγγελίου 'in the beginning of the gospel'?
>
> > 1. It refers to the time when they first received the gospel [Alf, Bg, Blm, Ea, EGT, GNC, ICC, Lg, Lt, MNTC, Mou, NIC, NTC, Pl, TH, TNTC, WC]: when you first received the gospel. It also includes the beginning of their participation in the gospel ministry [GNC].

2. It refers to the period from the time when the gospel was first preached to them down to the present, some ten years later [My]: during this period of the beginning of the gospel among you.

3. It refers to the fact that only when Paul came to Macedonia was he fully in charge of his gospel ministry, since previously he had been subservient to Barnabas [WBC].

QUESTION—What is the phrase ὅτε ἐξῆλθεν ἀπὸ Μακεδονίας 'when I went out from Macedonia' connected with?

1. It is connected with the preceding phrase ἐν ἀρχῇ τοῦ εὐαγγελίου 'in the beginning of the gospel' [Alf, Ea, GNC, ICC, Lg, Ln, MNTC, My, NTC, TH; REB, TEV]: in the beginning of the gospel; that is, when I went out from Macedonia.

1.1 He left Macedonia soon after preaching in Philippi, and on that specific occasion (as indicated by the aorist ἐξῆλθον 'I went out' [EBC, My]) only the Philippians helped him [Ea, EBC, El, GNC, ICC, MNTC, My].

1.2 The reference is to help given after he had left Macedonia [Lt]: after I had left Macedonia you alone helped me.

2. It is connected with the following statement [Bg, NIC]: when I went out from Macedonia no other church helped me.

no church shared[a] with-me in/for[b] (the) matter[c] of-giving[d] and receiving[e] except[f] you only,

LEXICON—a. aorist act. indic. of κοινωνέω (GEL 57.98) (BAGD 2. p. 438): 'to share' [GEL, WEC; NAB, NASB, NIV, NRSV, REB], 'to give a share' [BAGD], 'to contribute a share' [BAGD], 'to contribute' [ICC], 'to make (someone) (one's) partner' [BAGD], 'to enter into partnership with' [HNTC, NTC, WBC], 'to participate with' [Mou], 'to make common account with' [NJB], 'to have fellowship with' [Pl], 'to fellowship' [Ln], 'to take practical interest' [TNT], 'to help . . . to share' [TEV], 'to communicate' [Ea; KJV].

b. εἰς with accusative object (GEL 89.57; 89.76) (BAGD 4.g. p. 229): 'in' [HNTC, Mou, NTC, WBC, WEC; NASB, NIV, NJB, NRSV, REB, TNT], 'for' [BAGD], 'for the purpose of' [GEL], 'in order to' [GEL], 'as regards' [Ln], 'to' [Ea], 'by' [GEL], 'by means of' [GEL], 'through' [GEL], 'concerning' [GEL], 'with respect to' [GEL], 'with reference to' [GEL], 'about' [GEL], not explicit [TEV]. The phrase εἰς λόγον 'in the matter' is translated 'as regards' [Pl], 'as concerning' [KJV]. The phrase εἰς λόγον δόσεως καὶ λήμψεως 'in the matter of giving and receiving' is translated 'to my necessities' [ICC], 'by giving me something for what it had received' [NAB]. This word specifies the area of sharing [Bg].

c. λόγος (GEL 13.115) (BAGD 2.b. p. 478): 'matter' [GEL, Mou; NASB, NIV, NJB, NRSV], 'matters' [WEC], 'account' [Ea, Ln, NTC], 'accounting' [HNTC, WBC], 'settlement' [BAGD], not explicit [REB, TEV, TNT].

d. δόσις (GEL 57.71) (BAGD 2. p. 205): 'giving' [BAGD, GEL, Ln, Mou, Pl; KJV, NASB, NIV, NRSV, REB], 'gift' [Ea], 'expenditure' [WEC; NJB, TNT], 'expenditures' [HNTC, NTC, WBC], 'losses' [TEV], 'debit' [BAGD].

e. λῆμψις (GEL 57.125) (BAGD p. 473): 'receiving' [BAGD, GEL, Ln; KJV, NASB, NIV, NRSV, REB], 'receipt' [Ea], 'receipts' [HNTC, NTC, WBC; NJB], 'taking' [Mou, Pl], 'profits' [TEV], 'income' [WEC; TNT], 'credit' [BAGD].

f. εἰ μή (GEL 89.131): 'except' [Ln, NTC, WBC, WEC; NAB, NIV, NRSV], 'except that' [GEL], 'with the exception of' [Pl], 'but' [Ea, GEL, HNTC, Mou; KJV, NASB], 'but only' [GEL], 'other than' [NJB]. The phrase οὐδεμία ἐκκλησία εἰ μὴ ὑμεῖς μόνοι 'no church except you only' is translated 'you were the only church' [ICC, TNT]. The phrase οὐδεμία ἐκκλησία ἐκοινώνησεν εἰ μὴ ὑμεῖς μόνοι 'no church shared except you only' is translated 'yours was the only church to share' [REB], 'you were the only church to help . . . you were the only ones who shared' [TEV].

QUESTION—What is meant by the phrase εἰς λόγον δόσεως καὶ λήμψεως 'in the matter of giving and receiving'?

1. The Philippians gave material help and Paul received it [Alf, Bg, ICC, Lt, Mou, My(D), NTC, Pl, TH]: the matter of your giving to me and my receiving from you. Paul's expression here is in harmony with his reluctance to speak overtly of financial matters, but none of the commentaries mention this point.

2. The Philippians gave him material help, Paul gave them spiritual help [EGT, El, Lg, MNTC, TNTC; NAB]: the matter of our mutual giving, you materially to me and I spiritually to you.

3. The Philippians gave him material help and received spiritual blessing from their gift; Paul received material help from them [My].

4. The Philippians gave him material help and they received a receipt from Paul [WBC].

4:16

because/that even[a] in[b] Thessalonica both[c] once[d] and[c] twice[e] for[f] the need[g] to-me you sent.[h]

TEXT—Instead of εἰς τὴν χρείαν μοι ἐπέμψατε 'you sent *to me* for the need', some manuscripts read εἰς τὴν χρείαν μου ἐπέμψατε 'you sent for *my* need', and other manuscripts omit εἰς 'for' and read 'you sent to me the need' (i.e., 'the needed things'). GNT includes εἰς 'for' and μοι 'to me' ('you sent to me for the need') with a C rating, indicating a considerable degree of doubt; this text is read by Alf, Ea, EGT, El, ICC, Lg, Lt, My, NTC, WBC, and probably by HNTC, NRSV, TEV, TNT. The second form ('you sent for *my* need') is probably read by Ln, Mou, Pl, WEC, KJV, NAB, NASB, REB; and the third form ('you sent to me the need') by NIV, NJB; however, some of these renderings may be merely stylistic differences rather than indicating a reading differing from the GNT text.

LEXICON—a. καί (GEL 89.93): 'even' [Ea, GEL, HNTC, ICC, Ln, Mou, NTC, Pl, WEC; all translations except NJB, TEV], not explicit [WBC; NJB, TEV]. It is emphatic, emphasizing how soon they had helped him [El, Lg, MNTC, My, TH, TNTC, WBC]; it emphasizes the fact that even though he was working in the larger and richer city of Thessalonica the help had come from Philippi [ICC, Pl].

   b. ἐν with dative object (GEL 83.13): 'in' [Ea, GEL, HNTC, ICC, Ln, Mou, NTC, Pl, WBC, WEC; all translations except NAB, REB], 'at' [NAB, REB].

   c. καί ... καί (GEL 89.102) (BAGD I.6. p. 393): 'both ... and' [BAGD, Ea, GEL, Ln]. The phrase καὶ ἅπαξ καὶ δίς 'both once and twice' is translated 'more than once' [HNTC, ICC, Pl, WBC; NASB, NRSV, REB, TEV, TNT], 'once and again' [NTC, WEC; KJV], 'again and again' [NIV], 'not once but twice' [NAB], 'twice' [NJB], 'twice over' [Mou]. The καί ... καί 'both ... and' implies emphasis [Ea, Ln, My] to praise the Philippians [My].

   d. ἅπαξ (GEL 60.70) (BAGD 1. p. 80): 'once' [Ea, Ln, NTC; KJV, NAB]. The phrase ἅπαξ καὶ δίς 'once and twice' is translated 'more than once' [BAGD, GEL], 'several times' [GEL], 'again and again' [BAGD], 'once and again' [KJV].

   e. δίς (GEL 60.69): 'twice' [GEL; NAB], 'a second time' [Ea].

   f. εἰς with accusative object (GEL 90.41) (BAGD 4.d. p. 229): 'for' [BAGD, Ea, GEL, Ln, WEC; NAB, NASB, TNT], 'on behalf of' [GEL], 'unto' [KJV], 'to' [ICC, Mou; REB], 'to meet' [HNTC, WBC], 'to alleviate' [NTC], 'to minister to' [Pl], different text [NIV, NJB]. The phrase εἰς τὴν χρείαν 'for the need' is translated 'help for my needs' [NRSV], 'when I needed help' [TEV]. The meaning is 'for the purpose of supplying' [Alf]. It indicates the destination of the help [Ea, El].

   g. χρεία (GEL 57.40) (BAGD 2. p. 885): 'need' [BAGD, GEL, Ln, Mou, NTC], 'needs' [HNTC, Pl, WBC, WEC; NAB, NASB, NRSV, REB, TNT], 'necessity' [Ea; KJV], 'necessities' [ICC], 'lack' [BAGD, GEL], 'want' [BAGD], 'aid' [NIV], 'what I needed' [NJB]. The article with this noun refers to the specific need which Paul felt at that time [El, ICC, Lg, My] and implies the possessive pronoun 'my' [El, ICC, Lg] and the fact that the need was known to the Philippians [Lg].

h. aorist act. indic. of πέμπω (GEL 15.193) (BAGD 2. p. 642): 'to send' [Ea, HNTC, Ln, Mou, NTC, Pl, WBC, WEC; all translations except REB], 'to send (something)' [GEL], 'to send (something to someone)' [BAGD], 'to send (by someone)' [GEL], 'to contribute' [ICC; REB].

QUESTION—What relationship is indicated by ὅτι 'because/that'?

1. It indicates the grounds for the statement in the preceding verse [Alf, Ea, EBC, ICC, Lg, NIC, TH]: you were the only ones who shared, because you helped me even as soon as when I was in Thessalonica. This verse is a supporting statement for 4:15 and the gifts referred to in 4:16 are the same as the ones mentioned in 4:15 [MNTC, TH].

2. It indicates the grounds for the statement ἐν ἀρχῇ τοῦ εὐαγγελίου 'in the beginning of the gospel' [El]: you helped me in the beginning of the gospel work, because you helped me even in Thessalonica.

3. It indicates the content of οἴδατε 'you know' in the preceding verse, telling further what they knew [EGT, WBC]: you know that you sent me help in Thessalonica.

4. It explains 'except you only' [Ln]: no church shared except you; namely, you sent for my need.

QUESTION—What does the phrase ἐν Θεσσαλονίκῃ 'in Thessalonica' modify?

1. It modifies μοι 'to me' [Lg]. It is a brachylogy (a shortening) [El], expressed from Paul's point of view, telling where he was when he received the gifts [El, Lg, My]: you sent the gifts, and I received them in Thessalonica.

2. It modifies the verb of action ἐπέμψατε 'you sent' and means that the messengers had gone *into* Thessalonica and had given him the gifts *in* that city [Ea].

QUESTION—What is meant by ἅπαξ καὶ δίς 'once and twice'?

1. It means that they had sent gifts on two occasions [Alf, Bg, EGT, El, ICC, Lg(H), Ln, Mou, My, Pl, WBC; NAB, NJB]: you sent once and then a second time. This is an emphatic idiom [El].

2. It means that they had sent gifts on several occasions [NIC; NIV]: you sent gifts on several occasions.

3. It means merely 'more than once' with no indication of the number of times [GNC, Lt, TH, TNTC, WC; NASB, NRSV, REB, TEV, TNT].

QUESTION—Why does ἐπέμψατε 'you sent' have no expressed object?

It is because the readers knew what they had sent [My]; it is implied by the context [Ea].

4:17

Not that I-seek[a] the gift,[b]

LEXICON—a. pres. act. indic. of ἐπιζητέω (GEL 25.9) (BAGD 2.a. p. 292): 'to seek' [HNTC, NTC; NASB, NRSV], 'to seek for' [Ea], 'to look for' [NIV, TNT], 'to be in quest of' [Mou], 'to be out for' [Ln], 'to want to receive' [GEL; TEV], 'to desire' [GEL, Pl; KJV], 'to wish for' [BAGD], 'to be eager for' [NAB], 'to set one's heart on' [REB], 'to have one's heart set on' [WBC], 'to be interested in receiving' [WEC], 'to value most' [NJB]. This verb is also translated 'my chief interest' [ICC]. The prefixed preposition ἐπι- is intensive [Lt, TH]; it implies the direction of the desire [Alf, Ea, El, ICC, Lg, My, Pl], although this sense is weak [El]; it is both intensive and directional [WBC]. The present indicative implies a continuing attitude of mind [Alf, Ea, El, ICC, Lg, MNTC, My].

b. δόμα (GEL 57.73) (BAGD p. 203): 'gift' [BAGD, Ea, GEL, HNTC, ICC, Ln, Mou, NTC, Pl; all translations except TEV], 'gifts' [WEC; TEV], 'giving' [WBC].

QUESTION—Why is this clause mentioned?

It is included to avoid any misunderstanding about his comments [EBC, El, Ln, Lt, MNTC, My, NIC, NTC, TNTC, WBC, WEC], and to make it clear that he was concerned not for his benefit from their gifts to him but for the spiritual benefits to them [Alf], for their generous spirit [NIC], for their growth in the grace of giving [EBC], for the gift as evidence of God's grace in their lives [GNC]. He was not concerned for the gift itself [Lg]. He wants to discourage the Philippians from sending him more gifts [WEC].

QUESTION—What is meant by τὸ δόμα 'the gift'?

1. It refers to a gift of money.

1.1 It refers to the gift which Paul had just received [Alf; NJB, REB]: the gift which you have just now sent to me.

1.2 It refers to any gift similar to what he had received [Ea, ICC, MNTC, My; TEV]: any gift such as the one you have sent to me.

1.3 It refers to possible future gifts [WEC; KJV, NIV]: not that I am looking for a gift.

2. It refers to the act of giving [EGT, WBC]: your act of giving.

but[a] I-seek[b] the fruit[c] the-(one) abounding[d] to[e] your account.[f]

LEXICON—a. ἀλλά (GEL 89.125): 'but' [Ea, GEL, ICC, Ln, Mou, Pl, WBC; KJV, NASB, NIV, NRSV], 'instead' [GEL], 'on the contrary' [GEL], 'rather' [NAB, TEV], not explicit [NJB, REB, TNT].

b. pres. act. indic. of ἐπιζητέω: 'to seek'. See this word in the preceding phrase.

c. καρπός (GEL 42.13) (BAGD 2.b. p. 405): 'fruit' [Ea, Ln, NTC, Pl; KJV], 'result of deeds' [GEL], 'profit' [NASB, NRSV, TEV, TNT], 'advantage' [BAGD], 'interest' [HNTC, Mou, WBC; NJB, REB], 'proceeds' [WEC], 'spiritual blessing' [ICC]. The phrase τὸν καρπὸν τὸν πλεονάζοντα 'the fruit the one abounding' is translated 'the ever-growing balance' [NAB], 'what may be credited' [NIV], 'profit added' [TEV]. The fruit will be like the harvest from a seed sown [Lg].

d. pres. act. participle of πλεονάζω (GEL 59.67) (BAGD 1.a. p. 667): 'to abound' [Ea; KJV], 'to increase' [BAGD, Ln, NTC, WBC; NASB], 'to increase considerably' [GEL], 'to become more and more' [GEL], 'to multiply' [GEL], 'to go on multiplying' [HNTC], 'to cause to be more' [GEL], 'to accumulate' [Mou, Pl; NRSV], 'to accrue' [WEC], 'to mount up' [NJB, REB]. This verb is also translated 'that God is adding' [TNT]. The phrase τὸν πλεονάζοντα εἰς τὸν λόγον ὑμῶν 'the one abounding for your account' is translated 'which your acts of ministry will bring to you' [ICC]. The present tense implies a continual blessing [ICC]. The word itself implies abundance [MNTC].

e. εἰς with accusative object (GEL 84.22; 90.41): 'to' [Ea, HNTC, Ln, Mou, NTC, Pl, WBC, WEC; KJV, NASB, NIV, NRSV, TEV, TNT], 'into' [GEL], 'in' [NAB, NJB, REB], 'for' [GEL], 'on behalf of' [GEL]. It indicates the destination of the 'abounding' [My].

f. λόγος (GEL 57.228) (BAGD 2.b. p. 478): 'account' [BAGD, Ea, GEL, HNTC, Ln, Mou, Pl, WBC, WEC; all translations], 'credit' [GEL, NTC].

QUESTION—What is implied by the repeated ἐπιζητῶ 'I seek'?

It implies emphasis [Alf, Ea, ICC, Lg, Lt, MNTC, My, Pl, TH, WBC] and solemnity [Alf, El], to emphasize both thoughts [Lt, TH, WBC], to emphasize what he does seek [ICC, Lg]: I do not seek for the gift, but I do definitely seek for the fruit.

QUESTION—What is implied by the phrase τὸν καρπόν 'the fruit'?
1. It refers to the spiritual benefit for their gift which they will receive from the Lord [Alf, Blm, El, My, WBC] and from people [Blm]: I do seek for the benefit which will come to you.
2. It refers to the increasing spiritual benefit to them from their generous spirit [Ea]: I do seek for you the increasing spiritual benefits from your generous spirit.

QUESTION—What is the meaning of the phrase τὸν καρπὸν τὸν πλεονάζοντα εἰς τὸν λόγον ὑμῶν 'the fruit which abounds to your account'?

It means the spiritual advantage which is being added to their spiritual account [EBC, Lg, Lt, MNTC, NIC, TH] and increases with each gift as a manifestation of their love [Lt, MNTC, NIC], a development of their spirit of generosity [Mou], a deposit in heaven to which interest will accrue for their benefit [GNC, My, TH, TNTC, WBC] and which is now paying them dividends [NTC], the benefit to be received when the Lord returns [MNTC, Mou, My, TNTC].

QUESTION—What is the phrase εἰς λόγον ὑμῶν connected with?

It is connected with τὸν πλεονάζοντα 'which abounds' [Alf, Ea, El, Ea, EBC, EGT, HNTC, ICC, Lg, Lt, MNTC, Mou, My, NTC, Pl, TH, WBC, WEC; all translations]: the fruit which abounds to your account.

4:18
But I-have-in-full[a] everything and am-abounding;[b]
LEXICON—a. pres. act. indic. of ἀπέχω (GEL 57.137) (BAGD 1. p. 84): 'to have in full', 'to have' [Ea, Ln; KJV], 'to receive in full' [BAGD, GEL, Mou; NASB], 'to be paid in full' [GEL; REB], 'to receive payment' [HNTC]. The phrase ἀπέχω πάντα 'I have in full' is translated 'I have received payment in full' [NTC], 'here is my receipt for everything' [TNT], 'here is my receipt for everything you have given me' [WBC; TEV], 'I can give a receipt in full for all that you owed me' [Pl]. This entire phrase is translated 'I have received all I need and more' [WEC], 'I have all that I need and more' [NJB], 'my need is fully met' [ICC], 'I have been paid in full and have more than enough' [NRSV], 'I have been paid in full; I have all I need and more' [REB], 'I have received full payment and even more' [NIV], 'herewith is my receipt, which says that I have been fully paid and more' [NAB]. This verb is emphatic [Alf]; it is Paul's receipt to the Philippians [Bg, GNC, MNTC]; this technical use gives the present tense used here the sense of 'I have received' [MNTC, TH].

b. pres. act. indic. of περισσεύω (GEL 57.24) (BAGD 1.b.α. p. 651): 'to abound' [Ea, Ln; KJV], 'to have enough and to spare' [HNTC], 'to be more than enough' [TEV], 'to have more than enough' [BAGD, GEL, WBC; TNT], 'to have an abundance' [NASB], 'to have an overabundance' [GEL], 'to have abundance over' [Pl], 'to enjoy abundance' [NTC], 'to have all one needs and more' [REB], 'to run over' [Mou]. This verb amplifies the preceding ἀπέχω 'I have in full' and means that he has over and above what he needs [Alf, Lg, Lt, My, TH, TNTC], they have more than repaid their debt to him [MNTC].

QUESTION—Why is this clause mentioned?

1. It indicates (by δέ 'but' [Ea]) that even though it was not their gift that he desired, he has been helped by it [Alf, Ea, El] and now has all he needs [Ea]: it was not that I desired the gift, but the gift has helped me to have everything I need.

2. This clause tells further why he did not seek the gift but rather the benefit to the Philippians [ICC, My]: and as for my needs, I have enough.

3. It means that their gift makes Paul feel rich and also is a spiritual benefit to the Philippians [Ln].

QUESTION—What relationship is indicated by ἀπέχω πάντα 'I have all things'?

1. It means that he has all he wants or needs and is content [Alf, ICC, Lg, Lt, Pl]: I have all I want. It tells the Philippians how rich he feels [Ln].

2. It means that he is giving the Philippians a figurative receipt for their gifts to him [Bg, EGT, GNC, MNTC, NIC, TH, TNTC, WBC, WC, WEC; NRSV]: I hereby give you a receipt for everything. However, no aloofness, but rather friendliness, is implied [EGT, WEC].

I-am-filled,[a] having-received[b] from[c] Epaphroditus the-(things) from[d] you,

LEXICON—a. perf. pass. indic. of πληρόω (GEL 35.33; 59.37) (BAGD 1.b. p. 671): 'to be filled' [Ea, GEL, Ln], 'to be filled full' [Mou], 'to be full' [KJV], 'to be fully provided' [NJB], 'to be fully provided for' [GEL], 'to be fully taken care of' [WEC], 'to be well supplied' [BAGD; NAB], 'to be amply supplied' [NTC; NASB, NIV], 'to be fully supplied' [HNTC, Pl, WBC], 'to be fully satisfied' [NRSV], 'to have all one needs' [TEV], 'to have plenty' [TNT], not explicit [ICC; REB]. This verb repeats and intensifies the sense of περισσεύω 'I abound' [Alf, Blm, My, WBC] and is added to indicate that he does not desire any further gifts [Blm, WBC]. It refers to inward satisfaction, not material abundance [Lg]. The perfect tense indicates that he continues to be full [Ln].

b. aorist mid. (deponent = act.) participle of δέχομαι (GEL 57.125) (BAGD 1. p. 177): 'to receive' [BAGD, Ea, GEL, HNTC, Ln, NTC, Pl, WBC, WEC; all translations except TEV], 'to accept' [Mou]. The phrase δεξάμενος παρὰ 'Επαφροδίτου 'having received from Epaphroditus' is translated 'now that Epaphroditus has brought me' [TEV]. The phrase δεξάμενος παρὰ 'Επαφροδίτου τὰ παρ' ὑμῶν 'having received from Epaphroditus the things from you' is translated 'by this gift which Epaphroditus brought from you' [ICC]. This participle tells how he had become filled, as well as telling when he had become filled [Ea].

c. παρά with genitive object (GEL 84.5; 90.14) (BAGD 1.3.b. p. 610): 'from' [Ea, GEL, HNTC, Ln, Mou, NTC, Pl, WBC, WEC; NASB, NIV, NJB, NRSV, REB, TNT], 'from (the side of)' [BAGD], 'through' [NAB], 'of' [KJV]. It refers to Epaphroditus as the transmitter of the gift [Lt]. The double use of παρά 'from' indicates the double relationship, from Epaphroditus and from the Philippians [Ea].

d. παρά with genitive object (GEL 84.5; 90.14) (BAGD 1.4.b.α. p. 610): 'from' [Ea, GEL, HNTC, ICC, Ln, Mou, NTC, Pl; KJV, NAB], 'from (the side of)' [BAGD]. The phrase τὰ παρ' ὑμῶν 'the things from you' is translated 'what (you) give' [BAGD], 'what you sent' [WEC; REB], 'what you have sent' [NASB], 'the gifts you sent' [NIV, NRSV], 'the gifts you sent me' [WBC], 'your gifts' [TNT], 'all your gifts' [TEV], 'the offering that you sent' [NJB]. This preposition indicates transmission from the giver to the receiver [ICC].

QUESTION—Why is this clause mentioned?

It further explains the preceding clause [ICC, Ln]: that is to say, I am filled, because I have received your gift.

QUESTION—What relationship is indicated by the use of the aorist participle δεξάμενος 'having received'?

1. It indicates the reason for his being filled [ICC, TH; NAB, NIV, NJB, NRSV, REB]: I am filled because I have received your gift. (It is called temporal but translated as expressing the reason [El].)

2. It indicates the means by which he has become filled [Lg, Ln]: I am filled by having received your gift.

a-scent[a] of-fragrance,[b] a-sacrifice[c] acceptable,[d] well-pleasing[e] to-God.

LEXICON—a. ὀσμή (GEL 79.45) (BAGD 2. p. 586): 'scent' [GEL], 'odor' [BAGD, Ea, GEL, HNTC, ICC, Ln, Mou, NTC, Pl, WBC; KJV], 'smell' [GEL; NJB], 'fragrance' [BAGD, WEC;

TNT], 'offering' [BAGD; NAB, NIV, NRSV, REB, TEV], 'aroma' [NASB].

b. εὐωδία (GEL 79.46) (BAGD p. 329): 'fragrance' [BAGD, GEL], 'fragrancy' [Mou], 'aroma' [BAGD], 'sweet smell' [Ea, Pl; KJV], 'sweet odor' [Ln]. This noun is also translated as an adjective: 'fragrant' [BAGD, NTC, WBC; NAB, NASB, NIV, NRSV, REB], 'beautiful' [WEC], 'sweet' [ICC; TNT]; as a participle 'sweet-smelling' [TEV], 'pleasing' [HNTC; NJB].

c. θυσία (GEL 53.20) (BAGD 2.b. p. 366): 'sacrifice' [BAGD, Ea, GEL, HNTC, ICC, Ln, Mou, NTC, Pl, WBC, WEC; all translations except TNT], not explicit [TNT].

d. δεκτός (GEL 25.85) (BAGD p. 174): 'acceptable' [BAGD, Ea, GEL, HNTC, ICC, Ln, Mou, NTC, Pl, WEC; all translations], 'pleasing' [GEL], 'welcome' [BAGD]. This adjective is also translated as a phrase: 'that (God) accepts' [WBC].

e. εὐάρεστος (GEL 25.94) (BAGD 1. p. 318): 'well-pleasing' [Ea, HNTC, Ln, NTC, Pl; KJV, NASB], 'pleasing' [BAGD, Mou, WEC; all translations except KJV, NASB], 'pleasing to' [GEL], 'acceptable' [BAGD], not explicit [ICC]. This adjective is also translated as a phrase: 'that pleases' [WBC].

QUESTION—What relationship is indicated by the two phrases ὀσμὴν εὐωδίας, θυσίαν δεκτήν 'a scent of fragrance, a sacrifice acceptable'?

Both phrases (the first phrase [Ea, El, ICC, My]) are in apposition to τὰ παρ' ὑμῶν 'the things from you', further describing Paul's opinion of their gift [Ea, El, Lg, My]: your gift is a fragrant offering (and an acceptable sacrifice).

QUESTION—How are the two nouns related in the genitive construction ὀσμὴν εὐωδίας 'a scent of fragrance'?

The noun εὐωδίας 'fragrance' is a genitive of quality [El, ICC, My]: a scent which has a fragrant quality. This phrase implies that their gift was of the highest quality [WBC].

QUESTION—What relationship is indicated by the phrase εὐάρεστον τῷ θεῷ 'well-pleasing to God'?

It means that Paul regarded the gift to him as an offering to God as well [Ea, EGT, GNC, Lg, Ln, MNTC, My, NIC, NTC, TH, TNTC, WC]: God also is pleased with your gift to me.

QUESTION—What is τῷ θεῷ 'to God' connected with?

It is connected with both δεκτήν 'acceptable' and εὐάρεστον 'well-pleasing' [Ea, El, GNC, ICC, Lg, MNTC, My, NIC, NTC, TH, TNTC; NAB, NJB, NRSV, TEV, TNT] and also with ὀσμὴν εὐωδίας 'a scent of fragrance' [El, ICC, MNTC, My, NIC, TH; TEV]: (a scent of fragrance to God,) acceptable to God and well-pleasing to him.

DISCOURSE UNIT: 4:19-20 [NIC, NTC, Pl]. The topic is the assurance that God loves and cares for them [NTC], the sufficiency of God for all their needs [NIC], a requital and doxology [Pl].

4:19
And my God will-fill[a] every need[b] of-you according-to[c] the riches[d] of-him in[e] glory[f] in[g] Christ Jesus.

LEXICON—a. fut. act. indic. of πληρόω (GEL 35.33) (BAGD 1.a. p. 670): 'to fill' [BAGD, Ln], 'to fill up' [Mou], 'to fulfil' [NJB], 'to supply' [Ea, ICC, NTC; KJV, NASB, REB, TEV], 'to supply fully' [GEL, HNTC, Pl; NAB], 'to provide for completely' [GEL], 'to satisfy fully' [NRSV], 'to take care of fully' [WEC], 'to meet' [WBC; NIV], 'to see that (needs) are met' [TNT]. The future indicative indicates assurance [Alf, Bg, Ea, El, Ln, My, Pl, WEC]; it expresses Paul's wish or prayer, as the variant reading, the aorist optative πληρώσαι 'may he fill', makes specific [WBC]. See this word at 4:18.

b. χρεία (GEL 57.40) (BAGD 2. p. 885): 'need' [BAGD, Ea, GEL, HNTC, ICC, Ln, Mou, NTC, WBC; KJV, NRSV], 'needs' [Pl, WEC; all translations except KJV, NRSV], 'lack' [BAGD, GEL], 'what is needed' [GEL]. God will meet the Philippians' need (χρείαν) just as they have met Paul's need (4:16). Both spiritual and temporal needs are included [Blm, Ea, El, HNTC, Lg, MNTC, My, NIC, Pl, TH, TNTC, WEC], or only material needs are included [WBC].

c. κατά with accusative object (GEL 89.8): 'according to' [Ea, Ln, Mou, NTC, Pl, WEC; KJV, NASB, NIV, NRSV], 'in accordance with' [GEL, HNTC, WBC], 'in a way worthy of' [NAB], 'as befits' [ICC], 'in relation to' [GEL], 'out of' [NJB, REB, TNT], 'with' [TEV]. This preposition introduces the measure of the supply [Ea, ICC, MNTC, Mou, Pl]; it will be commensurate with God's infinite riches [EBC, HNTC, ICC, MNTC, My, NTC, TNTC, WBC, WC]. It introduces the source of the supply [NJB, REB, TNT].

d. πλοῦτος (GEL 57.30) (BAGD 2. p. 674): 'riches' [Ea, GEL, ICC, Ln, NTC, WEC; all translations except TEV, TNT], 'wealth' [BAGD, GEL, HNTC, Mou, Pl, WBC; TEV, TNT], 'abundance' [BAGD, GEL]. The reference is to riches of grace and beneficence [Blm].

e. ἐν with dative object (GEL 83.13): 'in' [Ea, GEL, ICC, Ln, Mou, Pl, WEC; KJV, NASB, NRSV], 'of' [NJB]. The phrase ἐν δόξῃ 'in glory' is translated 'glorious' [NIV, TNT], 'gloriously' [HNTC, NTC], 'abundant' [TEV], 'marvelous' [WBC], 'magnificent' [NAB], 'magnificence of' [REB].

f. δόξα (GEL 1.15; 79.18) (BAGD 1.a. p. 203): 'glory' [BAGD, Ea, GEL, ICC, Ln, Mou, WEC; KJV, NASB, NJB, NRSV], 'the kingdom of glory' [Pl], 'heaven' [GEL]. The glory is the manifestation of God's love and grace [Ln, Mou].

g. ἐν with dative object (GEL 83.13; 89.119; 90.6): 'in' [Ea, GEL, HNTC, ICC, Mou, NTC, Pl, WBC; NAB, NASB, NIV, NJB, NRSV, REB], 'in union with' [GEL, WEC], 'in connection with' [Ln], 'by' [GEL; KJV], 'through' [TEV, TNT].

QUESTION—What relationship is indicated by δέ 'and'?

The conjunction δέ 'but' introduces a different aspect of the preceding topic [Ea]; it adds this comment which implies God's approval [ICC]. God will meet their needs as a result of their generosity to Paul [TH]. It is an assurance to the Philippians [Alf, Bg, GNC, MNTC, NTC]: and I assure you that God will meet your needs. As they had filled Paul's needs, so God will fill theirs [Alf, EGT, El, Lg, MNTC]. This follows from God's pleasure with their gift to Paul (4:18) [Lg, My]. God will fill their needs (πληρώσει 'he will fill') just as their gifts have enabled Paul to be filled (πεπλήρωμαι 'I am filled', 4:18) [Alf, EGT, El, Lg, MNTC].

QUESTION—What is meant by ὁ θεός μου 'the God of me'?

1. It refers to Paul's intimate relationship with God [TH], his long experience of God's supply of all his needs [GNC], and the importance of God in his life [NTC].

2. Paul's use of μου 'my' implies that 'just as you have supplied *my* needs, so God on my behalf will supply *your* needs [Lt, Pl, TH, TNTC].

3. Paul says μου 'my' because he himself was the recipient of the gifts from the Philippians, and it is *his* God who will fill their needs [My].

QUESTION—What is meant by ἐν δόξῃ 'in glory'?

1. It is connected with πληρώσει 'he will supply' [Alf, Ea, El, HNTC, ICC, Lg, NTC].

1.1 It tells how and when the needs will be met [Alf, Lg, NIC, Pl].

1.1.1 God will fill their needs by giving them Christ's great riches, both now and at Christ's return [Alf, Lg, NIC, Pl]. It refers to the heavenly riches of Christ [Alf].

1.1.2 It means that their needs will be met in the coming Messianic glory [EGT, Lg(H), Lt, My]: he will meet your needs in the world of glory. This phrase is instrumental [My]. He will meet their needs by placing them in glory [Lt].

1.1.3 It means that their needs will be met in this life [NTC]: he will meet your needs in this life.

1.2 It tells the manner in which the needs will be met [Ea, El, HNTC, ICC, Lg, NIC, NTC]: he will meet your needs gloriously, generously. The needs are those of this life [HNTC, NTC].

2. It describes πλοῦτον 'riches' [Blm, EBC, TH, TNTC, WBC; NAB, NIV, REB, TEV, TNT]: his abundant, glorious riches. Christ's heavenly glories are the source of the supply [EBC].

3. It tells where the riches are located [Ln]: the riches located in glory. However, the needs of this life are referred to [Ln].

4. It describes both the riches and the manner of God's bestowing them [Bg]: God will gloriously bestow his glorious riches.

QUESTION—What is meant by ἐν Χριστῷ Ἰησοῦ 'in Christ Jesus'?

1. It is connected with πληρώσει 'he will fill'.

1.1 It means that Christ is the medium through whom the needs will be met [Alf, Blm, Ea, El, GNC, HNTC, ICC, Lg, MNTC, My, TH, TNTC, WBC, WC]: God will meet your needs through Christ Jesus. This phrase is emphatic by word order [WBC].

1.2 It means that they will receive these benefits because they are in union with Jesus Christ [Lg(H), Lt, NTC].

2. It is connected with ἐν δόξῃ 'in glory' [Ln, Mou]: glory manifested in Christ Jesus.

DISCOURSE UNIT: 4:20 [NTC, WC]. The topic is the doxology [NTC, WC].

4:20

Now to-the God and Father of-us (be) the glory[a] into[b] the ages[c] of-the ages.[c] Amen.[d]

LEXICON—a. δόξα (GEL 33.357; 87.4): 'glory' [Ea, HNTC, ICC, Ln, Mou, NTC, Pl, WBC, WEC; all translations], 'praise' [GEL], 'honor' [GEL]. This word includes both 'praise' and 'honor' [TH]. It refers to God's absolute perfection which calls for praise [NIC]. The article identifies the 'glory' as specifically God's glory [Ea, El, Ln, WBC, WC], the glory to which he is entitled, as is common in doxologies [MNTC, WBC], and the glory which we render to him [Ln, MNTC]. It is something which God already possesses and which we simply acknowledge [WBC].

b. εἰς with accusative object (GEL 67.95; 84.22): 'into' [GEL], 'unto' [HNTC], 'for' [Ln]. The phrase εἰς τοὺς αἰῶνας τῶν αἰώνων 'into the ages of the ages' is translated 'for ever and ever' [Ea, GEL, Mou, NTC, Pl, WBC, WEC; all translations except NAB], 'for evermore' [BAGD], 'forever' [ICC], 'for unending ages' [NAB]. This phrase imitates a Hebrew phrase

and implies an immeasurable eternity [Ea], all ages following
one another for ever [NIC, Pl, WBC].

  c. αἰών (GEL 67.95; 67.143) (BAGD 1.b. p. 27): 'age' [GEL,
HNTC], 'era' [GEL], 'eon' [Ln].

  d. ἀμήν (GEL 72.6) (BAGD 1. p. 45): 'amen' [BAGD, Ea, HNTC,
Ln, Mou, NTC, Pl, WBC, WEC; all translations], 'truly'
[BAGD, GEL], 'indeed' [GEL], 'so let it be' [BAGD], not
explicit [ICC]. This word is a transliteration of a Hebrew word
[EBC, TNTC, WC]; it implies assent to what has been said
[EBC, NIC, TH, TNTC, WBC, WC]. By this word Paul adds a
concluding "So be it!" [Ea, NIC, TH].

QUESTION—Why is this clause included?

It is motivated by Paul's realization of God's rewards for believers,
the grand consummation of God's plans at the last day [Alf, WC],
the realization of God's great salvation [My], God's care for his
children [HNTC, ICC, NIC, NTC], God's goodness [MNTC, TH],
God's glory [TNTC], the close of the epistle [Alf, GNC, Lg, Ln] or
of the expression of thanks [TH], and as an appropriate conclusion
to his expression of thanks [GNC]. It springs from the joy that
characterizes this entire epistle [Bg, TNTC], from the emotional
overflow of Paul's feelings [Ea, NTC]. There is a contrast here,
indicating that regardless of our good works the glory belongs to
God [Alf].

QUESTION—What is the relationship of the words in the phrase τῷ
θεῷ καὶ πατρὶ ἡμῶν 'to the God and Father of us'?

  1. It is one title [Ea, Ln], as is indicated by the one article
covering both nouns [EBC, Ln, TH], making it clear that only
one person is meant by both titles [EBC, Lg, Ln, Mou, TH,
TNTC; all translations except KJV, NJB], and ἡμῶν 'our'
belongs to both nouns [ICC, Ln, Pl, TH, TNTC; all translations
except KJV, NJB], joining Paul with the Philippians [Lt, Mou,
NIC, Pl, TH]: to the one who is both God and Father of us.

  2. The definite article τῷ 'the' refers only to θεῷ 'God' [WBC];
and ἡμῶν 'our', including Paul and the Philippians, refers only
to πατρί 'Father' [WBC; NJB]: to the one God, who is our
Father.

QUESTION—What verb is to be supplied in this sentence?

  1. The optative εἴη 'may it be' is understood here [Ea, El, HNTC,
ICC, Lg, Mou, My, NIC, NTC, Pl, WC; all translations]: may
there be glory to our God and Father.

  2. The indicative ἐστιν 'is' is to be supplied [WBC, WEC]: to God
is/belongs the glory.

DISCOURSE UNIT: 4:21–23 [Alf, EBC, EGT, HNTC, ICC, Lg, Ln, Lt, MNTC, NIC, NTC, Pl, TH, WBC, WC, WEC; GNT, NAB, NIV, NJB, TEV]. The topic is the conclusion with greetings and benediction [Lg, NIC, Pl, WC], greetings and final benediction [Alf, EGT, HNTC, Lt, MNTC], greetings and final wish [NJB], closing greetings [EBC, ICC, TH; GNT, NIV, TEV], farewell [NAB], conclusion [Ln, NTC, WBC, WEC].

DISCOURSE UNIT: 4:21–22 [NTC, TNTC]. The topic is greetings [NTC, TNTC].

4:21
Greet[a] every saint[b] in[c] Christ Jesus.
>   LEXICON—a. aorist mid. (deponent = act.) impera. of ἀσπάζομαι (GEL 33.20) (BAGD 1.a. p. 116): 'to greet' [BAGD, GEL, HNTC, NTC, Pl, WEC; NASB, NIV, NRSV, TNT], 'to send greetings' [GEL], 'to give greetings' [WBC; NAB, REB], 'to salute' [Ea, Ln, Mou; KJV]. This verb is also translated 'greetings' [TEV], 'my greetings' [NJB], 'my salutations' [ICC].
>   b. ἅγιος (GEL 11.27): 'saint' [Ea, HNTC, Ln, Mou, NTC, WBC, WEC; KJV, NASB, NIV, NRSV], 'Christian' [Pl], 'member of the church' [ICC; NAB], 'devoted follower' [TNT]. The phrase πάντα ἅγιον 'every saint' is translated 'God's people' [GEL; REB, TEV], 'God's holy people' [NJB]. This word means that the persons belong to God rather than describing their moral condition [TH]. The singular ἅγιος 'saint' implies Paul's love for each individual [Alf, NIC, TH, WBC]; each individual saint was to be greeted [Bg, Ea, EBC, El, HNTC, ICC, Lg, MNTC, Mou, My, NIC, Pl, TH, TNTC, WBC] with universal affection [Ea].
>   c. ἐν with dative object (GEL 83.13; 89.119): 'in' [Ea, GEL, HNTC, Ln, Mou, NTC, Pl, WBC; KJV, NAB, NASB, NIV, NJB, NRSV], 'in the fellowship of' [REB], 'in union with' [GEL], 'joined closely to' [GEL], 'who belong to' [TEV], 'in the name of' [WEC], 'of' [TNT], not explicit [ICC].
>   QUESTION—Who are the implied subjects of the second person plural verb ἀσπάσασθε 'greet'?
>   Paul is here requesting the church leaders to pass his greetings to the other believers [EBC, HNTC, NTC, WBC]: you leaders greet each saint for me.
>   QUESTION—What is the phrase ἐν Χριστῷ Ἰησοῦ 'in Christ Jesus' connected with?
>   1. It is connected with ἀσπάσασθε 'greet' [Alf, Ea, EGT, Lg, Lt, My, WC; NAB, REB]: greet them in Christ Jesus. This makes it a specifically Christian greeting [My].

2. It is connected with ἅγιον 'saint' [EBC, El, GNC, ICC, Ln, NIC, TH, WBC; TEV, TNT]: greet every saint who is in Christ Jesus.
3. It is connected with both of the above [HNTC]: greet in Christ Jesus every saint who is in Christ Jesus.

the brothers[a] with[b] me greet[c] you.

LEXICON—a. ἀδελφός (GEL 11.23): 'brother' [Ea, HNTC, ICC, Ln, Mou, NTC, Pl, WBC, WEC; all translations except NRSV, REB], 'fellow believer' [GEL], '(Christian) brother' [GEL], 'friend' [NRSV], 'colleague' [REB].

b. σύν with dative object (GEL 89.107) (BAGD 1.c. p. 781): 'with' [BAGD, Ea, GEL, HNTC, ICC, Ln, Mou, NTC, WBC, WEC; all translations except NAB, REB], 'together with' [GEL]. The phrase οἱ σὺν ἐμοὶ ἀδελφοί 'the brothers who are with me' is translated 'my brothers here' [NAB], 'my colleagues' [REB], 'all the brethren who are my companions here' [Pl].

c. pres. mid. (deponent = act.) indic. of ἀσπάζομαι (GEL 33.20) (BAGD 1.a. p. 116): 'to greet' [BAGD, Ea, GEL, NTC, WEC; KJV, NASB, NRSV, TNT], 'to send greetings' [GEL, HNTC, Pl, WBC; NAB, NIV, NJB, REB, TEV], 'to send greeting' [ICC], 'to salute' [Ln, Mou].

QUESTION—Who are the ἀδελφοί 'brothers'?

1. These brothers are Paul's colleagues [EBC, GNC, ICC, Ln, Lt, NTC, WBC], not the resident Christians [EBC, Lt, WBC].
2. It refers to Roman Christians [EGT].
3. It refers to those who were more closely associated with Paul [Alf, El, Mou, My, NIC, Pl, WC], including both his traveling companions and local Christians [Lg].
4. It refers to Jewish believers who were with Paul [Bg].

4:22

all the saints[a] greet[b] you, and especially[c] the-(ones) of[d] the household[e] of Caesar.[f]

LEXICON—a. ἅγιος (GEL 11.27) (BAGD 2.d.β. p. 10): 'saint' [BAGD, Ea, HNTC, Ln, Mou, NTC, WBC; KJV, NASB, NIV, NRSV], 'Christian' [Pl]. The phrase οἱ ἅγιοι 'the saints' is translated 'those who believe' [NAB], 'the members of the church' [ICC], 'God's people' [GEL; REB, TEV, TNT], 'God's holy people' [NJB], 'the whole sanctified community' [WEC].

b. pres. mid. (deponent = act.) indic. of ἀσπάζομαι (GEL 33.20) (BAGD 1.a. p. 116): 'to greet' [BAGD, GEL, NTC; NASB, NRSV, TNT], 'to send greetings' [BAGD, GEL, HNTC, ICC, Pl, WBC, WEC; NAB, NIV, NJB, REB, TEV], 'to salute' [Ea, Ln, Mou; KJV].

c. μάλιστα (GEL 78.7) (BAGD 1. p. 489): 'especially' [BAGD, GEL, HNTC, ICC, Ln, NTC, Pl, WBC; NASB, NIV, NJB, NRSV, TEV, TNT], 'particularly' [GEL, Mou; NAB, REB], 'in particular' [WEC], 'chiefly' [Ea; KJV]. Paul uses this word because the persons referred to were in closer contact with him [EGT, El, Ln], because they were from the region of Philippi [HNTC], or because this group had asked with special earnestness that their greetings be sent [Lg(H), My].

d. ἐκ with genitive object (GEL 63.20; 84.4) (BAGD 3.d. p. 235, 395): 'of' [Ea, GEL, HNTC, ICC, NTC, WBC; KJV, NASB, NJB, NRSV, TNT], 'a part of' [GEL], 'from' [GEL, Ln], 'out of' [GEL], 'who belong to' [BAGD, Mou, WEC; NIV, TEV], 'who are come from' [Pl]. The phrase οἱ ἐκ τῆς Καίσαρος οἰκίας 'the ones of the household of Caesar' is translated 'those in Caesar's service' [NAB], 'those in the emperor's service' [REB].

e. οἰκία (GEL 7.3; 10.8) (BAGD 3. p. 557): 'household' [BAGD, Ea, GEL, HNTC, ICC, Ln, Mou, NTC, Pl, WBC, WEC; KJV, NASB, NIV, NJB, NRSV, TNT], 'house' [GEL], 'residence' [GEL], 'palace' [TEV]. It refers to the imperial residence [Ea].

f. Καίσαρ (GEL 37.74; 93.208) (BAGD p. 395): 'Caesar' [Ea, GEL, HNTC, ICC, Ln, NTC, WEC; KJV, NAB, NASB, NIV, NJB, TNT], 'the emperor' [BAGD, GEL, Mou; NRSV, REB, TEV]. This noun is alos translated as an adjective: 'imperial' [Pl, WBC].

QUESTION—Who are implied by πάντες οἱ ἅγιοι 'all the saints'?
It refers to all the Christians of the church where Paul was [Alf, EBC, HNTC, ICC, Lg, Ln, Lt, MNTC, NIC, NTC, WBC, WC]—in Rome [Alf, EBC, HNTC, ICC, Lg, Ln, Lt, NIC, NTC, Pl, WC], in Ephesus [MNTC], in Caesarea [WBC]: all the Christians here.

QUESTION—Who are implied by οἱ ἐκ τῆς Καίσαρος οἰκίας 'of the household of Caesar'?

1. They were members of the staff of the imperial residence [El, Lg, Mou, My, TH], including slaves [Alf, Ea, ICC, Ln, Lt, NIC, Pl, TNTC, WC] and freed or free persons [Ea, ICC, Lt, NIC, Pl, TNTC, WC].

2. They were persons in the service of the emperor [GNC, HNTC, NTC; NAB, REB], including slaves and freedmen [EBC, GNC, HNTC, MNTC, NTC, WBC], in Rome [EBC, HNTC, NTC] or elsewhere [EBC, MNTC, WBC].

DISCOURSE UNIT: 4:23 [NTC, TNTC]. The topic is benediction [NTC, TNTC].

4:23

The grace[a] of-the Lord Jesus Christ (be) with[b] the spirit[c] of-you.

TEXT—Instead of τοῦ πνεύματος 'the spirit', some manuscripts read πάντων 'all'. GNT does not deal with this variant. 'All' is read by only Blm, My, and KJV.

TEXT—Some manuscripts add ἀμήν 'amen' at the end of this verse. GNT omits this word with a B rating, indicating some degree of doubt. 'Amen' is included by Blm, EGT, Lg, MNTC, Mou, WBC, KJV, NAB, and NIV.

LEXICON—a. χάρις (GEL 88.66) (BAGD p. 877): 'grace' [BAGD, Ea, GEL, HNTC, ICC, Ln, Mou, NTC, Pl, WBC, WEC; all translations except NAB], 'favor' [BAGD; NAB], 'kindness' [GEL], 'graciousness' [GEL]. This grace is God's unmerited favor [NIC, NTC] with all its attendant gifts [Ln, NIC] which blesses, encourages, and strengthens [Ea], bestowing his saving love [WBC], his love and mercy, on undeserving people [TH].

    b. μετά with genitive object (GEL 90.60) (BAGD A.II.1.c.γ. p. 509): 'with' [BAGD, Ea, GEL, HNTC, ICC, Ln, Mou, NTC, Pl, WBC, WEC; all translations].

    c. πνεῦμα (GEL 26.9) (BAGD 3.b. p. 675): 'spirit' [BAGD, Ea, GEL, HNTC, ICC, Ln, Mou, NTC, Pl, WEC; all translations except KJV, TEV], 'self' [BAGD]. The phrase τοῦ πνεύματος ὑμῶν 'the spirit of you' is translated 'you all' [TEV], 'you each one' [WBC]. The reference is to the highest part of their nature [El] which was receptive to God's grace [Ea], their inner nature [MNTC, NIC] which governs the entire being and is dependent on God for help [NIC]. It is merely an emphatic way of saying 'you' [GNC, WBC, WEC], or in the sense of 'person' or 'self' [TH]. The singular noun implies that one spirit characterizes them all [HNTC]; the singular is generic [Pl, WBC], emphasizing the spirit of each individual [WBC].